THE COMPLE

Star...

Yve Menzies was born in England but spent much of her time living and working abroad before settling near San Remo on the Italian Riviera dei Fiori some ten years ago. Trained as an interpreter/translator, she later became a journalist and copywriter for many of the big food companies. She is the author of *Living in Italy* and co-author of *Living in France*, two highly successful guides to living abroad. She is also the author of *Mediterranean Gardening* and regularly broadcasts on Radio Riviera on cookery and gardening. In addition to Britain, she has also had her work published in the United States, Australia and the Far East.

By the same author
Living in Italy

THE COMPLETE BOOK OF
Starters

An International Collection

YVE MENZIES

Illustrations by Maggie Redfern

ROBERT HALE · LONDON

© *Yve Menzies 1988*
First published in Great Britain 1988
First paperback edition 1994

ISBN 0 7090 5305 3

Robert Hale Limited
Clerkenwell House
Clerkenwell Green
London EC1R 0HT

2 4 6 8 10 9 7 5 3 1

Printed and bound in
Malta by Interprint

Contents

For Anthea Stoneham
(whose idea this book was)
with love and regard.

Acknowledgements

This book owes a great deal to my travels, which I started at the age of three weeks and hope to continue for ever, and to my many friends who have been so generous with their recipes from places I have never visited.

I should like to take this opportunity to thank Priscilla Nimr Aranian, Mollie Berwick, Ikka Boyd, Aase Brown-Thomson, Lucie Descloux, Madelena Ramirez de Gúzman, Márta Karácsonyi, Gaby Lambert, Gaby Lassière, Fiona MacKenzie, Consuelo Ramirez do Oldechea, Patricia Price, Margit Ritchie, Elva Conceicão Silva, Anthea Stoneham, Colette Thurillet, Jelena Vuletić, Ian Wallace, Gwen Waller and Marjorie Young.

I would also like to thank Maggie Redfern for illustrating the book so beautifully.

Finally, last but not least, my husband remains to be thanked for having been such a willing guinea-pig and for having sometimes eaten whole meals comprised of first courses.

YMM

Introduction

When I began the research for this book, I soon came across a number of problems which could easily militate against an imaginative (let alone international) selection of recipes. The first was that many Europeans start their meals with soup, and this was to be more than a book about soups.

Hors d'œuvres were another problem, since many countries – such as Great Britain, Germany, Austria and the Netherlands – consider such a course as an excuse to serve cooked or raw vegetables, cooked meat or fish etc in the same commercial mayonnaise for everything. In certain cases even the Scandinavians are guilty of this sin. As far as Europeans are concerned, Americans appear to have the rather distressing habit of setting cooked meat, fish, vegetables etc in sweet, artificially flavoured jellies and calling them salads. Few Europeans would relish starting a meal with prawns and cottage cheese set in cherry lime jello.

Pickled and smoked fish presented another problem, since there is no wine on earth which will really go with them, and you should not fall for the old *canard* that champagne goes with everything, since in this case it would be a very expensive mistake. Some form of schnapps or beer is possibly the answer.

Once all the recipes had been collected, an interesting pattern emerged. It was one which reflected the generally accepted view on food and *cuisine* generally. The French came out on top for sheer variety in every one of the sections. Northern Europe was best for smoked and pickled fish, and southern Europe and the Levant for the use of vegetables in first courses. Italy was strong in this section also, and in many cases her hams and pork products are better even than those of France.

The tremendous variety available in the United States shows that the Americans have a very open attitude to what constitutes a good or interesting (or both) first course. They appear to be prepared to try almost anything at the start of a meal, whereas they tend to become ultra-conservative in their main courses, often limiting themselves to grills and roasts, usually of steak, chops or chicken, only to become imaginative again at dessert. As few of these first courses are really indigenous to the USA, I have labelled them with their country of origin rather than call them 'American'. *Guacamole* is a case in point: its origin is Mexican but 'Texmex' cookery has a *guacamole* of its own which is never found in Mexico.

As for the rest of the world, the variety which is offered is immense but not all the food is necessarily acceptable to people of principally European extraction, which includes inhabitants of countries as far apart as Australia and South Africa. The old colonizing powers from Europe took their cooking habits with them, and even today this is evident. The cooking in Martinique and Guadaloupe, both French possessions, is noticeably better than that of Jamaica and Trinidad.

Over much of Europe and particularly in France, a new fashion has emerged – the *entrée chaude*. There are many good reasons for adopting it. It can be a relatively economical way of serving luxury food such as scallops, salmon, sole, lobster, crayfish, veal sweetbreads etc whose use in the main course would be prohibitively expensive. It can also roll the first course and fish course into one. Indeed, it can get you to use fish which is used too rarely nowadays because it can appear so expensive. It is a course which, more often than not, can be prepared in advance which is important for people who have not all day to prepare for a dinner party.

All recipes are for eight people.

1   Ready-made First Courses

Caviare and Fish Roes

The word comes from Turkoman and applies specifically to sturgeon roe and no other. In Russian the word is *ikra* or *eekra* and applies to any sort of fish roe. The best sturgeon roe comes from the Caspian Sea, which is under the aegis of Soviet Russia and Iran – which does not bode well for caviare-lovers.

My husband used to have several Iranian clients who always brought large amounts of caviare back from Teheran with them. One does not look gifthorses in the mouth but the champagne or vodka needed to accompany this amount of caviare (sometimes as much as a kilo) was quite an expense. Moreover, one had to decide whether to give a proper dinner party with caviare as the first course or just a rather plush champagne party with generous caviare canapés and then go out to a restaurant afterwards – either way quite an expense. I would love to relive the experience today, since I was not sufficiently aware of my good fortune in the mid-1970s!

Xan Smiley reports from Moscow that in Russia it is possible to buy caviare for as little as £60 per kilo, provided it is bought through a state-controlled factory or collective (and for something as important to celebrate as Lenin's birthday) but normally it will cost £325 per kilo – 'only a shade less', as he nicely puts it, 'than at Fortnum and Mason's'. Petrossian in New York, who seems to have a monopoly on caviare importation in the United States, does rather better on price but in France, where anything excellent is prohibitively expensive, it costs somewhere around £600 per kilo, put another way, £30 per head for a standard serving of 50 g. Indeed, the most expensive thing you can do in

France is to eat caviare accompanied by imported Russian vodka watching a pornographic film – all of them carry an *extra* tax of well over 30 per cent. Most countries slap a large tax on caviare, including Great Britain, where it is currently around 30 per cent, but that figure includes VAT whereas the French figure does not. Strangely, for such an expensive product, caviare is priced according to appearance rather than taste, larger-grained caviare obtaining the higher price. Beluga has the largest grain and is dark steel-blue to stagnant pond-green in appearance. This is followed by Ocietrova, usually even more pond-green than Beluga. Sevruga has the smallest grain, and the colour ranges from dirty green to black. Apparently connoisseurs buy Ocietrova more than the others since it is reputed to have the finest taste. However, many who cannot live without the stuff manage to assuage their yearning with pressed caviare which, by comparison with the granular sort, comes very cheap indeed. This is the sort you use in blinis and on toast for cocktail parties. It looks pretty horrible and black but, mixed with sour cream (when it looks pretty horrible and grey), tastes divine.

Caviare comes in both fresh and pasteurized form, and the latter keeps longer – ideally it should be kept just above freezing, i.e. in the coldest part of the refrigerator. Freezing destroys caviare. It is best to buy caviare where you know there is a quick turnover or from a dealer who orders it specially for you from a large importer or wholesaler – this latter is common in France.

Of course, there are all sorts of other fish roes masquerading under the name of caviare, from salmon and lumpfish through cod and grey mullet to tuna. Some make excellent eating and some do not. Lumpfish roe looks like caviare but is more or less tasteless, although there are now firms which flavour lumpfish roe to taste quite like real caviare. A real caviare-lover would not be fooled, however.

Real caviare should be served with light rye bread, Hovis or toast with plenty of unsalted butter (there is enough salt in the caviare) and accompanied by any dry white wine, not necessarily champagne. Iced vodka is much liked by some but caviare connoisseurs frown on it. No hard-boiled eggs and certainly no chopped onion.

We all know smoked cod's roe from which endless tons of *taramasalata* is made, but in Greece, the home of this dish, real *tarama* comes from the grey mullet (a very boring and tasteless fish) and tastes very different and infinitely more subtle. *Poutargue* in French, *botarga* in Italian and *batarek* in Arabic, this richly flavoured, orange-coloured dried roe is highly thought-of throughout the Mediterranean Basin. It is sometimes known as

'Arab caviare'. Claudia Roden, in her *Book of Middle Eastern Food*, describes how to make it, indeed the only problem is to find mullet roe – and female at that!

The Italians dry and smoke tuna roe into a granular, orange-to-brown crumbly mass which has its devotees, and they sell it at about double the price of the best-quality San Daniele *prosciutto* so magic is the idea of roe as a first course.

Salmon roe is bright, bright orange and tastes much like cod's roe but commands a considerably higher price. From an appearance point of view it makes interesting canapés and hors d'œuvres but the taste is not in keeping with the price.

I am none too fond of snails but can eat them when given them at a dinner party – the butter being the best thing for me, but snails' eggs are a delicacy I think I shall forego. They are ridiculously expensive for something that is inherently unattractive – but for that matter 'raw sturgeon roe' sounds very unappetizing, whereas the word caviare has a certain magic about it. What price semantics?

Foie Gras

Real *foie gras* comes only from France and only from over-fed geese (not necessarily any longer forced-fed or *gavées*, as in the past). Geese anyway are happy to stuff themselves. The French also produce a *foie gras* of duck liver, frequently sold *mi-cuit*, which they consider the best way to eat it. It is from these over-fed ducks that the popular *magret de canard* comes, the breast of an ordinary farmyard duck being considerably less flavoursome and plump.

It is a matter of personal taste whether you prefer *foie gras* from Alsace or the south-west of France, though personally I would choose that from the west and south-west, if only because I prefer the wines from that region. Some people err towards a medium sweet, slightly fruity wine such as Sauternes, Barsac or a really good Gewürztraminer, whilst others prefer Champagne, Riesling or a good white Burgundy. Probably the only rule is not to drink red wine with it, as it tends to deaden the taste.

Foie gras comes in several guises. The real thing is simply the goose liver whole. It is seldom on the market and, when it is, is ruinously expensive. The most common way to buy *foie gras* is '*en bloc*' in a tin. You open each end and push the *foie gras* out, using one of the lids as a pusher. A good 60 per cent of the *foie gras* from the Périgord is *truffé*, and the percentage of truffles must by law be marked on the box. Whole truffles in *foie gras* add a great deal to the price.

The most modern guise is *mousse de foie gras*, which is a mixture of unevenly shaped livers and pieces of liver put through a blender. Compared with whole goose liver, the price seems staggeringly reasonable and you are getting precisely the same product (there are no additives), except, possibly, for the texture. Goose liver is, in fact, so smooth in texture that I defy anyone to tell the difference from a taste point of view between *foie gras* and *mousse de foie gras*. Serving the mousse sort is much easier because it very seldom fails to slice absolutely evenly.

To slice *foie gras*, have a basin of very hot water into which you dip your slicing knife. Wipe dry before you slice. Allow 1½-2 oz (40-50 g) per person – it is very rich. Never serve it on lettuce or with any sort of salad. In the Périgord they serve it with thin slices of orange and a few fresh grapes with melba or ordinary toast. If the *foie gras* has been put in aspic, nothing else is needed. *Foie gras* can be served hot, though for many this defeats the purpose of such a luxury and it becomes murderously rich for modern stomachs.

For those interested in producing and processing *foie gras* themselves, there are courses offered on Périgord farms either over a weekend or, for the really enthusiastic, for a week. Accommodation and full board are included in the price, which works out at about £100 a weekend plus the fare (in 1988); of course, such courses are available only in the autumn. The French Tourist Office in all big cities will supply names and addresses.

Foie gras apart, many countries in Central Europe make a speciality of goose liver, Hungary and Czechoslovakia in particular. Usually it is simply steamed or fried (in its own fat or butter) and served hot, but there are recipes for goose liver in aspic and with *különléges* paprika, the best and most expensive paprika of all.

Before the Second World War my grandmother always went back to Hungary for her birthday in October. The menu was always the same: *foie gras* in Tokay aspic, *fogas* (a freshwater fish peculiar to Lake Balaton and now all but disappeared due to pollution) and partridge. I went once with her. I cannot recall all the food at that birthday lunch but I vividly remember watching my grandmother getting down to her treat. Goose liver in Tokay is obviously a Hungarian variant of the French classic *aspic de foie gras au Sauternes* and for aspics of this kind most well-made, fruity, slightly or definitely sweet wines will do well. Even certain white or tawny ports are excellent. Madeira aspic (the real thing, not from a packet) is a classic for *foie gras*. Recipes will be found on p. 180 ff.

Foie gras de canard as opposed to duck liver is served in much the same way as ordinary *foie gras* except that the French urge you not to cook it completely, and therefore you are rather more limited. The more you cook duck liver, the more it melts (which shows just how fat it is) and disappears. Being half cooked means that it is very perishable (never freeze it!), and so it should be bought on the day or day before you are going to eat it.

Oysters

'Poverty and oysters always seem to go together,' said Dickens in the last century, and to a degree it still holds true today, though for different reasons. Buy your dinner guests half a dozen per head and imminent poverty rears its head. Oysters, because of careful farming, are beginning to get (relatively) cheaper but are still in the luxury food class. Luckily the average host or hostess can take refuge in the fact that they are a rather dangerous first course, since so many people cannot eat raw shellfish.

The French and the Australians have the largest oyster farms in the world, smartly followed by the Japanese, who have them for pearl-making purposes. Pearl-producing oysters are usually very tough and unattractive to eat. Some restaurants in Australia include a baroque pearl in every serving of oysters but Sydney Bay oysters, in common with all the other edible sort, do not produce pearls. The Americans have large oyster farms on both the east and west coasts but much of the produce is taken off the shell and frozen. For dishes such as Oysters Rockerfeller, stuffed oysters, oyster chowder etc, they are positively economical compared with oysters on the shell. Great Britain and Italy both have an oyster-farming industry but not on the scale of the French or even the Americans. The vagaries of the weather off the British coast will probably always keep the native oyster expensive.

Which is the finest oyster to eat? It depends on the country you live in – Whitstables in Britain, the Belon or Marennes in France (in spite of their awful green colour due to the algae they eat), the Hunter Oysters from near Sydney in Australia, and the Blue Point from the American eastern seaboard, though there are many Americans who would argue for the oysters particular to their region. The whole subject of choice is very subjective, as is the question of what to drink with them. Chablis is considered *the* correct wine but frankly its price, anywhere, would rule it out for me. Muscadet, which is frequently offered instead, I find is too often like refined battery acid. You need quite a strong, rich, white wine and it does not matter which country it comes from. White Graves and hock are my favourites. Because of my origins, for years I avoided drinking Guinness or stout with oysters until I was forced to in Ireland, and it was a very pleasant revelation.

To open an oyster, unless you are an adept, wear rubber gloves or wrap your non-opening hand in a clean cloth. Hold the oyster in the palm of one hand and arm yourself with a short-bladed, very tough knife. (These are available in France at give-away prices and are worth bringing back since I have never seen them commonly in the UK or elsewhere for that matter.) Insert the knife at the side of the hinge at the point where the growth rings start. Twist the knife and with an upward movement prise the two shells apart – not always easy to achieve. Cut the hinge muscle through once you have got inside, and separate the two shells. Discard the flat shell and keep the oyster on the deeper of the two with its juice. For the sake of the diner, you will need to remove the oyster and turn it over, so it is easier to eat. The Americans market a special oyster-opening wedge which for oyster addicts is a good buy though most confirmed addicts have probably mastered the art of opening. For people like me with useless wrists such gadgets are a godsend. The French now have an electric oyster opener.

Other shellfish

In France and much of the Mediterranean a great deal of shellfish is eaten raw including mussels, clams (*praires* in French rather than the large American sort), sea urchins, cockles, etc, the huge platter of which usually includes some form of crab or spider crab and/or prawns and lobster. Not everyone likes raw shellfish and it is probably safer to make a mixture of 50 per cent cooked and 50 per cent raw if you wish to serve a shellfish platter. Oysters can of course be included.

Smoked Fish

There are no bargains with this sort of fish – you get what you pay for. Best Scotch smoked salmon has always been expensive and deserves care in carving and presentation. Smoked trout can be bought in fillets, but it is better bought as a fish, and then if you do not wish to serve a whole trout per person, which is rather a lot, you can divide it into fillets very easily.

Smoked salmon comes in three basic varieties – Baltic or

Scandinavian. Scotch and American/Canadian. Dismiss this last first: it is the sort used with bagels and cream cheese in the States for Sunday brunches and is, in its way, delicious but it is in no way related to the finest Scotch smoked salmon eaten with Hovis or rye bread and butter.

Up to about twenty years ago, people in Scotland who had access to salmon water (either owning it or poaching it) used to smoke their own salmon. Now few seem to do it, yet smoked salmon commands such a price that it would be even more worthwhile. The very finest smoking is done from Scotch or Irish salmon not in Scotland or Ireland but in England, mainly in Suffolk and the East End of London and to a lesser extent in the north-west of England. The end product is slightly salt, very slightly sweet and not at all wet. This is because the Scottish way of smoking a salmon is to cut it in half lengthwise, fillet it except for the gill (or collar) bones, and pickle it for 48 hours in an equal mixture of brown sugar and salt and a minute amount of saltpetre (see Gravadlax, p. 73). Then it is washed well and hung up by the gill bones to dry in a special drying-room for 12 to 24 hours. Thereafter it has a day or two in the smoking-room. How long the fish spend there depends on size, but nothing under 15 lb (approx. 7 kilos) is considered worth smoking.

Baltic or Scandinavian smoked salmon is quite different from Scotch. It is wetter (some say juicier), paler (some say anaemic) and distinctly sweeter. It is not dried before being smoked. Depending on the country in which you buy it, the price is higher or lower than Scotch smoked salmon. In the United Kingdom it is much used for mixed hors d'œuvres and by all the sandwich shops, being almost half the price of the Scotch. In France, however, the best Norwegian smoked salmon commands 600 francs a kilo (almost £60, in 1988), and in spite of the love-affair between Scotland and France (as opposed to France and Scotland), the French have little good to say for their smoked salmon. Just over the border in Italy, the best and most expensive smoked salmon is Scotch again, and Italians have a poor opinion of Nordic salmon. I have a theory that the French tend to buy Scotch salmon at the bottom end of the market, thus perpetuating the idea that Nordic smoked salmon is best. Moreover, the wholesale price of Scotch smoked salmon, to anyone, is higher than its equivalent in Scandinavia, thus leaving less profit margin for the French.

Smoked salmon requires a steady hand and a very sharp knife to cut well. Slice from the tail towards the head the whole length of the fish. To stop it moving all over the place, nail it down at the tail end onto the board. Just a wedge of lemon and brown bread and butter is all you need.

There are always tremendous arguments about which wine to serve with smoked salmon. With the combination of smoked food and lemon juice I personally do not think any wine goes particularly well. Keep it white and keep it innocuous and don't waste champagne or Chablis on it.

Several other fish are smoked but not all are worth buying. Smoked tuna is rather overrated in my opinion and very expensive. Good smoked trout is delicious served with sour cream and horseradish sauce. Again the wine problem is the same as for smoked salmon – this time the smoke and horseradish are the culprits.

Smoked eel is an expensive but delicious delicacy. The best comes from the Netherlands. Like the best smoked salmon, raw ham etc, smoked eel must be carved in very long, thin slices going from tail to head. Never be tempted to buy smoked eel in chunks in blister packs. They are very difficult to cut up and manage to give a couple of bones in every mouthful. For those going to the Netherlands it is something worth bringing back. You eat it much as smoked trout – in very small portions, since it is very rich and very filling – with or without a sauce (such as you would have for smoked trout) or just with lemon and pepper, brown bread and butter (the Dutch put everything on bread and butter, even strawberries and cream), and probably spirits are better than wine with it.

I have never seen smoked sturgeon in the United Kingdom or the United States but it is quite common (albeit expensive) on the Continent. It should be cut and eaten in exactly the same way as smoked salmon. Too often it is cut, or blister-packed, in chunks. When cut like this, it does not taste at all nice (in the same way as a chunk of smoked salmon or Italian raw ham tastes dreadful). There is little you can do to save the situation, except that the blister-pack piece can still be sliced in the horizontal fashion, which will redeem it slightly.

Sprats, particularly smoked, are almost a thing of the past and have become unbelievably expensive. On their home ground, around Hamburg and Kiel they are easier to buy in chocolate than their natural state. Like smoked and pickled herring they have become luxury food yet they still retain the aura of a poor man's dish. They are best served as part of a mixed smoked fish platter since a few go a long way. Best of all marinade them as you would kippers and serve 12 hours later.

I find smoked mackerel too rich to eat on its own and, like most people, tend to make a pâté of it – in any event, it is more economical that way, which makes one feel virtuous.

Other smoked fish, such as haddock, kippers, herrings etc, will be found in various recipes throughout the book, as will anchovies and sardines.

Tuna or Tunnyfish

The tuna or tunnyfish, offering large potential for starters, lives in both temperate and tropical seas and comes in three colours, white, beige and red.

The white tuna is fished young; it usually weighs only 50 lb (25 kilos) and is called germon in the trade. It is also the most expensive. The Albacore tuna (pinky-beige in colour) is what is mostly used for canning and is the most commonly encountered. Depending on the cut and the method of canning (whether it is with or without oil, and whether the oil is olive or otherwise), the price varies enormously.

The red tuna is what you see all over Mediterranean markets in summer. When it is young, the flesh is a beige colour but age reddens it. A fully adult tuna of this type can weigh almost a ton in old age, when much of it would be uneatable. The fish is actually sliced into steaks, and for a good and not too strong flavour these slices should not be more than about 6 inches (15 cm) across. Many French and Italian housewives preserve this sort of tuna in small preserving (Mason) jars. It is much like bottling plums and is much less expensive than buying tins of tuna. You will find that you will not be able to use more than a maximum of 1 lb (500 g) at any one time, since it is a dense and filling fish, so do not be tempted to use too large a jar. About 40 minutes at 400°F/200°C/Gas 6 for 3-4 jars of 1 lb (500 g) each. Test the seals before putting in the store cupboard or larder.

Tuna in cans comes in all sorts of guises. The most expensive – and the most difficult to find – are the fillets of white (germon) tunny from the Azores in what at first look like sardine tins. The price will quickly tell you the difference. Unless you are going to serve it in a mixed fish hors d'œuvres, it is not worth the money. After that comes white tunny, either *au naturel* (cooked in a *court bouillon*) or in olive oil, then white tuna in a mixture of peanut or other oil with olive oil and so on. Whole tuna is more expensive than pieces (*miettes* in French), although this usually means the tuna pieces have been pressed together and are extruded in one piece, in much the same way as we get square ham nowadays from a joint which is far from square. Red tuna is the cheapest, and red tuna in a special marinade or sauce should be cheapest of all. French, American, Japanese and Italian, in that order, are the

best canned tuna to buy whatever the colour, although all
Japanese tuna tends to be white.

Smoked tuna has become fashionable and commands a rather
fancy price. It has a pleasant taste but can be somewhat dry. It is
usually vacuum-packed, pre-sliced, and sometimes comes in
olive oil, which is an improvement. Since the price is about the
same for smoked eel and smoked tuna, I would plump for the
former as better value.

Ham and other Prepared Meats

Real ham, the salted and sometimes smoked back legs of a pig,
basically comes two ways – raw and cooked. After that there are
thousands of different sorts of raw and cooked ham. Dismissing
the extruded, rectangular, pressed variety as child-fodder or
flavoured pink rubber, let us look at cooked ham.

To cook ham at home, one must begin with it raw, and the
British, in common with much of Europe and the east coast states
of America, still have a vast choice of raw hams, from Bradenham
to Wiltshire, Suffolk to Cumberland to say nothing of Virginia and
Smithfield hams in America. Used as is, or in any of the recipes
which call for ham in this book, this ham will be a great
improvement on any ready-cooked variety. Ham purchased on
the bone is very much nicer, though more wasteful (to the
retailer) than pressed ham. Baked ham usually tastes nicer than
boiled only – but not always.

The problem is that a ham, or even half a ham, is very large, and even if one freezes some, it seems to go on for ever. It is worth bearing in mind that raw ham freezes much better than cooked, and with no loss of flavour. We always used to have a whole ham when I was cooking for a local charity dinner or fête – that way we had a festive dinner party and I made endless ham vols-au-vent or ham mousses out of the left-overs. Strangely it worked out cheaper than buying packeted, tasteless ham for the same purpose. Luckily there are still shops left where you can buy cooked ham on the bone.

Raw ham has become so expensive that you buy it by the slice. France, Switzerland, Germany, Spain, Portugal, Belgium and Italy all are famous for their raw hams. To anyone who has lived in Italy, the problem with raw ham elsewhere is that it is usually sliced too thickly. Thickness is inimical to raw ham. The French are the worst offenders but, if you insist, they will slice it thinner. They do not like doing it because, since it is bought by the slice rather than by weight, the slices will weigh less. The Spaniards also tend to cut their *jamon serrano* rather too thick, but again by insisting you can get it thinner.

It is generally acknowledged that Italian raw ham, *prosciutto crudo*, is best. For most non-Italians, raw ham is from Parma, a city famous for three things: cheese, ham and Verdi. Not all Parma ham is made from pigs reared in Parma – a lot of hams are sent there from all over the Emilia Romagna and the Po Plain to be 'ripened' in the valley of the Magra near Parma, where they are said to lose the taste of pickle and pick up the scent of chestnut woods. Most Italian raw ham seen abroad is Parma ham.

However, in Italy raw ham from San Daniele in the Friuli (near Venice) is considered better, leaner and sweeter; naturally it is more expensive. The main reason is that there are fewer producers of San Daniele than of Parma ham, and they are very jealous of the quality of their produce. It is rare to find a San Daniele ham that is not good, and if such a thing happens, it is usually the fault of the wholesaler or retailer rather than the supplier. The Friuliani are renowned for their honesty and reliability.

Many other regions in Italy produce *prosciutto crudo*, Tuscany among them, but this ham is not to everyone's taste – highly salted with added pepper and cut rather too thickly for non-Tuscans. Although most raw ham is produced in factories by highly mechanized methods, there are one or two firms producing raw ham by old-fashioned methods, which include massaging the hams by hand to remove particles of blood and/or water rather than pressing them out between rubber rollers. In the Val de Susa in Piedmont, right on the French border, San Giuliano ham is produced. It is in all the best Piedmontese restaurants (Piedmont is known for its gourmets) and occasionally gets to France and Switzerland. Not more expensive than Parma ham it is one of the best hams available in Italy today.

'Credit-card thin' is often used to describe the method of slicing raw ham. (Some credit cards are thicker than others! I once thought you could not cut it *too* thin, but you can, and it is almost as horrible as too thick. Slightly thinner than the average credit card (Access or Visa) is probably best – if you can see the design of the plate easily through the ham, it is too thin.

To keep sliced raw ham, it should always be interleaved with cellophane, waxed paper or film; put it in the freezer and remove half an hour to an hour before use. It freezes like a dream. Kept in the refrigerator for any length of time, it develops an odd, tired taste and also, because of Italian wrapping methods, has a tendency to dry out at the edges. Served with slices of melon – or, better still with figs – it is a delicious first course. Pickles, salads, mustard etc are absolutely forbidden.

If you are feeding a lot or the price of raw ham is too much, try good *coppa*, which is made from the shoulder and, although expensive, is considerably cheaper than Parma ham.

Germany produces exceedingly good ham for eating raw – some of the best is from Westphalia: it is smoked and has quite a different taste from Italian, which is not. It is eaten on thickly buttered pumpernickel bread and washed down with Steinhager – a fiery sort of German gin. It goes well with beer also. Northern Germany also produces cottage-industry-type ham, known as *Katenschinken*, but it is one of those items where you have to be friends with people who know where to go for the best. Nearer the Danish border, Holstein is also a famous region for ham.

The best-known raw ham of France, *jambon de Bayonne*, is made not at Bayonne but at Orthez nearby. Sliced finely (which often it is not), it is a delicious, very lightly smoked ham, still tasting slightly of the wine which was part of the pickle. There are plenty of country hams in France, often called *jambon de pays* or *jambon de montagne* – some are superb but many are rather tasteless and indifferent. The better the restaurant or *traiteur*, the better the ham. Again there are no bargains in this field, for ham-making is an onerous task and one in which there is a lot of chance. A change in the weather, too high humidity or an electricity breakdown (as in the winter of 1985) can all cause hams to go bad.

Germany, France and Italy are all famous for their sausages. Many of them are too hearty to serve as a first course. Salami is an exception, and the finest comes from near Parma and is called

Felino. It commands a very high price indeed, though luckily you need very little – 25 g (just under an ounce) per person is quite generous. Most places will allow you to taste salami or sausage before buying. The Danes make excellent bacon and pork products but alas, salami is not one of them. For a slightly larger outlay you can get something you will really enjoy from Italy or France. Some of the best sausages in France come from around Lyons and there are also good ones from Alsace. Austria, Hungary and Yugoslavia all produce sausages and salami which are excellent but usually not exported. Hungarian in particular is well worth buying if you see it. None should be sliced until virtually the last minute. Like raw ham, sliced salami freezes well, and if you want to keep it for more than twenty-four hours this is a better way than just using the refrigerator. This applies *only* to sliced salami and not to the whole sausage, which will keep quite well out of the refrigerator. It is easier to slice if you cool the salami slightly beforehand.

Another delicacy from both Italy and Switzerland is air-dried beef. This must be sliced as thinly as raw ham and is usually served as part of a mixed platter of cold meats. In Italy it is known as *Bressaola* and in Switzerland *bœuf des Grisons* or *viande sechée des Grisons* and sometimes as *Bündnerfleisch*. The price is quite horrific (the strong Swiss franc being partly to blame) but only very small amounts are served. The Swiss also do air-dried ham.

Except for goose liver, duck liver etc, I feel that armed with the right book one can make better pâté at home than one can buy in the average delicatessen or *traiteur*. Of course there are exceptions. Jane Grigson's book *Charcuterie and French Pork Cookery* is a mine of information on this branch of cookery, and it has a section devoted to this subject. The best thing is that you *know* exactly what has gone in to your pâté or terrine, and you *know* there are no taste-modifiers/enhancers, preservatives, artificial colourings etc in it.

Quails' and Gulls' Eggs

For some reason I cannot fathom, there are people who like the fishy taste of gulls' eggs. Thank goodness the eggs are less fashionable than they used to be – perhaps they are protected in many countries. In Germany they are not, and they are a speciality around Hamburg. Served as part of a mixed hors d'œuvre, they come accompanied by a very strong-tasting (of mustard?) mayonnaise and equally strong cottage-industry sausage.

Quails' eggs (being farmed) are generally available and are often served as a cocktail-party snack accompanied by celery salt. In themselves they are rather tasteless (as most eggs are) but they make a very pretty first course done in aspic – you follow the recipe for ordinary eggs this way but use 4 quails' eggs per person instead. They are also excellent done as for *Oeufs à la Tripe* (p. 41) but you leave the eggs whole – for 8 people you will need 3 dozen eggs. A quail's egg takes about 1½ minutes to soft-boil, and 2½ to hard-boil.

Fruit

GRAPEFRUIT

I think there are few people nowadays who would dare to serve a plain half grapefruit as a first course. Even soaked in brandy or grilled with brown sugar and port (when such preparation takes it out of the ready-made first course class) grapefruit just on its own has become hackneyed and unacceptable. Yet, in its own right it is just as delicious as the ubiquitous avocado. When absolutely ripe and perfectly presented it can make a delicious, clean start to a meal. *Larousse Gastronomique* states that the Americans copied the idea of starting a meal with grapefruit from the Chinese. Since grapefruit is grown only around Swatow in south China I doubt that this was a common occurrence and it seems so very un-Chinese and no-one I know (including myself) has ever come across it in China or among the Chinese. *Larousse* is not infallible since in the next paragraph it describes Grappa as a Piedmontese spirit with rue when in fact it is native to the Italian Veneto and it is *only* in this part of Italy that rue is added. Elsewhere, it is left without additional flavouring.

Always separate the flesh from the half grapefruit before serving or you risk your guests having to battle to get a bite or worse, getting a jet of juice in the eye. To choose grapefruit, pink or normal, go by weight because a grapefruit should be fairly heavy for its volume. Florida and Israel are probably the best places for this fruit. The near relations *ugli* from the West Indies and the *pomelo* from south-east Asia are more suitable for breakfast.

AVOCADOS

I have never fathomed how a food can be called 'common' in the social sense but a lot of people think that serving *any* form of avocado as a first course is simply not done. What a pity since avocados are something I can eat twice a day, everyday. Certainly, served on its own with just an oil and vinegar dressing, it can be a bit boring, and perhaps the serving of it filled with prawn cocktail in a too ketchup-y sauce has become something to be dreaded in both restaurants and private houses. Avocado seems to go well with so many things from hard or soft boiled eggs, smoked fish, smoked or cold meats, other salads and even some fruits. It is probably best to use avocado in combination with other ingredients rather than on its own for a dinner party, but, just every now and again, you should enjoy an avocado on its own.

MELONS AND FIGS

Figs feature here as an alternative to melons for serving with thinly sliced raw ham. White figs are almost better than purple but it is better to use melon where you have any doubts about the maturity of the figs. Since figs should be picked at their perfect moment of ripeness and served sun-warm, it is difficult to reproduce this perfection in non-fig-growing countries. Figs are notoriously bad travellers and are, therefore, picked slightly unripe, packaged in cotton wool, plastic *excelsior* or pre-formed plastic packs and flown to northern Europe. They do not ripen properly and tend to be rather tasteless.

It is not particularly easy to tell when melons are ripe even in their country of origin. There should be a fairly strong perfume and the top and bottom of the melon should give slightly to pressure from the fingers. However, it is also a question of taste, since in northern Europe melons are eaten in what would be considered an unripe state by Italians, French and Spaniards.

Melons will ripen to a degree away from the mother plant but a really green, unripe melon will never make a perfect first course no matter how long you keep it.

Canary melons are dark green with a pale green and peach interior and the hardest of all to test for ripeness – their shell remains firm to the end. They are also the least perfumed – though doubtless in the Canaries their flavour improves. It is a matter of taste which French melon is best – probably Charentais or Cavaillon – both have deep orange flesh and are easy to test for ripeness. Then there are the 'netted melons' of central Europe and the Middle East which have flesh ranging from pink through peach to almost red. Most melons in the UK are from Spain or Israel and highly priced. Pleasant mixtures can be made with prawns, watercress or mild cheese or by mixing it with other fruits. Although it may seem wasteful to remove the flesh with a melon-baller, it is in fact quite an economy since small balls in a glass take up quite a lot of room and look generous even when one is allowing only a quarter of melon per person. A slightly sweetened lemon-vinaigrette is quite a good dressing.

The most delicious way of serving melon is with thinly sliced, raw ham, be it Italian, Spanish, German or French. The melon should be peeled rather than left as is and the ham placed *over* it so the ham does not sit in a bath of melon juice. Plenty of freshly-ground black pepper is all that is needed.

2 Eggs

Poached and Soft-boiled

Many of these recipes are interchangeable. Certainly soft-boiled eggs (*œufs mollets*) can be substituted for poached eggs and vice versa. Also, provided you are careful, most of the poached and soft-boiled egg recipes will allow you to use baked eggs instead – i.e. you just break an egg over your vegetable, fish or meat base, top with cream and bake. It is always a good idea to have this base hot before you start the baking, otherwise you may have to overcook the egg to be sure of having the whole thing hot.

There appears to be an awful lot of snobbery surrounding the subject of poached eggs. It takes a great deal of skill and often a prodigious amount of eggs to get eight perfectly poached eggs by the traditional method, and for the slight difference in taste I think one is justified in using a non-stick egg-poacher instead. Of course, the end result is *not* the same, since the egg is more like a steamed or baked egg but, provided it is not overcooked, I think such a result is acceptable, and it is certainly tidier than many of the raggedy poached eggs I have had.

I prefer soft-boiled eggs – what the French call *œufs mollets* – to poached. Provided you time them properly and are careful in peeling them, they are fail-proof, which is more than can be said about poached eggs. The great thing about eggs, particularly cold, is not to overcook them – unless you are after the hard-boiled sort.

The first two recipes, for the record and for those who wish to try their hand at this particular skill, are for poached eggs, one French and one American – needless to say, the latter is the easier of the two.

The French poached eggs are round and totally covered by the white, whereas the American sort are more like those produced by a British egg-poacher – though the taste is very similar. The choice is yours.

CLASSIC POACHED EGGS

Have your egg ready on a flat saucer or plate. Do one at a time and use a wide-ish, shallow pan rather than a saucepan. Half fill with water and put in a little salt and 2 tablespoons vinegar. Bring to a rolling boil, lower the heat and with a wooden spoon swish the water round to make a hollow in the centre. Pour your egg into this space. Take the pan off the heat, cover and let stand 3-4 minutes – 3 if you are going to re-heat the egg later, 4 if you are going to use it immediately. Just-set poached eggs can be re-heated by steeping in really hot, but not boiling, water for 30 seconds – no longer or the result will be tough.

AMERICAN POACHED EGGS

Again use a shallow pan: half fill with salted water and add 2-3 tablespoons of white vinegar. Slide the eggs in one by one carefully – it does not matter if they touch but the yolks should be sufficiently far apart, one from the other, that you are able to cut out rounds of white with a yolk properly in the middle later on. Do not try to do more than 4 at a time. Reduce the heat immediately so that the water just judders (if using electricity, you will have to take the pan off the heat) and cover with a lid. In 3 minutes your whites should be set – if not, let the eggs steep a little longer. Cut round the eggs and lift out one by one. Trim with a pastry cutter (or a knife) and serve with the desired sauce.

EGGS BENEDICT (USA)

POACHED EGGS, HAM AND SAUCE HOLLANDAISE

Delicious but a bit tricky.

Imperial/Metric	*American*
8 crumpets	8 English muffins
8 eggs, poached	8 eggs, poached
8 circles of ham	8 circles of ham
1 recipe *sauce hollandaise*, (see p.395)	1 recipe *sauce hollandaise* (see p.395)

Make your sauce first and keep warm. Cut small squares of ham into circles with a pastry cutter. Poach the eggs and keep warm. Toast the crumpets (muffins), butter them and put a round of heated-through ham on each. Top with a poached egg and then cover with *sauce hollandaise*.

EGGS IN ANCHOVY SAUCE

There are many versions of this recipe – some use poached eggs some soft-boiled and others baked, so the choice is up to you. (Baked eggs with this sauce come out rather strong-tasting and are not recommended.) For the freshest taste use poached or soft-boiled eggs with the hot sauce ladled over them.

Serve on toast or fried bread if you wish, though it is not necessary to have bread at all.

Imperial/Metric	*American*
8 eggs	8 eggs
8 fl. oz (240 ml) cream	1 cup cream
½ pint (300 ml) *sauce béchamel*	1¼ cups *sauce béchamel*
(see p.391)	(see p.391)
10-12 anchovy fillets	10-12 anchovy fillets
1 tablespoon tomato con-	1 tablespoon tomato con-
centrate	centrate
parsley (to decorate)	parsley (to decorate)

The sauce will wait; the eggs will not. So prepare your sauce first and keep it hot whilst you prepare the eggs as you wish. (The sauce can also be prepared in advance and reheated at the last moment.)

Keep the *béchamel* on the thick side and do not add salt. In a liquidizer or food processor put the anchovy fillets, the cold sauce and cream, and whizz up together. Turn into a saucepan and heat through. When ready, pour over the eggs, sprinkle with parsley and serve.

ŒUFS EN GELEE

EGGS IN ASPIC

For the following recipes you may use *œufs mollets* (soft-boiled eggs) or poached eggs at your choice.

Imperial/Metric	American
8 eggs	8 eggs
1 pint (600 ml) Madeira jelly	2½ cups Madeira jelly
(see Quick aspic p.180)	2 or 3 thin slices of ham
2 or 3 thin slices of ham	tarragon or chives (to decorate)
tarragon or chives (to decorate)	

Cut the ham to fit the bottom of the moulds you are using. Put a little melted jelly in the base of each and, once set, lay the ham on top. Lay the cooked egg on top of this and decorate with long pieces of chives or a couple of tarragon leaves. Pour over the rest of the Madeira jelly and refrigerate. Turn out and serve on a bed of lettuce or other salad greens.

EGGS IN ASPIC WITH LOBSTER (UK)

Follow the previous recipe but instead of ham put a slice of lobster in the base of each mould and make the jelly with a slightly sweet white wine instead of Madeira.

MENIMEN (Turkey)

This is a dish which is found all over the Middle East – whether taken to their colonies by the Turks or not is debatable. In some countries it is called *Chakchouka* and in Algeria it becomes *Frita aux œufs*, a French colonial dish. The pepper, tomato and onion part can be done in advance, and the eggs can be cooked at the last minute. This recipe is best made with poached eggs surrounded by the mixture, but it is also quite good with cold *œufs mollets* (soft-boiled eggs), particularly if you add a little vinegar to the mixture and sprinkle the whole with parsley.

Imperial/Metric	American
8 eggs	8 eggs
2 large red peppers, chopped	2 large red bell peppers,
2 large green peppers, chopped	chopped
1 large onion, chopped	2 large green bell peppers,
1 lb (500 g) tomatoes, chopped	chopped
olive oil	1 large onion, chopped
salt and pepper	1 lb tomatoes, chopped
	olive oil
	salt and pepper

Starting with the onions on their own, fry all the ingredients until they are soft, with the tomatoes making a sort of thick sauce. Either poach the eggs and serve surrounded by this mixture or drop the eggs into it (in 2 pans of 4 eggs each) and cook until the white is well set and the yolk still a little wobbly – in the Middle East the egg is almost raw.

ŒUFS A LA BEARNAISE (France)

EGGS WITH SAUCE BEARNAISE

Unbelievably rich but delicious. The sauce can be made slightly in advance and, instead of traditional poached eggs, use the American sort for speed. Keep what follows very plain.

Imperial/Metric	*American*
8 eggs, poached	8 eggs, poached
8 slices toast or fried bread	8 slices toast or fried bread
1 recipe *sauce béarnaise* (p.392)	1 recipe *sauce béarnaise* (p.392)

Trim the poached eggs with a pastry cutter and keep warm while you make the toast or fried bread. Heat the sauce in a double boiler or *bain-marie*. Put a poached egg on each piece of bread and pour the *sauce béarnaise* over. Serve at once.

ŒUFS A LA BRUXELLOISE (Belgium)

An ideal starter for fans of cooked chicory.

Imperial/Metric	*American*
8 eggs, poached or soft-boiled	8 eggs, poached or soft-boiled
purée of 1 lb chicory (Belgian endive)	purée of 1 lb chicory (Belgian endive)
8 bread *croûtes*, made in the oven	8 bread *croûtes*, made in the oven
2 medium slices of home-cooked ham	2 medium slices of home-cooked ham
8 fl. oz (240 ml) double cream	1 cup heavy cream
salt, pepper and nutmeg	salt, pepper and nutmeg
paprika or parsley, chopped (to decorate)	paprika or parsley, chopped (to decorate)

Paint the bread *croûtes* with melted butter, put in a hot oven and let slightly brown – do not overcook. Before making the chicory into purée, make sure it has been well drained. Cut the ham into small pieces and add to the chicory purée. Add half the cream to this mixture and heat up. Divide it between the 8 *croûtes*. Heat the rest of the cream and add salt, pepper and nutmeg. Have the eggs re-heated and place one in each *croûte* on top of the chicory/ham mixture. Pour over the cream, sprinkle with parsley or paprika and serve immediately.

Hard-boiled eggs can be used and the whole thing can then be re-heated in the oven, but the taste is not so subtle.

POACHED EGGS WALDORF (USA)

Imperial/Metric	American
8 eggs, poached or soft-boiled	8 eggs, poached or soft-boiled
4 oz (125 g)chopped mushrooms	4 oz chopped mushrooms
8 large mushroom caps	8 large mushroom caps
½ pint (300 ml) single cream	1¼ cups light cream
scant 1 tablespoon flour	scant 1 tablespoon flour
2 tablespoons butter	2 tablespoons butter
small amount of dry white wine	small amount of dry white wine
salt and cayenne pepper	salt and cayenne pepper
parsley, chopped (to decorate)	parsley, chopped (to decorate)

Make a sauce by frying the chopped mushrooms in the butter, then adding the flour and finally the cream and white wine so that you get a not-too-thick sauce. Cook until any raw flour taste has disappeared. Cook the mushroom caps either by grilling or frying in butter. Have the poached or soft-boiled eggs hot and put one in each mushroom cap, pour over the sauce, sprinkle with parsley and serve.

ŒUFS MOLLETS AUX ARTICHAUTS (France)

ARTICHOKES AND SOFT-BOILED EGGS

Imperial/Metric	*American*
8 eggs, poached or soft-boiled (5 minutes)	8 eggs, poached or soft-boiled (5 minutes)
8 large artichokes*	8 large artichokes*
8 oz (225 g) ham, chopped (not minced) small	8 oz ham, chopped (not minced) small
1 recipe *sauce aurore* (p.391)	1 recipe *sauce aurore* (p.391)
2 oz (60 g) flour	2 oz flour
1 or 2 lemons	1 or 2 lemons
parsley, chopped (to decorate)	parsley, chopped (to decorate)

* Use the large Breton artichokes, the type which is exported under the name Black Prince among others. Smaller artichokes will not have enough room to contain the fillings.

Cut off the stalk of the artichoke and then turn it on its side and cut through the top half of the leaves (a serrated knife works well for this). Then remove all the leaves one by one so that you are left with only the heart and the choke. Remove the choke with a teaspoon or, if you find it easier, pull it out bit by bit – everyone has a different method. Rub the artichoke bottoms with the cut lemon to prevent darkening. Alternatively put into a bowl of water to which you have added the juice of 2 lemons.

Mix the flour with a little water, gradually adding the rest. Put on to boil and cook the artichoke bottoms for approx, 15 minutes. Test for 'done-ness' and give a little more time if necessary.

Have ready (and hot) 8 poached or shelled soft-boiled eggs. Place the drained artichokes either on individual serving dishes or on one large dish. Divide the chopped ham into 8 and put a portion of ham under each egg. Coat them with the hot *sauce aurore*. Sprinkle with a little chopped parsley.

Variation
This dish can be eaten cold, in which case, instead of a *sauce aurore*, a home-made mayonnaise (p.404) is used, to which you add half its volume in whipping cream together with 2 tablespoons tomato ketchup. Think in terms of ¾ pint (½ litre/1 US pint) of mayonnaise to 8 fl. oz. (¼ litre/1 US cup) of cream.

ŒUFS PASHA (UK)

SOFT-BOILED EGGS WITH CONSOMME

This recipe, by John Seyfried, appeared in *Harper's Bazaar* in June 1962. It is extraordinarily good and has the advantage of being able to be prepared in advance.

Imperial/Metric	*American*
8 eggs, soft-boiled or poached (cold)	8 eggs, soft-boiled or poached (cold)
4 salmon or lumpfish roe	4 salmon or lumpfish roe
juice of 1 lemon	juice of 1 lemon
1 small onion, finely chopped	1 small onion, finely chopped
approx. 3 tins Campbell's Beef Consommé	approx. 3 tins Campbell's Beef Consommé
½ pint (300 ml) single or sour cream	1¼ cups pouring or commercial sour cream
sprig of chervil or parsley	sprig of chervil or parsley

Blend together the salmon roe, lemon juice and onion and divide between 8 ramekins. Put the cold poached or soft-boiled eggs on top. Refrigerate for about 15 minutes. Warm – do not make hot – the consommé until it just melts. Alternatively heat the consommé and let it cool down to just before its setting point. Pour it over each ramekin to come to the top. Let set and serve with a blob of cream, sour or otherwise, and a sprig of chervil or parsley.

SOFT-BOILED EGGS IN CRAB SAUCE (UK)

This can also be done with baked eggs if wished.

Imperial/Metric	*American*
8 eggs, soft-boiled	8 eggs, soft-boiled
8 oz (225 g) crab meat	8 oz crab meat
8 fl. oz (240 ml) double cream	1 cup heavy cream
1 teaspoon Tabasco	1 teaspoon Tabasco
salt if necessary	salt if necessary

Mix the crab into the cream, heat up, add the Tabasco and pour over the soft-boiled or poached eggs. If baking the eggs, mix the crab with half the cream and Tabasco and divide the mixture between the bases of 8 ramekins. Top with a raw egg, a tablespoon of cream and bake as usual.
  Sprinkle with parsley before serving.

ŒUFS MOLLETS NANTUA (France)

SOFT-BOILED EGGS WITH CRAYFISH SAUCE

Pour *sauce Nantua* (p.399) over hot soft-boiled eggs. Serve on fried bread or toast.

ŒUFS MOLLETS AU CURRY (France)

SOFT-BOILED EGGS IN A LIGHT CURRY SAUCE

A great improvement on the standard curried eggs.

Imperial/Metric	*American*
8 eggs, soft-boiled	8 eggs, soft-boiled
1 medium onion, finely chopped	1 medium onion, finely chopped
½ pint (300 ml) *sauce béchamel* (p.391)	1¼ cups *sauce béchamel* (p.391)
4 fl. oz (120 ml) double cream	½ cup heavy cream
2 teaspoons (or more) curry powder	2 teaspoons (or more) curry powder
1 tablespoon (or less) sugar	1 tablespoon (or less) sugar
2 tablespoons vinegar	2 tablespoons vinegar
1 sweet red pepper	1 sweet red pepper
butter	butter

Slice the pepper into thin strips, put in boiling water for a few minutes to soften and then set aside. Cook the onion in a little butter but do not let it colour. Add the *sauce béchamel*, the vinegar and then the cream. Finally add curry powder to your liking – it should not be too hot. Re-heat your soft-boiled eggs for 1 minute in boiling water and coat with the sauce. Place 2 strips of red pepper across the top of each egg in a cross shape and serve.

ŒUFS MOLLETS A LA NORMANDE (France)

SOFT-BOILED EGGS IN A MUSSEL SAUCE

Imperial/Metric	*American*
8 eggs, soft-boiled	8 eggs, soft-boiled
2 pints (1 kilo) mussels	2½ pints mussels
1 large onion, finely chopped	1 large onion, finely chopped
2 tablespoons flour	2 tablespoons flour
6 oz (190 g) butter	6 oz butter
½ pint (300 ml) single cream	1¼ cups light cream
2 tablespoons brandy or	2 tablespoons brandywine or
calvados	calvados
2 tablespoons parsley	2 tablespoons parsley
1 tablespoon chervil (optional)	1 tablespoon chervil (optional)

Clean and cook the mussels by steaming them open – the moment they do so, take them off the heat and remove them from their shells. Keep 8 aside for decoration. Strain the liquid through a fine muslin or through a coffee filter paper and set aside.

Cook the onion in the butter, stir in the flour and then make a sauce by using the mussel liquid, brandy (or calvados) and herbs, adding the cream at the end. The sauce should not be too thick. Stir in the cooked mussels.

Heat the soft-boiled eggs by putting them in boiling water for 1 minute (no longer), draining them on paper. Put the eggs either on a large dish or on individual dishes and cover them with the sauce, placing a mussel on top of each egg. Sprinkle the whole with parsley and serve.

Alternatively you can bake the eggs, using half the sauce under the egg and half above. Decorate with the mussel and parsley on taking them from the oven.

ŒUFS A LA BASQUAISE (France)

POACHED OR SOFT-BOILED EGGS WITH PEPPERS, TOMATOES AND ONIONS

This is somewhat like a *piperade*. The original recipe calls for goose fat as the cooking medium but I think oil makes a lighter dish.

Imperial/Metric	American
8 eggs, poached or soft-boiled	8 eggs, poached or soft-boiled
1 red pepper	1 red bell pepper
1 green pepper	1 green bell pepper
1 medium onion	1 medium onion
2 medium tomatoes	2 medium tomatoes
parsley, chopped	parsley, chopped
oil (for cooking)	oil (for cooking)

Cut everything up into small cubes and cook in oil until almost a mush. Put a portion on each dish and press a hot poached (best) or soft-boiled egg into it and serve sprinkled with parsley.

ŒUFS MOLLETS A LA CREOLE (France)

SOFT-BOILED EGGS ON PIQUANT RICE

The Creole garnish can be done in advance and heated up at the last moment. (Follow with something light!)

Imperial/Metric	American
8 eggs, soft-boiled	8 eggs, soft-boiled
1 red pepper, chopped	1 red bell pepper, chopped
1 green pepper, chopped	1 green bell pepper, chopped
1 onion, chopped	1 onion, chopped
2 slices ham	2 slices ham
2 oz (60 g) rice, raw	¼ cup rice, raw
pinch oregano and cumin	pinch oregano and cumin
salt and red pepper or Tabasco	salt and red pepper or Tabasco

Put the rice on to cook. Meanwhile cook the onion, peppers and tomatoes together. Once done, season with the oregano, cumin, salt and red pepper or Tabasco to your taste. Mix these vegetables with the cooked rice and keep hot.

Put a helping of Creole rice on each plate and place an egg, either soft-boiled or poached, in the centre of each and serve immediately.

ŒUFS A LA BENEDICTINE (France)

Not to be confused with Eggs Benedict, which is an American dish. I find the addition of fried bread a bit too much and just serve the soft-boiled egg in its bed of *brandade*.

Imperial/Metric	American
8 eggs, soft-boiled	8 eggs, soft-boiled
1 lb (500 g) *brandade de morue* (p.77) (purée of salt codfish)	1 lb *brandade de morue* (p.77) (pureé of salt codfish)
½ pint (300 ml) double cream	1¼ cups heavy cream
pepper and nutmeg	pepper and nutmeg
8 slices of truffle or black olives (for decoration)	8 slices of truffle or black olives (for decoration)
8 rounds of bread, fried at the last moment	8 rounds of bread, fried at the last moment

Beat down the *brandade* with the cream and then heat (preferably in a double saucepan or *bain-marie*). Add the pepper and nutmeg. Re-heat the soft-boiled eggs. On each slice of fried bread put a portion of *brandade* and press the soft-boiled egg into it. Decorate with a slice of truffle or a black olive and serve.

Hard-boiled and Scrambled

CASINO EGGS (Hungary)

This is part and parcel of every Hungarian cold buffet, and it has to be admitted that one quickly gets sick of the repetition. Nevertheless, provided one is not offered this dish *every* night in summer, it can be very good – and it can be prepared well in advance. I prefer Casino eggs without the addition of sardines, though this is fairly traditional.

Imperial/Metric	American
8 large eggs, hard-boiled	8 large eggs, hardcooked
1 recipe Spanish/Russian salad (pp.331-2)	1 recipe Spanish/Russian Salad (pp.331-2)
½ pint (300 ml) thick sour cream	1¼ cups thick sour cream
1 tablespoon Dijon-type mustard	1 tablespoon Dijon-type mustard
1 tablespoon vinegar (or more to taste)	1 tablespoon vinegar (or more to taste)
1 tin sardines (optional)	1 tin sardines (optional)
paprika	paprika
dillweed to taste	dillweed to taste

Hard-boil the eggs and put to cool immediately in running cold water. Cut a small slice off the side of each egg and scoop out the yolk. Mix this with *half* the sour cream, mustard, vinegar and a little paprika, and add the mashed sardines if using them. Stuff the egg whites with these.

On a large platter spread out the Russian Salad (the Spanish version is so close to the Hungarian as to be almost indistinguishable) and arrange the stuffed eggs on it. Some people arrange their eggs with the hole downwards, others with the hole facing upwards – the first is the more common.

Stir the dillweed into the remaining sour cream and pour this sauce over the eggs. Sprinkle with paprika and serve. The eggs can be done in advance, as can the salad, but they must be separated until the last minute. Both should be covered with clingfilm. Put the dressing and paprika on at the very last.

ŒUFS A LA TRIPE (France)

HARD-BOILED EGGS IN *SAUCE SOUBISE*

The finished dish looks something like tripe in onion sauce, hence its name.

Elizabeth David says these were often called Convent Eggs but I have recipes for Convent Eggs with nothing but eggs, cream, salt and pepper. However, my grandmother in Scotland called a first course (for lunch) of eggs baked in sieved *sauce soubise* Convent Eggs (see p.46). Rightly or wrongly called, it is very delicious.

Imperial/Metric	*American*
8-10 eggs, hard-boiled	8-10 eggs, hardcooked
1 recipe *sauce soubise* without sieving (p.400)	1 recipe *sauce soubise* without sieving (p.400)
2 oz (60 g) Gruyère cheese, grated	¼ cup Gruyère cheese, grated

Butter an ovenproof dish, pyrex or earthenware, and lay in it a thinnish layer of hot *sauce soubise*. Then put a layer of sliced hard-boiled eggs, then a layer of sauce, and so on, finishing up with sauce. (Alternatively you can carefully stir the hard-boiled eggs into the sauce.) Scatter with cheese, if liked, and brown in the oven at around 400°F/200°C/Gas 6 for 7-8 minutes.

ŒUFS TAPENADE (France: Provence)

HARD-BOILED EGGS WITH OLIVE SAUCE

Tapenade (olive sauce) is now sold in jars, and all that is needed is for it to be mixed down with a little oil and the anchovies. Otherwise here is the whole recipe.

Imperial/Metric	*American*
8 eggs, hard-boiled	8 eggs, hardcooked
8 oz (250 g) black olives	8 oz black olives
4 oz (125 g) anchovy fillets	4 oz anchovy fillets
2 oz (60 g) capers	2 oz capers
4 fl. oz (120 ml) best olive oil	½ cup best olive oil
plenty of freshly ground pepper	plenty of freshly ground pepper
2 fl. oz (60 ml) brandy (cognac)	¼ cup brandywine or cognac
teaspoon Dijon mustard	teaspoon Dijon mustard

Remove stones from olives. Drop olives into a liquidizer or food processor together with all the other ingredients except the eggs. You will end up with a most unattractive but delicious-tasting mess. You can now proceed one of two ways.

1. You can remove the cooked egg yolks and add them to the *tapenade* and then put the result back into the egg halves or

2. You can leave the hard-boiled eggs as they are, cut in half, and dilute the *tapenade* a little further and use it as a sauce for the eggs.

Tapenade keeps for a long time in a jar in the refrigerator.

CUMBERLAND EGGS (UK)

This is a most peculiar but delicious recipe I encountered when I lived in Suffolk. I cannot remember who gave it to me, so I apologize in advance! It can be made at least 24 hours ahead, if wished, and kept in the refrigerator covered with clingfilm.

Imperial/Metric	*American*
10 eggs	10 eggs
3 tablespoons Cumberland sauce	3 tablespoons Cumberland sauce
a little milk	a little milk
2 oz (60 g) butter	¼ cup butter
2 teaspoons tomato paste	2 teaspoons tomato paste
2 tablespoons mayonnaise	2 tablespoons mayonnaise
parsley (to decorate)	parsley (to decorate)

Scramble the eggs gently, using as much milk as necessary, but do not overcook. Halve the mixture. Into the first mixture put the Cumberland sauce (it need not be homemade), and into the second put the tomato paste and mayonnaise. Divide the Cumberland mixture between 8 ramekins and then top with the mayonnaise mixture. Sprinkle with parsley at serving time.

Baked Eggs

Baked eggs (*œufs en cocotte*) should always be covered with something, butter, cream, sauce etc, or the top will be hard and unappetizing. They need on average 5 minutes cooking – 7 at the most, depending on your personal taste and the vagaries of your oven. The yolk should not be absolutely set as it will continue to cook for a moment or two after being taken out of the oven. Always cook baked eggs by putting the ramekins in a large baking tin in which you have boiling water which comes half way up the sides of the containers.

ŒUFS EN COCOTTE (France)

BAKED EGGS IN CREAM

This is the basic recipe from which can be made many, many variations. Some follow but there is nothing against using your imagination. The eggs should be of the freshest, and the additions should not be any old left-overs but items specially chosen to enhance the egg-and-cream mixture.

Imperial/Metric	*American*
8 very fresh eggs	8 very fresh eggs
8 fl. oz (240 ml) double cream	1 cup heavy cream
approx. 2 oz (60 g) butter	¼ cup butter
salt and pepper	salt and pepper

Butter 8 ramekins well. Pre-heat the oven. Fill a large baking dish with hot water so that it comes half way up the sides of the ramekins. Heat the cream and stir in the salt and pepper. Break the eggs into the ramekins and divide the hot cream between them. Cook for 6-8 minutes at 375°F/190°C/Gas 5.

BAKED EGG TARTLETS (UK)

Imperial/Metric	*American*
8 individual tartlets	8 individual tartlets
8 eggs	8 eggs
1 onion, chopped	1 onion, chopped
2 tomatoes, peeled and chopped	2 tomatoes, peeled and chopped
pinch of marjoram and thyme	pinch of marjoram and thyme
8 fl. oz (240 ml) single cream	1 cup light cream
2 egg yolks	2 egg yolks
1 slice of ham (optional)	1 slice of ham (optional)
butter	butter

Fry the onion but do not let it brown. Add tomatoes and the ham if used. Finally add the herbs. Let cool. Beat the egg yolks and cream together, then add the tomato/ham sauce. Break an egg into each tartlet and divide the sauce between them. Bake at 400°F/200°C/Gas 6 for 7-8 minutes (or longer) but look at 5-6 minutes and make sure they do not over-cook.

BAKED EGGS WITH PRAWNS IN BRANDY AND CREAM (UK)

Imperial/Metric	*American*
8 eggs	8 eggs
8 oz (250 g) prepared prawns	1 cup prepared shrimps
3 tablespoons brandy	3 tablespoons brandy wine
8 fl. oz (240 ml) double cream	1 cup heavy cream
2 shallots, chopped	2 shallots, chopped
2 tablespoons chopped parsley	2 tablespoons chopped parsley
1 tablespoon tomato concentrate	1 tablespoon tomato concentrate
salt and pepper	salt and pepper
a little butter	a little butter

Heat the butter and cook the shallot. Add the prawns and then the brandy and ignite. Then add half the cream, parsley and tomato purée. Divide this mixture between 8 small ramekins and break an egg into each. Cover with the rest of the cream and bake as for basic recipe (p.44).

BAKED EGGS WITH SMOKED HADDOCK (UK: Scotland)

I have tried using smoked haddock on its own at the base of the baked eggs and also smoked haddock mixed with a little cream. Nothing works as well as the smoked haddock in *sauce béchamel*.

Imperial/Metric	American
8 large eggs	8 large eggs
approx ½ pint (300 ml *sauce béchamel*	approx. 1¼ cups *sauce béchamel*
6-8 oz (190-240 g) smoked haddock, cooked	6-8 oz smoked haddock, cooked
8 tablespoons double cream	8 tablespoons heavy cream

Incorporate the cooked smoked haddock into the hot *sauce béchamel* and then divide between the 8 ramekins. Break an egg on top of this mixture and then put a good tablespoon of cream on each. Bake as for basic recipe (p.44).

BAKED EGGS WITH SMOKED SALMON

Smoked salmon pieces will do for this dish. Stir 8 oz (240 g) of diced smoked salmon into the basic recipe (p.44), hot, and cook.

CONVENT EGGS

BAKED EGGS IN ONION SAUCE

Imperial/Metric	American
8 very fresh eggs	8 very fresh eggs
1 recipe *sauce soubise* (p.400), sieved	1 recipe *sauce soubise* (p.400), sieved
salt and pepper	salt and pepper

Put a little *sauce soubise* in each ramekin and then break an egg on it. Cover again with a thin layer of sauce and bake for 7-8 minutes at approximately 350°F/180°C/Gas 4.

Some people put a small round of ham under the egg but it is not necessary and makes it awkward to eat – better to chop it up into small pieces if you want this addition. This recipe can also be done with poached or soft-boiled eggs.

BAKED EGGS AND TOMATOES (UK)

You need very large, Marmande-type tomatoes for this, and you should half-cook them before putting the eggs in.

Imperial/Metric	*American*
8 eggs	8 eggs
4 very large tomatoes, halved	4 very large tomatoes, halved
butter	butter
salt and pepper	salt and pepper
parsley (to decorate)	parsley (to decorate)

Bake the tomatoes for 6-7 minutes in a hot oven. Scoop out the centre. (This can be done well in advance.) Break an egg into each half, put a piece of butter on each and bake for 5-7 minutes at 375-400°F/190-200°C/Gas 5-6. Sprinkle with parsley before serving.

BAKED EGGS IN SOUR CREAM (Hungary)

You will need to think a little in advance for this recipe. The sour cream should be mixed with ordinary double cream so you get the richness and so that it will resemble Hungarian sour cream, which is much thicker than the western European sort.

Imperial/Metric	*American*
8 large eggs	8 large eggs
8 fl. oz (240 ml) soured cream	1 cup soured cream
2 oz (60 g) butter	2 oz butter
salt	salt
paprika	paprika

A couple of days before the baked eggs are wanted, mix 4 fl. oz (125 ml/½ US cup) of sour cream with 4 fl. oz (125 ml/½ US cup) double cream – the culture in the first will turn the mixture into a much thicker sour cream. Pre-heat the oven to 375°F/190°C/Gas 5. Butter the ramekins well. Put a spoonful of sour cream in each dish and break an egg on top. Salt the egg. Divide the rest of the cream between the ramekins and bake 6-8 minutes, looking at around 5 minutes to see how things are going. Sprinkle with paprika before serving.

EGGS BIGARADE

BAKED EGGS

Imperial/Metric	American
8 very fresh eggs	8 very fresh eggs
2 oranges	2 oranges
2 tablespoons Grand Marnier liqueur	2 tablespoons Grand Marnier liqueur
juice of ½ lemon or of whole small one	juice of ½ lemon or of whole small one
1 recipe fresh tomato sauce (p.389)	1 recipe fresh tomato sauce (p.389)
salt and pepper	salt and pepper

Remove skin from orange with potato-peeler, slice into thin julienne strips and blanch for 3 minutes in boiling water, then strain. Slice the oranges horizontally into 8 pieces. (There will be some end-pieces over: use them squashed for extra juice.) Put a slice of peeled orange into each ramekin. Warm the tomato sauce and add, off the heat, the Grand Marnier, lemon juice and orange juice, if any. Add salt and pepper. Pour a layer of sauce on each orange slice and then break an egg into each ramekin. Very gently pour the rest of thé sauce on top of each egg and bake in oven at 340°F/175°C/Gas 3½ for 7-8 minutes. The whites should be firm to a probing skewer but the yolks should still be slightly wobbly. Serve with the blanched orange peel scattered on top of each.

ŒUFS A LA CRESSONIERE (France)

BAKED EGGS WITH WATERCRESS

Imperial/Metric	American
8 eggs	8 eggs
2 egg yolks	2 egg yolks
2 bunches watercress	2 bunches watercress
8 fl. oz (240 ml) single cream	1 cup light cream
watercress (to decorate)	watercress (to decorate)

Save a few sprigs of watercress and remove the stems from the rest. Chop up and pass through the liquidizer or food processor with the cream and egg yolks. Using half the mixture, divide between 8 ramekins and then break an egg into each. Add salt and pepper and then cover with the rest of the sauce. Bake 7-8 minutes at 400°F/200°C/Gas 6, checking at 5-6 minutes.

ŒUFS A LA PORTUGAISE (France)

BAKED EGGS WITH TOMATOES AND ONIONS

Imperial/Metric	*American*
8 fresh eggs	8 fresh eggs
1 medium onion, finely chopped	1 medium onion, finely chopped
3 medium tomatoes, chopped	3 medium tomatoes, chopped
pinch of marjoram or oregano	pinch of marjoram or oregano
salt and pepper	salt and pepper
4 fl. oz (120 ml) double cream	½ cup heavy cream
butter (for frying)	butter (for frying)

Sweat onions gently in a little butter. Add tomatoes and cook until a coarse sauce is made. Add salt, pepper and oregano to taste. Divide between 8 ramekins, break an egg on each and cover with cream. Bake at 350°F/180°C/Gas 4 for 7-8 minutes.

ŒUFS AUX CREVETTES (France)

EGGS WITH PRAWNS

Imperial/Metric	*American*
8-10 oz (250-300 g) prepared prawns	8-10 oz prepared shrimps
8 eggs	8 eggs
8 fl. oz (240 ml) double cream	1 cup heavy cream
1 tablespoon tomato con-centrate	1 tablespoon tomato con-centrate
4 tablespoons medium dry white wine	4 tablespoons medium dry white wine
a little salt	a little salt
cayenne pepper or Tabasco	cayenne pepper or Tabasco
1 teaspoon instant shallot	1 teaspoon instant shallot

Beat all the ingredients together except the prawns (shrimps). Butter 8 ramekins well. Chop the prawns fairly small and divide between the 8 dishes. It is better to do it this way to avoid one or two people getting all the prawns. Pour on the egg mixture and cook at 375°/190°C/Gas 5 for 7-8 minutes – but look at 5-6 minutes to see how it is going on: the centre should be very slightly wobbly. The dish should be fairly highly seasoned.

ŒUFS EN BRIOCHE (France)

BAKED EGGS IN BRIOCHES

Imperial/Metric	American
8 eggs	8 eggs
8 cooked brioches*	8 cooked brioches*
2 slices ham, chopped	2 slices ham, chopped
8 teaspoons double cream	8 teaspoons heavy cream
salt and pepper	salt and pepper
Tabasco	Tabasco

* If you can, use home-made brioches without sugar or bought brioches without sugar.

Cut the top off each brioche and reserve. Hollow out and put a little chopped ham in the base of each. Break an egg into each brioche, salt and pepper it and put a teaspoonful, no more, of cream on top of each. Cook for 8-10 minutes in a hot oven (400°F/200°C/Gas 6). 2 minutes before the end, pop back the top-knots. Serve with *sauce aurore* (p.391) to which you have added a little Tabasco.

ŒUFS EN COCOTTE AUX ASPERGES (France)

BAKED EGGS WITH ASPARAGUS

To the basic Cocotte recipe (p.44) add 8 oz (225 g) small asparagus tips. Heat them in a little butter and divide them between the 8 ramekins. Break the egg on top of them and then proceed in the usual way.

ŒUFS EN COCOTTE A LA CRECY (France)

BAKED EGGS WITH CARROTS AND CREAM

Use 8 oz (250 g) carrot purée (into which you have put a good knob of butter) and break the eggs on top. Then proceed with the basic recipe (p.44).

EGGS FLORENTINE (France and Italy)

BAKED EGGS WITH SPINACH

Imperial/Metric	*American*
8 large eggs	8 large eggs
1½ lb (750 g) spinach	1½ lb spinach
8 fl. oz (240 ml) double cream	1 cup heavy cream
½ teaspoon nutmeg	½ teaspoon nutmeg
salt and pepper	salt and pepper

Prepare your spinach first – the idea is to end up with just over ½ lb (250 g) once cooked. Squeeze all the water out of it and over the heat add the nutmeg, salt and pepper and three-quarters of the cream. Divide between 8 ramekins. Break an egg on top of the cream and spinach mixture and put a tablespoon of cream over each egg. Bake for 5 minutes at 400°F/200°C/Gas 6. The white should be just set. The egg will continue to cook in the hot dish, so it should seem slightly undercooked as you take it out of the oven.

ŒUFS EN COCOTTE A LA SUISSE (Switzerland)

SWISS BAKED EGGS WITH CHEESE

Imperial/Metric	*American*
6-8 eggs, depending on size	6-8 eggs, depending on size
8 fl. oz (240 ml) single or double cream*	1 cup light or heavy cream
4 oz (125 g) Gruyère cheese, finely grated	½ cup Gruyère cheese, finely grated
butter	butter
nutmeg and pepper	nutmeg and pepper

* The Swiss use double cream but single makes it less rich and is quite enough.

Butter 8 ramekins well. Beat up all the other ingredients well and bake as for cocotte eggs (p.44) but the whole thing should be *just* set when serving.

ŒUFS EN COCOTTE A L'ITALIENNE (France)

ITALIAN BAKED EGGS

To the basic cocotte recipe (p.44) add 4 oz (125 g) diced ham and use this as a base. Sprinkle grated Parmesan cheese on top of the cream before baking in the usual way.

ŒUFS EN COCOTTE A L'OSEILLE (France)

BAKED EGGS IN SORREL SAUCE

Not everyone likes sorrel but those who do know how well it marries with egg and cream, and all 3 are in this dish, which is a French classic.

Imperial/Metric	*American*
8 eggs	8 eggs
2 egg yolks	2 egg yolks
8 oz (250 g) sorrel	8 oz sorrel
½ pint (300 ml) double cream	1¼ cups heavy cream
4-6 slices white bread	4-6 slices white bread
4 oz (125 g) butter	½ cup butter
1 tablespoon sunflower oil	1 tablespoon sunflower oil
salt and pepper	salt and pepper

Cut the bread into small cubes and make croûtons of them by using a mixture of butter and oil – just enough to cover the bottom of each ramekin. Cook the sorrel as you would spinach, with only the water adhering to the leaves – 2 minutes should do the trick. Drain and squeeze out the water. Chop as finely as possible and then stir in the cream. Heat together but do not let boil, and add salt and pepper. Put a layer of this in the bottom of each ramekin, crack an egg on top and then cover with the rest of the cream and sorrel. Bake approximately 5 minutes at 400°F/200°C/Gas 6. The whites should be set, the yolks slightly wobbly.

BAKED EGGS AU GRATIN (UK)

BAKED EGGS IN CHEESE SAUCE

Imperial/Metric	*American*
8 eggs	8 eggs
1 recipe *sauce mornay*	1 recipe *sauce mornay*
4 tablespoons Gruyère cheese, grated	4 tablespoons Gruyère cheese, grated

Put a little of the hot *sauce mornay* in each ramekin (keep the sauce on the thick side). Break an egg into each, cover with more *sauce mornay* and strew with grated cheese. Bake 5-7 minutes at 375-400°F/190-200°C/Gas 5-6.

ŒUFS EN MEURETTE (France: Burgundy)

Whichever of the methods given below you use, this is a much nicer recipe than mere eggs in red wine.

Imperial/Metric	American
8 large eggs	8 large eggs
8 slices of green streaky bacon *or* 8 oz (250 g) chicken livers	8 slices green streaky bacon *or* 8 oz chicken livers
1 recipe *sauce meurette* (p.396)	1 recipe *sauce meurette* (p.396)
8 slices crustless bread	8 slices crustless bread
parsley, chopped (to garnish)	parsley, chopped (to garnish)
4 oz (125 g) wild mushrooms (added to the sauce if desired)	4 oz wild mushrooms (added to the sauce if desired)

Chicken livers can be substituted for bacon if wished and mushrooms are sometimes added also.

Divide the *sauce meurette* between two straight-sided sauté pans. Fry the bread in butter and keep it warm. Fry the bacon and cut each rasher into two. Heat the sauce through gently and adjust the seasoning if necessary. Gently break 4 eggs, one by one, into each of the sauté pans, and let them cook in the simmering sauce for 4-5 minutes until the whites are properly set and the yolks still slightly runny. They should not touch each other. Put each egg and its portion of sauce on a piece of fried bread, garnish with a half rasher each side, sprinkle with parsley and serve.

Alternatively you can divide the sauce between 8 two-handled, flat fireproof dishes (as for *œufs au plat*, rather than ramekins) and break the egg on top. Put half a slice of already cooked bacon each side of the egg. Cover each with buttered foil and bake 5 minutes or so. Serve with triangles of fried bread.

ŒUFS MARIE-LEONORE

BAKED EGGS WITH CELERIAC

This is named after my mother's family, where the eldest female was always named Marie-Léonore or Léonore-Marie. It was my grandmother's recipe. She admitted she could not cook – '... *mais je donne des conseils*,' she said. The vegetable part can be prepared in advance, in which case heat it through before putting on the eggs and cream.

Imperial/Metric	American
8 very fresh eggs	8 very fresh eggs
4 fl. oz (120 ml) double cream	½ cup heavy cream
1 large or 2 smaller celeriac	1 large or 2 smaller celeriac
2 oz (60 g) butter	¼ cup butter
salt and pepper	salt and pepper

Peel the celeriac with a knife (as opposed to a potato-peeler) and keep it under water whilst doing this or it will quickly turn brown and unattractive. Cut into smallish cubes, throw into boiling salted water and cook for approximately 15 minutes – it depends how small the cubes are. Beat in the butter and some salt and pepper. Divide the purée between 8 ramekins and break an egg on top of each. Put on a very little salt and pepper, and then put a tablespoon of the cream over each egg. Put the ramekins in a baking dish partly filled with hot water (to come half way up) and cook for 15 minutes in a moderate oven (350°F/180°C/Gas 4).

Roulades

ROULADE A LA MORVANDELLE (France)

HAM AND POTATO ROULADE

It is far easier to make 2 roulades than one large one. This recipe requires your last-minute attention, although the filling can be made in advance.

ROULADE

Imperial/Metric	American
5 large eggs, separated	5 large eggs, separated
8 oz (250 g) cooked potato	8 oz cooked potato
5 fl. oz (150 ml) single cream	5 fl. oz light cream
5 fl. oz (150 ml) milk	5 fl. oz milk
1 small onion, chopped very fine	1 small onion, chopped very fine
4 oz (125 g) flour	½ cup flour
butter	butter
salt and pepper to taste	salt and pepper to taste

Have the potatoes warm and mash them with the milk, cream, chopped onion and egg yolks. Add the flour, incorporating it carefully. Beat the egg white stiff and fold into the mashed potato mixture. Grease two Swiss roll (jelly roll) tins with butter and pour in the mixture – it will be very sloppy. (Alternatively use

baking parchment.) Bake at 375°F/190°C/Gas 5 in the middle of the oven until golden.
Meanwhile get the filling ready and heated through. Do not have too hot.

FILLING

Imperial/Metric	American
8 fl. oz (230 ml) thick *sauce béchamel* (p.391)	1 cup thick *sauce béchamel* (p.391)
8 oz (250 g) ham, chopped	8 oz ham, chopped
2 small gherkins, chopped small	2 small gherkins, chopped small
1 tablespoon Dijon mustard	1 tablespoon Dijon mustard
2 tablespoons parsley, chopped	2 tablespoons parsley, chopped

Heat the sauce (not to boiling point). Take it off the heat and add the other ingredients. Remove the roulade from the tins onto parchment paper and spread the filling over them both. Roll up quickly, using the paper to handle them, put them on their final serving dish and cook for 5 minutes or so longer. Serve decorated with parsley.

SCHINKENROULADE (Austria)

HAM ROULADE

Usually Austrian ham roulade is cold and served on picnics. This version is served hot with sour cream and dill mixed together as a sauce. Simple and delicious, it can be prepared in advance to the beaten egg white stage.

Imperial/Metric	American
Roulade Morvandelle (p.54)	*Roulade Morvandelle* (p.54)
2 oz (60 g) butter	¼ cup butter
8 oz (250 g) ham, finely chopped	8 oz ham, finely chopped
2 tablespoons freeze-dried dill	2 tablespoons freeze-dried dill

Make a *Roulade Morvandelle* (without egg whites), then add the butter and ham. Now fold in the beaten egg white and bake until golden brown at 375°F/190°C/Gas 5.
Serve with a large bowl of sour cream to which you have added a little salt and a generous amount of finely chopped fresh dill or approximately 2 tablespoons freeze-dried dill. If using the latter, it is as well to let the herb steep in the sauce for about an hour beforehand.

LIPTAUER ROULADE (Austria, Hungary and Czechoslovakia)

Although Liptauer cheese comes from Czechoslovakia, the recipe is strictly Viennese. (The Czechs and Hungarians would put the mixture into a dumpling – so would most Viennese for that matter.) There are 2 versions, one based on the potato roulade, the other on spinach. As stated elsewhere (p.157), real Liptauer is made from sheep's milk but it is rare to find such cheese today, so a mixture of cream and cottage cheese is substituted here.

For Potato Roulade, follow recipe in *Roulade Morvandelle* (p.54)

SPINACH ROULADE

Imperial/Metric	American
6 eggs, separated	6 eggs, separated
12 oz (375 g) cooked spinach	12 oz cooked spinach
large pinch nutmeg	large pinch nutmeg

Preferably mix the spinach, eggs and nutmeg in a food processor. Alternatively chop the spinach as fine as possible and add the egg yolks and nutmeg. Do not salt. Beat the egg whites stiff and fold them into the spinach. Line two Swiss roll (jelly roll) tins with baking parchment and grease slightly with melted butter. Pour in the spinach mixture (very sloppy) and bake 15-20 minutes at 375°C/190°C/Gas 5. Once cooked, turn out onto a board, spread with the Liptauer mixture and roll up. Bake at a lower temperature for 5 minutes in the serving dish.

'LIPTAUER' FILLING

Imperial/Metric	American
6 oz (190 g) cottage cheese	¾ cup cottage cheese
6 oz (190 g) cream cheese	¾ cup cream cheese
1 medium onion, grated	1 medium onion, grated
1 dessertspoon caraway seeds	1 dessertspoon caraway seeds
1 tablespoon or more paprika	1 tablespoon or more paprika
1 tablespoon or more sour cream	1 tablespoon or more sour cream
½ teaspoon salt	½ teaspoon salt

Cream everything together and keep at room temperature to ensure easy spreading.

SPINACH AND PEAR ROULADE WITH ROQUEFORT FILLING (France)

The pears intensify the spinach flavour. This is a delicious roulade but a little tricky.

SPINACH ROULADE

Imperial/Metric	*American*
6 eggs, separated	6 eggs, separated
12 oz (375 g) cooked spinach	12 oz cooked spinach
1 large pear	1 large pear
salt	salt

Peel, cube and cook the pear in as little water as possible. Purée with the cooked spinach in a food processor or liquidizer. Add the egg yolks and salt to make a very murky mixture, exactly like rotting pondweed. Fold in the beaten egg whites, divide between 2 prepared Swiss roll (jelly roll) tins and cook for 12-15 minutes at 375°F/190°C/Gas 5. Meanwhile prepare the filling.

FILLING

Imperial/Metric	*American*
approx. 4 oz (125 g) Roquefort cheese	¾ cup Roquefort cheese
4 fl. oz (120 ml) double cream	½ cup heavy cream
4 oz (125 g) curd cheese	½ cup curd cheese
1 medium onion, finely chopped	1 medium onion, finely chopped
parsley, chopped (if wished)	parsley, chopped (if wished)

Mix together in liquidizer or food processor. Turn cooked roulades onto sheet of baking parchment and divide the filling between them. Roll up quickly and serve at once, sliced fairly thickly.

WHITE FISH AND AVOCADO ROULADE (UK)

ROULADE

Imperial/Metric	*American*
1 lb (500 g) white fish*	1 lb white fish*
6 eggs, separated	6 eggs, separated
8 oz (250 g) smoked salmon, sliced	8 oz smoked salmon, sliced
2 tablespoons fresh chopped dill or 1 teaspoon freeze-dried dill	2 tablespoons fresh chopped dill or 1 teaspoon freeze-dried dill
salt and pepper	salt and pepper

* Any good-quality white fish will do, from sole or monkfish to cod or haddock.

Cook fish either wrapped in aluminium foil in oven or in a microwave oven, and let cool. Blend fish with egg yolks, salt and pepper in a mixer or food processor – but not too finely. Fold in egg whites and spread in prepared Swiss roll (jelly roll) tin. Bake in centre of oven for approximately 15 minutes at 375°F/190°C/Gas 5. Turn out onto a sheet of parchment or greaseproof paper and let cool under a damp cloth – or it will never roll up.

FILLING

Imperial/Metric	*American*
1 large or 2 medium avocados	1 large or 2 medium avocados
3-4 tablespoons sour cream	3-4 tablespoons sour cream

Prepare filling by mixing sour cream and dill together with the avocado in a mixer or food processor, but do not make it too liquid. Season to taste.

Spread over the cooled roulade and lay smoked salmon slices on top. Roll up and sprinkle with a little more chopped dill. Serve with a little more sour cream if wished.

3 Meat and Poultry

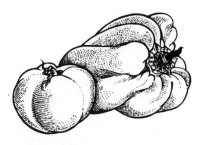

First courses comprised of meat and poultry are not only useful where the main course is to be a composite one or something without much substance, but also where to have a main course of something such as *satay* would be overpowering. It is also a way, as with expensive fish, of making a little meat or poultry go a long way.

Meat

ĆEVAPČIĆI (Yugoslavia)

GRILLED MEAT BALLS

Imperial/Metric	*American*
2 lb (1 kilo) best minced beef	2 lb best ground beef
salt and pepper	salt and pepper
olive or sunflower oil	olive or sunflower oil

The minced beef you buy from the butcher will not be sufficiently finely minced. In Romania and Yugoslavia some people put in a little bicarbonate of soda with lesser-quality meat to help soften it. It certainly gives it a different taste. Mince your meat very fine, preferably in a food processor. Form into elongated cylinders about 2 inches long by 1 inch thick (5 × 2.5 cm). Thread 5 or 6 on each skewer and cook under a fierce grill, turning once.

Serve with Aubergine and Pepper Salad (*Srpski Ajvar*) or ordinary *ajvar* (always served cold as an accompaniment to grilled meat and *ćevapčiči*) made as follows:

Imperial/Metric	American
2 lb (1 kilo) red peppers	2 lb red bell peppers
2 fl. oz (50 ml) olive oil	¼ cup olive oil
2 cloves garlic, crushed	2 cloves garlic, crushed

Cut the peppers into small pieces and fry together with the garlic until reduced to a purée. This will need constant watching. (I have done the first three-quarters of this in a hot oven with a lid on the casserole but the last bit must be done on top of the stove.) Stir constantly and watch it does not catch: an asbestos mat helps. The object is to get out all the residual liquid.

For keeping, you float a little oil on the top and put the jar in a larder. Alternatively, once you have got the purée 'dry', you can bottle it for the winter. If water is left in, the peppers ferment and explode.

VITELLO CRUDO CON BASILICO (Italy: Tuscany and Emilia-Romagna)

SLICED MARINATED VEAL IN BASIL SAUCE

This dish has a remarkably clean and fresh taste. The lemon juice 'cooks' the meat, and at first your guests will be hard put to guess exactly what they are eating. With the unadventurous, it is probably better to tell them afterwards.

Imperial/Metric	American
2 lb fillet of veal*	2 lb fillet of veal*
8 tablespoons lemon juice (2-3 lemons)	8 tablespoons lemon juice (2-3 lemons)
3 spring onions	3 scallions
1 tablespoon capers	1 tablespoon capers
peel/zest of lemon (optional)	peel/zest of lemon (optional)
1 large bunch of fresh basil	1 large bunch of fresh basil
black pepper (optional)	black pepper (optional)
8 tablespoons Tuscan, Ligurian or Provençal olive oil	8 tablespoons Tuscan, Ligurian or Provençal olive oil
parsley (to decorate)	parsley (to decorate)

* To obtain the cut of veal used for making medallions, usually you have to buy this in the piece and use the surrounding part for making veal escalopes. No other part will do.

Keep your meat in the refrigerator for at least 24 hours, covered, to make sure it is firm enough to be sliced easily. Some people pop it into the freezer for an hour but this can be dangerous if you forget it – which is very easy to do.

Cut the onions into 4 and chop with the basil and capers until a fine mush is obtained. Do not be tempted to use a machine for this, as it draws out too many juices – if you have a *mezzaluna*, this is the ideal utensil for achieving the right consistency. Add this mixture to the lemon juice plus a little black pepper if liked. Some Italians add either the grated peel of one lemon or the zest as well.

Slice your veal as thinly as possibly – rather the way Italians slice raw ham. A slicer makes life easier but is not vital. Lay these slices in a flat dish and pour over the lemon and herb mixture, making sure every slice of meat is coated. Leave in the refrigerator for 45 minutes to an hour. Thereafter, add the olive oil and a little salt and leave for a further hour before serving. Adjust seasoning to taste and serve on individual plates with a little parsley to decorate – nothing else.

VITELLO TONNATO (Italy)

This is ostensibly a rather expensive dish since you need the dearest cut of veal (fillet, loin or leg) but for a first course it becomes quite reasonable since you need allow only 3 oz (100 g) per person as it is somewhat rich. Italians slice the cooked veal *extremely* thin and then cover it with the sauce. Use the youngest veal you can buy.

Made in a larger quantity, this is perfect summer lunch food.

Imperial/Metric	*American*
1½ lb (750 g) fillet, leg or loin of veal tied into a neat shape	1½ lb fillet, leg or loin of veal tied into a neat shape
bunch of parsley	bunch of parsley
strip of lemon peel	strip of lemon peel
peppercorns	peppercorns
1 recipe stock (p.300) or use cubes	1 recipe stock (p.300) or use cubes

Cook the veal by simmering in the stock with the parsley and a strip of lemon peel. This will take around 1½ hours. Let cool (there are two schools of thought: some leave it to cool in the liquid, some out – I cool it out of the liquid). When cold, wrap in clingfilm and refrigerate until very cold.

SAUCE

Imperial/Metric	American
1 tin – approx. 4 oz (125 g) – tunnyfish (tuna)	1 tin – approx. 4 oz tuna
8 fl. oz (240 ml) mayonnaise	1 cup mayonnaise
1 tablespoon capers	1 tablespoon capers
juice of 1 large lemon	juice of 1 large lemon
2 or 3 anchovies, soaked in water or milk	2 or 3 anchovies, soaked in water or milk
thin cream	light cream
parsley and lemon (to decorate)	parsley and lemon (to decorate)

Chop the anchovies as finely as possible and mix into the mayonnaise. Add the capers and a little thin cream. You should have a slightly runny sauce. Do not put too much cream in it but instead use a little of the stock to thin it down if necessary. Stir in the capers and pour the sauce over the slices of meat.

Marinate for at least 24 hours. Serve sprinkled with parsley at the last moment and wedges or slices of lemon.

Poultry

POLLO EN NOGADA (Mexico)

CHICKEN IN WALNUT SAUCE

Imperial/Metric	American
2 whole chicken breasts	2 whole chicken breasts
8 oz (250 g) walnuts	1 cup walnuts
12 oz (375 g) cream cheese	1½ cups cream cheese (Philadelphia type)
12 fl. oz (360 ml) double cream	1½ cups heavy cream
Tabasco to taste	Tabasco to taste
4 fl. oz (120 ml) oil	½ cup oil
salt	salt
½ teaspoon cinnamon (optional)	½ teaspoon cinnamon (optional)

Cut chicken breasts into small cubes and put on skewers. Brush with the oil into which you have put salt and Tabasco to your taste. In a liquidizer or food processor blend together the cream cheese, cream, nuts and salt. If the mixture is too thick, add a little water. If liked, you can add ½ teaspoon of cinnamon. Grill the chicken until nicely done on both sides and serve on a bed of lettuce with the *nogada* sauce.

SKEWERED CHICKEN TERIYAKI (USA)

Teriyaki comes from the Hawaiians, who in turn got it from the Japanese. Normally it is done with steak but these cubes of chicken are now quite common – I've even had them with 'Mexican' *guacamole*!

Allow 2 or 3 small skewers per serving, with 3 or 4 pieces per skewer. Serve with sliced radish, salad greens etc.

Imperial/Metric	*American*
approx. 1½ lb (750 g) chicken breast	approx. 1½ lb chicken breast
2 cloves garlic, chopped	2 cloves garlic, chopped
6 medium spring onions, chopped	6 medium scallions
1 tablespoon fresh ginger root, chopped	1 tablespoon fresh ginger root, chopped
2-3 tablespoons brown sugar	2-3 tablespoons brown sugar
4 fl. oz (120 ml) dry sherry	½ cup dry sherry
8 fl. oz (240 ml) Japanese soy sauce	1 cup Japanese soy sauce

Make a marinade by mixing the chopped vegetables with the soy sauce and sherry. Marinate the 1 inch (2 cm) cubes (or smaller) of chicken in this for at least 2 hours but not more than 3. Grill under a fierce grill until done.

Satay

Everyone who has been to the Far East, even for a short visit, comes back with a liking for Satay (or Saté). Basically it is spiced, skewered meat served with a sauce. In Moslem countries such as Indonesia and Malaya it is made of lamb, beef or chicken but never pork, in Hindu communities never beef, and the Overseas Chinese have adopted it as their own and make it of pork. Fish satay is almost always Chinese in inspiration, though all Malays and Indonesians now cook fish this way.

Satay is nearly always served as an appetizer or early in the meal. It is usually accompanied by a peanut-based sauce bristling with birdseye chillies and a gentle turmeric pickle of cucumbers – though Indonesians have a sneaking tendency to put chillies in this dish as well. The fish satays (see Chapter 4) really do not need a separate sauce and can just have the cucumber pickle as an accompaniment.

MEAT SATAY

Imperial/Metric	American
1 lb (550 g) leg or shoulder of lamb or	1 lb leg or shoulder of lamb *or*
1 lb (500 g) fillet or rump steak or	1 lb fillet or rump steak *or*
1 lb (500 g) loin or leg of pork	1 lb loin or leg of pork
peanut or corn oil	peanut or corn oil

Cut the meat into small pieces approximately ¾ inch × ¾ inch (1.5 cm × 1.5 cm) and marinate for 2-3 hours.

MARINADE

Imperial/Metric	American
½ teaspoon turmeric	½ teaspoon turmeric
2 dried, preferably birdseye, chillies (or less)	2 dried, preferably birdseye, chillies (or less)
2 teaspoons ground coriander	2 teaspoons ground coriander
2 cloves of garlic crushed	2 cloves of garlic crushed
2 teaspoons fresh ginger, grated	2 teaspoons fresh ginger, grated
½ teaspoon ground cumin	½ teaspoon ground cumin
1-2 tablespoons brown sugar	1-2 tablespoons brown sugar
2 tablespoons dark Chinese soy sauce	2 tablespoons dark Chinese soy sauce
juice of half a lemon	juice of half a lemon
½ teaspoon salt	½ teaspoon salt

You will find this marinade is not very liquid: you need to coat every piece of meat with it by stirring carefully. Cover with film and give a stir every half hour or so.

Thread 6 or 7 pieces on small wood skewers 6-7 inches (15 cm) long or on proper satay sticks (which can be bought in most Chinese grocers). Cook under a hot grill (barbecue or charcoal is even better) for a few minutes each side – less for beef of course and more for pork. Baste if necessary with peanut or corn oil. Serve with the following sauce or with the cucumber dish *atjar ketimun*, p.265.

QUICK PEANUT SAUCE

Imperial/Metric	*American*
4 oz (125 g) crunchy peanut butter*	4 oz crunchy peanut butter*
6 fl. oz (180 ml) coconut milk (see p.102 on how to make coconut milk)	6 fl. oz coconut milk (see p.102 on how to make coconut milk)
1 chopped onion	1 chopped onion
1 tablespoon thick soy sauce	1 tablespoon thick soy sauce
1 tablespoon lemon juice	1 tablespoon lemon juice
1 tablespoon brown sugar	1 tablespoon brown sugar
Tabasco or chilli sauce (optional) to taste	Tabasco or chilli sauce (optional) to taste
1 piece lemon grass (optional)**	1 piece lemon grass (optional)**

* Note that smooth peanut butter does not give the right consistency.

** Lemon grass is obtainable at Chinese and Oriental grocers, sometimes in powder, sometimes fresh. If you cannot get it, substitute a little grated lemon or lime rind – about half a teaspoonful.

Fry the onion in some peanut oil. When almost cooked add the brown sugar and soy sauce, then all the other ingredients and heat through. The sauce should be quite thick. If you want to have it a little thinner, add a little stock.

MALAY CHICKEN OR BEEF SATAY

In all the big towns in Malaysia and all over the island of Singapore there are stalls set up in the evening for the sale of satay. If you cannot get to them, they will come to you – there are hundreds of itinerant vendors selling satay at drinks time. It is ideal cocktail party food, and hostesses often manage to get a satay man to come and do all the satay catering on their verandah when they give a cocktail party. Certainly in Singapore (which must be one of the cleanest cities in the world) the satay from such vendors is safe. There are frequent unheralded inspections of premises etc, and anyone found wanting in hygiene is quickly dispossessed of his vending licence.

Imperial/Metric	American
1 lb (500 g) chicken breasts or	1 lb chicken breasts or
1 lb (500 g) fillet of beef	1 lb beef tenderloin
1 medium onion, chopped	1 medium onion, chopped
3 or 4 teaspoons ground coriander	3 or 4 teaspoons ground coriander
1 teaspoon fennel seed	1 teaspoon fennel seed
1 teaspoon cumin	1 teaspoon cumin
2 cloves garlic	2 cloves garlic
1 tablespoon brown sugar	1 tablespoon brown sugar
6 oz (190 g) crunchy peanut butter	6 oz crunchy peanut butter
2 teaspoon Tabasco or 1 birdseye chilli	2 teaspoon Tabasco or 1 birdseye chilli
3 fl. oz (90 ml) coconut milk	3 fl. oz coconut milk
2 fl. oz (60 ml) tamarind water (optional)	2 fl. oz tamarind water (optional)
peanut oil	peanut oil
juice of a lemon	juice of a lemon

To make coconut milk, see p.102. To make tamarind water, put a piece of tamarind about the size of a grape into the amount of water given in the recipe. Tamarind is available at Indian Oriental grocers. It is not vital to the recipe but gives a more authentic flavour. Tabasco is used only because it is easier to control and certainly easier to handle.

Chop the onions very fine indeed and fry in a little peanut oil. Add the spices, tamarind water, peanut butter and last of all the coconut milk. Cook for 5-6 minutes on a low heat, with the lid off (or the coconut milk with curdle). Cut the meat into half-inch (1-1.5 cm) squares, and grill for a few minutes on both sides until done; the chicken will need slightly longer cooking than the beef. Put the skewers in a warmed dish, pour over the sauce, squeeze over the lemon juice and serve with chopped fresh cucumber.

CHICKEN LIVER SATAY WITH ATJAR KETIMUN

In Indonesia chicken livers are very small, coming mainly from bantam hens. Non-Oriental chicken livers will have to be cut into 3 or 4 pieces at least before putting onto skewers. Some people partially cook the chicken livers before cutting up since the handling becomes easier. Thereafter you follow the recipe for Indonesian satay and serve the finished dish with *Atjar Ketimun*, p.265.

Frogs

Now that frogs' legs are frozen and can be bought all over the world, it is not unreasonable to include a few recipes for them here. Frogs are protected in many European countries including France and, I believe, Belgium, where they are consumed in vast quantities. Most nowadays come from east Europe, Poland in particular. I loathe the idea of eating frogs or snails but the recipes given below are interesting in that they can serve for more or less any firm white fish, preferably cut into bite-sized pieces and are, therefore, worth trying by non-frog eaters.

Serve with either fried triangles of bread or hot French bread.

Imperial/Metric
24 pairs of frogs' legs (i.e. 48 legs altogether)
flour for dredging
8 oz (250 g) butter
1 tablespoon grape seed oil (*huile de pepins de raisin*) (sunflower oil will do, but not olive oil)
3 shallots, chopped
6 fl. oz. (180 ml) white wine (Chablis preferred)
good bunch of chives, snipped
chopped chervil to taste
salt and pepper

American
24 pairs of frogs legs' (i.e. 48 legs altogether)
flour for dredging
1 cup butter
1 tablespoon grape seed oil (*huile de pepins de raisin*) (sunflower oil will do, but not olive oil)
3 shallots, chopped
¾ cup white wine (Chablis preferred)
good bunch of chives, snipped
chopped chervil to taste
salt and pepper

Dredge the frogs' legs in flour and cook in a mixture of oil and enough butter – do not let brown: they should only become golden. Once cooked, keep in a warm place. Add a little more butter if necessary and cook the shallots, moisten with the Chablis and reduce by half. Remove the saucepan from the heat and add the rest of the butter, bit by bit. If you wish you can substitute double (heavy) cream for the butter. Pour the sauce over the frogs' legs and then scatter the chopped herbs over them.

CUISSES DE GRENOUILLES A LA PROVENCALE (France)

FROGS' LEGS A LA PROVENCALE

Imperial/Metric	*American*
24 pairs of frogs' legs	24 pairs of frogs' legs
olive oil for frying	olive oil for frying
1 recipe *sauce Provençale* (p.400)	1 recipe *sauce Provençale* (p.400)
parsley, chopped	parsley, chopped

Proceed as in previous recipe but instead pour over a *sauce Provençale* and scatter with parsley before serving.

Snails

Depending on your guests' appetites, allow 6, 9 or 12 snails per person. The following recipes allow 6 snails per person, i.e. 48 for 8 people, and can be doubled for hungry people.

It is assumed that you will be buying ready prepared snails with their shells in a separate packet. Preparing snails from scratch is hard work and, from personal experience, can prove a pretty violent appetite depressant!

The Austrians are second only to the French in their consumption of snails and have several recipes, some of which purport to come from France but seem unknown there. One requires last minute frying in hot lard which is the last thing any host or hostess wants to do before a dinner party.

ESCARGOTS A LA BOURGUIGNONNE (France)

SNAILS WITH BURGUNDY BUTTER

Imperial/Metric	*American*
1 lb (500 g) butter	1 lb butter
3 shallots	3 shallots
3 cloves garlic	3 cloves garlic
a good handful of parsley, finely chopped	a good handful of parsley, finely chopped
a little sea salt	a little sea salt
plenty of freshly ground black pepper	plenty of freshly ground black pepper

Either with a mixer or food processor or by hand, mix the above ingredients and, after placing each snail in its own shell, thoroughly 'seal off' each with a good spoonful of this butter. Range the snails as upright as possible or in special *escargot* dishes so the butter does not leak out. Bake in a hot oven (400°F/200°C/Gas 6) for 7-10 minutes, until the butter is bubbling.

CASSOLETTE D'ESCARGOTS A LA PROVENCALE (France)

SNAILS IN MUSHROOMS WITH SAUCE PROVENCALE

French bread is the best accompaniment.

Imperial/Metric	*American*
48 snails without their shells	48 snails without their shells
48 mushroom caps, finely chopped	48 mushroom caps, finely chopped
1 recipe *sauce Provençale* (p.400)	1 recipe *sauce Provençale* (p.400)
1 bunch parsley, chopped	1 bunch parsley, chopped
2 fl. oz. (60 ml) olive oil for frying	¼ cup olive oil for frying

Add the mushrooms to the sauce. Place a snail on each

mushroom cap and place each mushroom in the space allowed on the special snail plates. Alternatively use a small, flat ovenproof dish for each person. Divide the *hot sauce Provençale* between the 8 dishes and bake in a hot oven at around 400°F/200°C/Gas 6. Serve piping hot with parsley strewn over each portion.

SCHNECKEN NACH FRANZOSICHERART (Austria)

SNAILS IN THE FRENCH MANNER

Imperial/Metric	*American*
48 snails	48 snails
1 lb (500 g) butter	2 cups butter
4 oz (125 g) walnuts	½ cup walnuts
4 oz (125 g) breadcrumbs from a day-old loaf	½ cup breadcrumbs from a day-old loaf
4 oz (125 g) breadcrumbs to strew over the snails	½ cup breadcrumbs to strew over the snails
1 tablespoon parsley	1 tablespoon parsley
1 tablespoon Worcester sauce	1 tablespoon Worcester sauce
salt	salt

Mix all ingredients together, except the extra 4 oz breadcrumbs, which you sprinkle over the snail shells, and bake in a hot oven for 7-10 minutes (400°F/200°C/Gas 6).

SCHNECKEN NACH UNGARISHERART (Austria)

SNAILS IN THE HUNGARIAN MANNER

Imperial/Metric	*American*
48 snails	48 snails
1 lb (500 g) butter	2 cups butter
2 oz (60 g) Parmesan cheese	¼ cup Parmesan cheese
4 oz (125 g) dark mushrooms, chopped	½ cup dark mushrooms, chopped
1 tablespoon mild Hungarian paprika	1 tablespoon mild Hungarian paprika
good pinch of nutmeg	good pinch of nutmeg
2 teaspoons double tomato concentrate	2 teaspoons double tomato concentrate
4 oz breadcrumbs	½ cup breadcrumbs
2 cloves garlic, chopped	2 cloves garlic, chopped

Mix the garlic and mushrooms with other dry ingredients.

Gradually work in butter until a stiff paste is obtained. Seal off each snail shell with this, sprinkle the whole with paprika and bake at 400°F/200°C/Gas 6 for 7-10 minutes.

4 Fish

Fish is one of the most delicious foods and usually very easy and quick to prepare, yet we do not eat very much of it, compared with our meat and poultry consumption. Such fish as we do eat is mostly cod or coley (from fish-and-chip shops) or Dover sole or kipper pâté in posh restaurants. There are dozens of fish our grandparents used to eat which we never see nowadays, such as John Dory, ling, skate and brill. Brill is, in fact, now on many smart restaurant menus, since it cooks up like sole at about a third of the price – reader, take note, since brill tastes delicious and your guests won't know the difference. I suspect, though, that brill will become like monkfish – expensive. I can remember when monkfish was unknown less than 20 years ago that fishmongers had difficulty selling it at 3 shillings a pound when sole already commanded 15 or 16 shillings a pound.

Unless otherwise specified, all recipes for Dover sole can be done with lemon sole, witch or Torbay sole, the American flounder, plaice, turbot, halibut, brill or monkfish (*lotte*) and, at a pinch, the American red snapper. Whichever of these fish you use, the result will be delicious but of course very different one from the other.

For all these recipes the sole is skinned and filleted. An average Dover sole weighs around 12 oz-1 lb (375-500 g); occasionally they are much bigger. However, think in terms of a 4-6 oz (125-190 g) serving. It is unlikely you will feed more than two people from one sole. Get the fishmonger to fillet them for you – you will waste less – and keep the bones and trimmings. Then weigh the finished fillets and calculate your needs on the basis of trimmed fillets. If you do the filleting yourself, you will need to trim away the bones around the edge of the fillet as well. Much the same applies to plaice. Turbot (except for chicken or hen turbot), halibut, brill and even monkfish tend to come in small steaks which are easier to deal with. All these fish should be served skinned; nothing is more off-putting than the mackintosh quality of fish skin.

Freshwater Fish

GRAVADLAX (Sweden)

MARINATED SALMON WITH DILL

'Why,' asks a Swedish friend, 'does every foreign recipe for Gravadlax use the tail? This is party food, and we always have it for Midsummer Night, so we order either a whole salmon or certainly a *large* centre piece.' It is quite true, a great number of American, British and French recipes call for the tail end of a salmon. So herewith my friend's Swedish recipe which she says will comfortably feed 8 Swedes – you can halve it if you wish.

Although you cannot use frozen salmon for this dish, there is no need to use expensive wild salmon either (unless you have so much of it that you want to do something different); farmed salmon will do very nicely.

Imperial/Metric	American
3-4 lb (1.5-2 kilos) salmon	3-4 lb salmon
8 oz (250 g) rock or sea salt	1 cup rock or sea salt
12 oz (375 g) white sugar	1½ cups white sugar
dill, fresh or freeze-dried	dill, fresh or freeze-dried
freshly ground pepper	freshly ground pepper
2 tablespoons brandy	2 tablespoons brandy

Mix together the salt and sugar and add about a teaspoon of freshly ground pepper. If you are using a whole small salmon, gut it, take off its head and remove the backbone. Then remove the side bones; you may need a pair of tweezers to do so, but if you don't get all the bones out it makes it very difficult to carve afterwards. Rub the salt, pepper and sugar mixture into the flesh of the salmon. Sprinkle with brandy, teaspoon by teaspoon. The Swedes would lay several (12 or so) long branches of dill on the fish at this stage but, unless you grow your own, you must be content with 3-4 teaspoons of freeze-dried dillweed. Close the salmon up so you get flesh against flesh, cover with foil and weight down. 24 hours later baste the skin of the salmon with the juice which has flowed out. Do not serve before 48 hours have passed but eat it within 3 days. Drain and remove dill branches. The chopped dill you will have to leave mostly in place. You carve it in thin slices across, as you do for smoked salmon, and serve with a mustard sauce.

Some of the Swedish sauces are based on German mustard which for me ruins the whole freshness of the dish, and I use Dijon mustard. If your preference is for the German sort, you can substitute this for the French.

SAUCE

Imperial/Metric	*American*
2 egg yolks	2 egg yolks
1 tablespoon strong Dijon mustard	1 tablespoon strong Dijon mustard
8 fl. oz (240 ml) light olive oil	1 cup light olive oil
2 tablespoons white wine vinegar	2 tablespoons white wine vinegar
a little dill	a little dill
a little chopped onion (optional)	a little chopped onion (optional)

Mix the egg yolks and mustard as you would for a mayonnaise and add the oil, drop by drop. Finally add the vinegar and chopped onion. Serve separately

Variation
This marinated salmon can also be served grilled or even barbecued, in which case, cut the salmon into steaks from the start and then marinate them. Proceed as for ordinary cold Gravadlax except grill the steaks after 24-48 hours marinating. Serve with *cold* mustard sauce.

SALMON RAMEKINS (UK)

Quick, easy and fairly cheap to prepare. Fresh salmon can be used for this dish if available; tinned is suitable.

Imperial/Metric	*American*
1 lb (500 g) salmon	2 cups canned salmon
¼ pint (120 ml) single cream	scant ¾ cup light cream
1 onion, finely chopped	1 onion, finely chopped
4 oz (125 g) butter	½ cup butter
6 eggs, hard-boiled	6 eggs, hardcooked
¾ pint (450 ml) full cream milk	2 cups full cream milk
salt and pepper	salt and pepper
Worcester sauce to taste	Worcester sauce to taste
chopped parsley (to decorate)	chopped parsley (to decorate)

Cook the onion in the butter until soft. Add the flour and make a *roux*. Add the milk and the cream until a medium-thick *sauce béchamel* (p.391) is obtained. Mix in the roughly chopped eggs and salmon; some of the liquid can be included if liked, and add Worcester sauce to taste. Divide the mixture between individual pyrex dishes and bake for 10 minutes at 400°F/200°C/Gas 6. Decorate with parsley before serving.

TROUT IN HAZELNUT SAUCE (Turkey)

This is very similar to the Turkish *tarator* sauce used on fish and vegetables except that it has hazelnuts rather than walnuts as its main ingredient. The fish used are dry ones such as sturgeon, swordfish, tuna etc but inland trout would be available (though probably this sauce would not, since it is part of urban rather than country life). There is a Lebanese version of this dish but in that country yoghurt is *never* eaten with fish, so the sauce is lengthened by fish stock or water.

Imperial/Metric	*American*
8 trout fillets	8 trout fillets
4 slices white bread	4 slices white bread
6 oz (190 g) hazelnuts	6 oz hazelnuts
4 fl. oz (120 ml) light olive oil	½ cup light olive oil
4 fl. oz (120 ml) thick unfla-voured yoghurt	½ cup thick unflavoured yoghurt
2 tablespoons or more white wine vinegar	2 tablespoons or more white wine vinegar
salt and pepper	salt and pepper
freshly chopped parsley (to decorate)	freshly chopped parsley (to decorate)
lemon wedges	lemon wedges

From 4 large trout you will get 8 fair-sized fillets. Steam or poach them and let them cool. Place them on a serving dish, flesh side down, and remove the skin.

In a liquidizer or food processor mix the oil, yoghurt, vinegar, crustless bread, salt and pepper. Make sure the papery skin is off the hazelnuts: it can ruin the taste of the sauce. Drop the hazelnuts in and whizz for a few moments until a sauce is obtained. If it is too thick, add a little water or yoghurt. Pour this sauce over the trout fillets, decorate with chopped parsley and wedges of lemon.

COLD TROUT WITH HORSERADISH AND WALNUT MAYONNAISE

Imperial/Metric	*American*
8 cold trout, skinned	8 cold trout, skinned
4 fl. oz (120 ml) double cream	½ cup heavy cream
4 fl. oz (120 ml) mayonnaise (p.404)	½ cup mayonnaise (p.404)
3 oz (90 g) walnuts	3 oz walnuts
1 tablespoon vinegar	1 tablespoon vinegar
1 tablespoon fresh horseradish*	1 tablespoon fresh horseradish*

* Although you may prefer fresh horseradish, there is now available on the market freeze-dried horseradish which is excellent and very strong. Start with a teaspoon of this and work up gradually. The sauce should be slightly piquant – no more.

Pour boiling water over the walnuts and skin them if they are more than 6 months old. (You can tell their age from the colour.) Put them through the liquidizer or food processor or even mortar, with a little mayonnaise or vinegar. Whip the cream, fold in the mayonnaise and walnuts and add the horseradish last of all. Add salt if needed. If you like a slightly runnier sauce, do not whip the cream but stir all the ingredients together.

TROUT WITH MOUSSELINE SAUCE AND DILL (Sweden)

Imperial/Metric	*American*
8 trout	8 trout
1 recipe *sauce mousseline* (p.397)	1 recipe *sauce mousseline* (p.397)
1 teaspoon freeze-dried dill	1 teaspoon freeze-dried dill
court-bouillon for cooking trout (p.309)	*court-bouillon* for cooking trout (p.309)

Bone the trout but leave heads and tails on. Poach gently in the *court-bouillon*. Keep warm. Make a *sauce mousseline* and at the end add the dill. Serve either separately or poured over the trout. If you serve the trout on separate dishes, try to keep the sauce on the body only, as it looks prettier.

Sea Fish

BRANDADE DE MORUE (France)

PUREE OF SALT COD

Brandade is either served as it is with triangles of fried bread or used in other dishes such as *œufs à la benedictine*.

Imperial/Metric	*American*
1 lb (500 g) salt cod*	1 lb salt cod*
4 fl. oz (120 ml) olive oil	½ cup olive oil
4 fl. oz (120 ml) single cream	½ cup light cream
nutmeg	nutmeg
hot milk	hot milk

* Salt cod is not a cheap dish. The dried, salted fish comes either in the boned form in plastic or as a whole fish or fillet. Both need soaking in frequently changed water for 24 hours or they will be too salt to eat. Choose a middle cut if possible, where the flesh is thickest.

Having soaked your cod, cut it up roughly and poach in barely simmering water for 7-8 minutes. You can do the work by hand but a mixer or food processor is ideal for this. Drop the cooked cod into the food processor and add 4 fl. oz (120 ml) very hot oil, bit by bit. Then add the cream and finally warm milk until a medium-thick paste is obtained. It should be a little like very smooth mashed potato. Add nutmeg to taste.

PICKLED HERRING 1 (Baltic Coast)

Nowadays herrings are expensive, and commercially prepared herrings are unreasonably so. Alas! there are seldom gluts of herring but when they are at their cheapest it is worth pickling them for it is very easy to do and makes one feel virtuous at saving so much on the bought product. I use a plastic gallon container, with lid, to pickle herring. (It holds about 7 lb (3 kilos) gross weight of herring. Herring heads and bones appear to weigh quite a bit.) Alternatively you can use large glass jars (such as sweet jars) or proper pickling crocks, but earthenware will not do as it is too porous. It is not worth doing less than 5-6 lb (2-3 kilos) at a time.

Put the herrings, just as they are, into a large bowl of water with ice cubes in it and put into the refrigerator overnight. This whitens the flesh of the fish. Next day remove their heads and tails and gut them. Then pull out their backbone by working from the head towards the tail. (The other way you will lose a lot of fish.) The little bones at the side will melt later in the pickle, so do not worry about them. Whether you skin them or not is up to you. (I don't bother with herring but always skin mackerel.) Thereafter slice your boned herring in 1 inch (2-3 cm) or larger slices. Put these pieces back into iced water while you make and cool the pickle.

PICKLE

Imperial/Metric	American
8 fl. oz (240 ml) white wine vinegar	1 cup white wine vinegar
16 fl. oz (480 ml) water	2 cups water
8 oz (250 g) white sugar	1 cup white sugar
1 heaped tablespoon salt	1 heaped tablespoon salt
1 tablespoon pickling spice	1 tablespoon pickling spice
1 teaspoon mustard seed	1 teaspoon mustard seed
1 teaspoon coriander seed	1 teaspoon coriander seed

Put the water and vinegar on to boil and then add the other ingredients. Boil for 2-3 minutes and let cool at room temperature. (This takes longer than you would think.)

Cut 3 or 4 large onions in thin slices and put a layer of them on the bottom of your jar, then a layer of herring, a layer of onion and so on, finishing with onion. Pour over the *cold* pickle and put a plate on top of the herring to make sure they don't float. Push down daily for at least a week. The pickled herring will keep for at least six days in a refrigerator, less in a larder.

Serve the herring either on its own with wholemeal bread and butter or with any of the salads on pp. 321-51. Alternatively you can mix it with a little cream and dill and serve it like that.

PICKLED HERRING 2 (Northern Europe and USA)

Imperial/Metric	American
12 fl. oz (360 ml) vinegar (any sort)	1½ cups vinegar (any sort)
2 oz (60 g) salt	2 oz salt
4 oz (125 g) sugar	½ cup sugar
2 bayleaves	2 bayleaves
1 tablespoon pickling spice	1 tablespoon pickling spice
12 fl. oz (360 ml) water	1½ cups water
2 or 3 crushed juniper berries	2 or 3 crushed juniper berries

Proceed as for the Pickled Herring 1 and use in the same way.

MADEIRA MARINADE FOR HERRING (DENMARK)

For approx. 1-1½ lb (500-750 g) salt herring fillet:

Imperial/Metric	*American*
4 tablespoons water	4 tablespoons water
8 oz (250 g) brown sugar	1 cup brown sugar
8 fl. oz (240 ml) Madeira	1 cup Madeira wine
1 teaspoon coriander seed	1 teaspoon coriander seed
1 teaspoon mustard seed	1 teaspoon mustard seed
a few drops cochineal (optional)	a few drops cochineal (optional)

Soak the herrings until they are no longer unacceptably salty.

Melt sugar in the water and let it cool. Add the other ingredients and pour over the herrings. Leave in the marinade for the inside of a week. Serve with black pumpernickel bread.

SALTED HERRINGS (Denmark)

The Danes appear to like their herrings sweet as well as salted, and this recipe calls for equal amounts of sea or rock salt and sugar. You could halve the sugar.

You proceed as for pickled herrings except that you do not cut the fish into slices but into boned fillets, i.e. 2 to a herring. Mix the sugar and salt together (count approximately 1 lb (500 g) of salt for 5 lb (2.5 kilos) of herring plus the sugar in the amount you wish. Put a layer of salt/sugar on the bottom of the jar or crock then a layer of herring, then a layer of salt, then a layer of herring, so that it is skin to skin with the previous one. The next two layers of herring will be belly to belly. Continue like this until the jar is full. Put in a cold place more or less for ever if you wish but for at least a week.

You will need to soak these herring fillets before eating them – in plain water if you are going to put them into another marinade or in water for an hour, then in milk for a couple of hours, if you are going to eat them in a Baltic Salad or similar. They never need cooking – indeed, cooking would increase their saltiness to an uneatable degree.

HARENGS AU VIN BLANC (France)

HERRINGS SOUSED IN WHITE WINE

Herrings benefit from precisely the same treatment as mackerel but instead of a medium dry white wine use a very dry one. Also herrings in any sort of jelly are not very nice, so they should be served in the classic way.

SIERRA EN CEVICHE (Mexico)

PICKLED MACKEREL

A nice change from soused mackerel. Serve with onion rings and a little chopped fresh coriander or parsley to decorate. Guacamole sauce (p.395) is often served as an accompaniment.

Imperial/Metric	*American*
approx. 2 lb (1 kilo) mackerel	approx. 2 lb mackerel
½ pint (300 ml) lime juice	1¼ cup fresh lime juice
2 fl. oz (60 ml) pint sunflower oil	¼ cup sunflower oil
1 medium onion	1 medium onion
2 teaspoons Tabasco	2 teaspoons Tabasco
1 teaspoon fresh oregano or marjoram	1 teaspoon fresh oregano or marjoram

Head and tail, bone and then skin the mackerel, and cut it into bite-sized pieces. Mix the lime juice, Tabasco and oregano (or marjoram) together. Put in the mackerel and stir well, making sure every piece of fish is coated. Refrigerate for half a day before serving.

MAQUEREAUX AU VIN BLANC (France)

MACKEREL SOUSED IN WHITE WINE

The British and the Italians both souse their herrings and mackerel in violently strong vinegar. The British at least have the excuse that wine is expensive in their country. In Italy vinegar is almost as expensive as the wine one uses for this dish.

Imperial/Metric	American
4-5 fat mackerel	4-5 fat mackerel
6 shallots	6 shallots
2 large carrots, sliced	2 large carrots, sliced
2 large onions, sliced	2 large onions, sliced
1 bottle medium-dry white wine	1 bottle medium-dry white wine
1 teaspoon coriander seed	1 teaspoon coriander seed
1 teaspoon fennel seed	1 teaspoon fennel seed
a few parsley stalks	a few parsley stalks
a little cayenne	a little cayenne

Clean the fish and remove the heads. Make a broth with the wine, herbs and spice and reduce by at least a third and then strain. You can reduce it by as much as half if you wish, but you must have enough at this stage to cover your fish. Lay them in the wine stock and cook gently until done. Let them cool in the liquid. Remove the bones, skin them and fillet. Lay them in the dish in which they are going to be served and arrange a few pieces of carrot around them and a few sprigs of parsley. Reduce the wine stock further and pour over the fish. If you want to keep the fillets for a few days in the refrigerator, they must be completely covered; otherwise you do not need so much.

Some French cooks jelly the stock or even turn it into a sort of *chaud-froid* by making the broth stiff with gelatine and then adding cream to bring it back to a normal jelled consistency. However, the classic way to serve this fish is just in a little of the wine broth.

MONKFISH AND BACON BROCHETTES (Ireland)

When I first had this – in Dublin, many years ago – the monkfish was masquerading as lobster but the whole thing was so delicious that no one minded. An object lesson perhaps. Irish green bacon was used; I think smoked bacon would swamp the taste.

Imperial/Metric	American
1 lb (500 g) streaky green bacon, de-rinded	1 lb streaky green bacon, de-rinded
1½ lb (750 g) monkfish	1½ lb monkfish
2 shallots, chopped*	2 shallots, chopped*
2 lemons	2 lemons
1 tablespoon parsley, chopped	1 tablespoon parsley, chopped

* The shallot is not essential and is a bit of a performance to do. I have very successfully used chopped freeze-dried shallots for this dish.

Chop the shallots to a pulp. Stretch the streaky bacon as much as you can with the back of a knife and divide up into portions. Use the bacon to cover bite-sized pieces of monkfish on which you have first put a tiny bit of shallot, so they are completely wrapped. Thread onto a skewer (allow 2 skewers of 4 or 5 pieces per person) and grill until the bacon is more or less crisp and the monkfish inside cooked. Serve sprinkled with a little parsley and a wedge of lemon.

LOTTE AU POIVRE VERT (France)

MONKFISH WITH GREEN PEPPER SAUCE

Imperial/Metric	*American*
Approx. 3 lb (1.5 kilos) monkfish	Approx. 3 lb monkfish
1 recipe *sauce poivre vert* (pp.392-3)	1 recipe *sauce poivre vert* (pp.392-3)
½ glass white wine	½ glass white wine

Depending on the way your monkfish has arrived, cut it into small pieces or into small steaks and sauté in butter. Deglaze with a half glass of white wine. Keep warm for a few moments whilst you heat the sauce. Add the pan juices to the sauce and pour over the monkfish. Serve at once.

LOTTE AUX CHAMPIGNONS (France)

MONKFISH WITH MUSHROOMS

Imperial/Metric	*American*
approx. 3 lb (1.5 kilos) monkfish	approx. 3 lb monkfish
1 recipe mushroom sauce (p.398)	1 recipe mushroom sauce (p.398)
4 fl. oz (120 ml) brandy	4 fl. oz brandy
a little butter for frying	a little butter for frying

Cook the monkfish in a little butter and deglaze with the brandy. Do not flame. Add the hot mushroom sauce (which you have reduced slightly to make it thicker), then serve. This dish can be kept waiting a little in a warm oven without coming to harm.

LOTTE A L'ORANGE (France)

MONKFISH IN AN ORANGE AND HONEY SAUCE

This is a most delicious dish from the Auberge de Bellet in Nice, where it is served with a Blanc de Bellet (there is also a red), which is a wine actually grown in the Commune of Nice – something which surprises most non-Niçois. Any good dry-ish white wine will do, but nothing as dry as a Muscadet.

Imperial/Metric	*American*
3 lb (1.5 kilos) monkfish	3 lb monkfish
butter	butter
flour for dredging	flour for dredging

Depending on how your monkfish has arrived, cut it into individual steaks if this is possible or alternatively into bite-sized pieces. I usually find the latter easier to deal with from a serving point of view. Rinse the fish and dry well on paper towels. Then dredge in flour and fry it in sufficient butter. Do not let it colour. It will turn a brilliant white when cooked. Take out the fish and keep it warm.

SAUCE

Imperial/Metric	American
juice of 4 oranges	juice of 4 oranges
grated rind of 2 oranges	grated rind of 2 oranges
3 tablespoons honey	3 tablespoons honey
1 onion, thinly sliced	1 onion, thinly sliced
salt	salt
approx. 8 oz (250 g) butter	approx. 1 cup butter

Heat up the butter and cook the sliced onion in it but do not let it brown. De-glaze with the orange juice and add the orange rind. By now you should have a rather syrupy sauce. Add the honey and bring up to heat. If you have too much sauce, reduce a little – if not enough, add a little more butter.

   Put the fish back in or transfer it to an ovenproof dish and pour the sauce over. Do not keep warm for more than 10 minutes in a coolish oven or the fresh flavour will be lost.

COLD RED MULLET (Turkey)

Imperial/Metric	American
8 red mullet	8 red mullet
a little flour	a little flour
4 oz (125 g) long grain rice	4 oz long grain rice
2 oz (60 g) pinenuts	2 oz *pignoli*
1 medium onion, chopped	1 medium onion, chopped
8 oz (250 g) tomatoes, chopped	8 oz tomatoes, chopped
2 oz (60 g) currants	2 oz currants
olive oil	olive oil
flour for dredging	flour for dredging
water or stock	water or stock
juice of a lemon	juice of a lemon
parsley, chopped (optional	parsley, chopped (optional
lemons (to serve)	lemons (to serve)

Flour the red mullet and fry in olive oil. Let them cool. Cook the onion in a little oil and add the rice. Do not let it burn. Add the tomatoes and a little salt. Add the stock and cook until the rice is almost done, then add the currants and pinenuts (*pignoli*). Once the rice is cooked, the stock should be all used up – otherwise pour it off. Cool the rice down and then add the lemon and adjust the seasoning. (Although the recipe calls for no herbs, I put in some chopped parsley at this stage.) Arrange the cold mullet on top of the cold rice and serve with wedges of lemon. You can prepare this in the morning for serving in the evening.

TRIGLIE ALLA LIVORNESE (Italy)

RED MULLET LEGHORN STYLE

Imperial/Metric	*American*
8 small red mullet	8 small red mullet
4 fl. oz (120 ml) best olive oil	½ cup best olive oil
1 medium onion, chopped	1 medium onion, chopped
2 cloves garlic	2 cloves garlic
1 lb (500 g) tomatoes	1 lb tomatoes
pinch of thyme	pinch of thyme
pinch of ground bayleaf	pinch of ground bayleaf
3 tablespoons parsley, chopped	3 tablespoons parsley, chopped
flour for dredging	flour for dredging
2 lemons	2 lemons

Skin the tomatoes by using boiling water or by grilling them over a gas flame. Cut in half and remove seeds. Using a little oil, fry the tomatoes until cooked and continue to dry them out slightly. Put aside. Dredge the red mullets (heads on and liver in) in a little flour and fry gently on both sides. They will take 4-5 minutes each side at most. Keep warm on a serving dish. Separately fry the onion and garlic in some olive oil – do not let them brown. Add the herbs but only a quarter of the parsley, and the tomatoes. Cook for a few moments and then pour over the red mullet. Serve sprinkled with parsley and wedges of lemon.

ESCABECHE OF SARDINES (Portugal and Spain)

Allow 4-5 sardines per person, depending on size, i.e. 3 lb (1.5 kilos) sardines

Imperial/Metric	*American*
5-6 cloves garlic, roughly chopped	5-6 cloves garlic, roughly chopped
8 fl. oz (240 ml) wine vinegar	1 cup wine vinegar
juice of 2 lemons	juice of 2 lemons
bayleaf, parsley stalks and thyme	bayleaf, parsley stalks and thyme
3 tablespoons olive oil (optional)	3 tablespoons olive oil (optional)
parsley (to garnish)	parsley (to garnish)

Remove head and tails of sardines and clean them. Grill them about 4 minutes or less on each side and then lay them in a serving dish. Meanwhile put the vinegar, lemon juice, garlic and *bouquet-garni* in a pan and simmer for approximately 10 minutes. (Some people put 3 tablespoons of olive oil into the marinade. It certainly lessens the acidity of the dish, though the sardines are fairly oily in themselves.) Strain and pour hot over the dish of sardines. Let marinate over night. Serve very cold next day.

SKATE MAYONNAISE (USA)

This is a poor man's version of Lobster and Cucumber (p.119). Substitute 1½ lb (750 g) cooked skate (boned and well picked over) for the lobster, and instead of using ½ pint (225 ml) cream, use only half that amount and 5 fl. oz (140 ml) good mayonnaise (p.405). Otherwise proceed in the same way.

FILETS DE SOLE AUX ASPERGES A LA SAUCE MALTAISE (France)

SOLE WITH ASPARAGUS AND SAUCE MALTAISE

Imperial/Metric	*American*
8 or 16 fillets of sole, depending on size	8 or 16 fillets of sole, depending on size
1 lb (500 g) asparagus tips	1 lb asparagus tips
1 recipe *sauce hollandaise* (p.395)	1 recipe *sauce hollandaise* (p.395)
juice of 2 blood oranges*	juice of 2 blood oranges*
rind of 1 blood orange, grated	rind of 1 blood orange, grated
sprigs of parsley	sprigs of parsley

* Only blood oranges will do for this dish as ordinary oranges do not have the power to colour.

Poach your sole fillets or bake them *en papillote*. While they are cooking, make a *sauce hollandaise*, but keep back the juice of one of the lemons. Add the blood orange rind to the sauce, then add the juice of 2 blood oranges to it – bit by bit. Do this carefully or you will curdle your sauce. Put the fish fillets in a serving dish, pour over the sauce, decorate with the parsley and serve.

SOLE A LA SAUCE AURORE

Imperial/Metric	American
sole fillets for 8	sole fillets for 8
1 recipe *sauce aurore* (p.391)	1 recipe *sauce aurore* (p.391)
parsley, chopped (to serve)	parsley, chopped (to serve)

Poach the fillets and pour over the *sauce aurore*. Sprinkle with chopped parsley and serve.

SOLE AUX COURGETTES AVEC COULIS DE TOMATES FRAICHES (France)

SOLE WITH COURGETTES AND FRESH TOMATO SAUCE

Imperial/Metric	American
sole fillets for 8	sole fillets for 8
4 oz (125 g) butter	½ cup butter
1 large onion, finely sliced	1 large onion, finely sliced
1½ lb (750 g) courgettes	1½ lb zucchini
1 recipe *coulis de tomates* (p.389)	1 recipe *coulis de tomates* (p.389)
parsley and thyme, chopped (optional)	parsley and thyme, chopped (optional)

This is a dish which cannot be made ahead or the fresh taste is lost – though the courgettes could be cooked in advance and heated through.

Fry the onion in butter. Do not let it brown. Slice the courgettes as you would cucumbers, preferably with a mandoline. Cook these gently with the onions, adding a little water from time to time. You must end up with almost cooked courgettes and *no* water. Keep them warm. Poach the sole fillets (rolled up or not) in a mixture of fish stock and a glass of white wine. Put the courgettes in the bottom of a large, shallow serving dish with the sole fillets on top, and mask with the hot *coulis* before serving. Sprinkle with a little parsley or thyme if wished.

SOLE A LA MODE DE CHAMBERY (France)

SOLE IN CHAMBERY VERMOUTH

This must be done either in Chambéry vermouth or in dry Noilly Prat – no other sort of vermouth will do. The recipe looks more complicated and longer to do than it really is.

Imperial/Metric
8 medium or 16 small fillets of sole
8 fl. oz (240 ml) water or fish stock
8 fl. oz (240 ml) Chambéry vermouth
1 onion, sliced in rings
8 oz (250 g) butter
3 egg yolks
5 oz (155 g) small shrimp, shelled weight
1 tablespoon parsley, chopped

American
8 medium or 16 small fillets of sole
1 cup water or fish stock
1 cup Chambéry vermouth
1 onion, sliced in rings
1 cup butter
3 egg yolks
5 oz small shrimp, shelled weight
1 tablespoon parsley, chopped

Roll up the fillets of sole and secure with toothpick. In a large pan melt the butter in the vermouth and stock (or water) and put in the onion rings. Bring to the boil, then turn down heat and let simmer for 4-5 minutes. Then poach your fish. Once cooked, remove the fish to a dish and keep it in a warm place. Strain stock and then reduce to half. Beat 3 egg yolks in a bowl and pour on the hot stock. If it does not thicken enough, cook in a double boiler (or *bain-marie*) until it does. Add the parsley and the cooked, peeled shrimp and pour over the fish.

SOLE FLORENTINE (France)

SOLE WITH SPINACH AND CHEESE SAUCE

This is not the classic way to do this dish but not only is it remarkably easier but it tastes richer than the original dish.

Imperial/Metric
8 fillets of sole
1 recipe *sauce mornay* (p.397)
1 lb (500 g) cooked-weight spinach, chopped
4 oz (125 g) butter

American
8 fillets of sole
1 recipe *sauce mornay* (p.397)
1 lb cooked-weight spinach, chopped
½ cup butter

Do not put too much butter with your spinach. It is not necessary as some of the *sauce mornay* will work down into it. Put a layer of *sauce mornay* in a shallow ovenproof dish, then all the spinach, and then continue as for Sole Mornay (below).

SOLE AU GRATIN (Denmark)

SOLE IN *SAUCE SOUBISE* ·

Delicious and very simple as much of it can be prepared in advance.

Imperial/Metric	*American*
sole fillets for 8	sole fillets for 8
1 recipe *sauce soubise* (p.400)	1 recipe *sauce soubise* (p.400)
2 tomatoes, thickly sliced	2 tomatoes, thickly sliced
2 teaspoons fresh dill (1	2 teaspoons fresh dill (1
teaspoon freeze-dried)	teaspoon freeze-dried)
parsley, chopped	parsley, chopped

Roll up the raw sole fillets and secure them with a toothpick. Put in a buttered gratin dish. To a ready-made *sauce soubise* add the dill. Pour over the fish. Put the sliced tomatoes round the outside of the dish. Cook in a hot oven 400°F/200°C/Gas 6 for 20 minutes and serve sprinkled with parsley.

SOLE MORNAY (France)

SOLE IN *SAUCE MORNAY*

This is an unconventional way of cooking this recipe but I once did it in a hurry when there were many other things to prepare and it tasted so much better than the classic recipe that I have stuck to it ever since. Any firm white fish can be done like this.

Imperial/Metric	*American*
8 fillets of sole	8 fillets of sole
1 recipe *sauce mornay* (p.397)	1 recipe *sauce mornay* (p.397)
2 tablespoons dry white wine	2 tablespoons dry white wine
butter	butter

Put a layer of *sauce mornay* in the bottom of a shallow ovenproof dish (glass or ceramic but not metal) and lay the fish fillets on top. Alternatively you can use a smaller and less shallow dish and roll up your fillets (secured with a cocktail stick). Pour over the rest of the sauce, to which you have added 2 tablespoons dry white wine. Dot with butter and bake for 20 minutes at slightly under 400°F/200°C/Gas 6, on the middle shelf.

SOLE A LA CREME PERSILEE (France)

SOLE IN A PARSLEY AND CREAM SAUCE

This is a family recipe and was always made without flour, which meant it was liable to curdle. I have, therefore, put in a dessertspoon of flour to prevent this. More flour would turn it into an ordinary parsley sauce.

Imperial/Metric	*American*
sole fillets for 8	sole fillets for 8
1 dessertspoon flour	1 dessertspoon flour
2 oz (60 g) butter	¼ cup butter
15 fl. oz (450 ml) double cream	2 cups heavy cream
2 tablespoons parsley	2 tablespoons parsley
2 egg yolks	2 egg yolks
salt and pepper	salt and pepper

Melt the butter and add the flour to make a roux. Cook it a little and add the cream. Let it simmer at least 15 minutes on a very low heat. During this time cook the sole in the fish stock to which you have added a glass of dry white wine. Chop the parsley by hand (not in a machine) and rinse quickly again once you have chopped it. This stops the sauce going green. Press out as much water as possible and then add to the sauce. Finally add the two egg yolks and let it thicken up a little. Pour over the sole and serve at once.

VARIATION

My husband came across a similar dish in Denmark but the sauce was flavoured with dill (much less: probably a tablespoon would do) and lemon juice. He said it was excellent.

FILETS DE SOLE AUX SAUTERNES (France)

SOLE IN *SAUCE SAUTERNES*

This is a recipe from the nineteenth-century, when sweet wines were very popular with fish. There is no reason why you should not substitute something drier but choose a really full-flavoured wine, not one which is too dry, such as Muscadet. Serve the same wine as used in cooking.

Imperial/Metric	American
8 or 16 sole fillets	8 or 16 sole fillets
approx. 1 pint (600 ml) fish stock (p.308)	2½ cups fish stock (p.308)
8 fl. oz (240 ml) Sauternes	1 cup Sauternes
2 tablespoons flour	2 tablespoons flour
2 tablespoons butter, melted	2 tablespoons butter, melted
6 fl. oz (180 ml) double cream	1¼ cups heavy cream
3 egg yolks	3 egg yolks
sprigs of parsley	sprigs of parsley

Reduce the fish stock by half, then poach the sole fillets in it (rolled or not, as you wish). Keep warm. Reduce this stock down to about 4 fl. oz/120 ml/½ cup. In another saucepan melt the butter and make a roux with the flour. Do not let it brown. Add the fish stock and then the Sauternes. Cook a little longer and then add half the cream. Taste and adjust seasoning. Just before serving, beat up the egg yolks with the remaining cream and beat into the sauce. Pour over the sole fillets, decorate with a few sprigs of parsley and serve.

FILETS DE SOLE A LA SAUCE SURPRISE (France)

FILLETS OF SOLE IN RHUBARB SAUCE

Turbot would also do for this dish. The surprise sauce is that it is made of rhubarb rather than the traditional sorrel, and as a result it is the most beautiful rose colour, tasting as acid as, but slightly more gentle than, the classic sorrel sauce. I have put a tiny bit of flour in the sauce which is not in the original recipe, because without it the sauce 'turns' far too easily.

Poach or steam 8 medium or 16 small sole fillets.

SAUCE

Imperial/Metric	American
8 oz (250 g) best-quality rhubarb	8 oz best-quality rhubarb
4 oz (125 g) butter	½ cup butter
1 tablespoon flour	1 tablespoon flour
8 fl. oz (240 ml) double cream	1 cup heavy cream
3 or 4 egg yolks	3 or 4 egg yolks
salt and white pepper to taste	salt and white pepper to taste
parsley (to garnish)	parsley (to garnish)

Melt the butter and make a roux with the flour. Add the double cream and put on to simmer for 15 minutes, preferably on an asbestos mat or heat mat. Stir from time to time. Cook the rhubarb in as little water as possible. Once cooked, strain the rhubarb and put it through the liquidizer or food processor. Sieve the result – this is essential for the texture of the sauce. Add the rhubarb, bit by bit, to the cream sauce. Bring it up to heat. Beat the egg yolks in a bowl. Starting with 3, add them to the hot sauce and whisk in. Do not let boil but it should thicken a little. Taste. It should taste creamy but acid. If it is too acid, put in another egg yolk.

Pour the sauce over the hot fillets of sole and serve. (Alternatively serve the sole on individual plates and pour sauce over.) Garnish with parsley.

SOLE VERONIQUE (France)

SOLE IN A WHITE WINE SAUCE WITH GRAPES

Strictly, speaking, this dish should be made with muscatel grapes or seedless grapes. I found the most perfect grapes in the Austrian Weinviertel one September but alas no sole in that country, which still does not like anything but freshwater fish! Muscatel grapes usually have large pips and quite tough skins which involve a lot of hard work on the part of the cook. It is probably best to eschew this dish unless you can find the right seedless grapes.

Sole fillets for 8

SAUCE

Imperial/Metric	*American*
Fish stock (p.308)	Fish stock (p.308)
1 lb (500 g) seedless white grapes	1 lb seedless white grapes
4 oz (125 g) butter	½ cup butter
3 shallots, chopped	3 shallots, chopped
8 fl. oz (240 ml) dry white wine	1 cup dry white wine
10 fl. oz (300 ml) *sauce béchamel* (p.391)	1¼ cups *sauce béchamel* (p.391)
2 or 3 egg yolks	2 or 3 egg yolks
4 fl. oz (120 ml)double cream	½ cup heavy cream
salt and white pepper	salt and white pepper

Pour boiling water over the grapes and let them stand.

Fry the shallots gently in the butter, add the white wine and reduce by half. Then add the *béchamel*. Add the cream, salt and pepper and let simmer while you are poaching the fillets (rolled up) in fish stock (not *court-bouillon*). Once they are done, put them into a large, shallow serving dish and keep warm.

Strain the grapes well and put them around the fish. Add the egg yolks to the sauce and let it thicken a little – do not let it boil or it will curdle. Pour it over the fish and run it under a very hot grill for a minute or 2 to let it brown on top.

TUNA BRANDADE (France)

This is an inexpensive starter, but it must be prepared more or less at the last minute as it will not wait. However, the potatoes can be peeled in advance and the tuna can be mixed with the oil, garlic and egg yolks some hours beforehand without any harm coming to them. Serve warm, not hot, on a bed of crisp salad greens.

Imperial/Metric	*American*
approx. 12 oz (375 g) canned tuna	approx. 12 oz canned tuna
2 lb (1 kilo) mashed potatoes	2 lb mashed potatoes
6 tablespoons olive oil	6 tablespoons olive oil
2 egg yolks	2 egg yolks
3 cloves garlic	3 cloves garlic
salt and pepper	salt and pepper

Mash the potatoes and incorporate the oil and egg yolks gradually. Crush the garlic cloves with a little salt and mix well into the potatoes.

Drain the oil or *court-bouillon* off the tuna if the consistency of the mashed potato is right, otherwise add a little liquid from the can. Crush the tuna into small pieces. Fold into the mashed potato and serve at once.

COLD DOLMA WITH TUNA (Lebanon)

This dish used to be part of the wonderful cold table at the Hotel St Georges in Beirut which, alas, is no more. A similar dish was made with tuna and rice using vine leaves as the covering.

Imperial/Metric	American
1 lb (500 g) canned tuna	1 lb canned tuna
3 egg yolks	3 egg yolks
24 large lettuce leaves	24 large lettuce leaves
3 fl. oz (90 ml) double cream	3 fl. oz heavy cream
pinch of nutmeg, cinnamon and paprika	pinch of nutmeg, cinnamon and paprika
salt	salt
vinaigrette made with lemon (p.403)	vinaigrette made with lemon (p.403)

Blanch the lettuce leaves, rinse in cold water, dry on a paper towel and set aside. Mix tuna, egg yolks, cream and spices together by hand rather than in a mixer. Divide in 8 portions and wrap each portion in 3 thicknesses of lettuce leaves, rolling rather tightly. Place in a large dish, seam side down, and pour over the lemon dressing. Serve 2-3 hours later.

TURBOT WITH LEMON SAUCE (Sweden)

4-6 oz (125-190g) turbot per person

SAUCE

Imperial/Metric	American
3-4 egg yolks (depending on size)	3-4 egg yolks (depending on size)
2 oz (60 g) butter	¼ cup butter
1 shallot, chopped	1 shallot, chopped
juice of 2 lemons	juice of 2 lemons
grated peel of 1 lemon	grated peel of 1 lemon
8 fl. oz (240 ml) single cream	1 cup whipping cream
fresh parsley	fresh parsley
salt and sugar	salt and sugar

Poach or bake 'en papillote' small turbot steaks. Keep warm and prepare sauce.

Blanch the parsley on its stalk for a moment in boiling water and then dry and chop finely to make 3 tablespoons. Cook the shallot in the butter but do not let it brown. In a double boiler let the egg yolks and cream heat together, then add the shallot, lemon juice and rind. Taste and add sugar and salt to suit. Let the mixture thicken a little and finally add the parsley.

Serve over the fish fillets either in a large serving dish or on individual plates.

TURBOT A L'ORANGE (France)

TURBOT IN ORANGE AND HONEY SAUCE

This is cooked exactly the same way as the monkfish in orange and honey sauce (p.83). Halibut can be used equally well, as can sole or flounder, dab or plaice.

MERLANO E COZZE ALLA PIZZAIOLA (Italy)

WHITING AND MUSSELS IN A PIZZAIOLA SAUCE

Imperial/Metric	American
2 lb (1 kilo) whiting fillets	2 lb whiting fillets
1 lb (500 g) mussels in their shells	1¼ pints mussels in their shells
4 green and/or red peppers, sliced	4 green and/or red bell peppers, sliced
4 cloves garlic, chopped	4 cloves garlic, chopped
1 lb (500 g) ripe tomatoes, chopped	1 lb ripe tomatoes, chopped
¾ lb (750 g) peas in pod	¾ lb peas in pod
4 tablespoons olive oil	4 tablespoons olive oil
lemon and parsley (optional)	lemon and parsley (optional)
salt and pepper	salt and pepper

Clean and beard the mussels and set aside. Fry the garlic in the olive oil (you can use less of both if preferred), add the peppers and cook until half done. Meanwhile cook the peas separately in boiling salted water. Add the tomatoes to the pepper mixture and parsley if you wish. Butter a large, shallow dish and lay the whiting fillets on the bottom. Mix the cooked peas into the peppers and tomatoes and pour over the fillets. Cook in a hot oven (400°F/200°C/Gas 6) for 15 minutes.

Just before the dish is ready, open the mussels by putting them in a small amount of salted water in a saucepan with the lid on. Over a high heat the mussels will all open in 2-3 minutes. Discard those that are not. Remove one of the shells from each mussel and garnish the dish with them.

PESCADO EN SALSA VERDE (Mexico)

WHITING IN GREEN SAUCE

This recipe comes from Ensenada in Baja California and has no hot peppers in it. I understand the Vera Cruz version has plenty

of small hot chilli peppers in it. You can add them to your taste if
you wish, but it is also genuinely Mexican without.

Imperial/Metric	*American*
approx. 3 lb (1.5 kilos) whiting	approx. 3 lb whiting
3 tablespoons olive oil	3 tablespoons olive oil
1 teaspoon salt	1 teaspoon salt
1 large onion, finely chopped	1 large onion, finely chopped
3 or 4 cloves garlic	3 or 4 cloves garlic
1 lb (500 g) unripe green tomatoes, chopped*	1 lb unripe green tomatoes, chopped*
2 green peppers, chopped	2 green bell peppers, chopped
juice of 1 lemon	juice of 1 lemon
2 tablespoons vinegar	2 tablespoons vinegar
salt	salt
flour for dredging	flour for dredging

*The tomatoes should be just on the point of becoming red and
not completely unripe.

Dip the fish in flour and fry in olive oil. Remove to a shallow
dish and pour over lemon juice.

Fry the onion and garlic and, once soft, add the green tomatoes.
Add the green peppers, salt and vinegar. Taste, since it may need
more salt or olive oil. Pour this sauce over the fish and let get cold.
Chill for 3 hours before serving.

Various

CEYLON FISH CURRY (SRI LANKA)

I am not an admirer of airline food but I had this fish curry
between Colombo and Bangkok on one occasion and it was
delicious (and mild), though probably made for European taste.

Imperial/Metric	American
4-6 oz (125-190 g) very firm white fish per person	4-6 oz very firm white fish per person
4 oz (125 g) small shrimps, cooked and deveined	4 oz small shrimp, cooked and deveined
2 onions, very finely chopped	2 onions, very finely chopped
2 tablespoons mild curry powder	2 tablespoons mild curry powder
1 tablespoon turmeric	1 tablespoon turmeric
1 tablespoon ground coriander	1 tablespoon ground coriander
15 fl. oz (450 ml) coconut milk (p.102)	2 cups coconut milk (p.102)
a few slivers fresh ginger (optional)	a few slivers fresh ginger (optional)
salt	salt
butter for cooking the fish	butter for cooking the fish

Make the sauce first and cook the fish at the end.

In a little butter cook the onion until soft and almost disappearing. Add the spices, curry, salt and *half* the coconut milk. Cook for 15 minutes and then add the rest of the coconut milk. Cook the fish in a little butter then pour over the curry sauce. Add the shrimps and serve.

COLD FISH (Turkey)

My husband insists this is a Sephardi dish, and certainly I have come across it all over the Middle East, although ostensibly it is native to Turkey.

Imperial/Metric	American
8 whole small fish or 8 small fish steaks	8 whole small fish or 8 small fish steaks
olive oil	olive oil
2-3 tablespoons breadcrumbs	2-3 tablespoons breadcrumbs
1 green pepper, sliced	1 green pepper, sliced
2 onions, finely sliced	2 onions, finely sliced
3 cloves garlic, finely chopped	3 cloves garlic, finely chopped
1 lb (500 g) tomatoes, chopped	1 lb tomatoes, chopped
1 tablespoon tomato concentrate	1 tablespoon tomato concentrate
2 tablespoons white wine vinegar	2 tablespoons white wine vinegar
a handful of black olives	a handful of black olives
1 teaspoon dried dill weed (or parsley)	1 teaspoon dried dill weed (or parsley)
2 lemons	2 lemons

Cook the fish gently in plenty of olive oil. Drain and remove to another dish once cooked.

Cook the onions and pepper in this oil but do not let brown. Add the garlic and chopped tomatoes. Add the vinegar and tomato concentrate. Put in some breadcrumbs so that you have a just spreadable sauce. Smooth this over the fish, sprinkle on the dill (or parsley if liked) and decorate at the last moment with the olives and wedges of lemon. Chill for 2-3 hours before serving.

Variation
Because the swordfish or tuna usually used for this dish in Turkey are very dry, I tried doing thin slivers (escalopes) of chicken (turkey breast would be the same) this way: the result was excellent.

FISKEPUDDING (Norway and Sweden)

HOT FISH MOUSSE OR PUDDING

Don't be put off by the name, which sounds rather dull.

Imperial/Metric	American
1½ lb (750 g) sole or cod fillets	1½ lb sole or cod fillets
8 oz (250 g) prawns, shelled	8 oz shelled medium shrimps
8 fl. oz (240 ml) double cream	1 cup heavy cream
3 whole eggs	3 whole eggs
6 egg yolks	6 egg yolks
juice and rind of 1 lemon	juice and rind of 1 lemon
½ pint (300 ml) *sauce béchamel* (p.391)	1¼ cup *sauce béchamel* (p.391)
nutmeg	nutmeg
salt and pepper	salt and pepper
1 recipe shrimp sauce (p.401)	1 recipe shrimp sauce (p.401)

Put the fish fillets, *sauce béchamel* and egg in a liquidizer or food processor and mix. Add the cream. Turn into a bowl and add the shelled and deveined prawns. Salt and pepper and add the nutmeg, lemon rind and juice. Fill a shallow baking dish with about 2 inches (5 cm) and heat in an oven at 400°F/200°C/Gas 6. Turn the fish mixture into a fireproof dish or non-stick lined cake tin and bake for 30 minutes at this temperature; then turn down to 350°F/180°C/Gas 4 and continue to cook (on the middle shelf) another hour. Test with a knitting needle or the blade of a knife. It should not brown; if this happens cover it with some foil. Once cooked, turn it out onto a serving dish, handing the sauce separately.

OVERSEAS CHINESE FISH SATAY

Imperial/Metric	American
1½ lb (750 g) firm fish (monkfish is ideal)	1½ lb firm fish (monkfish is ideal)
1 clove garlic, crushed	1 clove garlic, crushed
4 oz (125 g) ground almonds	½ cup almonds, freed of their skins and ground *or* ½ cup Macadamia nut meats
4 fl. oz (120 ml) coconut milk (p.102)	
2 tablespoons lime or lemon juice	½ cup coconut milk (p.102)
2 teaspoons grated lemon rind	2 tablespoons lime or lemon juice
½ teaspoon or more Tabasco	2 teaspoons grated lemon rind
cucumber, peeled and chopped	½ teaspoon or more Tabasco
	cucumber, peeled and chopped

Cut fish into small pieces and thread onto satay skewers. Make sauce of other ingredients, except cucumber. Cover in the sauce and grill for a few minutes of each side until done. Serve with cucumber.

SEVICHE ANTILLAISE (Martinique)

CEVICHE OF WHITE FISH IN LIME JUICE

This can be made with any one white fish, absolutely fresh and never frozen, such as sole, turbot, halibut, brill, whiting, cod or monkfish. Monkfish is one of the best choices.

Limes are obtainable at most West Indian stores and certain supermarkets in the UK. Lemon juice will not do as a substitute for lime in this recipe.

Imperial/Metric	American
2-3 lb (1-1.5 kilos) white fish	2-3 lbs white fish
1 large onion, chopped	1 large onion, chopped
1 bunch parsley, chopped	1 bunch parsley, chopped
1 bunch chives, chopped	1 bunch chives, chopped
8 fl. oz (240 ml) double cream	1 cup heavy cream
2 tablespoons white wine vinegar	2 tablespoons white wine vinegar
juice of 6 fresh limes	juice of 6 fresh limes
salt	salt
Tabasco	Tabasco
hard-boiled eggs and lemon to decorate	hardcooked eggs and lemon to decorate

Cut the fish into 1 inch (2 cm) cubes and put to marinate in the lime juice for 20 minutes. The fish will lose its transparent look and will have become brilliant white. Drain well. Mix the cream, salt, chopped herbs and Tabasco and stir into the 'cooked' fish. Taste to see if it is sharp enough and if not add the wine vinegar. Put on an oval platter and decorate with quartered hard-boiled eggs, slices of lemon or tomato etc.

SOUTH PACIFIC FISH SEVICHE (South Pacific)

MARINATED RAW FISH

Imperial/Metric
2-2½ lb (1-1.25 kilos) firm fish
4 fl. oz (120 ml) lime and/or
  lemon juice
8 fl. oz (240 ml) coconut milk
  (see p.102)
salad of tomato, onion and
  cucumber
salt

American
2-2½ lb firm fish
4 fl. oz lime and/or lemon juice
1 cup coconut milk (see p.102)
salad of tomato, onion and
  cucumber
salt

Slice the fish into thin slices as you would for Japanese *sushi* (i.e. very thin). Cover with lime juice and let it 'work' for 3-4 hours. Pour off the lime juice and add coconut milk and some sliced onion. Chill for a further hour or so. Serve surrounded by chopped tomato, cucumber and onion.

VERA CRUZ ESCABECHE (Mexico)

Imperial/Metric
2 lb (1 kilo) white fish or red
  snapper
8 oz (250 g) white onion, sliced
8 fl. oz (240 ml) olive oil
3 cloves garlic, crushed
3 fl. oz (90 ml) wine vinegar
3 fl. oz (90 ml) white wine
2 teaspoons Tabasco
2 tablespoons chopped fresh
  coriander (or parsley)
salt
olive oil for frying the fish

American
2 lb white fish or red snapper
8 oz white onion, sliced
8 fl. oz olive oil
3 cloves garlic, crushed
¼ cup wine vinegar
¼ cup white wine
2 teaspoons Tabasco
2 tablespoons chopped fresh
  coriander (or parsley)
salt
olive oil for frying the fish

Cut the fish into bite-sized pieces and fry gently in some olive oil. In a separate pan, fry the garlic and onions for less than 2 minutes – they should just be slightly softened. Lay the fish pieces and onions in a dish and pour over the mixture of oil, vinegar, wine, salt and Tabasco. (There are two schools of thought about the coriander – some put half in at the marinating stage and some put it on at the end.) Cover and leave in the refrigerator for at least 48 hours before serving.

WHITE FISH ESCABECHE (All over the Caribbean)

Imperial/Metric	*American*
2 lb (1 kilo) any very fresh white fish, such as whiting, halibut or cod	2 lb any very fresh white fish, such as whiting, halibut or cod
8 fl. oz (240 ml) freshly squeezed lime juice	1 cup freshly squeezed lime juice
16 fl. oz (450 ml) milk	1 pint milk
8 oz (250 g) unsweetened desiccated coconut	8 oz unsweetened desiccated coconut
3 fl. oz (90 ml) light olive oil	3 fl. oz light olive oil
Tabasco	Tabasco
salt	salt
onion rings (to garnish)	onion rings (to garnish)
fresh coriander or parsley	fresh coriander or parsley

To make coconut milk, heat the milk to almost boiling, pour over the dessiccated coconut and leave to infuse until cool. Then pour through a very fine sieve. Press a little to extract all the flavour but throw away the pulp left over.

Skin, bone and cut the fish into thin slices or small squares. Pour over the lime juice (lemon juice will not do) and put in the refrigerator overnight turning once or twice. The fish should turn a brilliant white.

Next day pour off the lime juice. Mix the coconut milk with the Tabasco, olive oil and salt and pour over the fish. Decorate with the onions rings and fresh coriander or parsley.

Smoked Fish

CREAMED FINNAN HADDOCK (Scotland)

Allow 4-6 oz (125-190 g) off the bone per person. Please do not use coloured fillets since the taste is far too strong and salt. You may need to soak the Finnan Haddock a little but it is unlikely.

Imperial/Metric	American
approx. 3-3½ lb (1.5-1.75 kilos) Finnan haddock	approx. 3-3½ lb Finnan haddie
1 pint (600 ml) *sauce soubise* (p.400)	2 cups *sauce soubise* (p.400)
2 tablespoons double cream	2 tablespoons heavy cream
1 tablespoon parsley plus 1 sprig	1 tablespoon parsley plus 1 sprig
a little cayenne pepper	a little cayenne pepper

Cook, skin, bone and flake the fish, and set it aside while you make the sauce. Mix the haddock into the sauce, add the cream, parsley and pepper and put into ramekins or shells. Cook a few moments under a very hot grill to brown. Decorate with a sprig of parsley.

RAMEKINS ARNOLD BENNETT

SMOKED HADDOCK AND SOFT-BOILED EGGS

Imperial/Metric	American
8 fl. oz (240 ml) cooked smoked haddock	1 cup cooked smoked haddock
8 fl. oz (240 ml) thick *sauce béchamel*	1 cup thick *sauce béchamel*
8 eggs, soft-boiled	8 eggs, soft-boiled
8 tablespoons cream (optional)	8 tablespoons cream (optional)
a dash of Tabasco	a dash of Tabasco

Mix the smoked haddock, *sauce béchamel* and Tabasco (it should be fairly thick) and divide among 8 ramekins. Put a soft-boiled egg in each and top with cream. Heat through in a warm oven.

Variation
Break a raw egg on top of the smoked haddock mixture and then cover it with cream and bake for 8-10 minutes at 400°F/200°C/Gas 6.

MARINATED KIPPERS (UK)

Serve with Hovis or wholemeal bread and butter.

Imperial/Metric	American
4 large Craster or similar type kippers (kippered herrings)*	4 large Craster or similar type kippers (kippered herrings)*
1 recipe vinaigrette (p.401)	1 recipe vinaigrette (p.401)

*Frozen kipper fillets are not ideal for this recipe though it will improve them. Undyed Isle of Man or Craster, which are rather more beige than orange, are the sort to look for.

Pour boiling water over the kippers to cover and leave for 2 minutes, then pour off. Skin and bone them and cut into long, thinnish fillets. Put them to soak in the vinaigrette for 4 hours at least. (Alternatively you can skin and bone the kippers as they are and marinate them, but the first way I think is better.) Drain off most of the vinaigrette before serving.

Eels

Eels must be live until *just before* cooking. Either stun them with the back of a cleaver and then chop off the head (they sometimes wriggle frighteningly afterwards) or hand them back to the fisherman with instructions to report back when they have been despatched. To skin an eel, make an incision about 2 inches (5 cm) from the head right the way round its body. Then either hook the eel onto a hook or hold it in place with a fork thrust through it. Work the skin down a little so you can grip it with a pair of pliers and then peel it off. Alternatively buy your eel killed and skinned from a fishmonger.

MARINATED EEL (Italy)

Eels abound in Italian rivers (and probably most other rivers for that matter). This is a fishermen's recipe, useful for wives (or mothers) of coarse fishermen who go blank on what to do with what looks like a pretty dismal catch. Serve with wholemeal bread.

Imperial/Metric	American
approx. 2 lb (1 kilo) eel	approx. 2 lb eel
8 oz (250 g) onion, chopped	8 oz onion, chopped
4 fl. oz (120 ml) olive oil	½ cup olive oil
4 fl. oz (120 ml) wine vinegar	½ cup wine vinegar
4 fl. oz (120 ml) water	½ cup water
1 tablespoon parsley, chopped	1 tablespoon parsley, chopped
pinch oregano	pinch oregano
pinch nutmeg	pinch nutmeg
1-2 cloves garlic	1-2 cloves garlic
freshly ground pepper and salt	freshly ground pepper and salt
a little flour	a little flour

Chop your skinned eel into pieces about 1 or 2 inches (2.5-5 cm), dip them in flour and fry in the olive oil. Once done, remove them. Then fry the onions and garlic very slightly. Add the vinegar and water and bring to the boil. Taste – you may need a little more oil. Add the herbs and spices, salt and plenty of pepper and pour the marinade over the eel pieces. Refrigerate at least overnight once cooled down.

ANGUILLES AU VERT (Belgium)

COLD EELS IN A GREEN SAUCE

This is Antwerp's most famous dish although it is eaten all over Belgium and Holland. Some say you must use very dry white wine, others say slightly sweet. It is up to you.

Imperial/Metric	American
3 lb (1.5 kilos) freshwater eels	3 lb freshwater eels
8 shallots, finely chopped	8 shallots, finely chopped
3 tablespoons olive oil	3 tablespoons olive oil
8 fl. oz (240 ml) white wine	1 cup white wine
approx. 8 fl. oz (240 ml) water*	approx. 1 cup water*

1 lb (500 g) mixed greenstuff in equal proportions, such as spinach, sorrel, green celery and watercress, chopped

4 tablespoons parsley, chopped	4 tablespoons parsley, chopped
1 tablespoon chervil, chopped	1 tablespoon chervil, chopped
salt and pepper	salt and pepper

*My own family use no water – only 12 fl. oz (360 ml) wine – in this dish.

    Soften the shallots in olive oil. Add all the greenstuff and turn in the oil a few moments. Then put in 1 inch (2 cm) pieces of eel.

Pour over the wine and then just enough water to cover the eels (too much and the sauce will not set). Cook very gently indeed (preferably with an asbestos or similar mat), covered, for 20-30 minutes. Add the parsley, chervil, salt and pepper. Turn into a ceramic dish and let cool, then refrigerate. Eat 12 hours later.

5   Seafood

Mussels

In some countries mussels, and other shellfish for that matter, are sold by volume, in others by weight. A litre of mussels will weigh approximately 750 g; an imperial pint of mussels weighs approximately 15 oz; an American pint of mussels weighs approximately 12 oz. 1 pint (0.5 litre/US 1¼ pint) will serve one person generously, and you can count 3 imperial pints (1.8 litres/US 3¾ pints) for 4 people or 6-7 imperial pints (3.6-4.2 litres/7½-8¾ US pints) for 8.

Many people put their mussels in salted water with a little flour or oatmeal in it, so the mussels will rid themselves of any sand; some even change the water after 12 hours. In any event, you should always strain the resulting juice or the soup you have made, just to be sure. In parts of France, the Netherlands and Belgium (and maybe in Britain but I have never seen it) many fishmongers have a machine which will clean mussels of barnacles etc and de-beard them. Otherwise you will have to scrape each shell yourself – when you have 8 people for a dinner party, this operation can be a bit wearisome to say the least. Many people use a wire brush but I find this rips rubber gloves or is hell on the hands, which is scarcely surprising when it is designed to remove barnacles. A small sharp knife is best. If any of the mussels seems heavier than average, discard it – it usually means it is full of sand. Discard also those that are open before cooking and any that are closed after.

The coasts of Europe abound in mussels. Many are in farms (*moules du bouchot*) and are not for picking off by the public but there are plenty of rocky places where they abound when the tide is out. Make sure that the place is not polluted by a sewage outlet or some other horror and that only clean sea water (as clean as sea water can be in Europe nowadays) covers or splashes on to them. You can keep them up to 48 hours (24 in summer) in clean salted water (with or without the flour or oatmeal). Tinned mussels by and large are awful, rather expensive and usually full of sand.

MOULES MARINIERES (France)

You will need a large, wide pan (with lid) which will take all the mussels together.

Imperial/Metric
6 pints (3.5 litres) mussels, cleaned
3 medium onions, finely chopped
1 clove garlic, finely chopped
4 oz (125 g) butter
15 fl. oz (450 ml) dry white wine
a large bunch of parsley, finely chopped
pepper

American
8 US pints mussels, cleaned
3 medium onions, finely chopped
1 clove garlic, finely chopped
½ cup butter
1 pint dry white wine
a large bunch of parsley, finely chopped
pepper

Cook the onions and garlic in the butter in the open pan. Do not let the onions colour. Once cooked (they should be a little on the crisp side), add the wine and bring to the boil. Turn down heat and cook very gently for 3-4 minutes. Add the mussels, with the lid on this time, and shake the pan violently from time to time. Once all the mussels have opened (less than 5 minutes), take the pan from the heat immediately. Divide the mussels between 8 large soup plates, discarding any that have not opened. Sieve the juice to be sure there is no sand (a coffee filter, paper or otherwise, is excellent for this); divide this too between the 8 plates and serve with a good sprinkling of parsley on each.

MUSSELS WITH WALNUTS (Turkey)

Imperial/Metric	American
Between 64 and 80 mussels depending on size	Between 64 and 80 mussels depending on size
3 oz (90 g) parsley, chopped	⅓ cup parsley, chopped
3 oz (90 g) walnuts, ground	⅓ cup walnuts, chopped
2 fl. oz (60 ml) olive oil	¼ cup olive oil
2 fl. oz (60 ml) lemon juice	¼ cup lemon juice
1 clove garlic or more, crushed	1 clove garlic or more, crushed
salt and pepper	salt and pepper

Mix the walnuts, parsley, olive oil, lemon juice, garlic, salt and pepper in a bowl. Scrub and clean the mussels, open them with a knife and throw away the top shell of each. Arrange them on at least 2 trays to go under the grill. Put a teaspoonful of the mixture on each and run under really fierce heat for a couple of minutes. The moment they start bubbling, they are ready. Alternatively they can be done in the oven but this is less precise.

MOULES FARCIES (France)

STUFFED MUSSELS

Imperial/Metric	American
48 large mussels	48 large mussels
4 tablespoons dried breadcrumbs	4 tablespoons dried breadcrumbs
4 oz (125 g) butter	½ cup butter
handful of parsley, chopped	handful of parsley, chopped
3 cloves garlic	3 cloves garlic

Prepare mussels (p.107) and cook in a saucepan, without any additional liquid, over fast heat for 3-4 minutes, until shells open. The mussels need not be fully cooked at this stage – on the contrary, it is better that they are partially raw. You will need to shake the saucepan violently from time to time. Let cool and remove the top shell of each mussel.

Crush the garlic, add the dried breadcrumbs, parsley and softened butter and mix to a stiffish paste. Put a spoonful of this paste on each mussel, just enough to cover the fleshy part, and run it under a very hot grill until bubbling, or put in a very hot oven for 5 minutes. Some people sprinkle more breadcrumbs on top before heating but I think this produces rather a dry dish.

STUFFED MUSSELS (Spain: Valencia)

These are the large mussels they serve as *tapas* all down the east coast of Spain. Allow 6-8 per person.

Imperial/Metric	*American*
mussels for 8 persons	mussels for 8 persons
4 onions, chopped	4 onions, chopped
4 cloves garlic, crushed	4 cloves garlic, crushed
6 fl. oz (180 ml) white wine	¾ cup white wine
7 oz (220 g) ground almonds (blanched before grinding)	1 cup ground almonds (blanched before grinding)
4 oz (125 g) pine nuts	½ cup *pignoli*
4 fl. oz (120 ml) olive oil	½ cup olive oil
½ teaspoon cayenne pepper	½ teaspoon cayenne pepper
1 lb (500 g) tomatoes, chopped	1 lb tomatoes, chopped
large bunch of parsley	large bunch of parsley
breadcrumbs (if necessary)	breadcrumbs (if necessary)

Cook the mussels with 2 chopped onions, 2 cloves of garlic, and the wine, in a saucepan, discarding any that do not open. Strain off the juice and set aside.

Fry the other 2 onions in the olive oil. Add the tomatoes and simmer slowly. Meanwhile in a mixer (or a mortar in Spain) put the ground almonds, pine nuts (*pignoli*), parsley, cayenne and garlic. You should end up with a thick paste. Add the juice from the mussels to the tomato mixture and continue to cook. Pass through a fine sieve to avoid sand. The sauce should have the consistency of a *sauce béchamel*. Add the almond/pine nut mixture to the tomatoes and continue stirring over gentle heat. If it is not thick enough, put in a few breadcrumbs, as the Spaniards do. Divide between the mussels.

These can be served hot or very cold, but hot mussels are better.

Scallops

CEVICHE DE VIERAS (Chile)

CEVICHE OF SCALLOPS

A recipe from the sister of the person who supplied the recipe for *Vieras Guisadas* (p.112). Serve on lettuce or in avocado halves.

Imperial/Metric
1 or 2 scallops (*not* frozen) per person, depending on the size
1 onion, thinly sliced
2 tomatoes, chopped
2 hot green peppers (Jalapeño type in tins), sliced
½ pint (300 ml) lime (or lemon) juice
parsley, chopped (to decorate)
½ teaspoon oregano (optional)
a little olive olive oil (optional)

American
1 or 2 scallops (*not* frozen) per person, depending on the size
1 onion, thinly sliced
2 tomatoes, chopped
2 hot green peppers (Jalapeño type in tins), sliced
1¼ cups lime (or lemon) juice
parsley, chopped (to decorate)
½ teaspoon oregano (optional)
a little olive olive oil (optional)

Remove scallops and their coral from the shells and wash very thoroughly. Cut each scallop in two or four depending on the size; cut each coral in half. Mix the lime or lemon juice with the tomato, sliced peppers, onion, herbs and pour over scallops, stirring well to coat each piece. Leave for 3 hours until the scallop is opaque and glistening white. Drain well. Either serve as is or mix a little of the marinade with some olive oil as a dressing. Sprinkle with parsley.

COQUILLES ST JACQUES AUX COURGETTES (France)

SCALLOPS AND COURGETTES

Imperial/Metric
16 (or more) scallops
1 recipe *sauce aurore* (p.391)
1 lb (500 g) courgettes
1 tablespoon parsley, chopped
1 tablespoon shallot, chopped
4 fl. oz (120 ml) white wine
butter

American
16 (or more) scallops
1 recipe *sauce aurore* (p.391)
1 lb zucchini
1 tablespoon parsley, chopped
1 tablespoon shallot, chopped
½ cup white wine
butter

Clean the scallops and halve them, horizontally if possible. (Use the coral.) Fry them in a little butter and add the shallot. Deglaze with the white wine. Cook the peeled courgettes until almost done and drain well. Heat the *sauce aurore* and put in the scallops and courgettes. Turn into a serving dish when thoroughly heated through. Sprinkle with parsley and serve.

SCALLOPS AND BACON BROCHETTES (UK)

Delicious, simple, and I am afraid, expensive, this is very similar to the skewered scallops served in Overton's Fish Restaurant in London. Use small wooden brochettes.

Imperial/Metric	*American*
16 whole scallops*	16 whole scallops*
their weight in green bacon	their weight in green bacon
1 recipe *sauce tartare* (p.407)	1 recipe *sauce tartare* (p.407)
parsley, chopped	parsley, chopped
lemon wedges (optional)	lemon wedges (optional)
a little sunflower oil	a little sunflower oil

*Scallops vary greatly in size and you must be the judge of how much to give as a first course. They are also fairly filling, thank goodness.

Cut your bacon in ½-¾ inch (1-2 cm) slices. Cut your scallops into 4 or 2 (in which case you will need more scallops) and thread them onto skewers, alternating them with pieces of green bacon. Put a little oil over them and grill until done. Serve with *sauce tartare* or lemon wedges.

VIERAS GUISADAS (Spain: Santander)

BAKED SCALLOPS

Vieras Guisadas are a standard, if somewhat expensive, dish all along the Cantabrian coast. The scallop shell is the emblem of St James, who came from this part of Spain. Most towns in this region have a recipe similar to Santander's.

Imperial/Metric	American
1 large scallop per person*	1 large scallop per person*
approx. 4 oz (125 g) fresh breadcrumbs	approx. 1 cup fresh breadcrumbs
4 fl. oz (125 ml) full cream milk	½ cup full cream milk
2 or 3 cloves garlic, chopped	2 or 3 cloves garlic, chopped
1 medium onion, finely chopped	1 medium onion, finely chopped
a handful of parsley, chopped	a handful of parsley, chopped
a pinch of nutmeg	a pinch of nutmeg
salt and pepper	salt and pepper
6 fl. oz (180 ml) olive oil	¾ cup olive oil

* For this recipe frozen scallops can be used but then allow at least 2 scallops per person (per shell) as they always seem to be smaller than the fresh type.

Remove scallops from shells. If they are difficult to open, drop them into boiling water for a minute. Wash very thoroughly. Mix the onion, garlic, three-quarters of the parsley, nutmeg, salt, pepper and breadcrumbs and soak in the milk. Chop the flesh and coral of the scallops into fairly small pieces and mix into the breadcrumb mixture. Divide between 8 well-washed scallop shells and bake in a medium oven (350°F/175°C/Gas 4 for 20 minutes. (The Spanish tend to bake this at a hotter temperature which I think toughens the fish.) Sprinkle with the remaining parsley before serving.

Others

CLAM AND CREAM CHEESE DIP (USA)

Serve as a cocktail dip or as part of a mixed hors d'œuvre.

Imperial/Metric	American
8 oz (250 g) tins minced clams	8 oz can minced clams
1 lb (500 g) good-quality cream cheese	1 lb good-quality cream cheese
1 dessertspoon wine vinegar	1 dessertspoon wine vinegar
salt and pepper	salt and pepper
dill or parsley, chopped if liked	dill or parsley, chopped if liked

Strain the clams, and strain their juice and reserve. Stir into the cream cheese enough clam juice to make the consistency desired. Then add the herbs (if desired), vinegar, salt and pepper and the clams. Let stand 15 minutes before serving.

BLAFF D'OURSINS (French West Indies: Martinique)

SEA URCHIN 'BLAFF'

'The meal is memorable, apart from its other charms, by a first encounter with sea-eggs, the contents of smooth, hard white globes like spineless white sea-urchins, whose contents – a kind of reddish-brown roe – are scooped out and fried in butter.' (*The Traveller's Tree*, Patrick Leigh Fermor, Penguin, 1950.)

I am indebted to Dr Rose-Rosette of Martinique for this recipe. He is perhaps better known as the man who purchased and saved from total degradation what was left of the plantation belonging to the Empress Josephine's family, la Pagerie, and for creating a museum there.

These white sea-urchins are available all over the Caribbean and on the south-east coast of the United States. They sometimes appear in Paris markets as well, for those who cannot live without them. *Note that black urchins are poisonous.*

Imperial/Metric	American
approx. 50 white sea eggs	approx. 50 white sea eggs
2 cloves of garlic	2 cloves of garlic
2 red peppers (such as Scotch Bonnet), sliced	2 red peppers (such as Scotch Bonnet), sliced
1 onion, sliced	1 onion, sliced
juice of 2 lemons and strip of rind	juice of 2 lemons and strip of rind
parsley, thyme	parsley, thyme
salt	salt
1½ pints (900 ml) water	1 quart water

Put the sea eggs in a marinade composed of the red peppers, a clove of garlic, lemon juice, a little salt and possibly a little water. Leave for 30 minutes. Make a *court-bouillon* from the water, the onion, a clove of garlic, a strip of lemon rind and the herbs and some more hot pepper. Boil for a few minutes and then simmer the sea eggs in this for 10 minutes. Do not stir. Serve hot with a little butter and lemon juice.

CHUPE (CHILE)

BAKED SEAFOOD WITH MILK AND BREADCRUMBS

This can also be used most succesfully as a main course dish for a buffet supper in which case you will need to double the quantities. It can be prepared in advance. All the fish can be frozen but they should be thoroughly defrosted before cooking.

Imperial/Metric	*American*
1 lb (500 g) scallops	1 lb scallops
1 lb (500 g) medium prawns, shelled	1 lb shrimps, shelled
8-12 oz (250-375 g) white crab meat or lobster tails	8-12 oz white crab meat or lobster tails
5 medium white bread rolls	5 medium white bread rolls
1 pint (600 ml) milk	1¼ cups milk
2 large onions, finely sliced	2 large onions, finely sliced
1 tablespoon paprika	1 tablespoon paprika
1 teaspoon Tabasco	1 teaspoon Tabasco
2 hardboiled eggs	2 hardcooked eggs
salt to taste	salt to taste
butter and oil for frying	butter and oil for frying
parsley and oregano to taste	parsley and oregano to taste
2 oz (60 g) Gruyère cheese	¼ cup Gruyère cheese

Warm milk. Cut the rolls into cubes and leave to soak in the milk. Good quality bread can be used instead if wished. Meanwhile cook the sliced onions in a little butter and oil but do not let them colour. Add the scallops and cook for about 3 minutes until they are firm but entirely cooked through. Add the rest of the fish and cook another 3 minutes. Off the heat add the herbs and seasonings and the eggs, cut into quarters.

Mash the bread rolls into the milk to make a thickish purée – if there is not enough milk add some more to get the right consistency but allow for liquid coming from the fish during cooking. Depending on personal preference, you can either run this bread-and-milk purée through the blender or simply beat it. This dish was invented long before the modern kitchen. Mix the purée and fish together and put into a shallow dish. Sprinkle with the cheese and bake for 20 minutes at 400°F/200°C/Gas 6.

Sometimes this dish is decorated with a few whole prawns.

Crab

CRAB AND CUCUMBER MAYONNAISE (USA)

Imperial/Metric
2 lb (1 kilo) lump crab meat
1 pint (600 ml) mayonnaise
  (p.404)
2 cucumbers
half onion
2 teaspoons tomato concentrate
1 teaspoon Tabasco (optional)
parsley or dill

American
2 lb lump crab meat
2 cups mayonnaise (p.404)
2 cucumbers
half onion
2 teaspoons tomato concentrate
1 teaspoon Tabasco (optional)
parsley or dill

This can also be made from Japanese, French or American crab-flavoured 'sticks'.

Add the tomato concentrate to the mayonnaise as well as the tabasco if wished. Mix in the crab meat and cover with clingfilm. An hour before serving, peel the cucumbers, seed them and cut into small cubes. Sprinkle with salt and let them drain for an hour. Chop the onion and put to soak in cold, salted water. Just before serving, drain the cucumber and pat dry, and drain the onion. Mix in these 2 ingredients and serve on individual plates with a little parsley or dill.

CRAB LOUIS (USA)

To my mind this is just about the best way to eat cold crab. Ordinary crab will not do; it must be what is known as lump-crab, i.e. all white and claw meat; good-quality frozen will do.

Imperial/Metric
3 lb (1.5 kilo) lump crab meat
4 eggs, hard-boiled
4 artichoke hearts or half
  avocado sliced
15 fl. oz (450 ml) mayonnaise
8 fl. oz (240 ml) double cream
2 tablespoons onion, chopped
4 fl. oz (120 ml) chilli sauce*
dash of Tabasco
salt
2 tablespoons parsley, chopped
lettuce, finely shredded

American
3 lb lump crab meat
4 eggs, hardcooked
4 artichoke hearts or half
  avocado sliced
2 cups mayonnaise
1 cup heavy cream
2 tablespoons onion, chopped
½ cup chilli sauce*
dash of Tabasco
salt
2 tablespoons parsley, chopped
lettuce, finely shredded

* In the absence of commercial chilli sauce (the Mexican or Texmex sort rather than the Oriental sort), try using 1 dessertspoonful of Tabasco to 2-3 tablespoons tomato ketchup.

Chop the onions and pour boiling water over them. Let soak 5 minutes and drain. Pick over crabmeat but leave it in as big lumps as possible and arrange on a bed of shredded lettuce either in one big dish or on individual plates. Garnish with the hard-boiled eggs and avocado.

Whip the double (heavy) cream. Mix the chilli sauce, onions, salt, pepper and parsley together and fold into the whipped cream. Add the Tabasco if it is not already in the dressing. Taste – it should be creamy and piquant. Adjust if necessary and then pour over the crab.

CRABE MORNAY A LA CREOLE (USA)

CRAB IN A PIQUANT CHEESE SAUCE, CREOLE STYLE

Imperial/Metric	*American*
2 lb (1 kilo) lump crab meat	2 lb lump crab meat
1 recipe *sauce mornay* (p.397)	1 recipe *sauce mornay* (p.397)
1 hot green pepper, finely sliced	1 hot green pepper, finely sliced
1 hot red pepper, sliced, or 2 teaspoons Tabasco	1 hot red pepper, sliced, or 2 teaspoons Tabasco

This is best cooked in crab or scallop shells. Mix the crab meat with cold *sauce mornay*, add the pepper(s) and/or Tabasco. Put into 8 shells and bake for 15 minutes at 400°F/200°C/Gas 6.

CRAB NEWBURG (USA)

This is made in exactly the same way as Lobster Newburg (p.121) but substituting white crab claw meat for the lobster. Darker meat tends to melt into the sauce and you get a rather runny result. Crab-flavoured 'sticks' can be used very successfully.

CRAB RAMEKINS (UK)

Imperial/Metric	American
12 oz (375 g) white crab meat, flaked	12 oz white crab meat, flaked
2 oz (60 g) butter	¼ cup butter
4 oz (120 g) fresh brown breadcrumbs	½ cup fresh brown breadcrumbs
1 medium onion, finely chopped	1 medium onion, finely chopped
1 tablespoon Dijon-type mustard	1 tablespoon Dijon-type mustard
2 oz (60 g) Gruyère cheese, grated	¼ cup Gruyère cheese, grated
5-6 oz (155-190 ml) yoghurt	5-6 oz yoghurt
4 tablespoons double cream	4 tablespoons heavy cream

Melt the butter and fry the onion gently in it. Add the flaked crab and the breadcrumbs. Divide between 8 ramekins. Mix mustard, yoghurt and cream together and season with salt and pepper if needed. Put on top of the crab and breadcrumbs. Sprinkle with the grated cheese and cook for 25-30 minutes at 325°F/170°C/ Gas 3.

DEVILLED CRAB (USA)

Ideally this dish should be served in crab shell backs (which I always manage to break on removing the crab meat). Scallop shells will do just as well, as will large ramekins (around 6 oz/190 g capacity)

Imperial/Metric	American
1¼ lb (625 g) crab meat	2½ cups crab meat
2 tablespoons butter	2 tablespoons butter
2 tablespoons flour	2 tablespoons flour
8 fl. oz (240 ml) fish stock (p.308)	1 cup fish stock (p.308)
3 egg yolks	3 egg yolks
2 tablespoons sherry	¼ cup sherry
8 oz (250 g) mushrooms, sliced	8 oz mushrooms, sliced
6 tablespoons breadcrumbs	6 tablespoons breadcrumbs
5 tablespoons melted butter	5 tablespoons melted butter
1 teaspoon Tabasco	1 teaspoon Tabasco
1 teaspoon hot made mustard	1 teaspoon hot made mustard
parsley	parsley

Make a cream sauce with the fish stock, flour and butter. Add the egg yolks and let cool thoroughly. Stir in the chopped crab meat and the raw mushrooms. Add the sherry, parsley, mustard and Tabasco. Taste – it should be piquant. If it is not hot enough, add some more Tabasco. Put into 8 shells, sprinkle with breadcrumbs and top with melted butter. This dish can be made in advance up to this point. Before serving, it needs approximately 10 minutes in a hot oven (400°F/200°C/Gas 6).

Lobster

COLD LOBSTER AND CUCUMBER SAUCE (USA: Maine)

Lobsters are both more plentiful and very much cheaper in Maine than in Europe. As a first course, a decent-sized lobster (at least 1½ lb/750 g) should feed 4 people.

Imperial/Metric	American
2 or more lobsters depending on size	2 or more lobsters depending on size
2 medium cucumbers	2 medium cucumbers
½ pint (300 ml) double cream	1¼ cups heavy cream*
2 dessertspoons white wine vinegar	2 dessertspoons white wine vinegar
salt	salt
dill or parsley to decorate (optional)	dill or parsley to decorate (optional)

* Americans who are watching their weight often use sour cream instead of the richer heavy cream; if this is the case, do not try to whip it but stir in the other ingredients as they are.

Peel and remove seeds from cucumbers and cut into cubes. Sprinkle with salt and let drain well. Cook the lobsters, allow them to cool and remove meat and coral (if any). Divide between 8 plates. Just before serving, whip the cream fairly stiffly. Fold in the cucumber, vinegar and lobster and serve immediately sprinkled with dill or parsley.

HOMARDS ET COURGETTES AU THYM (France)

LOBSTERS AND COURGETTES WITH THYME

This is an excellent way of making two lobsters do for 8 people. Large prawns can be used instead.

Imperial/Metric	American
2 lobsters	2 lobsters
2 lb (1 kilo) courgettes	2 lb zucchini
4 shallots, chopped	4 shallots, chopped
10 fl. oz (300 ml) double cream	1¼ cups heavy cream
4 eggs	4 eggs
dill or parsley	dill or parsley
salt and white or cayenne pepper	salt and white or cayenne pepper
butter and oil for frying	butter and oil for frying

Cook the lobsters, let cool, extract the flesh and slice as well as possible. Peel the courgettes and slice into thin slices about the thickness of a coin. Salt and let drain as you would for cucumber, for approximately 30 minutes. Rinse and dry on paper towels. Sauté the shallots and add the sliced courgettes – do not let them brown. The dish can be prepared in advance up to here.

Beat up the eggs with the double (heavy) cream, add the salt and pepper and the dill or parsley. Take eight 5 oz (155 g) ramekins and fill approximately one-third full with the cooked courgettes. Put the lobster pieces on top and then add the savoury custard. Bake in a moderate oven (340°F/175°C/Gas 3½) for approximately 10-12 minutes. They should still be very slightly liquid in the middle. If they are too liquid, cook a little longer.

LOBSTER NEWBURG (USA)

A very rich but quick dish to do, though it needs your full attention at the last moment. Use a double boiler or a *bain-marie*.

Traditionally Lobster Newburg is served with triangles of toast or fried bread round the dish but it also makes a fabulous filling for vols-au-vent: heat them in the oven whilst stirring the mixture. You can use a parsley garnish if wished.

Imperial/Metric	American
1½ lb (750 g) lobster, cooked and diced	4 cups lobster, cooked and diced
2 oz (60 g) butter	¼ cup butter
4 fl. oz (100 ml) dry sherry	½ cup dry sherry
15 fl. oz (450 ml) double cream	2 cups heavy cream
8 egg yolks	8 egg yolks
1 teaspoon paprika	1 teaspoon paprika
pinch of nutmeg	pinch of nutmeg

Melt the butter in a double boiler and cook the lobster for a few moments. Add the sherry and heat through. Beat the egg yolks and cream together, preferably in a machine – they should be thick and syrupy; add them to the lobster mixture and stir constantly. During this time add the paprika and nutmeg. Taste and see if it wants salt and pepper. Normally it takes 8-10 minutes to thicken up.

Prawns and Shrimps

CAMERONES EN FRIO (Mexico)

PIQUANT PICKLED SHRIMP

Imperial/Metric	American
2 lb (1 kilo) medium prawns	2 lb medium shrimps
3 onions, chopped	3 onions, chopped
6 fl. oz (180 ml) olive oil	¾ cup olive oil
2 fl. oz (60 ml) vinegar	¼ cup vinegar
1 dessertspoon made mustard	1 dessertspoon made mustard
2 large tomatoes, sliced	2 large tomatoes, sliced
¼ tin Jalapeño chillies, sliced*	¼ tin Jalapeño chillies, sliced*

* If you cannot get Jalapeño chillies, use sweet (bell) peppers and at least 1 dessertspoon of Tabasco in the sauce, probably more, plus the juice of half a lemon or a whole lime.

Wash, de-vein and peel prawns. Fry one-third of the onion in a quarter of the oil, letting it go almost brown, and then add the prawns. Stir-fry for 8-10 minutes. Soak the rest of the onion in cold salted water for 2-3 hours before serving. While the prawns are still hot, pour over a sauce made of the rest of the olive oil, vinegar, herbs and chillies. Let cool thoroughly and then refrigerate for 3 hours. Serve garnished with sliced tomato and the drained onions.

CEVICHE DE CAMARONES (Ecuador)

PRAWNS MARINATED IN CITRUS JUICE

In Ecuador they always use bitter orrange juice from the Seville oranges which we use for marmalade. If you are a lover of the *ceviche* orange it is worth freezing a few pints of juice each winter to make this dish authentically. A good alternative is an equal mixture of ordinary orange and lemon juice or, better still, orange and lime juice.

Imperial/Metric
3 lb (1.5 kilos) medium prawns, deveined
2 medium onions, finely sliced
2 medium tomatoes, chopped
1 medium-size hot pepper or
2 teaspoons Tabasco
½ pint (300 ml) bitter orange juice or
half lemon and half sweet orange juice
fresh coriander or parsley (to decorate)

American
3 lb medium shrimps, deveined
2 medium onions, finely sliced
2 medium tomatoes, chopped
1 medium-size hot pepper or
2 teaspoons Tabasco
1¼ cups bitter orange juice or
half lemon and half sweet orange juice
fresh coriander or parsley (to decorate)

Shell the prawns. Keep half the sliced onions aside. Mix all other ingredients together and marinate the prawns in them for at least 2-3 hours before serving. Decorate with rings of onion and a little parsley or fresh coriander.

CHARLOTTE DE CREVETTES (France)

PRAWN CHARLOTTE

Use a 7½ inch (18 cm) charlotte mould in metal or ovenproof ceramic or glass. Serve on its own or with *sauce aurore* or *sauce Nantua* (pp.391 and 399).

Imperial/Metric
2-2½ lb (1-1.25 kilos) large prawns
court-bouillon (p.309)
12 eggs
1 small tin French prawn butter 3½-4 oz (100-125 g)
4 fl. oz (120 ml) double cream
2 pints (1.2 litres) full cream milk
2 oz (60 g) butter
salt and white pepper
2 or 3 prawns for decoration

American
2-2½ lb raw Gulf shrimps
court-bouillon (p.309)
12 eggs
1 small tin French prawn butter 3½-4 oz
½ cup heavy cream
2½ US pints full cream milk
¼ cup butter
salt and white pepper
2 or 3 shrimps for decoration

Cook the prawns in a *court bouillon* and let them cool. Remove their heads and throw these away but keep the shells. Devein each prawn. Rinse if necessary. Reduce the shells to a purée in the liquidizer with a little of the milk, warmed, and let it infuse for at least 15-20 minutes, then strain through a fine sieve. Put this with the prawns, prawn butter and milk. In a bowl whisk up the eggs, keeping back 2 of the whites for use later on. Add to the milk/prawn mixture and salt and pepper to taste. Butter a charlotte mould and pour in this mixture. Bake in a moderate oven (340°F/175°C/Gas 3½ with the charlotte mould in a baking pan with approximately 2 inches (5 cm) hot water for approximately 45-50 minutes. Turn out and serve.

CHINESE PRAWN SATAY

Quite an expensive dish as it looks mean to serve less than 2-3 satay skewers to each person which means a minimum of 8-9 prawns per person. You can do what a lot of Chinese do: mix prawn and fish on the same skewer. For a purely prawn satay, allow 8-12 prawns per person, depending on size. If the prawns are raw, so much the better.

Take off the heads and shells and devein. The black vein on their back is what causes most allergies to shellfish, and in any event it is the prawn's alimentary canal, which is not a pleasant idea. Thread on 6 inch (15 cm) satay skewers, leaving enough room for a handle.

Coat the prawns with half the sauce (p.64) and grill for a few moments until they are cooked (or warmed through in the case of cooked prawns) and then turn them over, using the rest of the sauce for the final grilling. Serve with chopped cucumber.

CHUPE DE CAMARONES (Peru)

PRAWNS IN MILK AND BREADCRUMBS

I always thought *chupe* was only Chilean until an English friend from Lima told me it was common to the whole of western South America. It is a cross between a stew and a soup. Peruvians like their food very hot – even more so than the Mexicans, so you can increase the amount of peppers you use ever upwards and still not have such a hot *chupe* as they would.

Imperial/Metric	American
4 lb (1.75 kilos) shelled prawns	4 lb shelled medium shrimps
4 eggs, hard-boiled	4 eggs, hardcooked
2 pints (1.2 litres) milk	5 cups milk
2 pints (1.2 litres) volume, fresh breadcrumbs	5 cups volume, fresh breadcrumbs
1 teaspoon oregano	1 teaspoon oregano
8 oz (250 g) white crab meat	1 cup white crab meat
2 medium onions, chopped	2 medium onions, chopped
1 dessertspoon sea salt	1 dessertspoon sea salt
2-3 serrano chillies *or*	2-3 serrano chillies *or*
Tabasco to taste	Tabasco to taste

Put the breadcrumbs to soak in the warmed milk. When all the liquid has been absorbed, add the salt, oregano and chillies or Tabasco and put aside. It is essential that all the liquid is absorbed; if it is not, add a few more breadcrumbs. Fry the onion in a little butter or oil but do not let it take colour. Add this and the prawns and crab meat to the breadcrumb mixture. Put into a well-buttered, not too deep ovenproof dish (you will need a large one) and bake for approximately 20 minutes in a hot oven (400°F/200°C/Gas 6).

CREVETTES A LA LOUISIANE (USA)

PRAWNS IN THE LOUISIANA STYLE

Serve with wedges of lemon and French bread.

Imperial/Metric	American
2½ lb (1.25 kilos) peeled prawns	2½ lb peeled Gulf shrimps
2 large onions, thinly sliced	2 large onions, thinly sliced

MARINADE

Imperial/Metric	American
8 fl. oz (240 ml) olive oil	1 cup olive oil
8 fl. oz (240 ml) wine vinegar	1 cup wine vinegar
4 fl. oz (120 ml) water	½ cup water
1 lemon or 2 limes, sliced	1 lemon or 2 limes, sliced
3 tablespoons Worcester sauce	3 tablespoons Worcester sauce
1 teaspoon salt	1 teaspoon salt
1 teaspoon Tabasco	1 teaspoon Tabasco
1 teaspoon dried garlic, minced	1 teaspoon dried garlic, minced
1 teaspoon mustard powder	1 teaspoon mustard powder
4 oz (125 g) sugar	½ cup sugar

Put the prawns (shrimps) and onions in alternate layers and pour marinade over them. Let stand at least 24 hours and not longer than 48 hours.

PRAWNS IN BRANDY AND CREAM (UK)

Quick, delicious and expensive – this dish requires last-minute attention but if you have a chafing dish it can be done quite dramatically in the dining-room. Serve with plenty of French bread.

Imperial/Metric	American
1½ lb (750 g) medium prawns*	1½ lb medium Gulf shrimps*
4 oz (125 g) butter	½ cup butter
1 clove garlic, crushed	1 clove garlic, crushed
1 medium onion, finely chopped	1 medium onion, finely chopped
4 fl. oz (120 ml) double cream	½ cup heavy cream
4 fl. oz (120 ml) brandy	½ cup cognac
salt, cayenne pepper and a little thyme	salt, cayenne pepper and a little thyme

* To make sure that the prawns (shrimps) are not overcooked, cook them yourself – you will need about double the quantity to get the prepared weight shown above.

Crush the garlic and fry it gently with the onion. Have the prepared prawns ready and heat them through with the onion/garlic mixture, then add the brandy and ignite. When the flames have subsided, add the cream and seasoning and serve at once.

ATJAR KETIMUN WITH PRAWNS (Overseas Chinese – Penang, Malaysia)

Imperial/Metric	American
1 recipe *atjar ketimun* (p.265)*	1 recipe *atjar ketimun* (p.265)
1 lb (500 g) dressed weight prawns	1 lb dressed weight medium shrimps

* It is better to have the chilli in the *atjar ketimun* for this recipe.

Cook the prawns in a little oil and when done add to the *atjar ketimun* and let stand for at least a couple of hours before serving.

DELICES DE LA MER (France)

PRAWNS, SCALLOPS AND VEGETABLES

One of the prettiest first courses and delicious too.

Imperial/Metric	American
8 oz (250 g) prawns, peeled and deveined	8 oz peeled shrimps
8 oz (250 g) scallops	8 oz scallops
2 or 3 small courgettes	2 or 3 small zucchini
2 or 3 small carrots	2 or 3 small carrots
2 shallots	2 shallots
8 eggs	8 eggs
4 oz (125 g) softened butter	½ cup softened butter
8 fl. oz (240 ml) double cream	1 cup heavy cream
butter	butter
parsley (to decorate)	parsley (to decorate)

Thickly butter the sides and base of 8 ovenproof ramekins. Slice the courgettes (unpeeled) and the carrots on a *mandoline* or cucumber slicer. Decorate the base of the ramekins with carrot, preferably not overlapping too much. Round the edge of each ramekin put a row of courgette slices. Stick them hard into the butter and refrigerate.

In a liquidizer or food processor mix the eggs and cream with the rinsed raw scallops and prawns. You should end up with a thick cream. Heat your oven to 325°F/170°C/Gas 3 and put in a baking tin with some water to heat up. Pour the mixture into 8 ramekins and bake in the oven in a baking tin for 20 minutes. Test with a knitting needle or skewer and if necessary give a little more time. Turn out each ramekin onto a dish and decorate with parsley.

MORETON BAY BUG TART (Australia)

In Singapore a great deal of luxury food such as really good beef, oysters and seafood is flown in from Australia. It was with some trepidation that we went to an Australian dinner party there where the highlight of the evening was to be Bug Pie. Our fears were unfounded since the dish was absolutely delicious. Moreton Bay bugs are rather like squat crayfish and, in the absence of the real thing, lobster or large prawns, can be used very successfully.

Imperial/Metric	*American*
1 recipe short-crust pastry, well salted (p.190)	1 recipe short-crust pastry, well salted (p.190)
1 lb (500 g) bugs, lobster or prawns (dressed weight)	1 lb bugs, lobster or shrimps (dressed weight)
1 recipe wine *court-bouillon* (p.309)	1 recipe wine *court-bouillon* (p.309)
2 medium shallots, chopped	2 medium shallots, chopped
½ pint (300 ml) *béchamel sauce* (p.391)	1¼ cups *béchamel sauce* (p.391)
8 fl. oz (240 ml) double cream	1 cup heavy cream
5 fl. oz (150 ml) sherry	good ½ cup sherrywine
2 egg yolks	2 egg yolks
2 tablespoons parsley, chopped	2 tablespoons parsley, chopped
salt and cayenne pepper	salt and cayenne pepper

Bake the pastry blind until almost done but do not let brown and then let it cool.

Cook the bugs, lobster or prawns in a wine *court-bouillon* until just done and set aside to cool. Then remove shells. Cook the shallots in a little butter or oil and add to heated *sauce béchamel*. Add the sherry and parsley and then, off the heat, the double (heavy) cream and egg yolks one by one. Stir in the bugs, lobster or prawns. Pour into the pastry shell and cook for 15 minutes (centre shelf) at 400°F/200°C/Gas 6. The result should be slightly wobbly (but not runny) in the centre.

6 Pâtés and Terrines

This particular first course makes one feel rather virtuous. One's guests are always so complimentary about one's efforts and yet pâtés and terrines are usually fairly simple things to produce, provided one takes care both with the making and the presentation.

The most common fault with pâtés is overcooking. It is a wise cook who tests the dish *at least* fifteen minutes before the end of the prescribed cooking time since ovens (and oven positions) differ greatly. Most pâtés containing liver go a rather dull grey once overcooked. Whilst this cannot be avoided in a pâté or terrine containing pig-liver, chicken liver pâtés should, by and large, be slightly rose-coloured when served. This lessens their life dramatically and much modern chicken liver develops an off taste within three or four days even with a good covering of clarified butter. Fish pâtés and terrines, except those made from smoked fish, need to be served within twenty-four hours of making and the same is true of those made with vegetables.

Presentation is very important. A rustic country terrine can be served straight from the container accompanied by lots of crisp French bread. If you did the same thing with a fish terrine or even a chicken liver pâté the dish would look most unappetizing after the third person had helped himself. When serving direct from the dish in which the terrine or pâté was cooked, always wash the dish before putting it on the table. There is no merit in showing all the baked-on spills and rings of congealed fat. The statutory limp lettuce leaf is not a decoration suitable for serving a slice of terrine (I swear it goes from customer to customer in some restaurants – never eat it!) and I personally dislike any form of salad as decoration except possibly a sprig of parsley if you must. A properly made pâté, terrine or galantine should be able to lie on a plate by itself and be appetizingly presentable.

Pâtés

CHICKEN LIVER PATE (Hungary)

By tradition, chicken livers are rather more cooked in Hungary than they are in France, so this pâté is less perishable than the French version.

Imperial/Metric	*American*
1 lb (500 g) chicken livers	1 lb chicken livers
8 oz (250 g) streaky bacon, without rind	8 oz streaky bacon, without rind
8 oz (250 g) pork dripping or real lard	8 oz pork dripping or real lard
2 tablespoons tomato concentrate	2 tablespoons tomato concentrate
2 tablespoons paprika	2 tablespoons paprika
2 cloves garlic, finely chopped	2 cloves garlic, finely chopped
1 carrot, grated	1 carrot, grated
1 tablespoon parsley, chopped	1 tablespoon parsley, chopped
2 tablespoons red wine	2 tablespoons red wine
salt to taste	salt to taste

Cook the chicken livers in the pork dripping or lard, together with the garlic and the carrot. When almost done, add the tomato concentrate, the paprika and finally the red wine (you may need a little more). Add the parsley. Whizz up in a liquidizer or food processor. Cut the streaky bacon into small pieces and grill or fry until crisp. (With present-day bacon you may need to use a little flour to get a crisp result.) Mix the bacon bits into the pâté and put everything into a serving dish. Once it is cool, refrigerate and float some melted lard on top to help it keep.

PATE DE FOIES DE VOLAILLE AUX BAIES ROUGES ET AU POIVRE VERT (France)

CHICKEN LIVER PATE WITH TWO PEPPERS

Imperial/Metric
1 lb (500 g) chicken livers
   (preferably the blond sort)
8 oz (250 g) butter
1 large onion, finely chopped
thyme and bayleaf, ground
2 egg yolks
2 tablespoons *poivre vert**
2 tablespoons *baies rouges* or
   Bourbon pepper
salt to taste

American
1 lb chicken livers
   (preferably the blond sort)
8 oz butter
1 large onion, finely chopped
thyme and bayleaf, ground
2 egg yolks
2 tablespoons *poivre vert**
2 tablespoons *baies rouges* or
   Bourbon pepper
salt to taste

* For this recipe the best *poivre vert* to buy is the freeze-dried sort, and the same goes for the *baies rouges* from the Ile de Bourbon – hence the other common name 'Bourbon pepper'. They are a rich rose colour and taste slightly sweet and scarcely hot. They are quite expensive, even in France, but you do not use many of them at a time. If you cannot get freeze-dried *poivre vert*, use the tinned sort but drain off the water. So far as I know, *baies rouges* only come freeze-dried except where they are produced.

Clean and chop the chicken livers. Cook the onion in the butter but do not let it brown. Add the chicken livers and cook until almost done. Whizz up in the liquidizer or food processor, add the two egg yolks, salt and herbs and 1 tablespoon of the *poivre vert*. Turn into a bowl and add the rest of the *poivre vert* and the *baies rouges*. Mix well and put into a terrine. Once cooled, refrigerate. Later run a small amount of melted butter, about half an inch (1 cm), on the top. Eat within 48 hours.

Variation
Alternatively this pâté can be made, as in France, with equal amounts of butter and chicken liver, but this makes it very rich. Also it can be made with rendered chicken fat if wished, though you may find it will be necessary to whizz it up once it has cooled (and possibly separated) and *then* put in the green and red peppers.

CHOPPED CHICKEN LIVER (Jewish: Central and Eastern Europe)

Serve with dark rye bread.

Imperial/Metric	American
1 lb (500 g) chicken livers	1 lb chicken livers
4 oz (125 g) chicken fat*	½ cup chicken fat
2 onions, finely chopped	2 onions, finely chopped
3 eggs, hard-boiled	3 eggs, hardcooked
salt and freshly ground pepper	salt and freshly ground pepper

* Chicken fat can be bought at Jewish butchers' shops and in some supermarkets, or can be made at home by rendering down the fat from inside the chicken as well as the drippings – it can be deep frozen with advantage. Soak the chicken livers for about an hour in salted water. Drain and dry on paper towels. Cook the onions until soft in the chicken fat. Clean the livers of any greenish bits and cut up into quarters. Cook thoroughly: there should be no pink left. Put into a food processor with the eggs, salt and pepper and mix. Pack into small pots or one large one.

QUICK CHICKEN LIVER PATE (USA)

Imperial/Metric	American
1 lb (500 g) chicken livers	1 lb chicken livers
8 oz (250 g) butter	1 cup butter
2 eggs, hard-boiled	2 eggs, hardcooked
a pinch of mace	a pinch of mace
thyme, parsley and sage	thyme, parsley and sage
2 teaspoons instant dried shallots	2 teaspoons instant dried shallots
2 tablespoons brandy	2 tablespoons brandy
salt and black pepper	salt and black pepper

Rinse the chicken livers and remove fat and any parts which are green or discoloured. Cut the livers into about 4 pieces each. Heat the butter and cook the chicken livers in it. They should be *slightly* pink. Tip the contents of the saucepan into the liquidizer or food processor. Add the hard-boiled eggs and process on high speed. Add the shallots, brandy, herbs, salt and plenty of freshly milled black pepper. Turn into a terrine or into individual pots and let cool. Eat within 24 hours.

Floating some melted butter on top once the pâté has cooled will help it keep for 72 hours. Nevertheless, once the butter has solidified it is best to cover or wrap in clingfilm as it can quickly pick up other odours from the refrigerator.

PIQUANT CHICKEN LIVER PATE (USA)

Imperial/Metric	American
1 lb (500 g) chicken livers	1 lb chicken livers
8 oz (250 g) rendered chicken fat	8 oz rendered chicken fat
2 cloves garlic, chopped	2 cloves garlic, chopped
2 teaspoons Tabasco	2 teaspoons Tabasco
1 tablespoon tomato concentrate	1 tablespoon tomato concentrate
1 tablespoon wine vinegar	1 tablespoon wine vinegar
1 teaspoon oregano	1 teaspoon oregano
2 tinned green chillies, deseeded and chopped	2 tinned green chillies, deseeded and chopped

Clean and chop chicken livers and cook to desired point in the chicken fat together with the garlic. Then add the vinegar, tomato paste, Tabasco and oregano, and put through the liquidizer or food processor. By hand add the chillies and serve next day. Keep covered at all times. You may wish to float a little fat across the top to prevent discoloration.

PATE DE CANARD AU POIVRE VERT (France)

DUCK PATE WITH *POIVRE VERT*

For this recipe you can use *poivre vert* either freeze-dried or tinned in water.

Imperial/Metric	American
1 medium duck and its liver	1 medium duck and its liver
1 lb (500 g) breast of veal	1 lb breast of veal
1 lb (500 g) belly of pork	1 lb fat pork
6 oz (190 g) fresh pork fat	6 oz fat back
4 tablespoons brandy	4 tablespoons brandy
4 tablespoons port or Madeira	4 tablespoons port or Madeira
1 tablespoon olive oil	1 tablespoon olive oil
1 large onion, chopped	1 large onion, chopped
2 eggs	2 eggs
1 tablespoon tomato concentrate	1 tablespoon tomato concentrate
1 teaspoon dried sage	1 teaspoon dried sage
2 bayleaves	2 bayleaves
2 tablespoons chopped parsley	2 tablespoons chopped parsley
salt	salt
2 tablespoons *poivre vert*	2 tablespoons *poivre vert*
aspic (optional)	aspic (optional)
strips of flare fat for lining	strips of flare fat for lining

Skin the duck. Slice the breast into long, thin *aiguilletes* – strips about half an inch (1 cm) thick. Chop the rest of the meat small (not in a mincer or machine). Put the duck into a marinade of the brandy, Madeira or port, olive oil, onion and herbs and refrigerate, covered, overnight. Try to keep the long breast pieces separate. Reserve the carcase if you are going to make an aspic.

Next day mince or process together the veal, pork and pork fat and add the liver. Add the duck bits and the marinade but *not* the duck strips. Stir in the 2 eggs.

Line a suitably sized terrine (smaller than you may at first think) with thin strips of pork flare fat which you have 'stretched' with the back of a knife, and put in a layer of the veal/pork/duck mixture. On top lay a third of the duck strips and one third of the *poivre vert*. Continue in this way until you have finished everything. Put the 2 bayleaves on top. Top with a strip of pork fat. Cook in a moderate oven for 1 hour at 375°F/190°C/Gas 5 or a little more, with the terrine in a baking dish of hot water. The terrine is cooked when it comes away from the sides. Weigh down when cooling.

You can either serve it in its present terrine decorated with parsley or decant it, clear it of fat, clean the container and then pour a Madeira aspic (p.180) around it.

PATE DE CANARD A LA MONTMORENCY (France)

DUCK PATE WITH CHERRIES

Imperial/Metric	American
2 breasts of duck (*magret de canard*) weighing a total of 1½ lb (750 g)	2 breasts of duck (*magret de canard*) weighing a total of 1½ lb
1 lb (500 g) pork belly	1 lb pork belly
1 lb (500 g) breast of veal	1 lb breast of veal
8 oz (250 g) green streaky bacon	8 oz green streaky bacon
1 small tin (20-30 black cherries, stoned	1 small can (20-30) black cherries, stoned
10 juniper berries	10 juniper berries
4 fl. oz (120 ml) gin	½ cup gin
½ teaspoon mace	½ teaspoon mace
pinch of thyme	pinch of thyme
3 cloves garlic, crushed	3 cloves of garlic, crushed
freshly ground black pepper and salt	freshly ground black pepper and salt
brandy for marinating duck (optional)	brandy for marinating duck (optional)

In a food processor or a mincer grind the pork and veal together with the garlic, juniper berries, mace, thyme, salt, pepper and gin. Remove to mixing bowl.

Strip the fat off the duck breasts and cut the meat into half-inch (1 cm) squares. Cut the rind off the streaky bacon, stretch the rashers out with the back of a knife and line out a suitably sized terrine. Mix the diced duck and cherries into the pork-veal mixture and put into the terrine. You can let this stand for a few hours in either the larder or the refrigerator for the flavours to develop, but it is not essential.

Cook in a pre-heated oven for approximately 1½ hours (it depends on the depth and size of your terrine) at 300-325°F/150-170°C/Gas 2-3, placing the terrine in a roasting tin in which you have put enough water to come half way up. This will stop the terrine drying out. If in doubt, put a piece of bacon or foil on the top or cook with a lid on the terrine.

The terrine is done when the sides have come away, but test after the first hour at 15-minute intervals. There is nothing more ghastly than an overcooked terrine.

Let cool for approximately 30 minutes, then cover with plenty of foil or clingfilm and weight down so that it will cut evenly. I cook my terrines in a loaf tin and weight them down by means of large cans of fruit or packets of beans placed in a similar loaf tin on top, thus distributing the weight fairly evenly.

LUCHEON PATE (Hungary)

This is traditionally eaten surrounded by aspic. It is very rich, and a little goes a long way, though my grandmother's note (1898) has it that it is very light (which it is not) and suitable for luncheon.

Imperial/Metric	American
1 lb (500 g) goose or chicken livers	1 lb goose or chicken livers
enough port and Madeira to marinate the above	enough port and Madeira to marinate the above
2 tablespoons goose fat or pure lard	2 tablespoons goose fat or pure lard
4 chopped shallots	4 chopped shallots
4 tablespoons double cream	4 tablespoons heavy cream
3 tablespoons Madeira	3 tablespoons Madeira wine
3 tablespoons port	3 tablespoons port wine
dried ground thyme	dried ground thyme
pinch of ground bayleaf	pinch of ground bayleaf
2 oz (60 g) minced truffles	2 oz minced truffles

Clean and cut up livers and put to marinate in the port and Madeira for 2-3 hours. Then heat the lard and cook the shallot in it; add the liver and cook until three-quarters done. Then add the marinade, thyme and bayleaf. Put through the liquidizer or food processor and then sieve. Let cool down. Add the port and Madeira carefully and then the cream. Season to taste with salt and a little paprika. Finally add the truffles. Put into separate containers or into one larger one (I keep an old *pâté de foie* tin for this) and let cool for at least 24 hours in the refrigerator. Once it is thoroughly cooled, you can cut it in thin slices like *pâté de foie gras* – used like that, it is not so expensive.

Variation

I have a friend who does the same recipe with duck livers from ducks specially bred for their *magrets* and livers. The difficulty is guessing from the sloppy mass you have in front of you when the duck liver is sufficiently cooked, since it continues to melt on cooking. If you want to take this risk (without the expense of truffles), follow this recipe and pour the whole into a small container (such as my *pâté de foie* tins) and let it cool. Slice as above. Once you are sure of the magic moment when to stop cooking, you can use the truffles – though the recipe is still very good without them.

GAME PATE (UK: Scotland)

Imperial/Metric
1 lb (500 g) fat pork or sausage meat, minced
1 lb (500 g) breast of veal, minced
1 pheasant or 2 partridges or 2 wild duck
8 oz (250 g) flare fat
2 medium onions, chopped
2 cloves garlic, chopped
8 fl. oz (240 ml) white wine
2 tablespoons gin or brandy
mace, juniper berries (crushed), bay leaf, parsley and sage to taste
grated rind and juice of 1 orange
2 tablespoons flour

American
1 lb fat pork or sausage meat, minced
1 lb breast of veal, minced
1 pheasant or 2 partridges or 2 wild duck
8 oz flare fat
2 medium onions, chopped
2 cloves garlic, chopped
8 fl. oz white wine
2 tablespoons gin or brandy
mace, juniper berries (crushed), bay leaf, parsley and sage to taste
grated rind and juice of 1 orange
2 tablespoons flour

Mix the meats, onion and garlic and put to marinate in the white wine and alcohol, together with the juniper, orange rind and herbs. Strip the flesh off the bird(s), chop coarsely and add to the other meat. If the birds are cooked, put them to soak separately in a little marinade of white wine, orange juice and gin. Next day pour a little of the juice off, mix the flour with it, return it to the meat mixture and bake as for *pâté maison*.

PATE DE LIEVRE (France)

HARE PATE

The problem with hare is that it has a tendency to be dry. The easiest way to overcome this fault is to mix it (closely) with a meat which is fat. Hence the very fine mincing and mixing of pork and hare. This is an ideal recipe for those who only like to eat a saddle of hare, as hare, and then wonder what to do with the rest.

Imperial/Metric	*American*
the (raw) remains of a hare	the (raw) remains of a hare
1 lb (500 g) fat pork belly	1 lb mixture of pork butt and fatback
1 onion, chopped	1 onion, chopped
2 eggs	2 eggs
2 tablespoons flour	2 tablespoons flour
mace, juniper and thyme to taste	mace, juniper and thyme to taste
4 fl. oz (120 ml) port	½ cup port wine
4 fl. oz (120 ml) brandy	½ cup brandy
salt and freshly ground pepper	salt and freshly ground pepper
streaky bacon to line terrine	streaky bacon to line terrine

Put the hare and pork to marinate overnight in a mixture of port and brandy. Next day mince the hare and pork as finely as possible. Add the onion, herbs and marinade. Line a suitably sized terrine and put in the mixture. Cover with aluminium foil and bake as for *Pâté de Campagne* (p.138).

With special treatment, as follows, this pâté will keep for a couple of months in a cool larder or refrigerator. Having removed all traces of exterior moisture, wash the container carefully. Pour in a layer of melted lard and let set. Put the hare pâté on top and then pour lard all round it and over the top. Once set, cover and keep cool.

PATE DE CAMPAGNE (France)

COARSE COUNTRY PATE

Imperial/Metric
1½ lb (750 g) fat pork or
  sausage meat*
1 lb (500 g) pork liver
8 oz (250 g) flare fat
2 medium onions, chopped
2 cloves garlic, chopped
8 fl. oz (240 ml) white wine
2 tablespoons gin or brandy
juniper berries, crushed
mace, parsley and sage to taste
bayleaf
2 tablespoons flour

American
1½ lb fat pork or sausage meat*
1 lb pork liver
8 oz flare fat
2 medium onions, chopped
2 cloves garlic, chopped
8 fl. oz white wine
2 tablespoons gin or brandy
juniper berries, crushed
mace, parsley and sage to taste
bayleaf
2 tablespoons flour

* The only objection to using British sausage meat is that it is sometimes made with bread and flavoured with pennyroyal, neither of which has any part in a classic French pâté.

Mince the meats, mix them with the onion and garlic and put to marinate in the white wine and gin or brandy, together with the crushed juniper and herbs. Next day pour a little of the juice off, mix the flour with it, return it to the meat and bake as for *pâté maison* (p.139).

If you float about half an inch (1 cm) pure lard over the top of this pâté, it will keep for a couple of weeks in the refrigerator.

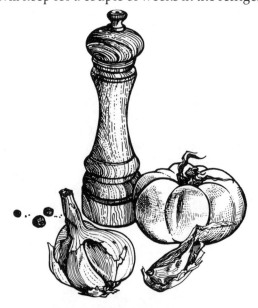

PATE MAISON (UK)

This makes a very good, everyday *pâté maison* to which you can add other ingredients, such as *poivre vert*, mushrooms, cold game, tongue, ham and even more bacon. The British are inclined to over-bacon pâtés and terrines, and the bacon is so heavily smoked that it shows. Such meat has no place in a classic pâté. Use only green (unsmoked) bacon.

Imperial/Metric	*American*
1 lb (500 g) pork belly or sausage meat	1 lb pork belly or sausage meat
1 lb (500 g) pork liver	1 lb pork liver
1 lb shoulder or breast of veal	1 lb shoulder or breast of veal
8 fl. oz white or red wine	8 fl. oz white or red wine
2 tablespoons brandy or similar	2 tablespoons brandy or similar
2 onions, chopped	2 onions, chopped
2 eggs	2 eggs
1 stick celery	1 stick celery
1 teaspoon dried oregano (or marjoram)	1 teaspoon dried oregano (or marjoram)
1 teaspoon dried thyme	1 teaspoon dried thyme
2 or 3 cloves garlic	2 or 3 cloves garlic
salt and pepper	salt and pepper
juniper berries (optional)	juniper berries (optional)
fat back pork, flare fat or green streaky bacon for lining	fat back pork, flare fat or green streaky bacon for lining

Mince all the meats and mix together with the herbs, garlic onion etc. Put everything (except the 2 eggs) to soak overnight in the wine and brandy. Next day add the eggs and put into a suitably sized terrine lined with either fatback pork, flare fat or stretched streaky (green) bacon. Cook for approximately 1 hour 15 minutes to 1 hour 30 minutes at 325°F/170°C/Gas 3. You must look frequently at the pâté towards the end of the cooking time to see that it is not over-cooked.

PATE DE RIS DE VEAU AU PORTO (France)

PATE OF SWEETBREADS WITH PORT

Imperial/Metric	American
2 pairs of veal sweetbreads	2 pairs of veal sweetbreads
8 oz (250 g) belly of pork	8 oz belly of pork
8 oz (250 g) slightly fat ham	8 oz slightly fat ham
8 oz (250 g) pork shoulder	8 oz pork shoulder
1 onion, finely chopped	1 onion, finely chopped
8 fl. oz (240 ml) dry white wine	1 cup dry white wine
8 fl. oz (240 ml) port	1 cup port wine
2 eggs	2 eggs
1 large carrot, grated	1 large carrot, grated
2 sticks celery, chopped	2 sticks celery, chopped
1 clove garlic, chopped	1 clove garlic, chopped
thyme and savory	thyme and savory
a little nutmeg	a little nutmeg
2 tablespoons brandy	2 tablespoons brandy
butter for frying	butter for frying
Madeira or port aspic (optional) (p.180)	Madeira or port aspic (optional) (p.180)
pistachio nuts (optional)	pistachio nuts (optional)

Soak sweetbreads in salted water for 30 minutes; rinse and cook in boiling salted water for just over 5 minutes. Drain; refresh with cold water. Trim any bits off and remove connective tissue. Weight down between 2 boards.

To make a *farce* of the minced lean pork, belly of pork and diced ham, add the onion, carrot, celery, 2 eggs, half the white wine and the brandy. Salt and pepper.

Trim the sweetbreads into neat medallions (you may have to slice them horizontally) and sauté them in the butter. Add the thyme, savory and nutmeg and pour over the rest of the white wine. Add the port and turn the heat up high. After 2 minutes take out the sweetbreads with a slotted spoon and put aside. Reduce the liquid in the sauce to half.

Put one-third of the pork-ham mixture in the terrine and lay over half the sweetbreads. Pour over half the juice in the saucepan, then put another layer of the *farce* and the other half of the sweetbreads. Pour on the rest of the juice and put on the final third of the *farce*. Cover the terrine with a lid or with aluminium foil and cook for just under 1½ hours in a moderate oven (340°F/175°C/Gas 3½). Weight down when cooling.

This terrine can be covered with Madeira or port aspic if wished. In any case you should turn it out and clean the container before serving. Pistachio nuts can be added for those who like them.

PATE OF ARBROATH SMOKIES (OR PINWIDDIES) WITH WHISKY (UK: Scotland)

This needs electricity to get the ingredients thoroughly amalgamated. Arbroath Smokies and Pinwiddies are *hot smoked*, unlike the more common Finnan haddock. The whisky replaces the more usual lemon juice.

Imperial/Metric	*American*
12 oz (375 g) Arbroath smokies or Pinwiddies	12 oz Arbroath smokies or Pinwiddies
12 oz (375 g) unsalted butter	1½ cups unsalted butter
½ fl. oz (30-60 ml) whisky	½ fl. oz whisky
cayenne pepper	cayenne pepper

Soften but do not melt the butter. Skin the smokies or Pinwiddies and cut up roughly. Put the pieces and the softened butter into the liquidizer or food processor and mix together. Add the whisky and some cayenne. Taste and adjust seasoning.

Variation
Alternatively you can use double (heavy) cream in the same amount instead of butter but you should mix these ingredients roughly before putting them in the machine. If you make this pâté with cream, you must eat it within 12 hours; made with butter it will keep for several days.

KIPPER PATE (UK)

Do please use proper kippers if possible – most frozen kippers are dyed. A kipper should be a tawny colour, not mahogany.

Imperial/Metric	*American*
12-16 oz (375-500 g) kippers	12-16 oz kippers
12-16 oz (375-500 g) unsalted butter	1½-2 cups sweet butter
juice of a lemon or 2-3 tablespoons whisky	juice of a lemon or 2-3 tablespoons whisky
cayenne pepper to taste	cayenne pepper to taste

Cook the kipper by your favourite method but preferably not by grilling. I leave mine in boiling water for a few minutes. Strip off the skin, bone them and put them, still warm, in the liquidizer or food processor. Add the lemon juice (or whisky), cayenne pepper and butter (which you cut up into small lumps). Process until thoroughly amalgamated. Pack into small pots or one large pot and let cool. Serve 12 hours later.

Variation
Proceed as for the previous recipe but substituting cream for the butter. However, everything should be very cold before processing in the machine or the cream will separate. Eat the same day if possible.

KIPPER PATE WITH CREAM CHEESE (UK)

Imperial/Metric	American
12-16 oz (375-500 g) cooked, cold kipper	12-16 oz cooked, cold kipper
12-16 oz (375-500 g) full cream cheese	12-16 oz full cream Philadelphia-type cheese
1 tablespoon onion or shallot, chopped	1 tablespoon onion or shallot, chopped
1 tablespoon lemon juice or wine vinegar	1 tablespoon lemon juice or wine vinegar
cayenne or freshly ground black pepper	cayenne or freshly ground black pepper

Do make sure every bone has been removed from your kippers, as there is no mixer to take care of stragglers. Mix the cream (Philadelphia) cheese, which should be creamy rather than cheesy, with the onion (or shallot) and lemon juice (or vinegar). Add freshly ground black pepper or cayenne to taste. Chop the kipper into half-inch cubes (2 cm) and fold them into the creamy (Philadelphia) cheese. Serve as soon as possible.

SMOKED MACKEREL PATE (UK)

Imperial/Metric	*American*
1 lb (500 g) smoked mackerel	1 lb smoked mackerel
6 oz (190 g) *unsalted* (sweet) butter	¾ cup sweet butter
juice and rind of 1 large lemon	juice and rind of 1 large lemon
plenty of freshly ground black pepper	plenty of freshly ground black pepper
aspic to cover (optional)	aspic to cover (optional)
1 dessertspoon white wine vinegar (optional)	1 dessertspoon white wine vinegar (optional)
parsley or dillweed (to decorate)	parsley or dillweed (to decorate)

This is best done in a mixer or food processor but can be done by hand with a little more effort. Skin and fillet the mackerel, if necessary, and mash together with the softened butter. Add lemon juice and rind and, if not sharp enough, add the vinegar. No salt should be needed.

Some people prefer to divide this into 8 separate portions and float a little aspic on top, I think it looks nicest in one dish with a bit of parsley or dill on top.

SMOKED HADDOCK AND CREAM PATE (UK)

This is a very light pâté for immediate consumption (it tends to separate after a time) but do make sure you get real smoked haddock and not dyed smoked fillets of some other fish. Probably it is preferable to buy it on the bone.

Imperial/Metric	*American*
12-16 oz (375-500 g) smoked haddock	12-16 oz smoked haddock
12-16 fl oz (360-480 ml) double cream	¾-1 pint heavy cream
juice and rind of 1 lemon	juice and rind of 1 lemon
Tabasco or cayenne pepper to taste	Tabasco or cayenne pepper to taste
milk	milk
sprigs of parsley to decorate	sprigs of parsley to decorate

Put the smoked haddock in a pan and cover it with milk. Bring to the boil and then turn down heat. Let simmer for 15-20 minutes.

(Keep the milk, as it can be the base of a good fish soup.) Take out and let cool. Remove skin and bones. Once cold, cut up roughly and drop into a liquidizer or food processor. Add the lemon juice and rind, a few drops of Tabasco or cayenne and then the cream. Process until it has blended. Either divide between ramekins or serve on one dish with sprigs of parsley to decorate.

SMOKED HADDOCK AND EGG PATE (UK: Scotland)

Imperial/Metric	*American*
12 oz (375 g) cooked smoked haddock	12 oz cooked smoked haddock
8 oz (250 g) unsalted butter	1 cup sweet butter
4 eggs, hard-boiled	4 eggs, hardcooked
1 tablespoon chopped parsley (or dill)	1 tablespoon chopped parsley (or dill)
a few drops Tabasco	a few drops Tabasco

Once the smoked haddock is thoroughly cold, put it in the liquidizer or food processor with the softened butter and the other ingredients. Process until everything is well mixed. Best served 3-4 hours later but can be served at once.

SMOKED SALMON PATE 1 (UK: Scotland)

Imperial/Metric	*American*
12 oz (375 g) smoked salmon	12 oz smoked salmon
12 oz (375 g) butter	1½ cups butter
a little cayenne	a little cayenne

Blend everything together in a liquidizer or food processor and pack into small ramekins.

Variation

Imperial/Metric	*American*
12 oz (375 g) smoked salmon	12 oz smoked salmon
12 fl. oz (360 ml) double cream	¾ pint heavy cream
a little cayenne	a little cayenne

Cut the smoked salmon into the smallest dice possible – do not mince or use a machine. Fold these into whipped cream to which you have added the cayenne.

SMOKED SALMON PATE 2 (Ireland)

Imperial/Metric	*American*
12 oz (375 g) smoked salmon	12 oz smoked salmon
12 oz (375 g) cream cheese	12 oz Philadelphia-type cheese
1 little cayenne	a little cayenne
1 tablespoon wine vinegar	1 tablespoon wine vinegar

Blend everything in the liquidizer or food processor and pack into small ramekins. Serve with hot toast.

PERTHSHIRE SMOKED TROUT PATE (UK: Scotland)

Imperial/Metric	*American*
1 lb (500 g) smoked trout preferably *not* in fillets	1 lb smoked trout preferably *not* in fillets
4 oz (125 g) walnuts (shelled weight)	4 oz walnuts (shelled weight)
8 fl. oz (240 ml) double cream	1 cup (heavy) cream
juice of 1 lemon	juice of 1 lemon
cayenne pepper or Tabasco to taste	cayenne pepper or Tabasco to taste
chives or parsley, chopped (to decorate)	chives or parsley, chopped to decorate)

Soak and peel the walnut pieces (the flavour is too strong if you omit this). Take the fish off the bone and either put in mixer or food processor with the lemon juice, peeled walnuts, and Tabasco or cayenne pepper or mix by hand – the mixture will be a little coarser. If you are doing it by hand, crush the walnuts with a rolling pin and flake the fish as finely as possible, then work in the lemon juice and Tabasco. Whip the cream and add it to the fish and walnut mixture. Keep it very cold and check before serving that the cream has not leaked any water. If it has, pour it off. Decorate with chopped chives or parsley.

SARDINE PATE (UK)

Imperial/Metric	*American*
2 tins Marie Elisabeth sardines, preserved in oil	2 tins Marie Elisabeth sardines, preserved in oil
12 oz (375 g) cream cheese	1½ cups cream cheese
2 tablespoons wine vinegar	2 tablespoons wine vinegar
cayenne pepper to taste	cayenne pepper to taste
parsley (optional)	parsley (optional)

Put everything into a liquidizer or food processor and mix. Adjust seasoning. Add parsley if you wish. Serve next day with very hot toast.

TUNA FISH PATE (USA)

Imperial/Metric
7 oz (220 g) tinned tuna fish
12 oz (375 g) butter
juice and rind of lemon
3 tablespoons parsley
1 tablespoon fresh coriander
    (optional)
good dash of Tabasco

American
7 oz canned tuna fish
1½ cups butter
juice and rind of lemon
3 tablespoons parsley
1 tablespoon fresh coriander
    (optional)
good dash of Tabasco

If you can get water-packed tuna, so much the better, otherwise drain all the oil off. Soften the butter but do not melt. In a liquidizer or food processor mix the fish, butter, lemon juice and Tabasco. Chop separately the parsley (and fresh coriander if you have it) and fold into the mixture by hand. (If you do everything in the machine, it comes out a very murky mess, though the taste is the same.) Taste and adjust seasoning if necessary. Cover and refrigerate for serving next day.

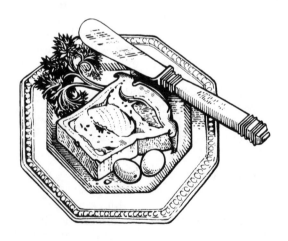

Terrines

TERRINE D'ARTICHAUTS FOURREE DE RIS DE VEAU (France)

ARTICHOKE TERRINE WITH A FILLING OF VEAL SWEETBREADS

Imperial/Metric	American
2 pairs of veal sweetbreads	2 pairs of veal sweetbreads
2 lb (1 kilo) artichoke hearts (frozen or fresh but not tinned)	2 lb artichoke hearts (frozen or fresh but not tinned)
3 or 4 shallots, chopped	3 or 4 shallots, chopped
1 onion, chopped	1 onion, chopped
1 tablespoon tomato concentrate	1 tablespoon tomato concentrate
4 fl. oz (120 ml) white wine	½ cup white wine
2 tablespoons Madeira	2 tablespoons Madeira wine
2 tablespoons olive oil	2 tablespoons olive oil
8 oz (250 g) sliced mushrooms	8 oz sliced mushrooms
15 fl. oz (450 ml) double cream	2 cups heavy cream
1 packet (0.4 oz/11-12 g) gelatine (see glossary)	Approx. 1 tablespoon gelatin* (see glossary)
butter for frying	butter for frying
thyme and parsley	thyme and parsley
salt and pepper	salt and pepper
flour (optional)	flour (optional)

Soak the sweetbreads in salted water for 2-3 hours, then blanch for approximately 10 minutes in acidulated water (i.e. with a little lemon juice added, but vinegar will do). Trim and weight under a board with a couple of heavy tins on top.

Fry the shallots in a little butter or oil, add the white wine and reduce a little. Set aside.

Cook the artichokes in boiling acidulated water until done and then drain and put through the liquidizer or food processor. Sieve the result if you think there are stringy bits. Melt the gelatine in a little water or white wine if wished and once it is liquid add to the artichoke mixture. Cool but do not let set. Whip the double cream and fold into the artichoke mixture. Coat the sides of your mould (round, square or oblong) with a layer of the artichoke/cream mixture, reserving sufficient to cover the top later on. Cover with clingfilm and refrigerate until set.

Fry the onion in a little butter (or butter and oil if wished), then add the sweetbreads cut into bite-sized pieces. (You might like to flour them; I prefer not to.) Add the mushrooms and cook for approximately 5 minutes on medium heat. Add the Madeira, herbs, salt and pepper. Do not overcook the mushrooms. Let cool slightly. Pour into the middle of the artichoke mould and top with remaining artichoke mixture. Cover with clingfilm and refrigerate overnight before serving.

TERRINE DE VEAU AUX FINES HERBES (France)

HERB AND VEAL TERRINE

Imperial/Metric	*American*
2 lb (1 kilo) breast of veal, minced	2 lb breast of veal, ground
8 oz (250 g) calves' liver	8 oz calves' liver
8 oz (250 g) unsmoked bacon, or *petit-salé*	8 oz unsmoked bacon, or *petit-salé*
1 medium onion	1 medium onion
2 tablespoons flour	2 tablespoons flour
small glass brandy or *marc*	small glass brandy or *marc*
4 oz (125 g) parsley, chopped	½ cup parsley, chopped
2 tablespoons basil, chopped	2 tablespoons basil, chopped
pinch each of ground rosemary, thyme, sage	pinch each of ground rosemary, thyme, sage
1 tablespoon tomato concentrate	1 tablespoon tomato concentrate
1 glass dry white wine	½ cup dry white wine
1 teaspoon sea salt	1 teaspoon sea salt
plenty of freshly ground pepper	plenty of freshly ground pepper

Cut up the onion and calves' liver roughly and drop into the liquidizer or food processor with the cognac, wine, rosemary, thyme, sage, tomato paste and half the salt and pepper. Although not called for in the recipe, I prefer to line the terrine in unsmoked streaky bacon (*petit-salé* in France) as I think it keeps the whole thing moister. Reduce to a purée, add the flour and whizz again. Cut the bacon or *petit-salé* into small cubes and mix in with the veal. Add the remaining pepper and salt. Finally stir in the parsley and basil. (The original recipe calls for 2 teaspoons of white pepper which seems rather a lot, but all the same don't stint on the pepper mill.) Into a suitably sized terrine put a layer of the veal forcemeat followed by a (rather wet) layer of the liver. Continue thus until all is used up, finishing with the forcemeat. Cover with aluminium foil and bake for about an hour at 375°F/190°C/Gas 5. Test for 'done-ness' with a skewer – the juices should be clear. Do not overcook – it is difficult to give an accurate time without knowing the size of the utensil used. Weight down when cooling with cans of foods placed in a slightly smaller utensil. This will help cutting the next day.

TERRINE COTE D'OR (France)

BURGUNDIAN RABBIT TERRINE

The Mersault wine recommended here is so expensive that I use Aligoté, which is approximately an eighth of the price, and it works very well. Instead of the *marc de Bourgogne* I use gin – the juniper in it gives a slightly gamey flavour to the rabbit.

Imperial/Metric	American
1 wild or farm young rabbit	1 wild or farm young rabbit
1 lb (500 g) fat pork (belly)	1 lb fat pork (belly)
1 lb (500 g) shoulder of veal	1 lb shoulder of veal
8 oz (250 g) shallots, chopped fine	8 oz shallots, chopped fine
½ bottle Mersault	½ bottle Mersault
4 fl. oz (120 ml) double cream	½ cup heavy cream
2 tablespoons parsley, chopped	2 tablespoons parsley, chopped
pinch of mace	pinch of mace
4 fl. oz (120 ml) *marc de Bourgogne*	½ cup *marc de Bourgogne*
12 oz (375 g) streaky green bacon	12 oz streaky green bacon

Mix the shallots, parsley, pepper and mace, and then add the white wine and *marc de Bourgogne*. Mince the veal and pork together, in either a mincing machine or a food processor. Strip the flesh off the rabbit and cut into half-inch (1 cm) cubes or twice as big – it is a matter of personal taste. Put everything except the bacon to marinate overnight.

Next day line a terrine with the stretched streaky bacon in such a way that the pieces overhang the receptacle. Put in the meat mixture which you have now salted and cover with the overhanging bacon. Put the terrine in a baking tin with water to come half way up and bake, covered with aluminium foil, for 1½ hours at 350°F/180°C/Gas 4.

SMOKED HERRING, ROE AND EGG TERRINE (Germany)

I find the best way to ensure this terrine turns out is to line the mould with Bakewell (sulphurized non-sticking) baking paper.

Some Germans cheat and put a little gelatine (melted first in some water) into the cream cheese mixture. If you are not 100 per cent sure of your cheese, this is probably a good idea.

Serve with pumpernickel or ordinary rye bread and butter.

Imperial/Metric	American
3 whole smoked herrings*	3 whole smoked herrings*
8 oz (250 g) smoked cod's roe or similar	8 oz smoked cod's roe or similar
6 eggs, hard-boiled	6 eggs, hardcooked
bunch of spring onions	bunch of scallions
1 lb (500 g) full cream cheese	2 cups full cream cheese
8 fl. oz (240 ml) double cream	1 cup heavy cream
juice of 1 large lemon	juice of 1 large lemon
freshly ground pepper to taste	freshly ground pepper to taste
chopped fresh herbs (optional)	chopped fresh herbs (optional)

* The smoked herring can be buckling (which the Germans use for this dish), kippers or the French type *harengs saurs* – the latter must be soaked before use unless the label says it is unnecessary. The aim is to have a *mild* herring – not too salty.

Beat the cream and cheese together (if necessary over heat) to a semi-liquid mass. Take 3-4 tablespoons of this and beat into the smoked cods' roe. Chop the spring onions and some of their stalk as small as possible. Slice the hard-boiled eggs. Skin the herring and put to soak if necessary.

Line a loaf tin with *cut* baking paper. Put in a layer of cheese/cream mixture. On top place some chopped-up herring. Sprinkle with spring onion (and herbs if wished), then put on a layer of hard-boiled egg, then a layer of cheese/cream. In the middle layer of the terrine spread the entire amount of cods' roe and then continue layering, finishing with cream cheese. Put a piece of baking paper on top and press down slightly. If you have another loaf tin, put a biggish weight in it and weigh down the terrine – but not as firmly as for a meat terrine. Leave 12 hours and turn out.

FRESH SALMON AND DILL TERRINE (Denmark)

Imperial/Metric
2 lb (1 kilo) fresh salmon
1 pint (600 ml) mayonnaise*
a few prawns (to decorate)
2 tablespoons fresh dill (and
 parsley, optional)
salt and pepper
½ pint (300 ml) strong fish
 stock (p.308)
2 tablespoons dry white wine
enough gelatine to set 1 pint
 (600 ml) liquid (p.413)

American
2 lb fresh salmon
2½ cups mayonnaise*
a few shrimps (to decorate)
2 tablespoons fresh dill (and
 parsley, optional)
salt and pepper
1¼ cups strong fish stock
 (p.308)
2 tablespoons dry white wine
enough gelatin to set 2½ cups
 liquid (p.413)

* Use 'real' mayonnaise ideally made with half olive oil and half sunflower oil.

Cook the salmon by poaching it in a little fish stock (which keep) or in foil in the oven. Skin, bone and flake it. Mix it with the mayonnaise. Melt the gelatine in a little of the fish stock and then add to the rest. Add the white wine. Put *half* the fish stock with the salmon and add 1 tablespoon chopped dill (and parsley, optional). Add the rest of the dill to the rest of the stock (and again some parsley if you wish) and pour a thin layer into the bottom of a suitably sized sandwich-loaf tin. Let set. Put in the salmon/mayonnaise mixture and let that set also. Later heat up the rest of the dill/fish stock to just above melting and pour it over the top. If the stock is too hot, it will sink into the salmon/mayonnaise part. Serve 12 hours later with fresh brown bread.

SALMON, MONKFISH AND SPINACH TERRINE (UK)

Serve with brown bread and butter.

Imperial/Metric
1 lb (500 g) salmon
1 lb (500 g) monkfish
1 lb (500 g) spinach, cooked
 weight
1 onion, chopped
pinch of nutmeg
3 eggs
15 fl. oz (450 ml) *sauce béchamel*
 (p.391)
4 fl. oz (120 ml) double cream
2 tablespoons parsley, chopped
2 tablespoons chervil or
 watercress, chopped

American
1 lb salmon
1 lb monkfish
1 lb spinach, cooked weight
1 onion, chopped
pinch of nutmeg
3 eggs
2 cups *sauce béchamel* (p.391)
½ cup heavy cream
2 tablespoons parsley, chopped
2 tablespoons chervil or
 watercress, chopped

Cut the salmon and monkfish into small cubes. Cook the spinach, drain well and chop. Add the nutmeg, a little salt and then the double cream. Butter a terrine well and put in a layer of cubed raw salmon. Then mix the parsley and chervil (or watercress) and put half of this over the salmon. Stir the monkfish into the white sauce, to which you have added the 3 eggs, and put half on top of the salmon and herbs. Put in another layer of salmon and herbs and follow it with the monkfish. Finally put on the spinach. Bake at 350°F/180°C/Gas 4 for 30 minutes in a baking tin with water to come half way up the sides of the terrine. Press down slightly when cooling, but much less than for a meat pâté. Turn out when cold (you may find it easier to dip the terrine in very hot water before turning it out).

TERRINE DE ST JACQUES (France)

SCALLOP TERRINE

Serve with a herb mayonnaise (p.407).

Imperial/Metric	*American*
2 lb (1 kilo) Dover sole	2 lb sole or flounder
8-10 scallops depending on size	8-10 scallops depending on size
8 oz (250 g) cooked white part of leeks	8 oz cooked white part of leeks
8 fl. oz (240 ml) white wine or Noilly Prat vermouth	1 cup white wine or Noilly Prat vermouth
8 fl. oz (240 ml) double cream	1 cup heavy cream
2 oz (60 g) butter	¼ cup sweet butter
1 tablespoon parsley	1 tablespoon parsley
1 tablespoon gelatine	1 tablespoon gelatin
2 shallots, chopped	2 shallots, chopped

Fillet the sole. Clean the scallops. Poach the sole gently in a mixture of the butter and white wine or vermouth with a little salt and pepper added. Set aside. Cook the scallops and their corals in the same mixture, adding the shallot if liked, drain and set aside.

In the remaining liquid, melt the gelatine and heat until thoroughly blended. Add the parsley. Mash down the sole roughly and add the gelatine/parsley mixture. Add the double cream. Pour half into a ceramic terrine, then place the cooked scallops and coral on top, pressing down slightly. Add the other half of the sole mixture. Cover with clingfilm and refrigerate, overnight if possible.

CRAB, SCALLOP AND AVOCADO TERRINE (USA)

Imperial/Metric	*American*
2 large ripe avocados	2 large ripe avocados
1½ lb (750 g) lump crab meat (frozen)	1½ lb lump crab meat (frozen)
12 large scallops and their coral	12 large scallops and their coral
1 recipe basic fish stock (p.308)	1 recipe basic fish stock (p.308)
1 recipe aspic jelly (p.180)	1 recipe aspic jelly (p.180)
8 fl. oz (225 ml) Sauternes or sweet white wine	8 fl. oz Sauternes or sweet white wine
2 tablespoons chives, chopped	2 tablespoons chives, chopped
2 tablespoons parsley, chopped	2 tablespoons parsley, chopped
1 teaspoon Tabasco	1 teaspoon Tabasco
salt to taste	salt to taste

Defrost the crab meat. Cook the scallops and coral in the basic fish stock to be used for the aspic. Take out with a slotted spoon and put aside. Reduce the stock by approximately one third and strain carefully. Off the heat add the Sauternes. Make the aspic in the usual way, let cool and pour a layer into the bottom of the terrine. Refrigerate and let set. On this place neat slices of avocado and scallop coral and pour another thin layer of aspic over and let set. Then put in a layer of crab meat, a layer of sliced avocado and a layer of cooked scallops and some of the coral. Sprinkle with half the chopped herbs. Pour over half of the rest of the aspic. Refrigerate until almost set, then continue the layering and finally add the rest of the aspic. Cover and refrigerate overnight.

Others

RILLETTES DU MANS (France)

The most famous *rillettes* come from le Mans, but for the life of me I cannot tell the difference between these and *rillettes* from elsewhere, though in the cheaper sort only belly of pork is used. Often *Rillettes du Mans* have rabbit added to them.

Imperial/Metric	*American*
1 lb (500 g) shoulder (or belly) of pork	1 lb shoulder (or belly) of pork
1 lb (500 g) fatback	1 lb fatback
a little mace and ground dried thyme	a little mace and ground dried thyme
salt	salt

Cut the meat up into the smallest possible cubes (do not mince), and do the same to the fatback. Put the whole mixture into a wide baking tin, pour over a little water (about 8 fl. oz. 240 ml/1 US cup) and cook in a very low oven for 4-5 hours, turning the meat from time to time. The meat should be falling apart, and the water should have evaporated. You may either put this through the food processor or beat it with a pair of forks – the object is to get the fat and meat thoroughly amalgamated. Flavour with mace (or thyme) and some salt and pack into individual containers. Run a little melted lard over the top of each if you are not going to serve the next day. Otherwise cover with cligfilm or foil.

RILLETTES DE CANARD (France)

DUCK RILLETTES

I have found that to make duck *rillettes* from a whole duck is a slightly dicey business and you tend to end up with totally melted meat plus hard bits of leg meat etc. I have used two *magrets de canard* for this duck *rillettes* and found it works very well though it is somewhat expensive.

Imperial/Metric	*American*
2 *magrets de canard* weighing in all approx. 1½ lb (750 g)	2 *magrets de canard* weighing in all approx. 1½ lb
1 lb (500 g) flare fat	1 lb fatback
salt and pepper	salt and pepper
pinch of dried sage (optional)	pinch of dried sage (optional)
clove of garlic (optional)	clove of garlic

Skin the *magrets*, then cut into small cubes, fat and all. Cube the flare fat (fatback) and mix with the duck. Chop the garlic if used and mix in. Sprinkle with sage if wished. Pour a wineglass of water over it, and cover with aluminium foil. Put in a very low oven (300°F/150°C/Gas 2) and cook covered for 3-4 hours. Take the foil off, stir the contents and then put back in the oven, uncovered, for a further 3-4 hours, by which time you should be able to shred the duck easily and beat it into the melted fat. You may have to turn down the heat a little to avoid browning the meat. It is better done this way than with a food processor. Add the salt and pepper to taste and let stand at least 24 hours before eating.

Covered with a layer of pure lard (not duck fat), these *rillettes* will keep for months in a cool place.

RILLETTES DE LAPIN (France)

RABBIT RILLETTES

Use the recipe for *Rillettes du Mans* but add approx. 1 lb (500 g) rabbit meat, and use belly of pork not shoulder. Also cover with approx. 12 fl. oz (360 ml) water.

POTTED CRAB (UK)

Serve with brown bread and butter or toast.

Imperial/Metric	*American*
1 lb (500 g) fresh crab meat*	1 lb fresh crab meat*
1 lb (500 g) butter	1 lb butter
juice of a lemon	juice of a lemon
1 teaspoon ground mace	1 teaspoon ground mace
½-1 teaspoon cayenne pepper	½-1 teaspoon cayenne pepper
2 tablespoons brandy	2 tablespoons brandy
sprig of parsley (to decorate)	sprig of parsley (to decorate)

* Ordinary crabs can be used for this dish and all the edible parts can be used.

Put ¾ lb (375 g) butter into a saucepan, add the spices and let melt gently. Chop/cream the crab meat and then add it to the butter, with the lemon juice. Off the heat add the brandy and stir well in. Pack into individual ramekins or a terrine. Separately melt the other butter and pour a film over each ramekin or over the terrine. Keep at least overnight before serving. Decorate with a sprig of parsley.

Variation

Imperial/Metric	*American*
approx. 1 lb (500 g) crab meat, light and dark	approx. 1 lb crab meat, light and dark
8 oz (250 g) butter	8 oz butter
pinch of cayenne pepper	pinch of cayenne pepper
1 tablespoon wine vinegar	1 tablespoon wine vinegar

Mix everything together and serve with hot toast.

POTTED SHRIMP (UK)

Using the smallest shrimps you can buy, peel them and proceed exactly as for Potted Crab (p.155) except that you should reduce the butter to ½ lb (250 g) for the shrimps and ¼ lb (125 g) for the covering.

PRAWN AND CURRY SPREAD (India)

In India they decorate this with a hot red pepper.

Imperial/Metric	*American*
1 lb (500 g) prawns, shelled and deveined	1 lb shrimps, shelled and deveined
8 oz (250 g) butter	8 oz butter
curry powder to taste – about 1 dessertspoon	curry powder to taste – about 1 dessertspoon
cucumber or radish to decorate	cucumber or radish to decorate

In a liquidizer or food processor mix the prawns and butter together and add the curry. No salt is needed, it seems.

HUMMUS BI TAHINI (Middle East)

CHICKPEAS WITH SESAME PASTE

Ostensibly you cannot overcook chickpeas, which is a good thing. However, it is all too easy to let them boil dry. Therefore, as there is no loss of flavour at all, I suggest using ready-prepared tinned chickpeas.

Our cook in Egypt used to make a trellis design on the *hummus* in chopped parsley and put paprika in the spaces. Black olives look beautiful with white *hummus bi tahini,* and the combination tastes wonderful. Serve with warm Arab bread (similar to pitta bread).

Although electricity is not essential for this dish, it makes everything very much quicker and easier.

Imperial/Metric	American
approx. 1 lb (500 g) drained weight tinned chickpeas	1 lb drained weight canned chickpeas
4 fl. oz (120 ml) *tahini* paste	½ cup *tahini* paste
juice of 2 lemons	juice of 2 lemons
1 or 2 cloves garlic	1 or 2 cloves garlic
cayenne pepper (optional)	cayenne pepper (optional)
2 tablespoons chopped parsley and/or paprika or sesame seed (to garnish)	2 tablespoons chopped parsley and/or paprika or sesame seed (to garnish)

Put the chickpeas, paste, lemon juice and garlic into the liquidizer or food processor and add approximately a wine glass of water (½ US cup). Whizz up and see what sort of consistency you get. It should just hold its shape on a flat plate, although some people in the Middle East like it quite runny. Taste and adjust the seasonings – I always use a little red pepper (cayenne) but it is not in the basic recipe. Turn onto a dish and sprinkle with a little paprika or sesame seed and/or chopped parsley.

LIPTÓI (Hungary)

LIPTAUER CHEESE SPREAD

Americans thin this down with sour cream to make a dip – unconventional and totally un-Hungarian but very good. In the old days the cheese was made of sheep's milk – there were more sheep in Slovakia, which was then part of Hungary and is where this cheese comes from, than there were people. Nowadays virtually everyone makes do with ordinary cream cheese.

Imperial/Metric	American
1 lb (500 g) good-quality cream cheese	1 lb good-quality cream cheese
4 oz (125 g) sour cream	½ cup soured cream
4 oz (125 g) butter	½ cup butter
1 teaspoon or more salt	1 teaspoon or more salt
1 teaspoon Dijon-type mustard	1 teaspoon Dijon-type mustard
1 tablespoon paprika	1 tablespoon paprika
1 tablespoon caraway seeds	1 tablespoon caraway seeds
1 small onion, grated	1 small onion, grated
1 tablespoon vinegar (optional)*	1 tablespoon vinegar (optional)*

* You will need the vinegar only if your cream cheese is very mild. You should end up with quite a sharp, full-tasting cheese and it should be a most beautiful pale peach pink.

Mix all the ingredients together either in a liquidizer or food processor or by hand, folding in the grated onion at the last. Sprinkle with a little more paprika at the end or make a pattern with the tines of a fork. Parsley is *never* put in Liptói.

CONFITURE D'OIGNONS (France)

ONION 'JAM'

For use with pâtés, *charcuterie* etc.

I came across this delicious accompaniment in the middle of the Cevennes, at la Guaribote near Joyeuse. We had it with cold stuffed quail as a first course.

Imperial/Metric	*American*
2 lb (1 kilo) onions, minced	2 lb onions, minced
just under 2 fl. oz (50 ml) grenadine syrup*	¼ cup grenadine syrup*
3½ oz (100 g) sugar	just under ½ cup sugar
1 tablespoon (20 g) butter	1 tablespoon butter
2 fl. oz (60 ml) sherry vinegar	¼ cup sherry vinegar
12 fl. oz (360 ml) full red wine**	1½ cups full red wine**
salt	salt

* Grenadine is available from good-quality grocers and speciality stores. It should be made from pomegranates only and not from the ubiquitous red fruit (*fruits rouges*) which is too often the case with cheap copies – even in France.
** The wine should be fairly heavy and not at all astringent.

Cook the minced onions very slowly in the butter until they are almost melted. Add the sugar, then the grenadine and finally the sherry vinegar. Let cook over an asbestos or heat mat (or even 2) for 1 hour. At the end of that time, add the red wine and bring up to heat. Then put back on the asbestos or heat mat and cook for a further hour stirring from time to time. Add salt at the end if needed. Pot into a warmed, dry jar and eat 48 hours later. Will keep for almost a year in the refrigerator.

Some people prefer more sugar and/or more vinegar. This is a matter of personal taste, and also it depends on the red wine used.

7   Soufflés

Providing you can trust your oven (and a lot of ovens are not worthy of such trust even in these modern times), there is very little to fear about making soufflés.

I never tie a band of buttered greaseproof paper round my soufflé dish, feeling that it is only asking for trouble when serving-time comes – 9 times out of 10 it will come off beautifully but on the tenth occasion it will let you down, so it is best to avoid such a possibility. Run your thumb or a knife round the edge of the filled soufflé dish, making a sort of moat, and your soufflé will rise spectacularly in a cottage-loaf fashion. Also, I think it is a *sine qua non* not to make a soufflé for more than 4 people in one dish. If you wish to make one for 8 in a large dish, you will need considerably longer at slightly less heat. Only trial and error can tell. My particular trials have been limited to cooking soufflés for 4 people in a soufflé dish of 2 imperial pints capacity, i.e. approximately 1.25 litres/5 US cups. The mixture should come just over half way up the dish before cooking.

There are certain rules to follow in soufflé-making, none of which is onerous.

The first is not to think of a soufflé as a vehicle for left-overs. (Game soufflé is probably the exception.) Eggs tend to potentiate flavours and anything tired or on the way out will taste more so in a soufflé. Eggs should be spanking fresh and on the cold side rather than at room temperature.

Another important rule is to beat up your egg whites if possible with a balloon whisk or with a hand beater. Electric beaters tend to make a very dense mass of egg white which is difficult to fold in nicely. I once had a Chinese cook who could beat up 5 or 6 egg whites *on a soup plate* with a pair of chopsticks in less than 5 minutes! I am not advocating this, but hand-beaten egg whites handle better. In the absence of a copper bowl, use a good pinch of cream of tartar which supplies the necessary acid to help up and keep up the egg whites.

The most important rule of all is to keep your guests rather than the soufflé waiting. Do not open the oven door until at least 15 minutes have passed or your soufflé will collapse, never to rise again.

Most soufflés are based on a *béchamel* base made with a roux containing equal amounts of butter and flour, and 1 egg per person. There are exceptions, of course, as for instance in the Gorgonzola Soufflé, but the principle remains more or less the same.

BASIC SOUFFLE

For 8 persons: *to be divided between two soufflé dishes.*

Imperial/Metric	American
3 oz (90 g) plain flour	3 oz plain flour
3 oz (90 g) butter	3 oz butter
12 fl. oz (360 ml) milk	1½ cups milk
8 egg yolks	8 egg yolks
8-10 egg whites	8-10 egg whites
flour	flour
salt and pepper	salt and pepper

Melt the butter and stir in the flour, making a roux – do not let it brown. Add the milk (hot or cold according to your own method) and cook gently for 5 minutes or so. Let cool for approximately 30 minutes or longer. The sauce should not be too thick; if it is, add a little more milk. Once cool, add the egg yolks one by one. Divide this mixture between 2 bowls at this stage.

Beat up the egg white until stiff but not dry and divide the mixture between the 2 bowls. Fold in with a metal spoon or palette knife, whichever you find easier. Turn the contents of each bowl into a buttered and floured soufflé dish and put into a pre-heated oven (375°F/190°C/Gas 5), on the lowest shelf, for 25-30 minutes. Some cooks use the *bain-marie* method when baking a soufflé. This is a matter of personal taste: I find it tends to make a slightly heavier soufflé.

Vegetable

ARTICHOKE SOUFFLE

Imperial/Metric	*American*
12 oz (375 g) artichokes (bottoms or hearts)	12 oz artichokes (bottoms or hearts)
basic soufflé recipe (p.160)	basic soufflé recipe (p.160)

You can use either artichoke bottoms or the entire hearts. If you use the latter, you must sieve them, since the result may be stringy. Purée the artichokes and add to the egg yolk mixture before adding the whites. Bake as for a normal soufflé.

ASPARAGUS SOUFFLE

Imperial/Metric	*American*
12 oz (375 g) asparagus	12 oz asparagus
basic soufflé recipe (p.160)	basic soufflé recipe (p.160)

Cook the asparagus. Once cooked, remove tips and set aside. Purée the rest of the asparagus (without any liquid) and then sieve. This last is essential or you may end up with a stringy soufflé. Fold the purée into the soufflé mixture before you add the egg whites. Divide between 2 mixing bowls and fold half the asparagus tips into each. Then add beaten egg whites. Bake as usual.

Can be served with *sauce hollandaise* (p.395).

SOUFFLE DE CHOUFLEUR AU GRUYERE (Switzerland)

CAULIFLOWER AND GRUYERE CHEESE SOUFFLE

I have to admit that the original recipe was done with a Vacherin cheese, which is available in Switzerland only in the winter and early spring months, and elsewhere usually not at all. Thus something has been lost in the translation, but the result is still delicious and different.

Imperial/Metric	*American*
8 oz (250 g) Gruyère or Beaufort cheese	8 oz Gruyère or Beaufort cheese
8 oz (250 g) cooked cauliflower in sprigs	8 oz cooked cauliflower in sprigs
basic soufflé recipe (p.160), slightly varied – see below	basic soufflé recipe (p.160), slightly varied – see below

Cook the cauliflower in the smallest sprigs you can make. Let cool. Having made your basic *sauce béchamel*, put in the grated Gruyère and stir until melted. Let cool. Add the egg yolks and divide the mixture between 2 bowls. Add half the cauliflower sprigs to each bowl. Then beat up the egg whites and fold in. Bake as for a normal soufflé.

CHESTNUT AND ONION SOUFFLE (Belgium)

Serve with a herbed tomato sauce (p.389).

Imperial/Metric	*American*
4 oz (125 g) onion, cooked and chopped	4 oz onion, cooked and chopped
4 oz (125 g) chestnuts, cooked, chopped or puréed	4 oz chestnuts, cooked, chopped or puréed
basic soufflé recipe (p.160)	basic soufflé recipe (p.160)

Follow the basic recipe, adding the onions and chestnuts after the egg yolks but before the whites.

SOUFFLE DE COURGETTES AVEC COULIS DE TOMATES (France)

COURGETTES SOUFFLE WITH FRESH TOMATO SAUCE

Serve with Tomato Coulis (p.389).

Imperial/Metric	*American*
8 oz (250 g) courgettes, cooked and puréed	1 cup zucchini, cooked and puréed
a little nutmeg	a little nutmeg
basic soufflé recipe (p.160)	basic soufflé recipe (p.160)

Following the basic soufflé recipe, add the courgette mixture and a pinch of nutmeg after incorporating the egg yolks. Divide, fold in the egg whites and bake as usual.

SCHWAMMERLSOUFFLE (Austria)

MUSHROOM SOUFFLE

Imperial/Metric	*American*
8 oz (250 g) mushrooms, sliced	8 oz mushrooms, sliced
basic soufflé recipe (p.160)*	basic soufflé recipe (p.160)*

When making your basic soufflé increase the butter to 4 oz/125 g/½ US cup, and fry the mushrooms in it. Then add the flour once they are more or less cooked, then the milk. Let cool and continue as for a normal soufflé in every way. No sauce is served with it.

Cheese

CHEESE SOUFFLE (France)

Imperial/Metric
8 oz (250 g) Gruyère cheese, grated
basic soufflé recipe (p.160)

American
8 oz Gruyère cheese, grated
basic soufflé recipe (p.160)

Bake in the normal way recipe. A pinch of nutmeg can be added. Some French cooks also add 4-8 oz (125-250 g) of minced ham, but this is not very common.

ITALIAN CHEESE SOUFFLE

This is served on its own but there is nothing to stop you serving a sauce with it.

It is an ordinary basic soufflé (p.160) except that you substitute 4 oz (125 g) cream cheese (in Italian *mascarpone*) for the butter and add 4 oz (125 g) grated Parmesan cheese, preferably the *stravecchio* type, though this is a counsel of perfection. Proceed as for an ordinary soufflé.

GORGONZOLA SOUFFLE (Italy)

Italians serve it on its own but it would also be good with a Tomato Coulis (p.389).

Imperial/Metric	American
4 oz (125 g) plain flour	4 oz plain flour
8 oz (250 g) Gorgonzola cheese	8 oz Gorgonzola cheese
12 fl. oz (360 ml) milk	1¾ cups milk
8 egg yolks	8 egg yolks
8 or 10 eggs whites	8 or 10 egg whites
salt and pepper	salt and pepper

Melt the Gorgonzola very gently (it catches easily) and stir in the flour to make rather a sloppy roux. Cook this for a good 5-6 minutes before adding the milk. Then proceed as for an ordinary soufflé.

Fish and Seafood

SMOKED HADDOCK SOUFFLE (UK)

Can be served with *sauce hollandaise*.

Imperial/Metric	American
12 oz (375 g) smoked haddock, cooked and flaked	12 oz smoked haddock, cooked and flaked
basic soufflé recipe (p.160)	basic soufflé recipe (p.160)

If you can use the milk in which you have cooked the smoked haddock in making the *sauce béchamel*, so much the better for flavour. Using the basic recipe, incorporate the flaked (or puréed) haddock into the soufflé mixture at the egg-yolk stage. Divide into 2 and fold in the egg whites. Bake as for a normal soufflé.

LOBSTER SOUFFLE (France)

Serve with *sauce hollandaise* or *sauce aurore*

Imperial/Metric	American
1 lobster weighing at least 1½ lb (750 g) or frozen lobster which has been thoroughly thawed.	1 lobster weighing at least 1½ lb or frozen lobster which has been thoroughly thawed.
basic soufflé recipe (p.160)	basic soufflé recipe (p.160)

Cook the lobster in the normal way, i.e. slightly under a quarter of an hour in boiling water; cool and remove meat. Discard the foamy, spongy mass near the head, and also the liver (though normally this can be eaten), but add the coral, if there is any, to your meat mixture. Remove the claw meat and separate from the rest. Let cool thoroughly. Purée about half the lobster meat with some of the soufflé/egg yolk mixture, keeping the nicest pieces for chopping up. Divide the mixture into 2, add half the chopped lobster to each and then fold in the egg whites. Bake in the normal way.

SOUFFLE DE BROCHET A LA SAUCE NANTUA (France)

PIKE SOUFFLE WITH *SAUCE NANTUA*

This is a classic dish from all round Lac Léman, both in France and in Switzerland. Serve with *sauce Nantua*.

Imperial/Metric	American
12 oz (375 g) pike fillets (uncooked)	12 oz pike fillets (uncooked)
basic soufflé recipe (p.160)	basic soufflé recipe (p.160)

Put fish through the liquidizer or food processor with some of the soufflé mixture before you have got to the egg-white stage. Pike are notorious for bones, so make sure you have none or that they are well ground up. Divide the soufflé/pike mixture into 2, fold in the beaten egg whites and bake in the usual way.

PRAWN SOUFFLE WITH SAUCE NANTUA (France)

Serve with *sauce Nantua* (p.399)

Imperial/Metric	American
12 oz (375 g) prawns, cooked and shelled	12 oz medium shrimps, cooked and shelled
basic soufflé recipe (p.160)	basic soufflé recipe (p.160)

Devein the prawns and purée half with some of the soufflé mixture before adding the egg whites. Chop the rest, not too small, and add to the mixture. Divide into 2 and fold in the egg whites. Bake in the normal way.

SMOKED SALMON SOUFFLE (UK)

Imperial/Metric
8 oz (250 g) good-quality
   smoked salmon
basic soufflé recipe (p.160)

American
8 oz good-quality smoked
   salmon
basic soufflé recipe (p.160)

Cut the smoked salmon into small dice (not bits) and incorporate into the basic soufflé recipe at the egg-yolk stage. Divide into 2 and fold in the egg whites. Bake as a normal soufflé but watch it does not get too dry.

TUNA SOUFFLE WITH ROSEMARY (Italy)

A *sauce aurore* (p.391) or *sauce hollandaise* (p.395) could be served with this if wished, though the original recipe called for no sauce.

Imperial/Metric
6-8 oz (190-250 g) tinned tuna
basic soufflé recipe (p.160)
juice and rind of 1 lemon
½-1 teaspoon powdered
   rosemary

American
6-8 oz tinned tuna
basic soufflé recipe (p.160)
juice and rind of 1 lemon
½-1 teaspoon powdered
   rosemary

Though the original recipe calls for rosemary, it is not a spice to everyone's liking (mine included) so oregano or dill could be substituted.

Following the basic soufflé recipe, purée the tunafish with the herb, lemon juice and rind together with a little of the *sauce béchamel* before the egg yolks have been added. Then proceed as for a normal soufflé.

Poultry, Meat and Game

CHICKEN OR TURKEY SOUFFLE WITH MUSHROOM SAUCE (UK)

Serve with mushroom sauce.

Imperial/Metric
12 oz (375 g) turkey or chicken,
   minced
basic soufflé recipe (p.160)

American
12 oz turkey or chicken, minced
basic soufflé recipe (p.160)

Using the basic soufflé recipe, at the *béchamel* stage add the turkey or chicken and proceed as for a normal soufflé.

CHICKEN LIVER SOUFFLE

Can be served with Madeira sauce (p.394), in which case leave out the Madeira in the soufflé.

Imperial/Metric	*American*
8 oz (250 g) chicken livers	8 oz chicken livers
garlic, chopped (optional)	garlic, chopped (optional)
pinch of thyme	pinch of thyme
2 tablespoons Madeira	2 tablespoons Madeira
basic soufflé recipe (p.160)	basic soufflé recipe (p.160)

Use basic soufflé recipe but before adding the egg whites add the barely cooked and chopped chicken liver, a little chopped garlic, a pinch of thyme and the Madeira. Cook in the normal way.

Do not be tempted to use the liquidizer or food processor for this: the result is positively sepulchral.

CHRISTMAS SOUFFLE (Hungary)

GAME SOUFFLE WITH MUSHROOMS

Nothing to do with Christmas time but named after a Hungarian cousin, Márta, whose surname means Christmas in English. She walked out of Hungary in 1956, along with thousands of others, and eventually set up a very successful home-catering business in Germany. Many of the Hungarian recipes in this book are hers.

This can be served with orange and port wine sauce (p.399).

Imperial/Metric	American
8 oz (250 g) winged game, chopped*	8 oz winged game, chopped*
3 medium shallots, chopped	3 medium shallots, chopped
3 oz (90 g) plain flour	3 oz plain flour
6 oz (190 g) butter	¾ cup butter
6 fl. oz (180 ml) milk	¾ cup milk
4 oz (125 g) mushrooms, sliced	4 oz mushrooms, sliced
4 fl. oz (120 ml) port or Madeira	½ cup port wine or Madeira wine
8 egg yolks	8 egg yolks
8 or 10 egg whites	8 or 10 egg whites
1 heaped teaspoon paprika	1 heaped teaspoon paprika
salt	salt

* The game should be partridge, pheasant, grouse or good-quality pigeon – not fishy birds such as wild duck, teal, snipe etc.

Mince or chop the game up small and put to marinate in the port.

Fry the shallots in half the butter. Add the mushrooms and cook until almost done. Strain off the liquid. Melt the rest of the butter and make a roux. You will need in all 12 fl. oz (375 ml) of liquid made up of milk, port wine and mushroom liquid – make up what is missing with additional milk. Stir in the minced game and port wine and cook a few moments. Then let cool and proceed as for an ordinary soufflé.

SPINACH AND HAM SOUFFLE (UK)

Good, if a little rich, with *sauce hollandaise* (p.395).

Imperial/Metric	American
8 oz (250 g) spinach, cooked and squeezed very dry	8 oz spinach, cooked and squeezed very dry
4 oz (125 g) ham, diced	4 oz ham, diced
basic soufflé recipe (p.160)	basic soufflé recipe (p.160)

Chop the spinach finely; do not purée as this turns the soufflé a horrible colour. Add it to the basic soufflé recipe after incorporating the egg yolks. Divide the mixture between 2 bowls and add half the diced ham to each. Then fold in the egg whites and bake in the usual way.

HAM SOUFFLE WITH ORANGE AND PORT WINE SAUCE (UK)

Serve with orange and port wine sauce (p.399).

Imperial/Metric	*American*
12 oz (375 g) ham, minced	12 oz ham, minced
basic soufflé recipe (p.160)	basic soufflé recipe (p.160)

To a basic soufflé at the *béchamel* stage add the ham and proceed as for a normal soufflé.

Sformati

These are basically a mixture of eggs, but in a lesser quantity than for soufflés, and either a vegetable or more unusually fish or meat. They are easier to do than soufflés because they do not collapse but they are also heavier, and the hostess always runs the risk, out of Italy, that her guests may think it is a heavy or failed soufflé. A *sformato* is baked in a charlotte mould but a pyrex basin will do just as well, I find non-stick cake tins and charlotte moulds excellent. They should always be baked in a *bain-marie*, i.e. with water in a baking tin to come half way up the sides of your *sformato*.

SFORMATO DI SPINACI (Italy)

BAKED SPINACH MOULD

Imperial/Metric	*American*
1 lb (500 g) spinach purée	2 cups spinach purée
scant 8 fl. oz (240 ml) thick *sauce béchamel* (p.391)	1 cup thick *sauce béchamel* (p.391)
6 eggs, separated	6 eggs, separated
½ teaspoon nutmeg	½ teaspoon nutmeg
1 tablespoon Parmesan or Gruyère cheese	1 tablespoon Parmesan or Gruyère cheese

Mix the spinach purée and *sauce béchamel* together. Add the egg yolks, one by one, mixing them well in, then the nutmeg. Beat the whites stiff and fold in carefully. Place in a well-buttered mould (or an attractive glass or earthware dish you can bring to table) and cook in the oven for 30 minutes at approximately 350°F/180°C/Gas 4. Wait a moment or two before turning out (quite unlike a soufflé).

SFORMATO DI CARCIOFI (Italy)

BAKED ARTICHOKE MOULD

Exactly as for the spinach *sformato* but use instead a purée made of either fresh or frozen artichokes. Tinned artichokes have an odd taste which is accentuated by cooking them this way.

SFORMATO DI FUNGHI PORCINI (Italy)

BAKED WILD MUSHROOM MOULD

There is no point in doing this with cultivated mushrooms, but British field mushrooms would do well, although the taste would be different.

Imperial/Metric	*American*
1 lb (500 g) mushrooms, finely chopped	2 cups mushrooms, finely chopped
8 fl. oz (240 ml) thick *sauce béchamel* (p.391)	1 cup *sauce béchamel* (p.391)
2 tablespoons Madeira or port	2 tablespoons Madeira or port
pinch of nutmeg	pinch of nutmeg
a little butter	a little butter
clove of garlic	clove of garlic
3 eggs, separated	3 eggs, separated

Make the *sauce béchamel*. Chop the garlic finely and cook in butter. Add the mushrooms and cook for a few minutes. Add Madeira or port, then strain the mushrooms, returning the liquid to the pan and reducing it by half. Add the *sauce béchamel* and the mushrooms once more. Cool. Add the yolks, one by one, incorporating them carefully. Beat the egg whites stiff and fold into this mixture. This is a very dicey *sformato* to turn out (though one of the most delicious), so better to bake it in an oven-to-table dish. Bake in a *bain-marie* at approximately 325°F/170°C/Gas 3 for 30 minutes or so.

8   Mousses and Aspics

Neither is less trouble than the other since aspics need great care taken over the jelly and its clearing and mousses need a fair amount of work so far as mincing the ingredients and beating the eggs. Neither keeps well and, like galantine, they should not be made too far in advance in hot summer weather.

Some people dislike the texture of jelly or aspic, but luckily they are rare, and most people enjoy mousses. Since these dishes are to be served cold, remember that chilling increases the saltiness but reduces the aroma of herbs and spices.

The most difficult thing is to get a full-bodied flavour to a mousse and until you have prepared a mousse a couple of times you should test it out on your family first. Eggs, particularly in quantity, can make the most strongly-flavoured food quite bland and tasteless and you will need to take this factor into account.

With the exception of *Jambon Persillé*, most aspics look better done in individual moulds, whereas with mousses it is quite the contrary. Both frequently require the addition of something crisp to provide texture contrast. There are of course exceptions such as the *foie gras* in aspic and the avocado dishes which rely on their unctuosity for their charm.

Mousses

ARTICHOKE MOUSSE (France)

Serve with brown bread and butter.

Imperial/Metric
approx. 2 lb (1 kilo) artichoke
　　hearts, cooked
1 pint (600 ml) mayonnaise
　　(p.404)
gelatine to set 1½ pints (900 ml)
8 fl. oz (240 ml) double cream
3 tablespoons tomato ketchup
salt and cayenne pepper

American
approx. 2 lb artichoke hearts,
　　cooked
2½ cups mayonnaise (p.404)
gelatin to set 3¾ cups
1 cup heavy cream
3 tablespoons tomato ketchup
salt and cayenne pepper

Melt the gelatine in hot water. Mix the mayonnaise together with the cream, tomato ketchup, salt and hot pepper in a liquidizer or food processor and add the melted gelatine. Chop the artichokes by hand, separating the bases from the rest of the hearts. Chop the bases by hand but put the rest of the artichoke in the mixer. Turn into a bowl and stir in the chopped artichoke bases. Turn into an oiled (or wetted) mould and let set over night. Next day turn out.

ASPARAGUS AND EGG MOUSSE (Belgium)

Serve with brown bread and butter.

Imperial/Metric
1 lb (500 g) tinned asparagus
　　spears
8 eggs, hard-boiled
1 pint (600 ml) mayonnaise
　　(p.404)
gelatine to set 1 pint (600 ml)
salt and cayenne pepper
salad greens for 8
French dressing (optional,
　　p.401)

American
1 lb tinned asparagus spears
8 eggs, hardcooked
2½ cups mayonnaise (p.404)
gelatin to set 2½ cups
salt and cayenne pepper
salad greens for 8
French dressing (optional,
　　p.401)

Melt the gelatine in hot water. Mix the eggs and mayonnaise together with the salt and hot pepper in a liquidizer or food processor and add the melted gelatine. Chop the asparagus spears by hand and stir into the egg mixture. Turn into an oiled (or wetted) ring mould and let set over night. Next day turn out and fill centre with salad greens. Pass a French dressing separately if wished.

GUACAMOLE MOUSSE WITH PRAWNS (Mexico)

AVOCADO MOUSSE WITH PRAWNS

Use a ring mould with a hole in the middle.

Imperial/Metric	*American*
4 large avocados	4 large avocados
12 fl. oz (360 ml) mayonnaise (p.404)	1½ cups mayonnaise (p.404)
8 oz (250 g) full cream cheese	8 oz full cream cheese
juice of 3 lemons	juice of 3 lemons
1 lb (500 g) medium prawns, shelled and deveined	1 lb medium shrimps, shelled and deveined
approx. 2 tablespoons gelatine	approx. 2 tablespoons gelatin
8 fl. oz (240 ml) double cream	1 cup heavy cream
2 tablespoons tomato ketchup	2 tablespoons tomato ketchup
3 teaspoons Tabasco	3 teaspoons Tabasco
4 oz (125 g) green chilli peppers (or less, to taste)	4 oz green chilli peppers (or less, to taste)

Put the lemon juice, half the mayonnaise, half the cream, the cream cheese and 2 teaspoons of the Tabasco into the liquidizer or food processor. Mix together. Melt the gelatine in hot water according to packet instructions and add to the mixture. Peel and pit the 4 avocados, chop roughly and add to the food processor. Blend together. Add the green chillies and blend further. Turn out into an oiled mould. Cover with clingfilm and let set. Do not worry about the slight discoloration as it will not show. Next turn out onto a serving dish. Mix the rest of the cream and mayonnaise with the teaspoon of Tabasco and the tomato ketchup and stir into the prawns (shrimps). Put in the centre and serve.

GUACAMOLE MOUSSE WITH CRAB (Mexico)

AVOCADO MOUSSE WITH CRAB

Follow recipe for Guacamole mousse with prawns (above) but substitute lump crab meat. Ordinary dark and light crab meat will not do. Chop into small pieces.

TOMATO MOUSSE (Portugal)

Imperial/Metric	American
2 lb (1 kilo) tomatoes	2 lb tomatoes
1 large onion, chopped	1 large onion, chopped
8 eggs	8 eggs
8 oz (250 g) cream cheese	8 oz cream cheese
basil	basil
butter	butter
gelatine to set 1½ pints (900 ml)	gelatin to set 3¾ cups
salt and pepper	salt and pepper
watercress or salad greens	watercress or salad greens

Fry the onion in some butter but do not let it take colour. Peel the tomatoes by dipping them in boiling water; chop roughly and fry with the onion. You will get a rather sloppy mixture, and this must be reduced a little. When it is, add the cream cheese. Get the mixture very hot. Tip everything into a liquidizer or food processor and whizz up. Add the eggs and finally the basil, seasonings and gelatine. Tip into a wetted mould and let set. Surround with watercress or salad greens.

FLANES DE QUESO (Spain)

COLD CHEESE CUSTARD WITH HAM AND CUCUMBER

Imperial/Metric	American
6 oz (190 g) grated Manchego cheese*	¾ cup grated Manchego cheese*
1 cucumber, sliced unpeeled	1 cucumber, sliced unpeeled
8 oz (250 g) ham, chopped	8 oz ham, chopped
8 eggs	8 eggs
15 fl. oz (450 ml) single cream	2 cups light cream

* It is difficult to find a substitute for Manchego cheese; probably Gouda or a very mild Cheshire would do.
   Butter the ramekins well. Put slices of cucumber around the inside edge, pressing well into the butter. Divide the ham between the ramekins. Beat the eggs into the warmed, not hot, cream and then strain through a sieve. Incorporate the Manchego cheese and pour into the dishes. Place in a *bain-marie* in a moderate oven (350°F/180°C/Gas 4) for 15 minutes. Let cool and turn out some hours later.

CRAB MOUSSE (UK)

Ordinary crab can be used for this but the decoration should be with lump crab meat. It is not meant to be turned out.

Imperial/Metric
1 lb (500 g) crab meat, light and dark
lump crab meat (to decorate)
15 fl. oz (450 ml) *sauce béchamel* (p.391)
juice of 1 lemon
2 sticks celery, chopped
2 tablespoons parsley, chopped
2 shallots, chopped
15 fl. oz (450 ml) double cream
approx. 2 tablespoons gelatine
1 teaspoon Tabasco
salt to taste
½ sweet red pepper (to decorate)

American
1 lb crab meat, light and dark
lump crab meat (to decorate)
2 cups *sauce béchamel* (p.391)
juice of 1 lemon
2 sticks celery, chopped
2 tablespoons parsley, chopped
2 shallots, chopped
2 cups heavy cream
approx. 2 tablespoons gelatin
1 teaspoon Tabasco
salt to taste
½ red bell pepper (to decorate)

Soften the gelatine in warm water. Put the *béchamel* on to heat. In a separate saucepan fry the shallot and celery and add to the sauce. Stir in the crab meat, Tabasco, lemon juice etc and finally the gelatine. Put in the refrigerator to set. Once it is on the point of setting, beat up the cream fairly stiff and fold it into the mixture. Let set for some hours, then decorate it with slices of sweet red pepper, the crab meat and a little parsley.

LOBSTER MOUSSE (UK)

Proceed exactly as for Crab Mousse (above), substituting lobster for crab. Decorate with a little claw meat and pepper rings.

MOUSSE DE LOTTE A L'ORANGE (France)

MONKFISH AND ORANGE MOUSSE

Delicious and unusual, this dish can be done with sole or lobster but the fish must not be too delicate in taste.

Imperial/Metric	American
1 lb (500 g) monkfish, cooked	1 lb monkfish, cooked
1 pint (600 ml) mayonnaise (p.404)	1 pint mayonnaise (p.404)
10 fl. oz (300 ml) fresh orange juice	1¼ cups fresh orange juice
gelatine to set 1½ pints (900 ml)	gelatin to set 3¾ cups
2 teaspooons sugar (if needed)	2 teaspooons sugar (if needed)
cucumber salad (to serve)	cucumber salad (to serve)
salt	salt

Melt the gelatine in warm water and set aside. In a liquidizer or food processor mix the mayonnaise and orange juice with the monkfish. Taste – it should not be too tart. Put in the necessary amount of salt. Taste again. Add the gelatine. Turn into individual moulds and serve next day surrounded by sliced cucumber.

PRAWN MOUSSE (UK)

Proceed as for Crab Mousse (p.175) but substitute prawns (shrimps) for crab and decorate with a few unshelled prawns.

PRAWN AND EGG MOUSSE WITH WATERCRESS (USA)

Serve with brown bread and butter.

Imperial/Metric	American
1 lb (500 g) prawns, shelled and deveined	1 lb shrimps, shelled and deveined
8 eggs, hard-boiled	8 eggs, hardcooked
1 pint (600 ml) mayonnaise (p.404)	2½ cups mayonnaise (p.404)
gelatine to set 1 pint (600 ml)	gelatin to set 2½ cups
salt and cayenne pepper	salt and cayenne pepper
2 or 3 bunches watercress	2 or 3 bunches watercress
French dressing (optional, p.401)	French dressing (optional, p.401)

Melt the gelatine in hot water. Mix the hard-boiled eggs and mayonnaise together with the salt and hot pepper in a liquidizer or food processor and add the melted gelatine. Chop the prawns by hand and stir into the egg mixture. Turn into an oiled (or wetted) ring mould and let set over night. Next day turn out and fill centre with cleaned watercress. Pass a French dressing separately if wished.

PAQUETS AUX DEUX SAUMONS (France)

SALMON IN PACKETS

This makes a very pretty first course; it is made up of fresh salmon, cream cheese and herbs in a smoked salmon 'case' with a small blob of caviare on top.

It should be made at least 12 hours before serving.

Imperial/Metric	*American*
8 slices smoked salmon	8 slices smoked salmon
cucumber (to decorate)	cucumber (to decorate)
1 small 3-4 oz (90-125 g) jar caviare or lumpfish roe	1 small 3-4 oz jar caviare or lumpfish roe
8 oz (250 g) cream cheese	1 cup Philadelphia-type cheese
8 fl. oz (240 ml) double cream	1 cup heavy cream
1 lb (500 g) cooked salmon	1 lb cooked salmon
1 teaspoon dill	1 teaspoon dill
1 tablespoon parsley	1 tablespoon parsley
1 teaspoon Dijon mustard	1 teaspoon Dijon mustard
2 tablespoons lemon juice	2 tablespoons lemon juice

Mix all the ingredients, except the first 3, and set aside.

Between 2 sheets of waxed paper bang out the smoked salmon slices so they can be used to line 8 ramekins and fold over on top. If the smoked salmon pieces are large enough, this will not be necessary. However, it is as well to have the wrap-over part a little thinner. Line the ramekins and divide the fish mixture between them, pressing down well. Fold the smoked salmon pieces across the top and press well down. Wrap in clingfilm and refrigerate.

At serving time turn out of the ramekins (you will have neat little dark pink 'packets') onto a plate, surround with cucumber slices and put a dab of caviare or lumpfish roe on the top of each.

WHITEFISH MOUSSE WITH SAUCE NICOISE (France)

Serve with sauce Niçoise (p.408).

Imperial/Metric	American
1½ lb (750 g) any cooked white fish	1½ lb any cooked white fish
15 fl. oz (450 ml) *sauce béchamel* (p.391)	2 cups *sauce béchamel* (p.391)
juice of 1 lemon	juice of 1 lemon
2 sticks celery, chopped	2 sticks celery, chopped
2 shallots, chopped	2 shallots, chopped
15 fl. oz (450 ml) double cream	2 cups heavy cream
approx. 2 tablespoons gelatine	approx. 2 tablespoons gelatin
1 teaspoon Tabasco	1 teaspoon Tabasco
salt	salt
2 tablespoons parsley, chopped (to decorate)	2 tablespoons parsley, chopped (to decorate)
½ sweet red pepper (to decorate)	½ red bell pepper (to decorate)

Soften the gelatine in warm water. Put the *béchamel* on to heat. In a separate saucepan fry the shallot and celery and add to the sauce. Stir in the chopped fish, Tabasco, lemon juice etc and finally the gelatine. Put in the refrigerator to set. Once it is on the point of setting, beat up the cream fairly stiff and fold it into the mixture. Let set for some hours then decorate it with slices of sweet red pepper and parsley.

SNAFFLES MOUSSE 1

Why it's called this I cannot imagine. You get it at a lot of dinner parties because it is quick and easy and tastes good. It is also relatively cheap.

Imperial/Metric	American
12 oz (375 g) cream cheese (this can be the Philadelphia type or Quark or St-Morez but not cottage)	1½ cups Philadelphia-type cream cheese
4 eggs, hard-boiled	4 eggs, hardcooked
3 tins Campbell's Beef Consommé	3 tins Campbell's Beef Consommé
1 heaped teaspoon curry powder (hot, medium or mild)	1 heaped teaspoon curry powder (hot, medium or mild)

Cut cheese roughly if it is the sort that will allow you to do this; otherwise use a spoon. Cut eggs into quarters. Heat 2 tins of the consommé to melting point and put into liquidizer or food processor. Add eggs, cheese and curry powder. Do *not* taste: at this warm stage it is revolting. Divide between 8 ramekins so that they are approximately two-thirds full. Put in refrigerator to set. At least 2 hours before serving, heat the remaining tin of consommé and divide between the ramekins so you have a thickish layer of clear jelly on each. Chill.

If you cover each ramekin so the contents do not pick up the refrigerator smells, this starter can be made up to 2 days beforehand.

SNAFFLES MOUSSE 2

Imperial/Metric	*American*
3 tins Campbell's Beef Consommé	3 tins Campbell's Beef Consommé
8 oz (254 g) cream cheese	1 cup Philadelphia-type cream cheese
4 fl. oz (120 ml) soured cream	½ cup commercial sour cream
chives or parsley, chopped	chives or parsley, chopped
dash of Tabasco	dash of Tabasco
1 dessertspoon wine vinegar	1 dessertspoon wine vinegar

Reserve one tin consommé and warm and mix the other 2 with the cream cheese and soured cream in a liquidizer or food processor. (This can be done by hand but a sieve must be used to avoid any lumps.) Add vinegar and Tabasco. Divide between 8 ramekins (you may have a little over) and set in refrigerator. Float melted consommé on top and sprinkle with chives or parsley before serving. Can be made in advance.

Aspics

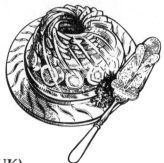

QUICK ASPIC (UK)

Imperial/Metric
1½ pints (900 ml) chicken broth
1 teaspoon salt
1 teaspoon sugar
2 fl. oz (60 ml) white wine or
    Madeira
6 to 8 peppercorns
6 stalks parsley
gelatine to set 32 fl. oz (960 ml)
    liquid (see *Glossary* for note
    on gelatine)

American
3¾ cups chicken broth
1 teaspoon salt
1 teaspoon sugar
¼ cup white wine or Madeira
6 to 8 peppercorns
6 stalks parsley
gelatin to set 4 cups liquid (see
    Glossary for note on gelatin)

Stir salt, sugar, herbs and peppercorns into the stock and bring to boil. Let steep 20 minutes and bring up to the boil once more. Off the heat melt the gelatine in a little of the warm liquid and add it to the rest of the stock. Make sure it is thoroughly amalgamated. Strain through a sieve and then through a piece of muslin previously wrung out in warm water. The liquid should be clear. If not, clarify it with egg whites (see p.300). Use as directed in the various recipes.

Tomato Aspic
Instead of using 1½ pints (900 ml) 4 cups of stock you can substitute ½ pint (300 ml) – 5 fl. oz of tomato juice for the stock. Basil is nice steeped in this mixture rather than parsley.

ASPIC DE FOIE GRAS AU SAUTERNES (France)

Unless you are cooking your own goose liver use the *bloc de foie gras* for this dish. The aspic should not be rigid but only just set and a pleasure to eat which often aspic is not.

Allow one or two small escalopes of *foie gras* per person – about 3 oz (75 g) altogether per person. If you use normal-sized ramekins you will find this amount plus the aspic will make a perfect serving.

Imperial/Metric	*American*
1 pint aspic (600 ml) (see recipe)	2½ cups aspic (see recipe)
1½ lb (750 g) approx. *foie gras*	1½ lb approx. *foie gras*
Sauternes	Sauternes
½ packet (1 tablespoon) gelatine	½ packet (1 tablespoon) gelatin

Reduce aspic by boiling to half, i.e. 10 fl. oz or 300 ml. Sprinkle half a packet of gelatine (1 tablespoon) and let it melt. Put back on the heat and let it thoroughly dissolve. Add enough Sauternes to bring it up to a pint (600 ml/2½ cups). Cool and let set. If it has not set enough then remove a quarter of the liquid and add a little more gelatine. Try the setting again. If too stiff add a small amount of Sauternes. Slice the *foie gras* carefully. The aspic should be cold, on the point of setting. Hot aspic will release the fat in the *foie gras*. Put a little aspic on the base of each ramekin and refrigerate. Once set paint the inside edges with aspic and set this. You will need two or three goes to get a thin coating. Alternatively, if there is space round your escalope you will not need to coat the edges. Place the *foie gras* on the aspic and pour over the rest to cover. Let set and then cover with clingfilm so that it won't pick up smells. Do not let get too cold – *foie gras* shouldn't be really iced – just cold. Turn out just before serving with hot toast. Drink the same Sauternes with it.

Variation
Since, depending on the *foie gras*, it can be difficult to make sure no fat is released when pouring over your jelly it is very acceptable to pour the jelly into a very large shallow pan, let it set and then surround the slices of *foie gras* with *chopped* jelly. I think this is almost prettier than the first version.

TERRINE DE ROQUEFORT AUX NOIX (France)

ROQUEFORT CHEESE AND WALNUT TERRINE

Serve in slices with wholemeal bread.

Imperial/Metric	*American*
12 oz (375 g) Roquefort cheese	12 oz Roquefort cheese
8 fl. oz (240 ml) *sauce béchamel* (p.391)	1 cup *sauce béchamel* (p.391)
6 egg yolks	6 egg yolks
8 fl. oz (240 ml) double cream	1 cup heavy cream
4 oz (125 g) walnuts, chopped	4 oz walnuts, chopped
gelatine to set ½ pint (300 ml)	gelatin to set 1¼ cups
parsley (to decorate)	parsley (to decorate)
a little cayenne pepper	a little cayenne pepper

Pour boiling water on the walnuts and peel if more than 6 months old. Save 2 or 3 halves for decoration. Chop the others roughly. Heat the *béchamel* and add the Roquefort cheese and cream. Stir constantly. Off the heat add the egg yolks one by one. Heat up a little but on no account let boil. Add the pepper and walnuts. Melt the gelatine in half a teacup of hot water and pour into the mixture. (If using a glass container, wet it thoroughly before pouring in the mixture, otherwise use a metal non-stick loaf pan.) Let cool and set and refrigerate over night. Next day turn out, put 2 or 3 walnut halves on top and surround with parsley.

LOTTE EN GELEE AUX HERBES (France)

ASPIC OF MONKFISH

Serve with a mayonnaise (p.404) thinned down with some single cream.

Imperial/Metric	*American*
3 lb (1.5 kilos) monkfish	3 lb monkfish
1 recipe aspic (p.180)	1 recipe aspic (p.180)
1 sweet pepper, red or green	1 bell pepper, red or green
8 oz (250 g) chopped mixed herbs*	8 oz chopped mixed herbs*

* Choose parsley, chives, tarragon, chervil etc and use approximately equal parts to make up the amount. Chop finely.

Put a little aspic in the bottom of the mould and put in a design of red or green pepper. Let set. Steam the monkfish and cut into bite-sized pieces. Let cool. Roll each piece in the chopped herbs and then put layers of herbed monkfish in the mould. Make sure the aspic is cold but not quite jellied – pour on a little at a time and let set from time to time, otherwise the fish will float to the top. Continue in this fashion until mould is full. Pour over the rest of the aspic and let set until next day.

SALMON AND CUCUMBER IN ASPIC (UK)

One of the prettiest aspics and not difficult to make – though somewhat time-consuming. Serve with brown bread and butter.

Imperial/Metric
1½ lb (750 g) cold, poached
    salmon
1 cucumber
1 recipe aspic (p.180)
1 tablespoon lemon juice or
    more to taste
a little Tabasco

American
1½ lb cold, poached salmon
1 cucumber
1 recipe aspic (p.180)
1 tablespoon lemon juice or
    more to taste
a little Tabasco

Do not peel cucumber but slice thinly on a mandoline or special cucumber cutter. Depending on the size of the cucumber, you may need more than one. Add the lemon juice to the aspic and cool to almost setting point. Pour a little aspic over the bottom of the mould and let set. Put on a design of cucumber rings and pour over a little more aspic. Let set. Put on some salmon and a layer of cucumber, then some aspic, and let set. Continue in this fashion until everything is used up. Let set thoroughly and turn out.

JELLIED TROUT (UK)

Serve with mayonnaise (p.404) and brown bread and butter.

Imperial/Metric
8 trout
1 recipe fish stock (p.308)
2 egg whites
2 tablespoons white wine
    vinegar
sprigs of tarragon or parsley
gelatine

American
8 trout
1 recipe fish stock (p.308)
2 egg whites
2 tablespoons white wine
    vinegar
sprigs of tarragon or parsley
gelatin

Cook the trout (in 2 lots of 4) in the fish stock. Put onto a plate to cool and cover with clingfilm while still warm. Once cool enough to handle, remove the skin from both sides between the head and the tail but leave the heads on. You can, if you wish, bone the fish but it is not necessary. Take approximately 2 pints (1.2 litres/5 US cups) of the fish stock and clarify it by heating and pouring it onto the whipped egg whites. Strain, preferably through a paper coffee-filter. Then add the vinegar and gelatine (enough to set the amount). Make a design on each trout with the tarragon or parsley and pour over enough jelly to cover. Let set.

POULET EN GALANTINE (France)

GALANTINE OF CHICKEN

You will need a large piece (maybe 2) of clean muslin.

This recipe is easier than boning out a chicken and stuffing it as a galantine but it still takes some care. You can make the Madeira jelly from the stock in which you cook the galantine, but you must clear it of all fat and particles first.

Imperial/Metric	*American*
1 medium chicken, about 2½ lb (1 kilo)	1 medium chicken, about 2½ lb
2 whole chicken breasts	2 whole chicken breasts
8 oz (250 g) pork shoulder	8 oz pork shoulder
8 oz (250 g) veal shoulder	8 oz veal shoulder
8 oz (250 g) ham, diced	8 oz ham, diced
1 medium onion, chopped	1 medium onion, chopped
4 whole chicken livers	4 whole chicken livers
8 fl. oz (240 g) (volume) fresh breadcrumbs	1 cup fresh breadcrumbs
3 eggs	3 eggs
4 fl. oz (120 ml) milk	½ cup milk
2 tablespoons parsley, chopped	2 tablespoons parsley, chopped
1 bayleaf	1 bayleaf
pinch of nutmeg	pinch of nutmeg
juice of 1 lemon	juice of 1 lemon
1 recipe Madeira jelly (p.180)	1 recipe Madeira jelly (p.180)

Skin the chicken breasts and the whole chicken. Remove its breast. Chop the rest of the flesh in the food processor or mincer with the pork, ham and veal and add the onions, herbs and nutmeg. Soak the breadcrumbs in the milk and drain slightly. Mix in with meat. Mix the whole with the 3 eggs and put aside.

Cook the chicken livers in a little stock. Bone out the chicken breasts and beat them into twice their previous size between 2 sheets of waxed paper. Take a large piece of clean muslin and lay the chicken breasts on it in such a way that you will be able to put the *farce* in the middle, bring over the sides and ends and make a neat parcel. Bring up the muslin and tie it to hold the chicken parcel. You may need another piece of muslin to close the parcel thoroughly.

Put the juice of a lemon into the stock and bring to the boil. Lower the parcel in and cook for approximately 1½ hours at simmering point only. Let cool in the liquid. When cold, lift out, drain and unwrap coverings. Put on a plate, seam side down, and paint on a coat of just-setting jelly. Once this is cold, continue to put further coats on until you have at least a half-inch (1 cm) coating over it all. Surround with the rest of the jelly, chopped up. Served sliced next day.

JAMBON PERSILLE A LA DIJONNAISE (France: Burgundy)

HAM IN PARSLEY JELLY

It is possible to make this recipe in half quantities and also to use green gammon – the taste will be quite different but equally delicious. Do check though on the saltiness; most joints should be soaked for at least 2 hours before being cooked. In parts of Burgundy this recipe is made with equal portions of ham and slightly salted pork available at any *charcutier*.

Excellent served with fresh home-made walnut bread. Served with salad and a baked potato it makes a wonderful informal lunch.

The ingredients for this dish are expensive and it's worth making it in quantity, a 6 lb joint will probably do 3 dinners for 8 people.

Imperial/Metric
5-6 lb (2-2.5 kilos) uncooked
  ham or equal amount of
  shoulder and ham
2 onions stuck with 4 cloves
1 veal trotter
1 pig's trotter
3 or 4 carrots
1 bottle white wine, preferably
  Bourgogne Aligoté
2 tablespoons white wine
  vinegar
10-12 oz (315-350 g) parsley,
  chopped fine – keep the
  stalks
gelatine
bouquet garni (optional)

American
5-6 lb uncooked ham or equal
  amount of shoulder and ham
2 onions stuck with 4 cloves
1 veal trotter
1 pig's trotter
3 or 4 carrots
1 bottle white wine, preferably
  Bourgogne Aligoté
2 tablespoons white wine
  vinegar
10-12 oz parsley, chopped fine
  – keep the stalks
gelatin
bouquet garni (optional)

Put all the ingredients into a large pan, except the chopped parsley and wine vinegar, together with the parsley stalks and *bouquet garni* (if used). Cook, covered, until the meat is thoroughly tender. Let it cool in the cooking liquid. Once cold, either cut into half-inch (2 cm) squares or tear and crush the meat, rather as for *rillettes* (p.153). This is a matter of personal taste: both methods are 'right' in Burgundy.

Layer the meat in a terrine or a square dish with the parsley, a layer of meat, a layer of parsley and so on ending with a parsley layer. You may well need a bit more parsley.

Strain the cooking liquid, and taste to see if it is too salty or not. If it is just right, do not reduce but use a little gelatine to make it set, following the instructions on the packet as to quantities. You will need enough liquid to cover the top layer of parsley. Add the wine vinegar and pour gently over the layered meat and parsley. If the liquid is not at all salt, you can reduce it to about approximately 15 fl. oz/450 ml/1 US pint. Test it for saltiness again, and its setting capacity, and add gelatine if needed. It is impossible to give an exact amount for the final jelly liquid since it depends on the volume of the dish you have used. The jelly should not be too stiff.

This keeps several days in the refrigerator so can be made in advance – but keep it covered as the jelly tends to absorb other flavours from the refrigerator.

9 Pastry Dishes

With the advent of the food processor, anyone can make pastry but, whether it is made by machine or by hand, there are a few basic rules which must be adhered to.

1. The flour should be plain flour.

2. The pastry should not be handled too much – do not over roll and do not re-roll and re-roll. Roll on one side only – do not turn pastry over if you can avoid it.

3. Everything should be as cold as possible, including the cook's hands.

4. The richer the pastry (except a sweet pastry), the hotter the oven.

5. The richer the pastry, the longer it should rest between rollings (puff-pastry and rough puff-pastry), and if possible let it rest before baking.

In France and Belgium ready-to-bake puff pastry made with all butter can be purchased fresh or frozen but I have yet to see this elsewhere. Bought puff pastry, other than that made with all butter, is suitable for eating hot only – cold, it has a rather unpleasant greasy taste.

For the basic recipes which follow, it is essential to follow either imperial, metric or US all the way through, since the equivalents are very rough and ready, and mixing them will lead to disaster.

Basic Recipes

PATE A CHOUX
CHOUX PASTRY

Imperial/Metric	*American*
6 oz (200 g) plain flour	6 oz plain flour
6 oz (200 g) unsalted butter	¾ cup sweet butter
5 fl. oz (150 ml) water	5 fl. oz water
6 medium eggs	6 medium eggs
pinch of salt	pinch of salt

Cut the butter into cubes and put on to boil with the salted water. Once boiled, put in the flour and mix in well, off the heat. Put back on the heat and cook until the mass comes away from the sides of the saucepan in a ball. Remove from heat and beat in the eggs one by one. Beat really well. Let cool and then either drop blobs onto an oiled baking tray or pipe them out (éclair shaped if you prefer them that way). Cook on the middle shelf in a hot oven (around 425°F/220°C/Gas 7) with the door *very slightly* open to let the steam escape. (If you keep the door totally closed, the choux come out heavy and steam-laden and collapse on cooling.) 15 minutes should do the trick.

CHEESE PASTRY (Russia and Poland)

This cheese pastry is used for certain tarts (particularly in the spring), piroshki (p.194) etc, – in the Ukraine they use sour cream and butter in equal quantities instead of the two types of cheese. In any event it is an ideal pastry for those with a food processor – alternatively you need everything very cold – the day, the kitchen, the ingredients and the cook's hands!

Imperial/Metric	*American*
4 oz (125 g) butter, cut into small cubes	½ cup butter, cut into small cubes
4 oz (125 g) rich cream cheese	½ cup rich cream cheese
4 oz (125 g) cottage cheese	½ cup cottage cheese
1 teaspoon salt	1 teaspoon salt
½ teaspoon white pepper	½ teaspoon white pepper
1 egg white	1 egg white
12 oz (375 g) plain strong flour	12 oz plain strong flour

If you are making the pastry in a food processor, simply process until everything is mixed and then pat out the ball a little, cover with film and refrigerate for at least 30 minutes – longer if possible.

If making by hand beat everything together except the flour and then beat this in bit by bit, ending by kneading in the final amount of flour with your hands. Refrigerate for at least 1 hour.

When you come to use this flour, it should be rolled out on a very cold, highly-floured surface and the cut-out shape should be lifted onto the baking tray with a palette knife or egg turner. It will need from 25-35 minutes in a hot oven (350°F/180°C/Gas 4) depending on the size. Piroshkis, of course, take less time than tarts.

CHEESE ROUGH PUFF PASTRY (Poland)

My stepmother used to make this pastry for piroshki and vegetable tarts. I have always supposed it to be Polish because she was, but in fact it turns out to be her own invention. Very good, very light and very rich, but not easy to work with. It is equally good with meat and fish fillings.

Imperial/Metric	*American*
4 oz (125 g) butter	½ cup butter
4 oz (125 g) cream cheese	½ cup cream cheese
12 oz (375 g) plain strong flour	1¾ cups plain strong flour
2 tablespoons iced water	2 tablespoons iced water
1 tablespoon white vinegar	1 tablespoon white vinegar
salt	salt

Rub the butter into the flour. Mix the vinegar and water and use enough of this mixture to make a stiff dry pastry dough. Roll out, cover with film or waxed paper and refrigerate for 30 minutes. Alternatively refrigerate the ball of dough for up to an hour and roll out. Cut the cream cheese into small cubes or, if it is not stiff enough, use about ½ teaspoon at a time. Roll out the dough into a long rectangle and mark into thirds. In the central third put 3 or 4 lines of blobs or cubes of cheese using half the amount. Bring up one of the other thirds on top to cover this cheese and pastry mixture and do the same with the rest of the cheese. Finally bring up the last third of the pastry to cover the second layer of cheese. If you find it easier you can cut the pastry into three and do it that way but the cheese has a tendency to ooze out at the edges. Refrigerate, covered, for at least 30 minutes. Roll out quickly on a well floured board and use at once. Refrigerate the piroshki or tart for at least 15 minutes before putting in the oven. Really easier to do than to describe.

COTTAGE CHEESE PASTRY (Lithuania, Finland and Scandinavia)

Imperial/Metric	*American*
8 oz (250 g) cottage cheese	1 cup cottage cheese
4 oz (125 g) butter	½ cup butter
12 oz (375 g) plain flour	1½ cups plain flour
1 teaspoon sea salt	1 teaspoon sea salt

Blend the cheese with the butter. This is easy in a food processor but if done by hand you can warm the bowl which will help the process. Mix in the flour and knead well. You may need a minute amount of water to get a good dough. Roll out thinly and use where required. This pastry requires brushing with beaten egg yolk before baking at about 400°F/200°C/Gas 6. Do not overcook or the result will be bitter.

PATE BRISEE

SHORT CRUST PASTRY

The best pastry for quiches and the most traditional. The word for pastry in French is pâte. An almost fail-proof pastry provided it is not handled too much.

Imperial/Metric	*American*
8 oz (250 g) plain flour	1 cup plain flour
4 oz (125 g) butter	½ cup butter
½ teaspoon salt	½ teaspoon salt
1½-2 fl. oz (approx. 50 ml) iced water	1½-2 fl. oz iced water
1 medium egg (optional)	1 medium egg (optional)

Either by hand or in a food processor mix the butter into the flour to which you have added the salt. Add enough water to make a firm pastry (the amount depends on the quality of the flour) and chill for at least 30 minutes. Roll out quickly before use. A medium egg can be used instead of water to make a richer pastry if wished.

PUFF PASTRY

Since the making of puff pastry is time-consuming, it is worth making in double quantities and freezing half. Puff pastry will keep for up to 3-4 days in the coldest part of the refrigerator, properly wrapped. It freezes marvellously, both uncooked and cooked. The golden rule is never try to hurry the process. Always mark the direction (with an arrow mark made with a knife) in which you last rolled the dough.

This recipe will make 9-12 vol-au-vent cases.

Imperial/Metric	*American*
1 lb (500 g) plain flour	2 cups plain flour
8 oz (250 g) butter	1 cup butter
½ teaspoon salt	½ teaspoon salt
10 fl. oz (300 ml) iced water	1¼ cups iced water
2 tablespoons lemon juice	2 tablespoons lemon juice

Mix the lemon juice and water together. Keep the butter in one pat (for the avoirdupois measurements you will have to cut a little off the pat). Roll the butter in the flour, pressing the flour well in, so it is entirely coated. Cover with film and refrigerate for a quarter of an hour.

Mix the rest of the flour with the salt and the lemon juice and water. You should have a slightly sticky dough (not as dry as you would for pastry), and you may not need all the water – it depends on the absorbing capacities of the flour. Knead this dough as you would for bread (this is where a machine comes in useful) for at least a quarter of an hour by hand and slightly less than 5 minutes by machine. You should end up with a very elastic dough. Put in refrigerator and let rest for a quarter of an hour.

Take out and roll roughly into a thick rectangle. Place a small coffee saucer or something similar in the middle of the rectangle as a guide, and from that roll out in 4 directions, leaving a central mound. Place the butter pat on this mound and then bring the 4 pieces up to meet it, overlapping them where necessary. You should end up with a piece of butter cushioned top and bottom. Refrigerate again for a quarter of an hour.

Flour a board or work surface well or flour a cloth as you would for strudel – whichever you find easier. Roll your pastry/butter block into a rectangle which will be approximately 18-20 inches (45-50 cm) long by 9-10 inches (23-25 cm) wide. Roll evenly and always in the same direction. It requires practice not to roll too wide and too short. Mark gently with a knife the middle of the rectangle. Bring each end to it and then fold the double end nearest to you onto the top of the other one – thus obtaining 4 layers. Mark with an arrow the direction of your last fold. Wrap in clingfilm or a damp teatowel and refrigerate for half an hour.

Bring your rectangle of dough out of the refrigerator and roll it at *right angles* to the arrow you have made, i.e. in the opposite direction to before. Keep much to the same size as before. Fold into 4 as before. Mark with an arrow the rolling direction, then refrigerate half an hour.

Do this turning, rolling, folding and chilling at least 4 times (6 is better). The final chilling should be for at least 2½-3 hours. So you see that before baking, puff pastry takes at least 6¼ hours, which is why it is a good idea to make a double quantity.

For final use, roll as thinly as possible – ¼-⅛ inch (6-4 mm) – and bake at 450°F/230°C/Gas 8 for the first 10 minutes, then reduce the heat to 350°F/180°C/Gas 4 until cooked. Puff pastry should always be glazed with beaten egg yolk but this must be done with the utmost care. If any is allowed to drip down the sides, this will prevent the pastry from rising.

To use up bits of left-over puff pastry, always mark the direction of the last rolling with an arrow and pile these on top of each other so that the arrows are all facing in the same direction. That way they will all rise up – otherwise it will be total anarchy and awful to see!

ROUGH PUFF PASTRY OR HALF-PUFF PASTRY

Imperial/Metric
12 oz (375 g) plain flour
6 oz (180 g) butter
1 egg, beaten
milk or water
salt

American
1½ cups plain flour
¾ cup butter
1 egg, beaten
milk or water
salt

This can be used for quiches. Divide the butter in half and rub one half into the flour and salt. Mix in the egg and enough water to make a normal, dryish pastry. Roll out into a long rectangle. With a knife, mark gently into thirds and on the centre third put tiny pieces of butter in 4 or 5 rows. Bring up the other two-thirds on top, press the edges together and roll out into another rectangle. Fold into 3 again and roll again. Do this twice more, handling the pastry as little as possible and always keeping in the same direction. Put in refrigerator for at least 1 hour before using. The secret of this pastry is to roll quickly and chill well before using.

Cook at 425°F/220°C/Gas 7 for 15-20 minutes – watching

carefully that it does not get too brown.

To use uncooked scraps up, always stack them in the direction you have been rolling.

YEAST PASTRY

Imperial/Metric
1 lb (500 g) plain flour
1 oz (30 g) fresh yeast or 1
   packet dried yeast
1 dessertspoon salt
Scant 8 fl. oz (225 ml) tepid
   water
2 tablespoons olive or
   sunflower oil
1 teaspoon sugar

American
2 cups plain flour
1 oz fresh yeast or 1 packet
   dried yeast
1 dessertspoon salt
Scant 1 cup tepid water
2 tablespoons olive or
   sunflower oil
1 teaspoon sugar

Mix yeast with sugar and a small amount of water in a teacup and put to prove. Bubbles should form within 5 minutes if the yeast is good. If at the end of 10 minutes the yeast has not doubled in volume discard it and start with some fresh. Sift the flour with the salt into a large bowl and make a well in the centre. Mix the yeast with the oil and three-quarters of the water and pour into the well. Mix into flour until you get a ball of elastic dough. You may need a little more water but add drop by drop in order to avoid getting too wet a dough. Turn the ball of dough onto a floured board and knead for approximately 10 minutes. Alternatively if you have a food processor or a mixer with a dough hook the dough can be kneaded fast for 5 minutes. Put the kneaded dough back into a clean bowl, cover with a cloth and let rise in a warm (not hot), draughtproof place. This will take anything from 45 minutes in summer to 1½ hours in winter in a cool kitchen. 'Knock down' the dough by plunging your fist or a wooden spoon into the mixture. Turn on a floured board and roll out to the size and shape wanted. Before rising the dough should be about ⅛ inch thick, i.e. very thin indeed. Yeast dough is horrifically elastic with a will of its own and needs a firm hand to keep it flat and well rolled out. Place on the baking dish and let rise once more. It should at least double in size before being baked in a very hot oven 450°F/230°C/Gas 8.

PIROSHKI (Russia and Poland)

Eaten in prodigious quantities with various soups or on their own Russians and Poles seem to live on piroshki. They can be made as tiny cocktail nibbles and served hot or slightly larger for soup and even larger as a first course in which case have some sour cream or sauce to hand. They freeze wonderfully.

Use either of the cheese pastries or ordinary shortcrust. A tumbler makes an excellent cutter for the first course size and a sherry glass for the soup size. Put the filling onto one side of the circle, moisten the edge all round with egg white or water and press the other half over to form a half moon shape.

Piroshki can be filled with minced beef, pork, veal, chicken liver, game, etc or mushrooms in sour cream or chopped cooked cabbage with hard boiled eggs. Virtually all the strudel and dumpling fillings work equally well for piroshki. The only rules are that the filling should not be too bulky and that it should be cold before being used. Always refrigerate or cool piroshki before baking – depending on size they take anything from 20-40 minutes in a hot oven 325-350°F/170°-180°C/Gas 3-4.

Quiches and Flans

The pastry for all these quiches can be Pâte brisée (Shortcrust) or Rough Puff Pastry. I always bake the pastry blind for 15 minutes without letting it brown. This, coupled with brushing the base with yolk of egg, helps prevent a stodgy base. You can use puff pastry or half-puff pastry (pp.190-2) and again you should partially bake it. I always use butter for pastry but there is no reason why you should not use a mixture of butter and lard or all lard – but please never margarine, which makes awful-tasting pastry.

Rather than baking 1 huge tart or quiche, I prefer to use 2 tins, each measuring 7½ inches (18 cms) × 1½ inches (3-4 cms) deep.

QUICHE AUX ENDIVES (Belgium)

This is made in precisely the same way as the Flamiche (p.217) but the endives are braised in butter beforehand and allowed to colour slightly before being stirred into the egg and cream mixture. No nutmeg is used but a little parsley instead.

MUSHROOM TART (UK)

Imperial/Metric	*American*
quiche pastry for 8 (p.190)	quiche pastry for 8 (p.190)
1 lb (500 g) mushrooms	1 lb mushrooms
1 packet (1 oz/30 g) Italian dried mushrooms	1 packet (1 oz) Italian dried mushrooms
2 tablespoons flour	2 tablespoons flour
4 eggs	4 eggs
½ pint (300 ml) double cream	1¼ cups heavy cream
pinch of thyme	pinch of thyme
1 teaspoon instant shallots (optional)	1 teaspoon instant shallots (optional)
butter for frying	butter for frying
2 tablespoons Madeira	2 tablespoons Madeira wine
salt and pepper	salt and pepper

Soak the dried mushrooms well, drain, rinse and chop small. Clean the other mushrooms, slice and sauté in the butter until three-quarters done. Sprinkle the flour over the mushrooms and carefully mix in. Add the cream, thyme, Madeira, salt and pepper and blend well. Let cool slightly. Beat in the eggs one by one and then add the dried mushrooms and instant shallots. Pour into a partly cooked pastry shell and cook at 350°F/180°C/Gas 4 for 30 minutes.

SIENISALAATTI (Finland)

A TART OF MUSHROOMS IN SOUR CREAM

This is often served on toast or with rye bread instead.

Imperial/Metric	American
2 fully cooked quiche shells for 4 persons (p.190)	2 fully cooked quiche shells for 4 persons (p.190)
4 lb (2 kilos) mushrooms	4 lb mushrooms
4 shallots, finely chopped	4 shallots, finely chopped
4 oz (125 g) butter	4 oz butter
1 pint (600 ml) sour cream	2½ cups commercial sour cream
1 pint (600 ml) double cream	2½ cups heavy cream
2 egg yolks (if required)	2 egg yolks (if required)
generous grating of nutmeg	generous grating of nutmeg
salt and pepper	salt and pepper

Two days before you cook this dish, mix the creams together; refrigerate in summer but leave in a cool place in winter. You will end up with thick sour cream. Some cream simply will not thicken up sufficiently, and in that case you will need to thicken it in a *bain-marie* with a couple of egg yolks and then add this mixture to the hot mushrooms. It is worth experimenting with this dish beforehand since even the sloppy failures taste divine and once you know how your particular cream reacts you will not be let down at a dinner party.

On the day, cook the shallots in the butter and then add the sliced mushrooms. These will take approximately a quarter of an hour to cook. Pour off the juice and reduce it to about 2 tablespoons. Heat the quiche shell. Stir in the nutmeg and some white pepper. Add the cream and heat through – do not let boil. Pour the whole into the shell and serve at once.

QUICHE AUX OIGNONS (France)

ONION QUICHE

Imperial/Metric	American
quiche pastry for 8 (p.190)	quiche pastry for 8 (p.190)
1 lb (500 g) onions, finely sliced	1 lb onions, finely sliced
8 eggs	8 eggs
1 pint (600 ml) double cream	2½ cups heavy cream
nutmeg	nutmeg
salt and pepper	salt and pepper
butter for frying	butter for frying
parsley, chopped	parsley, chopped

Half-bake your pastry shell.

Fry the onion very gently and allow to cool slightly. Meanwhile pre-heat the oven to 400°F/200°C/Gas 6. On your half-baked pastry arrange the sliced onion. Beat together the other ingredients and pour gently into the pastry shell (tricky: it must not slop over the edge). Cook for 15 minutes at this heat, then lower the temperature to 325°F/170°C/Gas 3 and continue cooking for up to a further 30 minutes. Serve immediately.

PISSALADIERE (France: Comté de Nice and Provence)

PROVENÇAL ONION TART

This can be made on a base of short-crust pastry, puff pastry, bread or brioche dough or the local sort which is a mixture of flour, salt, olive oil and water.

Imperial/Metric	*American*
1 recipe of pastry (p.190 or p.191) or	1 recipe of pastry (p.190 or p.191) or
12 oz (375 g) plain flour*	1½ cups plain flour*
2 fl. oz (65 ml) olive oil*	¼ cup olive oil*
enough cold water to make a paste*	enough cold water to make a paste*
2-2½ lb (1-1.25 kilos) onions, finely sliced	2-2½ lb onions, finely sliced
approx. 30-35 black olives	approx. 30-35 black olives
30-35 anchovy fillets**	30-35 anchovy fillets**
olive oil to cook onions	olive oil to cook onions

* To make the Niçois/Italian pastry, mix the flour and salt with the olive oil and slightly warmed water. Knead the pastry well and refrigerate before using. Roll very thinly indeed.
** Soak the anchovies in warm milk to rid them of their saltiness.

Cook the onions in olive oil. Do not let them take colour – they should simply soften. Roll out the pastry and use an oblong baking tray. Spread the cooled onion mixture on top. Make a trellis of the anchovy fillets. In the middle of each trellis put a black olive. (Alternatively you can put the black olives on after the *pissaladière* has cooked.) Cook in a very hot oven 475°F/250°C/Gas 9 for 20 minutes and then reduce the heat a bit and cook until you are sure the base is cooked. It is eaten warm, tepid or cold.

CHOLERA (Switzerland)

ALPINE POTATO TART

Only the Swiss would dare to put such a name on an hotel menu! Heaven knows where this name originates but it has nothing to do with the disease. This is a famous dish of the Valais and what they call a *mets alpage*. *Fromage de Conches* is not easy to get outside Switzerland but a mixture of Gruyère and a mild cheese like Bel Paese will do quite well. Bake in a large tin about 12 inches (30 cm) in diameter. It is quite filling, so follow with something light such as grilled meat and salad or fish.

Imperial/Metric	*American*
1 lb (450 g) quiche pastry (p.190)	1 lb quiche pastry (p.190)
2 or 3 potatoes, partially cooked	2 or 3 potatoes, partially cooked
1 large onion, finely chopped	1 large onion, finely chopped
2 oz (60 g) butter	¼ cup butter
1 large or 2 medium eating apples	1 large or 2 medium eating apples
4 oz (120 g) Gruyère cheese	½ cup Gruyère cheese
3 oz (90 g) mild cheese	3 oz mild cheese
6 fl. oz (180 ml) double cream	¾ cup heavy cream
1 egg yolk	1 egg yolk
1 whole egg	1 whole egg
salt and pepper to taste	salt and pepper to taste

It is not essential to bake or partially cook the pastry but I think it makes for a better result. Cook the chopped onion in the butter but do not let it brown. Grate or cut the potatoes into tiny cubes. Peel the apples, cut into 4, remove the pips and slice finely. Grate the Gruyère cheese and grate or cut the other cheese. Spread the onion on the base of the pastry, follow with the potatoes, then the cheese and finally the sliced apples.

With the left-over bits of pastry make thin strips and arrange them criss-cross fashion over the top. Paint with yolk of egg and cook for 30 minutes at 425°F/220°C/Gas 7. Beat the egg together with the rest of the egg yolk and the double (heavy) cream and add salt and pepper. Pour this mixture into the spaces left by the pastry strips and cook for a further 10 minutes at 350°F/180°C/Gas 4.

KULBIAKA OF RED CABBAGE (Russia)

RED CABBAGE IN A PASTRY CASE

If you and your guests are red cabbage fans (and many are not), this is one of the prettiest first courses imaginable. By tradition it is made with a yeast and egg pastry (i.e. unsweetened brioche) but ordinary shortcrust, puff or half-puff pastry will do just as well.

Use an enamelled or stainless steel pan only.

Imperial/Metric
1 recipe quiche pastry (p.190)
1 red cabbage, approx. 2 lb (1 kilo)
2 onions, finely chopped
lard or oil
2 tablespoons vinegar
2 tablespoons sugar
caraway seed (optional)
8 oz (250 g) minced veal (optional)
no salt but plenty of pepper
sour cream

American
1 recipe quiche pastry (p.190)
1 red cabbage, approx. 2 lb
2 onions, finely chopped
lard or oil
2 tablespoons vinegar
2 tablespoons sugar
caraway seed (optional)
8 oz minced veal (optional)
no salt but plenty of pepper
sour cream

Fry the onions in the lard or oil until limp. Add the veal if used. Slice or finely grate the red cabbage, discarding the woody centre bits. Cook gently in the fat or oil with the onions and meat, with the lid on, for approximately 20 minutes, stirring from time to time. (It catches very easily.) Once it is almost cooked, stir in the sugar and then the vinegar. Taste and adjust seasoning: it should be sweet and sour. Add the caraway seeds (optional) and plenty of freshly ground pepper. Let cool thoroughly.

This dish can be made in advance up to this point and in fact improves by resting overnight. Roll out the dough in 2 rectangles as described in the salmon recipe on p.203 and put your cabbage and/or cabbage/meat mixture on it. Put on the top and trim. Brush with beaten egg, make 2 or 3 holes in the top and bake at 350°F/180°C/Gas 4 for 35-40 minutes, turning it round once so that one side does not brown more than the other.

QUICHE AUX EPINARDS (France)

SPINACH QUICHE

Imperial/Metric	*American*
quiche pastry for 8 (p.190)	quiche pastry for 8 (p.190)
1 lb (500 g) spinach, cooked and chopped	1 lb spinach, cooked and chopped
8 eggs	8 eggs
1 pint (600 ml) double cream	2½ cups heavy cream
nutmeg	nutmeg
salt and pepper	salt and pepper

Half bake your pastry shell. Pre-heat your oven to 400°F/200°C/ Gas 6.

Beat the chopped spinach into the other ingredients and pour gently into the pastry shell (tricky: it must not slop over the edge). Cook for 15 minutes at this heat, then lower the temperature to 325°F/170°C/Gas 3 and continue cooking for up to a further 30 minutes. Serve immediately.

LEIPZIGER ALLERLEITORTE (Germany)

TART OF SPRING VEGETABLES IN BUTTER SAUCE

Imperial/Metric	*American*
quiche pastry for 8 (p.190)	quiche pastry for 8 (p.190)
1 lb (500 g) vegetables*	1 lb vegetables*
1 pint (600 ml) *sauce béchamel* (p.391)	2½ cups *sauce béchamel* (p.391)
3 egg yolks	3 egg yolks
2 tablespoons cream	2 tablespoons cream
1 tablespoon parsley, chopped	1 tablespoon parsley, chopped
salt and pepper	salt and pepper

* For your mixed vegetables, choose from peas, carrots, baby turnips, parsnips, asparagus, artichoke, courgettes, broad beans, celery, spring onions etc.

Half-bake your pastry shell. Cook vegetables (separately from each other). Pre-heat oven to 375°F/190°C/Gas 5.

Dice the cooked vegetables and combine them with the *sauce béchamel* into which you have stirred the egg yolks, parsley and cream. Add salt and pepper to taste. Turn into the pastry shell and bake for 20-25 minutes.

QUICHE AU VACHERIN (Switzerland)

VACHERIN CHEESE QUICHE

This is remarkably similar to a Quiche au Maroilles which the French have, although this latter has no onion in it, which I think is an improvement. Serve with a small green salad as decoration.

Imperial/Metric
quiche pastry for 8 (p.190)
4 oz (125 g) lightly smoked
  bacon
8 eggs
8 oz (225-250 g) Vacherin
  cheese
1 medium onion, finely
  chopped
½ pint (300 ml) double cream
nutmeg
salt and pepper

American
quiche pastry for 8 (p.190)
4 oz lightly smoked bacon
8 eggs
8 oz Vacherin cheese
1 medium onion, finely
  chopped
1¼ cups heavy cream
nutmeg
salt and pepper

Half bake your pastry shell. Pre-heat your oven to 400°F/200°C/ Gas 6.

Fry together the onion and bacon until half done. Arrange on the pastry shell. Remove rind from Vacherin, beat together with the other ingredients and pour gently into the pastry shell. Cook for 15 minutes at this heat, then lower the temperature to 325°F/170°C/Gas 3 and continue cooking for up to a further 30 minutes. Serve immediately.

QUICHE AU GRUYERE (Switzerland)

Exactly as for Quiche au Vacherin (above) but substitute approx. 8 oz (250 g) grated best-quality Gruyère for the Vacherin.

QUICHE LORRAINE 1 (France: Nancy, Lorraine)

BACON AND EGG FLAN

Although very rich, this is an amazingly light tart.

Imperial/Metric
quiche pastry for 8 (p.190)
8 oz (225 g) lightly smoked
  bacon or lightly smoked
  belly of pork
8 eggs
1 pint (600 ml) double cream
nutmeg
salt and pepper

American
quiche pastry for 8 (p.190)
8 oz lightly smoked bacon or
  lightly smoked belly of pork
8 eggs
2½ cups heavy cream
nutmeg
salt and pepper

Half bake your flan. Cool.

Pre-heat your oven to 400°F/200°C/Gas 6. On your half-baked pastry arrange the chopped bacon (or pork). It should be slightly on the fat side but less so than streaky bacon. Beat together the other ingredients and pour gently into the pastry shell (tricky: it must not slop over the edge). Cook for 15 minutes at this heat then lower the temperature to 325°F/170°C/Gas 3 and continue cooking for up to a further 30 minutes. Serve immediately.

Variation

Although this is not strictly speaking a true *quiche lorraine*, it is the type most commonly encountered under that name.

To the recipe for Quiche Lorraine add 6 oz (170 g) grated Gruyère cheese and lessen the bacon (or belly of pork) by 2 oz (50 g).

KULBIAKA OF VEAL AND HAM (Russia)

VEAL AND HAM IN PASTRY

This is not unlike a very superior veal-and-ham pie but served hot with a sour cream and dill sauce.

Imperial/Metric
quiche dough for 8 or puff
  pastry (p.190)
1½ lb (750 g) best-quality ham,
  cubed
1½ lb (750 g) shoulder of veal,
  cubed
3 medium onions, sliced fine
5 eggs, hard-boiled and sliced
4 oz (125 g) butter
8 fl. oz (240 ml) stock (cubes
  will do)
a pinch each of nutmeg and
  thyme
3 tablespoons parsley, chopped

American
quiche dough for 8 or puff
  pastry (p.190)
1½ lb best-quality ham, cubed
1½ lb shoulder of veal, cubed
3 medium onions, sliced fine
5 eggs, hardcooked and sliced
½ cup butter
1 cup stock (cubes will do)
a pinch each of nutmeg and
  thyme
3 tablespoons parsley, chopped

Cook the onions until almost done, then add the veal, nutmeg and thyme. Stir in the ham and add enough stock to make the whole stick together. Put in a layer of meat mixture followed by egg and parsley, and continue this way. Put on the top piece of dough and paint with egg etc. Cook for 45 minutes at 350°F/180°C/Gas 4.

SAUCE

Imperial/Metric	American
1 pint (600 ml) sour cream	2 cups sour cream
2 teaspoons dried dillweed	2 teaspoons dried dillweed
1 teaspoon vinegar	1 teaspoon vinegar
salt	salt

For the sauce, stir the dried dillweed, vinegar and some salt into the sour cream. Let this stand at least an hour before use. Almost better next day re-heated.

KULBIAKA OF SALMON (Russia)

SALMON IN PASTRY

This is served hot with a sauce or sour cream as an accompaniment, or with cucumber in sour cream. It is filling, so thin slices are enough if you do not want to stuff your guests full from the start. Sometimes, to make the fish or meat go further, it has rice or *kasha* in it but the luxurious versions never do. This can also be made in exactly the same way with high-quality ground beef, as a main course.

It can be made the day before and re-heated for approximately 15 minutes in a hot oven at 400°F/200°C/Gas 6.

Imperial/Metric	American
quiche pastry (p.190) or puff pastry (p.191) for 8	quiche pastry (p.190) or puff pastry (p.191) for 8
3 lb (1.5 kilos) raw salmon or trout	3 lb raw salmon or trout
3 onions, finely chopped	3 onions, finely chopped
4 eggs, hard-boiled	4 eggs, hardcooked
2 tablespoons parsley, finely chopped	2 tablespoons parsley, finely chopped
2 tablespoons dill, finely chopped	2 tablespoons dill, finely chopped
approx. 8 fl. oz (240 ml) double cream	approx. 1 cup heavy cream
juice of 1 lemon	juice of 1 lemon
1 egg yolk beaten with a little water	1 egg yolk beaten with a little water
salt and white pepper	salt and white pepper

Roll out the dough into a large rectangle and cut it in half so that you have 2 narrow rectangles considerably longer than wide. Fry the onions gently but do not let them colour. Cut the salmon into half-inch (1 cm) cubes. Mix with the onion but do not cook. Pour on the lemon juice and enough cream to make the mixture stick together. Add a little salt and plenty of white pepper. Paint the dough with egg yolk. Put on a layer of cubed salmon and onions, then a layer of hard-boiled egg sprinkled with herbs. Continue in this fashion until everything is used up. Then put on the other strip of pastry and pinch the edges together, using a little egg yolk to help stick. Trim the edges and then press them again with the tines of a fork. Paint the whole packet with egg-yolk glaze, slash 2 or 3 holes to let the steam escape, and bake at 350°F/180°C/Gas 4 for 40-45 minutes on the middle shelf. You may need to turn the baking tray round once so that one side does not brown more than the other.

JUNE FISH PIE (UK: Scotland)

SALMON AND CUCUMBER PIE

Imperial/Metric	*American*
quiche pastry for 8 (p.190)	quiche pastry for 8 (p.190)
12 oz (375 g) salmon cooked and flaked	12 oz salmon cooked and flaked
approx. 8 oz (250 g) cucumber	approx. 8 oz cucumber
8 eggs	8 eggs
½ pint (300 ml) double cream	1¼ cups heavy cream
butter (for frying)	butter (for frying)
nutmeg	nutmeg
salt and pepper	salt and pepper
fennel leaves, freshly chopped	fennel leaves, freshly chopped

Half bake pastry shell.

Peel and remove seeds from cucumber. Cut into small cubes, sprinkle with salt and let drain for approximately 30 minutes. Then fry in a small amount of butter. Let cool. Meanwhile pre-heat your oven to 400°F/200°C/Gas 3. On your half-baked pastry shell arrange the chopped cucumber and flaked salmon. Beat together the other ingredients and pour gently into the pastry shell. Cook for 15 minutes at this heat, then lower the temperature to 325°F/170°C/Gas 3 and continue cooking for up to a further 30 minutes. Serve immediately.

QUICHE AU THON (France)

TUNNYFISH (TUNA) PIE

Imperial/Metric	*American*
quiche pastry for 8 (p.190)	quiche pastry for 8 (p.190)
12 oz tuna	12 oz tuna
8 eggs	8 eggs
½ pint (300 ml) double cream	1¼ cups heavy cream
nutmeg	nutmeg
salt and pepper	salt and pepper

Half bake your pastry shell. Pre-heat oven to 400°F/200°C/Gas 6.

Separate yolks from whites and beat whites stiffly. Liquidize the tunnyfish with the other ingredients and fold in the beaten egg whites. Pour gently into the pastry shell and cook for 15 minutes at this heat, then lower the temperature to 325°F/170°C/Gas 3 and continue cooking for up to a further 30 minutes. Serve immediately.

QUICHE AU CRABE (France)

CRAB QUICHE

Imperial/Metric	*American*
quiche pastry for 8 (p.190)	quiche pastry for 8 (p.190)
approx. 12 oz (750 g) crab meat*	approx. 12 oz crab meat*
8 eggs	8 eggs
1 pint (600 ml) double cream	2½ cups heavy cream
nutmeg	nutmeg
salt and pepper	salt and pepper
a little parsley or chopped dill (optional)	a little parsley or chopped dill (optional)

* Fresh or frozen – tinned crab hardly tastes in a quiche.

Half bake your quiche pastry. Pre-heat your oven to 400°F/200°C/Gas 6. On your half-baked pastry arrange the chopped crab meat. Beat together the other ingredients and pour gently into the pastry shell. Cook for 15 minutes at this heat, then lower the temperature to 325°F/170°C/Gas 3 and continue cooking for up to a further 30 minutes. Serve immediately.

QUICHE AUX FRUITS DE MER (France)

SHELLFISH QUICHE

Imperial/Metric	*American*
quiche pastry for 8 (p.190)	quiche pastry for 8 (p.190)
12 oz (375 g) lobster, crayfish or prawns	12 oz lobster, crayfish or shrimps
8 eggs	8 eggs
1 pint (600 ml) double cream	2½ cups heavy cream
nutmeg	nutmeg
salt and pepper	salt and pepper

Half bake your pastry shell. Pre-heat oven to 400°F/200°C/Gas 6.

On your half-baked pastry shell arrange the chopped shellfish of your choice. Beat together the other ingredients and pour gently into the pastry shell (tricky: it must not slop over the edge). Cook for 15 minutes at this heat, then lower the temperature to 325°F/170°C/Gas 3 and continue cooking for up to a further 30 minutes. Serve immediately.

Choux

Virtually any filling suitable for vol-au-vent is suitable for choux puffs. The most important thing to remember is not to have the filling too liquid since it will become more so on cooking unless there is an egg liaison to take into account. The recipe for making choux pastry is on p.188.

The following fillings are based on a recipe of *sauce béchamel* (p.391) plus added ingredients. Often, as below, egg yolks and cream are added but this need not always be the case. For instance, where there is a Madeira or other wine sauce, it is used on its own. The filling should be put in *hot* and the whole thing baked in a medium oven – around 350°F/170-175°C/Gas 4 for 7-10 minutes. Whether you pipe out your choux shells or just drop small heaps is not important (I know someone who rolls hers out but personally I get a very wodgy result from that technique), nor does it matter if you do not bother to brush an egg glaze on before baking. Overcooking of the shells results in a somewhat too crisp product rather than something really ruined. I find cutting off approximately a quarter for the lid is the easiest way to fill the choux, and this lid can be replaced once they have been filled.

Any filling given for choux, vols au vent etc will also do for bread croûtes if wished.

SCHWAMMELCHOUX (Austria)

MUSHROOM CHOUX

Imperial/Metric	American
1 recipe choux pastry, shells, baked (p.188)	1 recipe choux pastry, shells, baked (p.188)
1 recipe *sauce béchamel* (p.391), cold	1 recipe *sauce béchamel* (p.391), cold
8 fl. oz (240 ml) double cream	1 cup heavy cream
1 lb (500 g) mushrooms, raw, sliced	1 lb mushrooms, raw, sliced
8 oz (225 g) ham, diced	8 oz ham, diced
1 shallot	1 shallot
1 tablespoon Madeira	1 tablespoon Madeira
2 egg yolks	2 egg yolks

Crush the shallot and cook it in a little butter in a small saucepan. Add the Madeira and set aside. To the cold *sauce béchamel* add half the cream, then the shallot and Madeira mixture, the 2 egg yolks and finally the mushrooms and ham. The mixture should be stiff. If it will take it, add the rest of the cream but the mixture should remain stiff to allow for the liquid from the mushrooms. Heat through in a saucepan and then fill the choux with the mixture. Bake 7-10 minutes at 350°F/180°C/Gas 4.

GOUGERES BOURGUINONNES (France)

CHEESE CHOUX

A lot of people think *gougère* is similar to Yorkshire pudding. It is not, since it is based on choux pastry.

A very useful first course as it demands a red wine (preferably a Burgundy) from the start and avoids having to serve a white wine, as so often is the case with many hot first courses.

Imperial/Metric	American
1 recipe choux pastry (p.188)	1 recipe choux pastry (p.188)
4 oz (125 g) Gruyère or Comté cheese	½ cup Gruyère or Comté cheese
good pinch of nutmeg	good pinch of nutmeg
egg yolk (optional)	egg yolk (optional)
salt and pepper to taste	salt and pepper to taste

To your still-warm choux pastry add the cheese cut into small dice, rather than grated, and mix very thoroughly. Divide into about 24 small heaps or pipe them through a coarse piping nozzle. (For piping purposes it is better, of course, to use grated cheese.) If you want shining choux, paint them with beaten egg yolk. Place on a well greased baking sheet and cook in a hot oven at 425°F/220°C/ Gas 7 for 15-20 minutes.

CHOUX AUX POIREAUX EN SAUCE MORNAY (Belgium)

CHOUX FILLED WITH LEEKS IN A CHEESE SAUCE

This recipe usually fills a dozen large shells.

Imperial/Metric	*American*
choux for 12 large shells (p.188)	choux for 12 large shells (p.188)
1½ lb (750 g) leeks*	1½ lb leeks*
1 recipe *sauce mornay* (p.397)	1 recipe *sauce mornay* (p.397)
a little butter for cooking the leeks	a little butter for cooking the leeks
salt and pepper	salt and pepper

Bake the shells.
* You will need at least 3 lb (1.5 kilos) leeks, if not more, to produce 1½ lb (750 g) of cooked vegetable.

Soak, clean and drain leeks well. Cut the white part into thin rounds and stew them in some butter. Watch carefully as they 'catch' very easily. Equally do not let them disintegrate. Stir in the *sauce mornay* and fill the shells. Cook for approximately 10 minutes at 375°F/190°C/Gas 5.

CHOUX AU BLANCS DE POULET ET AUX ASPERGES (France)

CHICKEN AND ASPARAGUS CHOUX

A lovely summer first course when asparagus is still too expensive to give to 8 people. Out of season tinned asparagus does quite well.

Imperial/Metric	American
1 recipe choux (p.188)	1 recipe choux (p.188)
1 lb (500 g) chicken breast, cooked and diced	1 lb chicken breast, cooked and diced
8 oz (250 g) asparagus tips, cooked	8 oz asparagus tips, cooked
1 recipe *sauce aurore* (p.391) or *sauce suprème* (p.392)	1 recipe *sauce aurore* (p.391) or *sauce suprème* (p.392)
salt and pepper	salt and pepper

Bake the shells.

Heat the chicken and the almost-cooked asparagus pieces in whichever sauce you choose to use and fill the choux. Bake 7-10 minutes at 350°F/180°C/Gas 4.

CHOUX AUX FOIES DE VOLAILLES ET AU MADERE (France and Switzerland)

CHOUX WITH CHICKEN LIVER IN MADEIRA SAUCE

Imperial/Metric	American
1 recipe choux (p.188)	1 recipe choux (p.188)
8 oz (250 g) chicken livers, cut up	8 oz chicken livers, cut up
1 lb (500 g) mushrooms, finely sliced	1 lb mushrooms, finely sliced
2 shallots (or onions), finely chopped	2 shallots (or onions), finely chopped
2 oz (60 g) butter	¼ cup butter
pinch powdered thyme	pinch powdered thyme
2 tablespoons parsley, chopped	2 tablespoons parsley, chopped
3 tablespoons Madeira	3 tablespoons Madeira

Bake the shells.

Soften the shallots (or onions) in half the butter. Turn up heat slightly, add the cut-up chicken livers and cook until stiffened. In the rest of the butter start cooking the mushrooms. Quite a lot of liquid will come out. Once the mushrooms have stopped losing their liquid, drain them and mix in with the chicken livers. Reduce the mushrooms liquid to about 2 tablespoons by rapidly boiling in a wide pan. Some people add *beurre manié* at this stage but it makes for a floury and heavier end product. Pour this liquid into the mushrooms and add the Madeira. Heat through and divide between 8 shells. Cook for 7-10 minutes at 375°F/190°C/ Gas 5.

CRAB AND CUCUMBER CHOUX (USA)

Imperial/Metric	American
1 recipe choux (p.188)	1 recipe choux (p.188)
1 lb (500 g) frozen white crab*	1 lb frozen white crab*
2 shallots	2 shallots
1 cucumber, peeled, de-seeded, chopped and drained	1 cucumber, peeled, de-seeded, chopped and drained
half recipe *sauce béchamel* (p.391)	half recipe *sauce béchamel* (p.391)
2 tablespoons double cream	2 tablespoons heavy cream
1 teaspoon dillweed	1 teaspoon dillweed
a little butter for frying	a little butter for frying
salt and pepper	salt and pepper

* Use a white Alaska crab or similar (the Japanese have a good one). Or you can substitute minced clams, in which case use some of the clam liquid for the *sauce béchamel*.

Bake the shells.

Chop cucumber, sprinkle with salt and drain for 1 hour. Defrost the crab and cut into small pieces. Fry the cucumber and shallots in the butter until half cooked. Mix with crab and *sauce béchamel* and add dillweed, salt and pepper. Bake for 7-10 minutes at 375°F/190°C/Gas 5.

CHOUX AUX CREVETTES A LA CREME (France)

CHOUX FILLED WITH PRAWNS IN A CREAM SAUCE

Imperial/Metric	American
1 recipe choux (p.188)	1 recipe choux (p.188)
1 lb (500 g) prepared prawns	1 lb prepared large shrimps
1 recipe *sauce béchamel* (p.391)	1 recipe *sauce béchamel* (p.391)
8 fl. oz (240 ml) double cream	1 cup heavy cream
2 teaspoons double-concentrate tomato purée	2 teaspoons double-concentrate tomato purée
1 teaspoon fresh or freeze-dried dillweed	1 teaspoon fresh or freeze-dried dillweed

If using frozen prawns (shrimps) defrost and let drain well before use. Bake the shells. Combine all ingredients, heat through and fill shells. Cook the shells for 7-10 minutes in a moderate oven (375°F/190°C/Gas 5).

Vols-au-Vent

Vols-au-vent are made with puff pastry (p.191).

HAM VOLS-AU-VENT (UK)

Imperial/Metric	*American*
8 vol-au-vent cases (p.191), baked and cooled	8 vol-au-vent cases (p.191), baked and cooled
1 lb (500 g) or more ham, diced	1 lb or more ham, diced
1 pint (600 ml) enriched *sauce béchamel* (p.391)	2½ cups enriched *sauce béchamel* (p.391)
2 tablespoons parsley, chopped	2 tablespoons parsley, chopped

Preheat the oven 375°F/190°C/Gas 5. Mix the parsley and ham into the *sauce béchamel* and divide between the vol-au-vent cases. Bake for 20 minutes.

VOLS-AU-VENT A LA GENEVOISE (Switzerland)

VOLS-AU-VENT WITH HAM IN MADEIRA SAUCE

I find that port is just as good as Madeira in this dish.

Imperial/Metric	*American*
8 vol-au-vent cases (p.191), baked and cooled	8 vol-au-vent cases (p.191), baked and cooled
1 lb (500 g) good-quality ham	1 lb good-quality ham
1 pint (600 ml) Madeira sauce (p.394)	2½ cups Madeira sauce (p.394)
4 oz (125 g) mushrooms, chopped and cooked	4 oz mushrooms, chopped and cooked

Make the Madeira sauce on the thick side. Stir in the chopped mushrooms and ham and turn into the vol-au-vent cases. Cook 15 minutes at 350°F/180°C/Gas 4.

VOLS-AU-VENT A LA SAVOYARDE

VOLS-AU-VENT WITH HAM AND CHEESE FILLING

Imperial/Metric	*American*
8 vol-au-vent cases (p.191), baked and cooled	8 vol-au-vent cases (p.191), baked and cooled
12 oz (375 g) good-quality ham	12 oz good-quality ham
1 pint (600 ml) *sauce béchamel* (p.391)	2½ cups *sauce béchamel* (p.391)
2 tablespoons (*yes!*) strong Dijon mustard	2 tablespoons (*yes!*) strong Dijon mustard
4 oz (125 g) Gruyère cheese, grated	½ cup Gruyère cheese, grated

Mix the mustard and Gruyère cheese into the just-cooked *sauce béchamel*. Cook a little longer, then add the diced ham. Divide between the 8 vols-au-vent and bake at 400°F/200°C/Gas 6 for 15 minutes. The mustard loses a great deal of its strength in cooking, and the result is not hot.

CRIEFF VOLS-AU-VENT (UK: Scotland)

SALMON VOLS-AU-VENT

This can be made with tinned salmon, in which case use a few more prawns and leave them whole, since the salmon rather melts into the sauce.

Imperial/Metric	*American*
8 medium vol-au-vent cases (p.191), baked and cooled	8 medium vol-au-vent cases (p.191), baked and cooled
1 lb (500 g) cooked salmon	1 lb cooked salmon
4 oz (125 g) mushrooms, sliced	4 oz mushrooms, sliced
8 oz (250 g) medium prawns	8 oz medium shrimp
6-8 anchovy fillets, chopped	6-8 anchovy fillets, chopped
1 pint (600 ml) enriched *sauce béchamel* (p.391)	2½ cups enriched *sauce béchamel* (p.391)
2 tablespoons whisky (or brandy)	2 tablespoons whisky (or brandy)
butter (for cooking)	butter (for cooking)

Make the *sauce béchamel*. Cook the mushrooms in a little butter and save the liquid. Mix into the sauce together with the flaked salmon, prawns and anchovy fillets. Add the whisky and divide between the 8 vol-au-vent cases. Bake at 350-375°F/180-190°C/Gas 4-5 for 20 minutes.

VOLS-AU-VENT A LA DIEPPOISE (France)

VOLS-AU-VENT WITH A SOLE AND PRAWN FILLING

Imperial/Metric
8 vol-au-vent cases (p.191), baked and cooled
1 lb (500 g) sole fillet
1 lb (500 g) medium prawns, deveined
½ pint (300 ml) white wine
½ pint (300 ml) double cream
2 shallots
4 oz (125 g) butter
2 scant tablespoons flour
a little parsley, chopped

American
8 vol-au-vent cases (p.191), baked and cooled
1 lb sole fillet
1 lb medium shrimps, deveined
1¼ cups white wine
1¼ cups heavy cream
2 shallots
½ cup butter
2 scant tablespoons flour
a little parsley, chopped

Soften the shallots in some of the butter. Then cook the sole and the prawns in a mixture of butter and white wine. Once done, remove with a slotted spoon and keep aside. Reduce this mixture to half its volume, add the flour and make a roux. Then add the cream. If it is too thick, add a little more wine. Cut the sole into small pieces, and the prawns in half. Mix into the sauce and divide between the cooked vols-au-vent. Cook for 20 minutes at 350-375°F/180-190°C/Gas 4-5.

VOLS-AU-VENT DE HOMARD (France)

LOBSTER VOLS-AU-VENT

Imperial/Metric
8 vols-au-vent cases (p.191), baked and cooled
1 lb (500 g) cooked lobster (including its coral, if any)
1 pint (600 ml) *sauce aurore* (p.391)
2 tablespoons double cream
2 egg yolks
2 tablespoons brandy
a little chopped fennel leaf

American
8 vols-au-vent cases (p.191), baked and cooled
1 lb cooked lobster (including its coral, if any)
2½ cups *sauce aurore* (p.391)
2 tablespoons heavy cream
2 egg yolks
2 tablespoons brandy
a little chopped fennel leaf

Make the sauce and let it cool. Keep everything cold. Mix the cream and brandy into the sauce and add the cream and 2 egg yolks. Finally stir in the chopped lobster. Divide between the 8 vols-au-vent and bake 20 minutes at 375°F/190°C/Gas 5.

VOLS AU VENT AUX FRUITS DE MER (France)

VOLS-AU-VENT WITH SEAFOOD

This is an unconventional way of making this dish but it avoids overcooked shellfish, which can be very unattractive.

Imperial/Metric	*American*
8 vol-au-vent cases (p.191) baked and cooled	8 vol-au-vent cases (p.191) baked and cooled
4 scallops and their coral	4 scallops and their coral
1 small lobster	1 small lobster
4 oysters	4 oysters
8 giant prawns	8 giant shrimps
24 mussels, cooked	24 mussels, cooked
1 pint (600 ml) *sauce americaine* (p.390)	2½ cups *sauce americaine* (p.390)

Into a *cold sauce americaine* mix in the just-cooked mussel, chopped lobster and chopped giant prawns. Half fill the vol-au-vent cases with this mixture and place in the middle of each half an oyster and half a scallop. Pour on the rest of the mixture. Pop on the vol-au-vent lids and bake 25 minutes at 375°F/190°C/Gas 5.

Strudel and Filo

KÁPOSZTATÖLTELÉK (Hungary)

CABBAGE STRUDEL

In Hungary cabbage strudel is often made with butter and sugar (no caraway) and served as a pudding or tea-time treat. It is in fact delicious once the immediate prejudice is overcome and well worth trying. My grandmother's family always included sultanas in them and served them with whipped cream. You could serve them with sour cream.

Imperial/Metric	American
approx. 1 lb (450 g) strudel or filo or burek dough	approx. 1 lb strudel or filo or burek dough
2 lb (1 kilo) white cabbage	2 lb white cabbage
8 oz (250 g) butter or pork dripping	1 cup butter or pork dripping
2 teaspoons caraway seeds	2 teaspoons caraway seeds
salt and plenty of freshly ground pepper	salt and plenty of freshly ground pepper
garlic (optional)	garlic (optional)

Grate the cabbage, salt it and let it drain in a colander. Rinse after about 30 minutes. Shake as dry as possible and cook gently in the butter or pork dripping. Add the caraway seeds, garlic (optional), salt and plenty of black pepper and let cool. Brush the strudel sheets with butter and fill with the cooked cabbage. Brush tops again with melted butter and bake at 375°F/190°C/Gas 5 for approximately 30 minutes.

SCHWAMMERLSTRUDEL (Austria)

MUSHROOM STRUDEL

If you can buy large sheets of strudel dough, so much the better. Otherwise you will probably have to make 4 strudel and give your guests half each. An average commercial strudel sheet size (3 thick) will feed 2 but they vary from country to country, so no precise instructions can be given. If you use burek or boreka pastry which is often round, you should count 2 sheets per person. If in doubt, the easiest thing is to divide your mushroom mixture into 4 or 8 portions and work out the pastry covering from there.

Imperial/Metric	American
2 lb (1 kilo) mushrooms	2 lb mushrooms
8 oz (250 g) butter	1 cup butter
2 tablespoons Madeira (optional)	2 tablespoons Madeira (optional)
8 fl. oz (240 ml) double cream	1 cup heavy cream
2 tablespoons parsley	2 tablespoons parsley
good pinch marjoram	good pinch marjoram
salt and pepper	salt and pepper

Cook mushrooms in approximately half the butter. Reduce any liquid left separately down to about 2 tablespoons. Alternatively you can add 2 tablespoons of Madeira. Add the parsley, marjoram and, once a little cooler, the cream. Set aside while you deal with the strudel.

Brush the sheets of strudel with melted butter and count on 2 or 3 sheets of strudel per roll. Put a line of the mushroom and cream filling on the strudel and roll up. Brush again with melted butter and put on a greased baking sheet. Continue thus until you have used all your ingredients up. Once the strudel is rolled up and painted with butter, bake it at 375°F/190°C/Gas 5 for approximately 30 minutes.

GIBANICA (Yugoslavia: Serbia)

BAKED CHEESE TART

In Yugoslavia this dish is made with a very rich cheese called kačkavalj and often spinach is included in it. Count on approximately 8 oz (250 g) cooked, drained spinach and put it between the first layers of pastry before pouring on the mixture in quantity.

Imperial/Metric	American
1 lb (500 g) strudel or filo pastry	1 lb strudel or filo pastry
8 oz (250 g) rich cream cheese	1 cup rich cream cheese
8 oz (250 g) Gruyère cheese, grated	1 cup Gruyère cheese, grated
5-6 eggs, separated	5-6 eggs, separated
1½ pints (900 ml) full cream milk	3¾ cups full cream milk
4 oz (125 g) lard or butter or oil	½ cup lard or butter or oil
a little pepper (no salt)	a little pepper (no salt)

Ideally this should be done in a liquidizer or food processor but it can be made without. Grease a large tart tin well (for 8 persons).

Mix cream cheese, Gruyère, egg yolks, etc. Beat egg whites separately and fold into the mixture. Dip a sheet of strudel or filo into the mixture and lay on bottom of dish. Continue in this fashion until only 3 or 4 sheets of pastry are left. Then pour *half* the remaining cheese mixture in, top with 3 or 4 sheets of pastry and pour on the rest. Heat the fat or oil and sprinkle the tart with it. Put into a hot oven (400°F/200°C/Gas 6 and bake approximately 30 minutes until the top crust is browned and the tart has come away slightly from the sides of the dish.

SPANAKOPITTA (Greece)

CHEESE AND SPINACH FLAN

Ideally you should buy the round *feuilles de brik* or round filo pastry rather than the oblong sort. If you use the oblong sort, you must use a tin or dish to match. Some people put their spinach in 2 layers, others in a single layer. I feel nothing is added by the rather soggy middle layer.

Imperial/Metric	*American*
10 leaves filo or burek pastry	10 leaves filo or burek pastry
1 lb (500 g) cooked spinach, chopped	1 lb cooked spinach, chopped
4-6 oz (125-190 g) butter	½-¾ cup butter
6 oz (190 g) Greek feta cheese	6 oz Greek feta cheese

Melt the butter and brush the sheets of pastry and the dish or tin you are using. Put 5 sheets of the pastry in the base of the tin, one on top of another. Chop the spinach well, add the chopped feta and any butter you may have over. Put the remaining buttered pastry leaves on top and tuck in. Cook for 30 minutes at 375°F/190°C/Gas 5. Remove from oven and carefully invert the pie onto a ovenproof serving dish and bake 5-10 minutes longer at 325°F/170°C/Gas 3.

Other Pastries

FLAMICHE (Belgium)

LEEK TART

There must be dozens of recipes for this dish: the only constant is leeks. The tart can be open or closed. In northern France the pastry is sometimes made with a mixture of cream cheese and butter or even Brie and butter. My mother's family always used a very short-crust pastry (a food processor is ideal for this type of pastry) which you cannot roll out but have to pat into shape in the baking tin itself. It may seem to have a prodigious amount of cream but there are few eggs. There is no reason why you should not lessen the cream and increase the eggs.

Imperial/Metric	American
12 oz (375 g) very short pastry using equal amount of butter and flour with 1 egg yolk	12 oz very short pastry using equal amount of butter and flour with 1 egg yolk
approx. 12 oz (375 g) leeks, trimmed and cooked*	approx. 12 oz leeks, trimmed and cooked*
8 fl. oz (240 ml) double cream**	1 cup heavy cream**
3 egg yolks	3 egg yolks
pinch nutmeg, salt and pepper	pinch nutmeg, salt and pepper

* Start with about 2 lb (1 kilo) leeks. By the time you have trimmed and cooked them (in rounds – sweat them soft in a little butter: they catch very easily), you should be left with approximately the right amount.

** I find a mixture of single and double cream better and less rich than purely double cream but that is a matter of personal taste.

Beat the cream and egg yolks together and stir in the leeks. Flatten the ball of dough as much as possible and line out the baking tin. Do not worry that it looks untidy; the only important thing is that the pastry should be more or less the same thickness throughout. Pour in the *flamiche* mixture and cook for 30-35 minutes in a hot oven (375-400°F/190-200°C/Gas 5-6), middle shelf.

SMOKED HADDOCK AND BROCCOLI TART (UK)

Imperial/Metric	American
1 recipe short-crust pastry (p.190)	1 recipe short-crust pastry (p.190)
1 lb (500 g) smoked haddock fillet	1 lb smoked haddock fillet
12 oz (375 g) broccoli spears	12 oz broccoli spears
1½ pints (900 ml) milk	3-4 cups milk
4 eggs	4 eggs
6 oz (190 ml) double cream	¾ cup heavy cream
pepper and nutmeg	pepper and nutmeg

Preheat the oven 400°F/200°C/Gas 6.

Soak the smoked haddock for 30 minutes and then cook in the milk. Keep the milk for later. You may need less milk – it depends on the size of the fish.

Line a tin with the pastry and bake blind for 15 minutes in a moderately hot oven, 400°F/200°C/Gas 6. Cool.

Arrange the smoked haddock pieces and broccoli spears which you have cut into very small pieces. Beat the eggs, cream and a very little of the milk together. Add pepper and nutmeg (*not* salt). Cook in a medium to hot oven (340°F/175°C/Gas 3½) for 30 minutes.

SLOVENIAN MUSHROOM PASTRIES (Yugoslavia)

This dish can be prepared in advance and at the last moment can be assembled together.

Imperial/Metric	*American*
1 recipe rough puff pastry (p.192)	1 recipe rough puff pastry (p.192)
1 medium onion, chopped	1 medium onion, chopped
8 oz (250 g) mushrooms, chopped	8 oz mushrooms, chopped
3 tablespoons sour cream	3 tablespoons commercial sour cream
1 egg, beaten	1 egg, beaten
pepper, salt and dill to taste	pepper, salt and dill to taste
butter for frying	butter for frying

Sauté the onion in a little butter and add mushrooms. Add pepper, salt and dill and pour off any surplus liquid. Then add the sour cream. Cool.

Roll out your pastry and cut out into 2 inch (5 cm) squares. Beat the egg with a little milk or water. Put a spoonful of filling in each 'diamond'-shaped square. Brush with beaten egg. Fold the points towards each other so they meet in the middle and brush again with beaten egg. Bake in a very hot oven (475°F/240°C/Gas 9) for 12-15 minutes on the middle shelf.

CHAUSSONS DE RIS DE VEAU AU MADERE (France)

SWEETBREAD TURNOVERS

Allow half a sweetbread (or a whole lobe) per person – thus you will need 4 pairs of sweetbreads for 8 people.

Imperial/Metric	American
1 recipe puff or short-crust pastry (pp.190-1)	1 recipe puff or short-crust pastry (pp.190-1)
4 pair sweetbreads	4 pair sweetbreads
4 or 5 shallots, chopped	4 or 5 shallots, chopped
4 oz (125 g) butter	4 oz butter
4 tablespoons Madeira	4 tablespoons Madeira
2 tablespoons double cream	2 tablespoons heavy cream
pinch of thyme	pinch of thyme
1 tablespoon flour	1 tablespoon flour

The sweetbreads can be prepared in advance, as can the pastry and only need to be assembled just before cooking.

Soak the sweetbreads in salted water for 30 minutes. Rinse and drain and then cook for 8-10 minutes in boiling water. Weigh down, between boards, for at least 30 minutes. Cut the sweetbreads into cubes. Sauté the shallots in the butter and add the sweetbreads. Cook until done and then sprinkle a tablespoon of flour over the whole and mix well in. Pour on the Madeira and finally add the cream, salt, pepper and thyme. Let cool.

Preheat the oven (400°F/200°C/Gas 6 for short pastry; 425°F/220°C/Gas 7 for puff pastry). Roll out the pastry and divide into 8 portions. Roll each piece into a largish circle and put in one eighth of the sweetbreads and gravy. Fold over in a half-moon shape and bake for 20 minutes. Alternatively you can roll the pastry into oblongs and put the filling in one half and fold over the other. Ideally in both cases you should paint the pastry with beaten egg, watching carefully lest it run down the sides of the puff pastry: this can prevent its rising.

LOHIPIIRAKKA (Finland)

FISH PIE

This is a pie which is made with a top and bottom crust of cottage cheese pastry (p.190) and moulded freehand, as it were. Not for the unartistic but for those good at cutting pastry shapes it makes a stunning first course. You will see that its a near relation of a Kulbiaka from Russia (p.199).

Serve with cucumber mayonnaise.

Imperial/Metric	American
1 recipe cottage cheese pastry	1 recipe cottage cheese pastry
3 lb (1.5 kilos) salmon in fillets	3 lb salmon in fillets
8 oz (250 g) cooked rice	8 oz cooked rice
4 eggs, hard-boiled	4 eggs, hardcooked
4 oz (125 g) melted butter	½ cup melted butter
2 tablespoons parsley, chopped	2 tablespoons parsley, chopped
2 tablespoons chopped fresh dill or 2 teaspoons freeze-dried dill	2 tablespoons chopped fresh dill or 2 teaspoons freeze-dried dill
salt and pepper	salt and pepper
beaten egg for glazing	beaten egg for glazing

Trim the salmon fillets into a fish shape. Chop up the trimmed-off pieces and mix with the cooked rice, parsley, dill, salt and pepper.

Preheat the oven 375°F/190°C/Gas 5. Prepare the pastry and roll it out in two pieces. Cut them both into a large fish shape. Place one piece on a buttered baking sheet, and put the rice and salmon mixture on it. Then put a layer of hard-boiled eggs on top and finally the large pieces of salmon. Glaze round the edges with beaten egg. Top with the second piece of fish pastry and glaze all over. Trim fish into better shape and put on fins, gills etc and mark a tail. Make a hole for the eye and then a series of holes over the body to let the steam escape. They should look like scales. Glaze the finished fish again. Bake 35 minutes.

ZWIEBELKUCHEN (Germany)

ONION TART

This is served in autumn to accompany the new white wine – *federwein*, as its called.

Imperial/Metric	American
yeast pastry for 8 (p.193)	yeast pastry for 8 (p.193)
1 lb (500 g) onions, finely sliced	1 lb onions, finely sliced
8 oz (250 g) streaky bacon	8 oz streaky bacon
6 eggs	6 eggs
½ pint (300 ml) double cream	1¼ cups heavy cream
1 teaspoon caraway seeds	1 teaspoon caraway seeds
salt and pepper	salt and pepper
butter for frying	butter for frying

Prepare the yeast pastry. Pre-heat the oven to 325°F/170°C/Gas 3.

Fry the sliced onion very gently and allow to cool slightly. Add the diced bacon to the fat and cook slightly. Mix all ingredients together and pour onto uncooked yeast pastry. Cook for approximately 45 minutes. Serve immediately.

CROSTINI DI PORCINI (Italy)

MUSHROOM *CROUTES*

Imperial/Metric	American
8 *croûtes* made from a sandwich loaf	8 *croûtes made* from a sandwich loaf
2½-3 oz (75-90 g) dried mushrooms (*boletus edulis (cèpes)* or *porcini*)	2½-3 oz dried mushrooms (*boletus edulis (cèpes)* or *porcini*)
4 good slices of ham, diced	4 good slices of ham, diced
2 large eggs	2 large eggs
1 shallot, chopped	1 shallot, chopped
1 heaped tablespoon flour	1 heaped tablespoon flour
8 fl. oz (240 ml) double cream*	1 cup heavy cream*
6 oz (190 g) melted butter	¾ cup melted butter

* Some people substitute white wine for a quarter of the amount of cream, which makes for a slightly less rich result.

Use small sandwich loaves to make the *croûtes*. Cut bread to shape and line tartlet moulds. Coat inside and out with melted butter and put in a hot oven to bake for 7 minutes (400°F/200°C/Gas 6). Soak the mushrooms. Mix the flour into a little of the cream, then add the rest and heat, stirring all the time. (Alternatively, if you find it easier, make a roux with some butter and then add the cream.) Add the ham and the rinsed mushrooms. Off the heat add the 2 egg yolks. Divide between the 8 *croûtes* and bake for approximately 10 minutes at 340°F/175°C/Gas 3½.

The *croûtes* can be deep fried if you wish, but do not let them get too brown.

10 Vegetables and Fruit

Fruit is not commonly served as a first course, though sometimes it appears with ham in Italy (melons or, even better, figs). Occasionally grapefruit is served, the Mexicans (and subsequently the Americans) mix citrus fruits with avocado in wonderfully refreshing first courses.

Vegetable courses are something different altogether. They are very useful when you do not particularly want to serve a second (or even third) vegetable with the main course, or when you have fish as a main course. Game, for instance, is better with just a few potatoes and its various sauces, than loaded down with imperfectly boiled sprouts, cabbage or carrots. The same goes for things like *boeuf à la bourguignonne* or plainly grilled lamb cutlets or steak.

Moreover, when vegetables are not merely accompanying another dish they come properly into their own. Many of these recipes can be prepared in advance and one or two, such as the 'Bayeldi' way of cooking vegetables actually improve with keeping for 24 hours. Finally, vegetables are relatively inexpensive with the possible exception of asparagus and seakale.

ARTICHAUTS A LA BARIGOULE (France)

ARTICHOKES STUFFED WITH HAM AND MUSHROOMS

At the end of this recipe I have written 'Chamberlain, *Gourmet Magazine*' to whom I owe many thanks for this recipe, which I have used hundreds of times.

Imperial/Metric	American
8 plump artichokes – Black Prince type	8 plump artichokes – Black Prince type
8 oz (250 g)mushrooms	8 oz mushrooms
8 oz (250 g) minced ham	1 cup minced ham
4 oz (125 g) dried breadcrumbs	1 cup dried breadcrumbs
1 medium onion, finely chopped	1 medium onion, finely chopped
1 tablespoon parsley, chopped	1 tablespoon parsley, chopped
½ pint (300 ml) chicken stock	1¼ cups chicken stock
1 clove garlic	1 clove garlic
8 fl. oz (240 ml) dry white wine	1 cup dry white wine
small sliced carrot	small sliced carrot
bouquet garni	*bouquet garni*
2 fl. oz (60 ml) olive oil	2 fl. oz olive oil

Trim the base and the leaves of the artichokes and cook them in boiling salted water for 20 minutes. Once they are cool enough to handle, remove the centre leaves and the chokes. Make a stuffing of the ham, mushrooms, breadcrumbs, onion, garlic and parsley, and moisten with some of the stock. It should be fairly stiff. Stuff the artichokes. Pour a few drops of olive oil onto each artichoke and place them in a deepish container suitable for the oven. Heat up the rest of the stock and boil for 5 minutes or so on top of the stove with the carrot and *bouquet garni*. Pour *round*, not on, the artichokes and cook for 40 minutes in a low oven 300°F/150°C/Gas 2. Baste from time to time and serve the artichokes hot with the juice poured round them.

Chamberlain, *Gourmet Magazine*

ARTICHOKES WITH SAUCE HOLLANDAISE

One of the nicest ways of eating this vegetable.

Boil the artichokes until done (at least 30 minutes and anything up to 40) and have them really hot when served. For 8 people make at least 2 recipes of *sauce hollandaise* (p.395) and allow people to help themselves, though butter and lemon are a good alternative if you are in a dreadful hurry.

CARCIOFI ALL' ITALIANA (Italy)

ARTICHOKES STUFFED WITH HAM IN CHEESE SAUCE

Imperial/Metric	*American*
8 or 16 artichokes, depending on size	8 or 16 artichokes, depending on size
8 oz (250 g) ham, finely chopped	1 cup chopped ham
1 pint (600 ml) *sauce béchamel* (p.391)	2½ cups *sauce béchamel* (p.391)
4 tablespoons Parmesan cheese, grated	4 tablespoons Parmesan cheese, grated
4 tablespoons thick cream	4 tablespoons heavy cream

Cook the artichokes in boiling water and remove leaves and chokes as soon as they can be handled. Stir the ham and cheese into the hot *sauce béchamel* and fill each artichoke bottom generously. The sauce should be fairly stiff. Put a couple of teaspoons of thick cream on each and cook for 10 minutes at 400°F/200°C/Gas 6. They should come out brown and bubbling.

Alternatively you could run them under a very fierce grill. They could be done on individual dishes.

FONDS D'ARTICHAUTS – SAUCE SOUBISE (France)

ARTICHOKE BOTTOMS WITH *SAUCE SOUBISE*

Imperial/Metric	*American*
8 large artichokes	8 large artichokes
1 recipe *sauce soubise* (p.400), prepared	1 recipe *sauce soubise* (p.400), prepared
juice of 1 lemon	juice of 1 lemon
2 oz (60 g) flour	¼ cup flour
5 pints (3 litres) water	6½ pints water
8 oz (250 g) ham, diced	1 cup ham, diced
salt and pepper	salt and pepper

Mix the flour with a little cold water, then add the rest of the water. Trim half the leaves of the artichokes and rinse under cold tap. Put into the water and add lemon, bring to the boil and cook 20-30 minutes depending on size.

Once cooked, put in cold water and then remove all the leaves and the choke. Divide the chopped ham between the 8 artichokes and top with the *sauce soubise*. Dot with butter and put in oven for 15 minutes at 450°F/230°C/Gas 8.

STUFFED ARTICHOKES (Turkey)

Imperial/Metric	American
8 medium artichokes	8 medium artichokes
7 oz (220 g) mushrooms, thinly sliced	7 oz mushrooms, thinly sliced
4 oz (125 g) carrots, finely chopped	4 oz carrots, finely chopped
4 oz (125 g) onions, finely chopped	4 oz onions, finely chopped
4 oz (125 g) currants	4 oz currants
5 fl. oz (150 ml) white wine	good ½ cup white wine
3 fl. oz (90 ml) olive oil	scant ½ cup olive oil
pinch thyme and sage, preferably ground	pinch thyme and sage, preferably ground
1 teaspoon ground coriander	1 teaspoon ground coriander
juice and rind of 1 lemon	juice and rind of 1 lemon
salt and pepper	salt and pepper

Trim off the top half of the leaves and clean the artichokes under a running tap. Cook them in boiling water for 20-30 minutes depending on size.

Pour lemon juice over the mushrooms. Cook the onions and carrots slowly in the olive oil, together with the herbs and spices, salt and pepper. They should remain slightly crisp. At this stage add the mushrooms (reserving the lemon juice), stir and cook for 5 minutes. Add the white wine and currants. Cook for a further 5 minutes or so, until currants have plumped up.

Once the artichokes are cooked, strain them and remove the choke (wearing a pair of clean rubber gloves is a good idea). Put the artichokes back into boiling water to keep warm if necessary. Add the lemon juice to the vegetable mixture and adjust seasoning. It should taste slightly sweet and sour. Divide it between the 8 artichokes and serve.

ARTICHOKES WITH ŒUFS MOLLETS

Imperial/Metric	American
8 large artichokes*	8 large artichokes*
8 eggs, soft-boiled (5 minutes)**	8 eggs, soft-boiled (5 minutes)**
7 oz (220 g) ham, chopped (not minced) small	7 oz ham, chopped (not minced) small
1 recipe *sauce aurore* (p.391)	1 recipe *sauce aurore* (p.391)
2 oz (60 g) flour	¼ cup flour
1 lemon or juice of 2 lemons	1 lemon or juice of 2 lemons
parsley, chopped	parsley, chopped

* Use the large Breton artichokes, the type which is exported under the name Black Prince among others. Smaller artichokes will not have enough room to contain the filling.

** Poached eggs can be used instead if preferred.

Cut off the stalk of the artichoke, then turn it on its side and cut through the top half of the leaves (a serrated knife works well for this). Then bit by bit remove all the leaves so that you are left only with the heart and the choke. Remove the choke with a teaspoon or, if you find it easier, pull it out bit by bit – everyone has a different method. Rub the artichoke bottoms with the cut lemon to prevent darkening. Alternatively put into a bowl of water to which you have added the juice of 2 lemons.

Mix the flour with a little water, at first gradually, then adding more. Put on to boil with the artichoke bottoms, cooking for approximately 15 minutes. Test and give a little more time if necessary.

Have ready (and hot) 8 shelled soft-boiled (or poached) eggs.

Prepare the *sauce aurore*. Place the drained artichokes either on individual serving dishes or on one large dish, divide the chopped ham into 8 and put a portion of ham under each egg. Coat them with the hot *sauce aurore*. Sprinkle with a little chopped parsley.

Variation

This dish can be eaten cold in which case instead of a *sauce aurore* a home-made mayonnaise (p.404) is used, to which you add half its volume in whipping cream together with 2 tablespoons of tomato ketchup. Think in terms of ¾ pints/½ litre/1 US pint of mayonnaise to 8 fl. oz/250 ml/1 US cup of cream.

ASPERGES A LA POLONAISE (France and presumably Poland)

ASPARAGUS WITH EGG SAUCE

Most Poles will tell you that when they are fortunate enough to eat asparagus they do so with hot melted butter and lemon juice, but the hard-boiled egg finish is undoubtedly a Polish touch.

Imperial/Metric	American
5-8 asparagus spears per person	5-8 asparagus spears per person
6 eggs, hard-boiled	6 eggs, hardcooked
8 oz (250 g) butter	1 cup butter
3 tablespoons fresh breadcrumbs	3 tablespoons fresh breadcrumbs

Cook asparagus in the normal way. Towards the end of the cooking time, fry the breadcrumbs in half the butter until they are golden. Do not bother to separate them from the butter. Take the yolks of the hard-boiled eggs and push them through a small sieve so you cover the tips of the asparagus to about a third of the way down the spear. Heat the rest of the butter to the *noisette* stage, mix in with the butter and breadcrumbs and pour the whole over the asparagus. This is not as tricky as it sounds and the result is delicious. If you wish, you can pass more *noisette* butter separately.

ASPERGES A LA VINAIGRETTE (FRANCE)

ASPARAGUS IN OIL AND VINEGAR DRESSING

Allow 5-8 spears per person. This recipe is best for green rather than white asparagus.

Cook the asparagus carefully and dress it while still hot. Use a very plain French dressing with only oil, vinegar, salt and pepper. Before serving, sprinkle with a little parsley.

ASPERGES AUX DEUX SAUCES

ASPARAGUS WITH TWO SAUCES

There is a lot of argument about the 2 sauces to go with this classic dish. The only constant is that one of them is *sauce Maltaise* (*sauce hollandaise* in which blood-orange juice is substituted for the lemon, p.396) which is not always easy to do, since blood oranges are not always easily found when asparagus is in season. It is worth freezing blood-orange juice for just this dish – there is scarcely any difference in taste between fresh and frozen. Most people choose *sauce hollandaise* (p.395) as the other, but there are some who use a herb and cream sauce as an alternative or even *beurre blanc* which, if you have not tried it, is divine with asparagus.

Cook the asparagus well, preferably upright in a special saucepan so the tips get steamed and the woodier parts boiled, or in a steamer. They need a great deal of careful straining – hence the Edwardian asparagus dishes and the white napkins etc: nothing is worse than having cooling asparagus water running into your sauces. Allow between 5 and 8 spears per person depending on size, availability, price and your own generosity. Arrange the asparagus neatly on plates and put some of each sauce on either side. Your guests will undoubtedly need more, so have at least a sauce boat of each to hand round. Both *Maltaise* and *hollandaise* sauces should be warm, not hot.

ASPERGES – SAUCE HOLLANDAISE (France)

See recipe for *Asperges aux deux sauces* and omit the *sauce Maltaise*. People are greedy for *sauce hollandaise*, so provide plenty.

AUBERGINES A LA NICOISE (France)

AUBERGINES WITH TOMATOES AND ONIONS

To my mind this is almost identical with a *ratatouille* except that there are no courgettes or peppers. The result is less liquid.

Imperial/Metric	American
Approx. 2lb (1 kilo) aubergines	Approx. 2lb aubergines
2 lb (1 kilo) plum tomatoes	2 lb plum tomatoes
1 lb (500 g) onions, sliced	1 lb onions, sliced
4 cloves garlic, crushed	4 cloves garlic, crushed
thyme, summer savory, basil*	thyme, summer savory, basil*
salt to taste	salt to taste
4 fl. oz (120 ml) olive oil	½ cup olive oil

* The thyme used is *thymus serpyllum* or *serpolet*, and the savory known as *poivre d'âne*, both very Niçois herbs. Ordinary thyme and savory can be substituted.

Slice the aubergines with their skins on, salt them and let them drain for 45 minutes, then rinse and dry them well on paper towels.

Fry the onions gently in the olive oil with the garlic. Once half done, remove them with a slotted spoon (draining spoon) and set aside. In the same oil fry the aubergines gently both sides. Return the onions to the pan. In a *separate* pan cook the (peeled or not) tomatoes in the left-over olive oil (you may need to add some more) until you get a good, thick sauce. It is essential that the tomatoes are not mushy. Chop the savory, thyme and basil together and add to the tomatoes. Mix everything together and put in a ovenproof dish. Bake for 25-30 minutes at 375°F/190°C/ Gas 5.

AUBERGINES AU GRATIN (France)

AUBERGINES BAKED IN CHEESE SAUCE

Imperial/Metric	American
4 large aubergines	4 large aubergines
4 tablespoons sunflower oil	4 tablespoons sunflower oil
1 onion, finely chopped	1 onion, finely chopped
1 recipe *sauce mornay* (p.397)	1 recipe *sauce mornay* (p.397)
4 tablespoons Gruyère cheese, grated*	4 tablespoons Gruyère cheese, grated*
salt and cayenne pepper	salt and cayenne pepper

* Do not be tempted to use Cheddar cheese for this dish: the taste is too strong and cloying.

Depending on personal preference, have your aubergines peeled or unpeeled. Cut into half-inch (1 cm) cubes, salt well and let drain for 45 minutes or so in a colander. Rinse well and pat dry. Sweat the onion in the oil but do not let it take colour. Add the aubergines pieces and seal them. Discard any fat left over. Put the vegetables in a *hot sauce mornay* and then cook in a hot oven for 30 minutes at 400°F/200°C/Gas 6. If you feel the top is not brown enough, run it under a hot grill for a minute or two.

AUBERGINES IMAM BAYELDI (Turkey and the Middle East)

STUFFED AUBERGINES

In Egypt and Turkey this dish used to be cooked in an old-fashioned oil stove which kept a slow, steady heat. Every household employed a boy to watch the stove like a hawk in case it blew up and covered the kitchen in smuts. Needless to say, the boy scarcely ever watched like a hawk and occasionally he was caught out. Whilst virtually every dwelling in Egypt now has a modern stove, few can afford to cook much in or on it – a sign of the times.

Imperial/Metric	American
8 medium or 4 large aubergines	8 medium or 4 large aubergines
1 lb (500 g) onions, chopped	1 lb onions, chopped
1 lb (500 g) tomatoes, chopped	1 lb tomatoes, chopped
4 tablespoons parsley, chopped	4 tablespoons parsley, chopped
4 oz (125 g) currants	¼ cup currants
2 teaspoons dill	2 teaspoons dill
2 cloves garlic, chopped	2 cloves garlic, chopped
1 level dessertspoon sugar	1 level dessertspoon sugar
1 teaspoon ground coriander	1 teaspoon ground coriander
breadcrumbs (optional)	breadcrumbs (optional)
1 teaspoon vinegar	1 teaspoon vinegar

FOR COOKING

Imperial/Metric	American
4 fl. oz (120 ml) olive oil	½ cup olive oil
juice of 1 lemon	juice of 1 lemon
8 fl. oz (240 ml) water	8 fl. oz water
sugar and salt (optional)	sugar and salt (optional)

Cut the aubergines in half, remove the flesh and put aside. Leave approximately a half an inch shell (1 cm) thickness round. Sprinkle with salt and let drain for 45 minutes to get rid of the bitter juices. Do the same with the chopped-up flesh you have removed. At the end of this time rinse in a sieve and drain again. Pat dry with paper towels.

Prepare the stuffing by frying the onion and garlic in some olive oil. Sprinkle on the sugar and ground coriander. Add the chopped tomatoes and aubergine and cook a little longer. If there is too much liquid, drain it off. Stir in the currants (which will take up a little of the excess liquid) and add the herbs and vinegar.

Stuff the aubergine halves with this mixture (some people cheat and put in a few breadcrumbs). Arrange them in a Pyrex baking dish or ovenproof container (you will need a large one) and pour round the olive oil/lemon/water mixture. Cook in a low oven (300°F/150°C/Gas 2) for approximately 1 hour until virtually all the liquid is used up. Hotter, faster cooking produces a tough end-product.

BABA GHANNOUCHE (The Levant)

AUBERGINE CREAM WITH *TAHINA* PASTE

Thinned down considerably, this can be used as a party dip but be warned: *tahina* (sesame) paste is a devil to get out of carpets, so do not have it too liquid.

Imperial/Metric	*American*
2 lb (1 kilo) aubergines	2 lb aubergines
2 cloves garlic	2 cloves garlic
2-4 fl. oz (60-120 ml) olive oil	¼-½ cup olive oil
juice of 1 lemon	juice of 1 lemon
6 fl. oz (180 ml) *tahina* paste	6 fl. oz *tahina* paste
salt and pepper	salt and pepper
parsley or dried mint (to garnish)	parsley or dried mint (to garnish)

Bake the aubergines in a hot oven or grill them. (The skin should be blackened.) Put the cooked pulp in a liquidizer or food processor together with the other ingredients and process until a purée has been obtained. Add the *tahina* paste. At this stage you may need to add some water, as the result may be too stiff.

CAPONATA SPECIALE (Italy)

SAUTE OF AUBERGINES TOMATOES ETC

Imperial/Metric	*American*
2 lb (1 kilo) aubergines	2 lb aubergines
1 lb (400 g) ripe tomatoes, diced	1 lb ripe tomatoes, diced
2 or 3 sticks celery, diced	2 or 3 sticks celery, diced
2 large onions, diced	2 large onions, diced
8 oz (250 g) pitted green olives	8 oz pitted green olives
1 tablespoon pinenuts	1 tablespoon each of *pignoli*
1 tablespoon capers	1 tablespoon capers
1 tablespoon currants	1 tablespoon currants
1 tablespoon sugar	1 tablespoon sugar
wine glass of red wine vinegar	½ cup red wine vinegar
2 cloves garlic	2 cloves garlic
salt and pepper	salt and pepper

Put the currants to soak in warm water. Slice the aubergine (you may peel it if you wish), sprinkle with salt and let it drain for 30 minutes. Rinse, dry and dice.

Fry the onion and garlic in some olive oil and then add the celery, tomato, currants, pine nuts (*pignoli*), olives, capers and currants. Put in the sugar and vinegar and cook until the vegetables are done (not too soft). Fry the aubergine separately. Mix the vegetables together and let the whole thing cool well before serving. Better the next day.

PIZZETTE DI MELANZANE (Italy)

AUBERGINES WITH PIZZA TOPPING

Imperial/Metric	American
4 medium aubergines	4 medium aubergines
1 lb (500 g) fresh tomatoes, chopped	1 lb fresh tomatoes, chopped
2 cloves garlic, chopped	2 cloves garlic, chopped
basil and oregano	basil and oregano
olive oil	olive oil
3-4 oz (100 g) mozzarella cheese	3-4 oz mozzarella cheese
16 anchovy fillets	16 anchovy fillets
8 green olives, chopped	8 green olives, chopped
2 eggs, beaten	2 eggs, beaten
a little flour	a little flour
breadcrumbs	breadcrumbs

Cut the aubergines into slices about ¾ inch (2 cm) thick. (You should get at least 16 good slices.) Sprinkle with salt and let drain for half an hour.

Fry the garlic and tomato together until you get a thickish sauce. Add the basil, oregano, salt and pepper. Wash and dry the aubergines on a paper towel and dip them in flour, egg and then breadcrumbs. Fry in the olive oil until almost cooked and drain on kitchen towel. Lay the slices in a shallow baking dish and put a little of the tomato sauce on each slice, followed by a slice of mozzarella cheese, some chopped olive and an anchovy fillet. Bake in a hot oven (400°F/200°C/Gas 6) for 10 minutes and serve immediately.

POOR MAN'S CAVIARE (Balkans and Near East)

AUBERGINE PUREE

Imperial/Metric	American
2 lb (1 kilo) aubergines	2 lb aubergines
2 cloves garlic	2 cloves garlic
2-4 fl. oz (60-120 ml) olive oil	¼-½ cup olive oil
juice of a lemon	juice of a lemon
1 tablespoon parsley	1 tablespoon parsley
salt and pepper	salt and pepper
parsley, chopped, or paprika (to garnish)	parsley, chopped, or paprika (to garnish)

Bake the aubergines in a hot oven or grill them. (The skin should be blackened.) Put the cooked pulp in a liquidizer or food processor together with the other ingredients and process until a purée has been obtained. You may need to adjust the seasoning. Serve sprinkled with more parsley or a little paprika.

SRPSKI AJVAR (Yugoslavia: Serbia)

VEGETABLE CAVIAR – AUBERGINES AND PEPPERS

This is a little different from the normal aubergine purée (or Poor Man's Caviare) in that it has the addition of peppers – and a lot of them.

Imperial/Metric
3 big aubergines (at least 2 lb (1 kilo) in weight)
8 large green peppers, chopped
4 tablespoons wine vinegar
4-6 fl. oz (120-180 ml) olive oil
garlic to taste
salt and pepper

American
3 big aubergines (at least 2 lb in weight)
8 large bell peppers, chopped
4 tablespoons wine vinegar
½-¾ cup olive oil
garlic to taste
salt and pepper

Bake the aubergines and peppers (whole) in the oven. Prick them half way through cooking, which will take approximately 30-45 minutes at 450°F/230°C/Gas 8. On taking the pepper out of the oven, cover with a cloth or a large piece of clingfilm for 10 minutes: you will then find it easy to remove their skins. Cut each aubergine in half and remove the pulp. In a liquidizer or food processor liquidize the aubergine, garlic cloves, salt, pepper, olive oil and vinegar. Fold the peppers into the purée. Serve chilled.

BAKED AVOCADO WITH CRAB FILLING (USA)

Imperial/Metric	*American*
4 large avocados	4 large avocados
1 lb (500 g) white crab meat, cooked	1 lb white crab meat, cooked
8 oz (250 g) white fish, cooked*	8 oz white fish, cooked*
1 pint (600 ml) *sauce béchamel* (p.390)	2½ cups *sauce béchamel* (p.390)
4 fl. oz (120 ml) double cream	½ cup heavy cream
juice of 1 lemon or 2 limes	juice of 1 lemon or 2 limes
2 egg yolks	2 egg yolks
2 tablespoons parsley	2 tablespoons parsley
Tabasco to taste	Tabasco to taste

* The white fish can be cod, hake, whiting, snapper etc but nothing fine like turbot or sole.

Heat the sauce, add the cream, lemon, parsley and one by one the egg yolks. Taste and adjust seasoning. Add the flaked crab meat and fish. Cut avocados in half and stuff each half with the fish mixture. Cook in the oven (middle shelf) for 10-15 minutes (depending on the size of the avocados) at 375°F/190°C/Gas 5.

PALTAS CON SALSA CRUDA (Bolivia and Peru)

AVOCADOS WITH FRESH TOMATO SAUCE

Peruvians would have this hotter than the Bolivians.

Imperial/Metric	*American*
4 avocados	4 avocados
1 recipe *salsa cruda* (p.389)	1 recipe *salsa cruda* (p.389)
1 red pepper, finely chopped	1 red pepper, finely chopped

Chill both the avocados and the sauce before serving. Cut the avocados in half and fill cavities with *salsa cruda* with or without the additional pepper.

AVOCADOS WITH CAVIAR (USA)

Serve with freshly baked brown rolls.

Imperial/Metric	American
4 avocados	4 avocados
8 tablespoons caviar or lumpfish roe	8 tablespoons caviar or lumpfish roe
8 fl. oz (240 ml) sour cream	1 cup commerical sour cream

Choose absolutely ripe and perfect avocados for this. Mix the caviar or lumpfish roe with the sour cream and spoon into each cavity.

AVOCADO WITH TARAMA (Israel)

Imperial/Metric	American
4 avocados, halved	4 avocados, halved
4 oz (125 g) *tarama*	4 oz *tarama*
2 slices white bread	2 slices white bread
4 fl. oz (120 ml) whipped cream	½ cup whipped cream
caviar or lumpfish roe	caviar or lumpfish roe

Allow half an avocado per person. Cut in half and fill cavity with the *tarama* mixed with the whipped cream and breadcrumbs from the 2 slices of bread. Top with a little caviar or lumpfish roe.

AGUACATES RELLENOS (Ecuador)

STUFFED AVOCADOS WITH EGG AND CHICKEN

Imperial/Metric	American
4 avocados	4 avocados
1 whole chicken breast	1 whole chicken breast
6 eggs, hard-boiled	6 eggs, hardcooked
½ pint (300 ml) chicken stock	1¼ cups chicken stock
15 fl. oz-1 pint (450-600 ml) mayonnaise (p.404)	1-1¼ pints mayonnaise (p.404)
2 teaspoons tomato concentrate	2 teaspoons tomato concentrate
1 onion, finely chopped	1 onion, finely chopped
1 teaspoon Tabasco	1 teaspoon Tabasco
shredded lettuce	shredded lettuce
1 tablespoon wine vinegar (optional)	1 tablespoon wine vinegar (optional)
salt	salt
parsley (to decorate)	parsley (to decorate)

Poach the chicken breast gently in stock, let cool and cut into cubes. Chop the hard-boiled eggs. To the mayonnaise add the tomato concentrate and Tabasco (and salt if necessary). Bind all the ingredients with this mayonnaise and refrigerate. Shred the lettuce and divide it between 8 plates. Just before serving, *peel* and pit the avocados. Remove a thin slice from the bottom of each half so they will sit straight on the plate. Fill each cavity with the chicken/egg mixture; it may overflow slightly. Serve immediately, sprinkled with a little parsley.

ISRAELI STUFFED AVOCADOS (Israel)

Imperial/Metric	*American*
4 large avocados, halved	4 large avocados, halved
4 oz (125 g) black lumpfish roe	4 oz black lumpfish roe
8 fl. oz (240 ml) sour cream	1 cup commercial sour cream
4 oz (125 g) grey mullet roe or smoked cod's roe	4 oz grey mullet roe or smoked cod's roe
1 tablespoon tomato ketchup	1 tablespoon tomato ketchup
red or black pepper	red or black pepper

Mix down the *tarama* (mullet or cod's roe) with the sour cream and ketchup and fill the cavities of the avocados. Top with lumpfish roe and serve. Let people put on their own pepper.

PALTAS RELLENOS CON ARROZ Y CAMARONES (Chile)

AVOCADOS STUFFED WITH PRAWNS AND RICE

Imperial/Metric	*American*
5 avocados	5 avocados
8 oz (250 g) rice, cooked	1 cup rice, cooked
8 oz (250 g) prawns	1 cup shrimps
vinaigrette (p.401)	vinaigrette (p.401)
red peppers to taste (optional)	red peppers to taste (optional)
parsley, chopped, or fresh coriander	parsley, chopped, or fresh coriander

Cook the prawns; peel and devein. Cook the rice. Combine rice and prawns and dress with vinaigrette. Add 1 cubed avocado and fold in carefully. At this stage you must decide whether you want to add hot peppers or not. In Chile the dish is frequently eaten without peppers but in Peru never. Divide filling between 8 avocado halves and serve at once sprinkled with parsley or fresh coriander.

AVOCADO WITH CURRIED PRAWNS (India)

Imperial/Metric	*American*
4 avocados, halved	4 avocados, halved
1 lb (500 g) prawns, cooked	2 cups shrimp, cooked
scant pint mayonnaise (p.404)	good pint mayonnaise (p.404)
1 tablespoon sugar	1 tablespoon sugar
1 tablespoon wine vinegar	1 tablespoon wine vinegar
1 tablespoon tomato concentrate	1 tablespoon tomato concentrate
1 tablespoon curry powder	1 tablespoon curry powder
green salad or lettuce	green salad or lettuce

Devein each prawn. Mix into the mayonnaise all the ingredients except the avocados and lettuce, and then add the prawns. Fill the avocado halves with the prawn mayonnaise and serve well chilled on a bed of salad or lettuce.

BROAD BEANS AND ARTICHOKES (Lebanon, Syria and Egypt)

The Lebanese tend to use more sugar than the Egyptians. This dish also exists in Turkey but with an oil and vinegar dressing, and sometimes rice is included in the dish when it is served hot. Dill is usually used instead of dried mint.

Imperial/Metric	*American*
16 artichoke hearts (fresh or frozen)*	16 artichoke hearts (fresh or frozen)*
2 lb (1 kilo) fresh broad beans*	2 lb fresh broad beans*
dried mint or dill (to garnish)	dried mint or dill (to garnish)

DRESSING

Imperial/Metric	*American*
juice of 1 lemon	juice of 1 lemon
6 tablespoons light olive oil	6 tablespoons light olive oil
salt and sugar to taste	salt and sugar to taste

* If you use frozen broad beans, count on having at least a pound of them. Neither tinned artichokes nor tinned broad beans will do for this dish.

Boil the vegetables separately. You will find it easier to remove the choke after cooking rather than before. Dress while *hot* and let it cool. Sprinkle with mint (or dill) before serving.

LOBIO (USSR: The Caucasus)

WHITE BEAN (OR HARICOT) WITH WALNUTS

This can be served hot or cold, in which case you will need a little oil and vinegar. In its native land they use thick sheep's milk yoghurt as an accompaniment.

Imperial/Metric	American
approx. 1½ lb (750 g) haricot or white beans	approx. 1½ lb haricot or white beans
4 oz (125 g) walnuts	½ cup walnut pieces
1 bunch spring onions	1 bunch scallions
salt and pepper	salt and pepper
fresh coriander or parsley (to decorate)	fresh coriander or parsley (to decorate)

Wash and pick over the beans and then soak in water for 4-5 hours. Drain and cook in new water until tender. Chop the spring onions (with some of the green part) and walnuts or whizz them up in the food processor. Stir walnuts and onions into the hot beans. Season with salt and pepper and sprinkle with parsley or coriander.

BROCCOLI WITH SAUCE HOLLANDAISE

Use only home-grown broccoli, straight from the garden. Really good purple sprouting broccoli is excellent this way as well.

Simply steam or boil your broccoli or cook it in the microwave until just cooked. Serve with plenty of *sauce hollandaise* (p.395).

CELERY WITH ANCHOVY SAUCE (UK)

Imperial/Metric	American
½ head of celery per person	½ head of celery per person
6 or 8 anchovy fillets	6 or 8 anchovy fillets
4 tablespoons olive oil	4 tablespoons olive oil
4 tablespoons butter	4 tablespoons butter
5 oz (150 ml) sour cream	5 fl. oz commercial sour cream
juice of 1 lemon	juice of 1 lemon
a little pepper	a little pepper
parsley (to decorate)	parsley (to decorate)

While the celery is cooking (preferably by steaming or in a

microwave), mix the anchovy fillets with the olive oil, butter and sour cream. Add the lemon juice and a little pepper. Arrange the half hearts of celery on a dish and put a blob of sauce on each one and let it melt in. Sprinkle with parsley and serve.

Don't follow with anything too subtle after the anchovy!

CELERY HEARTS IN PAPRIKA SAUCE (Hungary)

A celery heart should feed 2 people for a first course unless it is very small, in which case allow one each but split it in half once cooked.

Imperial/Metric	American
4 or 8 celery hearts depending on size, almost cooked	4 or 8 celery hearts depending on size, almost cooked
1 recipe *sauce béchamel* (p.390)	1 recipe *sauce béchamel* (p.390)
1 tablespoon double-concentrate tomato purée	1 tablespoon double-concentrate tomato purée
1 tablespoon paprika	1 tablespoon paprika
3 tablespoons double cream	3 tablespoons heavy cream

To the *sauce béchamel* add the tomato purée and mix over heat, add paprika and off the heat add the cream. Pour over the celery hearts and bake for 10-12 minutes at 375°F/190°C/Gas 5.

CELERI A LA GRECQUE (France)

The preparing of vegetables *à la grecque* has thoroughly entered French cuisine, although this vegetable is never, or hardly ever, seen in Greece. Celeriac can be done the same way.

Imperial/Metric	American
3 or 4 heads of celery	3 or 4 heads of celery
1 pint (600 ml) water or more	2½ cups water
4 fl. oz (120 ml) olive oil	½ cup olive oil
juice of 1 large lemon	juice of 1 large lemon
8 oz (250 g) tomatoes, chopped	8 oz tomatoes, chopped
1 medium onion, chopped	1 medium onion, chopped
5 or 6 stalks parsley	5 or 6 stalks parsley
2 sprigs thyme	2 sprigs thyme
1 tablespoon coriander seeds	1 tablespoon coriander seeds
salt	salt

Cut the outer leaves of the celery off, and cut the celery stalks into 1 inch (2 cm) pieces. Put on to boil in the water – you may need more. Heat the oil and fry the onion in it, but gently. Add the tomatoes and cook a little longer. Finally add all the other ingredients. Strain the celery, reserving approximately ½ pint (300 ml/1¼ US cups) of the cooking water. Combine the celery and this water with the other ingredients and simmer for 15 minutes moderately fast. Let cool and serve next day. Adjust seasoning once cold – you may need a little more vinegar or, if it is too sharp, a little sugar.

COURGETTES AND HAM AU GRATIN (UK)

Imperial/Metric	*American*
8 medium-large courgettes	8 medium-large zucchini
1 pint (600 ml) *sauce béchamel* (p.390)	2½ cups *sauce béchamel* (p.390)
8 oz (250 g) ham, diced	8 oz ham, diced
2 tablespoons chopped parsley	2 tablespoons chopped parsley
4 tablespoons Gruyère or Cheddar cheese	4 tablespoons Gruyère or Cheddar cheese

Parboil the courgettes, cool slightly and cut in 2 lengthwise. Scoop out the central seeds and pith, and some of the flesh. Combine the ham and sauce, put in the parsley, then divide between the courgettes. Sprinkle with cheese and bake for 15 minutes in a hot oven, 400°F/200°C/Gas 6.

COURGETTES AND RICE (Mediterranean Countries)

Imperial/Metric	*American*
2 lb (1 kilo) courgettes peeled, cooked and chopped roughly	2 lb zucchini peeled, cooked and chopped roughly
2 tablespoons rice, uncooked	2 tablespoons rice, uncooked
5 eggs	5 eggs
8 fl. oz (240 ml) double cream	1 cup heavy cream
salt and Tabasco or pepper	salt and Tabasco or pepper
1 clove garlic (optional)	1 clove garlic (optional)
1 tablespoon tomato concentrate	1 tablespoon tomato concentrate

Beat up eggs, cream, tomato concentrate, garlic etc, preferably in a mixer. Stir the rice into the courgettes and then add the tomato custard. Put in a suitably sized dish. Bake for 40 minutes in a medium oven 375°F/190°C/Gas 5.

COURGETTES IMAM BAYELDI (Turkey and the Middle East)

STUFFED COURGETTES

Imperial/Metric	American
8 medium courgettes	8 medium zucchini
1 lb (500 g) onions, chopped	1 lb onions, chopped
1 lb (500 g) tomatoes, chopped	1 lb tomatoes, chopped
4 tablespoons parsley, chopped	4 tablespoons parsley, chopped
4 oz (125 g) currants	¼ cup currants
2 teaspoon dill	2 teaspoon dill
2 cloves garlic	2 cloves garlic
1 level dessertspoon sugar	1 level dessertspoon sugar
1 teaspoon ground coriander	1 teaspoon ground coriander
1 teaspoon vinegar	1 teaspoon vinegar
breadcrumbs (optional)	breadcrumbs (optional)

FOR COOKING

Imperial/Metric	American
4 fl. oz (120 ml) olive oil	½ cup olive oil
juice of 1 lemon	juice of 1 lemon
8 fl. oz (240 ml) water	8 fl. oz water
sugar and salt (optional)	sugar and salt (optional)

Cut the courgettes (zucchini) in half and remove the flesh, leaving approximately half an inch (1 cm) thickness round. Prepare the stuffing by frying the onion and garlic in some olive oil. Sprinkle on the sugar and the ground coriander. Add the tomatoes and cook a little longer. If there is too much liquid, drain it off. Stir in the currants (which will take up a little of the excess liquid) and add the herbs and vinegar.

Stuff the courgette halves with this mixture (some people cheat and put in a few breadcrumbs). Arrange them in a Pyrex, baking dish or ovenproof container (you will need a large one) and pour round the olive oil/lemon/water mixture. Cook in a low oven (300°F/150°C/Gas 2 for approximately 1 hour until virtually all the liquid is used up. *Test after 45 minutes.* Hotter, faster cooking produces a tough end-product.

ZUCCHINI RIPIENI (Italy)

STUFFED COURGETTES

Imperial/Metric	*American*
8 courgettes	8 zucchini
1 lb (500 g) fresh tomatoes	1 lb fresh tomatoes
4 tablespoons tomato concentrate	4 tablespoons tomato concentrate
12 oz (375 g) bacon, diced	12 oz bacon, diced
8 oz (250 g) cooked rice	1 cup cooked rice
2 tablespoons parsley, chopped	2 tablespoons parsley, chopped
2 tablespoons basil, chopped	2 tablespoons basil, chopped
2 tablespoons brown sugar	2 tablespoons brown sugar
4 fl. oz (120 ml) red wine	½ cup red wine
salt and pepper	salt and pepper

Do not peel the courgettes. Cut them through their length and scrape out the seeds and some of the flesh so that you are left with approximately half an inch (1 cm) thickness all round. Blanch in boiling water for 3 minutes.

Fry the onion and bacon in a little oil. Once soft, add the tomatoes, which need not be peeled. Add the rice and cook a few moments more. Finally add the wine, herbs and seasoning. Divide between the 8 courgette halves and put on a baking tray. Cook at 400°F/200°C/Gas 6 for 25 minutes.

ZUCCHINI FARCITI (Italy: Tuscany)

STUFFED COURGETTES

The tiniest courgettes are used for this dish in Italy which seem to be unobtainable elsewhere. However, that is no reason to deprive yourself of this dish – the large sort can be given the same treatment.

Imperial/Metric	*American*
8 medium courgettes or more	8 medium zucchini or more
approx. 1 lb (500 g) cooked spinach, chopped and dried	approx. 1 lb cooked spinach, chopped and dried
½ teaspoon nutmeg	½ teaspoon nutmeg
1 large packet Boursin-type cheese with herbs	1 large packet Boursin-type cheese with herbs
2 oz (60 g) butter	¼ cup butter
3 eggs, separated	3 eggs, separated
Parmesan cheese (optional)	Parmesan cheese (optional)

Partially cook the courgettes whole, let cool a little and split in half lengthwise. Remove the seeds, pith and some of the flesh leaving about half an inch (1 cm) all round. Heat the cooked spinach slightly and mix in the butter and cheese. Cool and mix in 3 egg yolks. Let everything cool down. This dish can be prepared in advance to this stage.

Just before cooking, beat the 3 egg whites stiff and fold them into the spinach/cheese mixture. Spoon carefully into the courgettes (zucchini boats). Arrange the boats in a non-stick (but still well-greased) baking dish and cook for 10 minutes at 375°F/190°C/Gas 5.

It does not matter if the mixture overflows slightly. This dish can be cooked in individual dishes which, of course, makes serving much easier.

BRAISED ENDIVES (Belgium and Northern France)

This is often served both at home and in restaurants when the main course is the sort that calls only for a few potatoes or rice and no other vegetable.

Imperial/Metric	*American*
16 small endives (Belgian *witloof*)	16 small chicory (*witloof*)
8 oz (225 g) butter	1 cup butter
juice of 1 lemon or 1 tablespoon wine vinegar	juice of 1 lemon or 1 tablespoon wine vinegar
salt	salt

Good-quality endives should not need washing and should not have sand in them but should be closely packed and clean. If they are slightly large, split them *after* cooking. If small, cook them whole. However, splitting them afterwards does enable the buttery juices to get inside. Just cut off any limp leaves and trim the bottom. Steam, boil or cook in the microwave until done. Drain well in a colander with the tips facing down. Lay them, split or not, in a large baking dish.

Heat the butter to the *noisette* stage, add the lemon juice off the heat, being careful of the spitting this will cause, and add the salt. Pour this mixture over the endives and cook for 7-8 minutes at 375°F/190°C/Gas 5. This dish can be prepared in advance – or can be reheated – but will need 10 minutes in a hotter oven, say 400°F/200°C/Gas 6.

ENDIVES IN TOMATO AND BUTTER SAUCE

My first cookery writing job was to compose 50 recipes, using a well-known brand of tomato ketchup in each. It strained the imagination somewhat, particularly as I was not – and still am not – a tomato ketchup fan. However, there were one or two recipes which stayed the course and this is one of them.

The ketchup taste in this amount is quite subtle and does not obtrude. If you overdo it, you will not taste the butter or the endive/chicory.

Imperial/Metric	*American*
16 small or 8 large Belgian endives	16 small or 8 large Belgian chicory
8 oz (225 g) butter	1 cup butter
4-5 tablespoons tomato ketchup	4-5 tablespoons tomato ketchup
1 tablespoon parsley, chopped (to decorate)	1 tablespoon parsley, chopped (to decorate)

Having cooked the endive/chicory cut the large ones in half and place flat side down, leave the small ones whole and serve 2 per person. They should be hot.

In a pan melt the butter gently and stir in the tomato ketchup. When it is bubbling, pour over the endives/chicory and run under a very hot grill until slightly browned. Sprinkle with parsley and serve.

FINOCCHIO CON OLIVE (Italy)

FENNEL WITH OLIVES

Imperial/Metric	*American*
8 whole fennel bulbs	8 whole fennel bulbs
16 anchovy fillets	16 anchovy fillets
2 dozen black olives	2 dozen black olives
5 oz (155 g) butter	½ cup butter
1 tablespoon flour	1 tablespoon flour
juice of a lemon	juice of a lemon
2 tablespoons wine vinegar	2 tablespoons wine vinegar
salt and pepper	salt and pepper

Remove any tired leaves and cut a cross in the base of each fennel. Cook for 15 minutes in boiling salted water to which you have added the lemon juice and a tablespoon of flour (this keeps the vegetable a good colour). Cut each fennel bulb into 4. Heat half the butter in a large pan and slightly brown half the fennel pieces – then slightly brown the other half. Put them all into one dish, sprinkle with chopped anchovy fillets and the whole olives. Run under a hot grill for 5-6 minutes until bubbling. Pour over the vinegar and serve hot sprinkled with freshly ground black pepper.

HARICOTS VERTS A LA BEARNAISE (France)

GREEN BEANS WITH BACON, TOMATO AND PEPPER

Serve with warm French bread.

Imperial/Metric	*American*
3 lb (1.5 kilos) French beans*	3 lb French beans*
1 red pepper, cut in strips	1 red pepper, cut in strips
1 medium onion, chopped	1 medium onion, chopped
3 medium tomatoes, chopped	3 medium tomatoes, chopped
8 oz (250 g) unsmoked streaky bacon, chopped**	8 oz unsmoked streaky bacon, chopped**
olive oil and butter	olive oil and butter

* The beans should be very new and very small and very tender.
** Ham can be substituted for bacon and gives a slightly more sophisticated though less rich tasting dish.

Cook the beans until done. Meanwhile fry the onion in a mixture of olive oil and butter and add the red pepper. Finally add the tomatoes and bacon. Drain the beans and mix in the sauce.

GREEN BEANS WITH TARATOR (Turkey)

GREEN BEANS IN A WALNUT SAUCE

This sauce is used throughout Turkey and the Middle East for plainly boiled vegetables. In Turkey it is made with walnuts and occasionally, but more expensively, hazelnuts. In the Lebanon it is usually made of almonds. Also in Turkey it is frequently mixed with thick yoghurt to make a less concentrated sauce. It can also be used on cold vegetables.

Imperial/Metric	American
3 lb (1.5 kilos) runner beans	3 lb string beans
8 oz (250 g) walnut pieces	1 cup walnut meats
6 fl. oz (180 ml) olive oil	¾ cup olive oil
4 tablespoons wine vinegar	4 tablespoons wine vinegar
2 tablespoons breadcrumbs	2 tablespoons breadcrumbs
1 clove garlic, chopped fine	1 clove garlic, chopped fine
½ teaspoon salt	½ teaspoon salt
pepper to taste	pepper to taste
10 fl. oz (300 ml) yoghurt, unflavoured (optional)	1¼ cups yoghurt, unflavoured (optional)

Cook the prepared beans in boiling water and drain. Mix all the other ingredients in a liquidizer or food processor. (Add the yoghurt if wished.) Stir into the beans, sprinkle with freshly ground pepper and serve.

This sauce is better made the night before.

TOPINAMBOURS AU GRATIN (France)

JERUSALEM ARTICHOKES IN CHEESE SAUCE

Not everyone likes Jerusalem artichokes, so make sure from your guests beforehand.

Imperial/Metric	American
2½ lb (1.5 kilos) cooked weight Jerusalem artichokes	2½ lb cooked weight Jerusalem artichokes
1 recipe *sauce mornay* (p.397)	1 recipe *sauce mornay* (p.397)
4 tablespoons Gruyère cheese, grated	4 tablespoons Gruyère cheese, grated
1 teaspoon Tabasco	1 teaspoon Tabasco

Put the vegetables into a *hot sauce mornay*, sprinkle with grated cheese and then cook in a hot oven for 20 minutes at 400°F/200°C/Gas 6. If the top is not brown enough, run it under a hot grill for a minute or 2.

POIREAUX A LA CREME (France)

LEEKS IN A CREAM SAUCE

Imperial/Metric	*American*
5 or 6 leeks per person*	5 or 6 leeks per person*
1 recipe *sauce suprème* (p.392)	1 recipe *sauce suprème* (p.392)
2 egg yolks	2 egg yolks
4 tablespoons Gruyère cheese	4 tablespoons Gruyère cheese

* Choose the new, small leeks, cut off the green and keep them whole.

Cook the leeks in boiling water until *just* done, or alternatively cook them in a microwave. Lay the cooked leeks in a large, shallow, fireproof dish and pour over the *sauce suprème* to which you have added 2 egg yolks. Cook for 10 minutes at 375°F/190°C/Gas 5. It should be brown on top – if not, run it under a very hot grill for a moment rather than cooking any more in the oven.

POIREAUX A LA VINAIGRETTE (France)

COLD LEEKS IN OIL AND VINEGAR DRESSING

Imperial/Metric	*American*
7 lb (3.5 kilos) leeks*	7 lb leeks*
1 recipe vinaigrette (p.401)	1 recipe vinaigrette (p.401)
1 teaspoon tomato concentrate or dessertspoon ketchup	1 teaspoon tomato concentrate or dessertspoon ketchup
a little sugar (optional)	a little sugar (optional)

* By the time you have discarded the green part of the leeks, you will be left with about 2½ lb (1 kilo) and not much more. The smaller and thinner these are, the better.

Wash the leeks thoroughly and put on to cook in plain boiling salted water. Cook approximately 10 minutes, but check so they are not overcooked, refresh them with cold water and drain once more. Stir a scant teaspoon of tomato purée into the vinaigrette. Cover and chill, overnight preferably.

LATTUGHE FARCITE (Italy)

STUFFED LETTUCE

Only for people who grow their own lettuces. Then it is inexpensive and delicious.

Imperial/Metric	American
8 small lettuces	8 small lettuces
8 oz (250 g) prepared prawns	8 oz prepared shrimps
4 oz (125 g) dried breadcrumbs	½ cup dried breadcrumbs
2 egg yolks	2 egg yolks
4 tablespoons double cream	4 tablespoons heavy cream
1 tumbler white wine	1 cup white wine
2 oz (60 g) butter	¼ cup butter
nutmeg, parsley, salt and pepper	nutmeg, parsley, salt and pepper

Boil a large saucepan of water and plunge the cleaned but still whole lettuces in for just under 2 minutes. Drain, rinse with cold water and squeeze as dry as possible. Put the lettuces in a shallow fireproof dish so that they are close together. Mix all the other ingredients together, except the wine, and divide between the 8 lettuces. Then pour the wine around them. Cut the butter into 8 pieces and put a piece on each lettuce. Cook for 15-20 minutes at 350°F/180°C/Gas 4.

CEPES MARINES (France)

MARINATED *BOLETUS EDULIS*

Some people add onion rings at serving time. This is quite a good idea where cultivated mushrooms are concerned but kills the subtlety of the wild sort.

Imperial/Metric	American
3 lb (1.50 kilos) *boletus edulis* or cultivated mushrooms*	3 lb *boletus edulis* or cultivated mushrooms*
1 lemon (for blanching wild mushrooms)	1 lemon (for blanching wild mushrooms)
5 cloves garlic	5 cloves garlic
1 or 2 bayleaves, according to taste	1 or 2 bayleaves, according to taste
2 or 3 sprigs of thyme	2 or 3 sprigs of thyme
bunch of parsley, tied up	bunch of parsley, tied up
1 teaspoon fennel seeds	1 teaspoon fennel seeds
1 bunch parsley, chopped (to decorate)	1 bunch parsley, chopped (to decorate)
6 fl. oz (180 ml) olive oil	¾ cup olive oil
6 fl. oz (180 ml) wine vinegar	¾ wine vinegar

* If using other than cultivated mushrooms, blanch them for 2-3

minutes in boiling water acidulated with the lemon, and strain.

Crush the garlic, add the herbs, vinegar and olive oil and bring to the boil. After a couple of minutes put in the mushrooms and turn off the heat. Let cool and refrigerate overnight. When serving, add some chopped parsley.

CHAMPIGNONS A LA BEARNAISE (France)

MUSHROOMS WITH *SAUCE BEARNAISE*

Imperial/Metric	*American*
24 large mushrooms, approx. 3 inches (7 cm) diameter*	24 large mushrooms, approx. 3 inches (7 cm) diameter*
1 recipe *sauce béarnaise* (p.392)	1 recipe *sauce béarnaise* (p.392)
2 tablespoons parsley, finely chopped (to decorate)	2 tablespoons parsley, finely chopped (to decorate)

* If smaller mushrooms are used, you will need proportionately more.

Make the *sauce béarnaise* in advance and heat in a double saucepan or *bain-marie*. Make sure it is quite warm at serving time. Brush both sides of the mushrooms with oil and grill the top side first (white side). Once cooked, pour over the warm *sauce béarnaise*, sprinkle with parsley and serve.

CATALAN MUSHROOMS WITH HAM (Spain)

In Catalonia either fresh *boletus edulis* (*cèpes*) or pine mushrooms would be used. This is an ideal recipe for British field mushrooms but cultivated mushrooms also taste good done this way. Hot French bread is the best accompaniment.

Imperial/Metric	*American*
3 lb (1.5 kilos) mushrooms	3 lb mushrooms
1 lb (500 g) best-quality ham	1 lb best-quality ham
1 onion, chopped	1 onion, chopped
4 cloves garlic	4 cloves garlic
8 fl. oz (240 ml) dry white wine	1 cup dry white wine
4 tablespoons breadcrumbs	4 tablespoons breadcrumbs
3 tablespoons chopped parsley (to decorate)	3 tablespoons chopped parsley (to decorate)
2 fl. oz (60 ml) olive oil	2 fl. oz olive oil
salt and fresh black pepper	salt and fresh black pepper

Keep the mushrooms whole if you can, since they lose less liquid that way. Cut the ham into thickish slices and then into cubes. Fry with the onion and garlic in the olive oil and then add the mushrooms. Pour off some of the liquid if there is too much. Add the breadcrumbs, stir, then add the white wine. Simmer gently for 15 minutes or so and serve with the parsley sprinkled on top.

CHAMPIGNONS A LA GRECQUE 1 (France)

MARINATED MUSHROOMS

Imperial/Metric	*American*
2½ lb (approx. 1 kilo) button mushrooms	2½ lb button mushrooms
6 fl. oz (180 ml) olive oil	¾ cup olive oil
6 fl. oz (180 ml) wine vinegar	¾ cup wine vinegar
6 fl. oz (180 ml) water	¾ cup water
bouquet garni of bayleaf, thyme and parsley	*bouquet garni* of bayleaf, thyme and parsley
1 teaspoon coriander seeds	1 teaspoon coriander seeds
1 teaspoon fennel seeds	1 teaspoon fennel seeds
salt and pepper	salt and pepper
parsley, chopped (to garnish)	parsley, chopped (to garnish)
2 tablespoons tomato concentrate	2 tablespoons tomato concentrate

Make a *court-bouillon* and boil for 3-4 minutes before adding the whole button mushrooms. Cook 5-10 minutes, depending on the size and type of mushroom used. Strain and reduce the liquid by at least three-quarters and pour over mushrooms. Cool and serve next day with parsley sprinkled on top.

CHAMPIGNONS A LA GRECQUE 2 (France)

MARINATED MUSHROOMS

Imperial/Metric	*American*
2½ lb (approx. 1 kilo) button mushrooms	2½ lb button mushrooms
juice of 1 lemon	juice of 1 lemon
6 fl. oz (180 ml) olive oil	¾ cup olive oil
bouquet garni of bay leaf, thyme, parsley	*bouquet garni* of bay leaf, thyme, parsley
6 fl. oz (180 ml) wine vinegar	¾ cup wine vinegar
6 fl. oz (180 ml) water	¾ cup water
1 teaspoon coriander seeds	1 teaspoon coriander seeds
salt and pepper	salt and pepper
parsley, chopped (to garnish)	parsley, chopped (to garnish)

As before, make a *court bouillon* of the above ingredients and add button mushrooms after 3-4 minutes of boiling. Cook for 5-10 minutes, depending on the size and type of mushrooms. Strain and reduce liquid by three-quarters and pour over mushrooms. Cool and serve next day with parsley garnish.

HOT MUSHROOM HORS D'ŒUVRES (Lebanon)

Serve with Arab or pitta bread.

Imperial/Metric	*American*
2 lb (1 kilo) large mushrooms, finely sliced	2 lb large mushrooms, finely sliced
4 fl. oz (120 ml) olive oil	½ cup olive oil
4 cloves garlic, crushed	4 cloves garlic, crushed
2 teaspoons Tabasco	2 teaspoons Tabasco
rind and the juice of 1 lemon	rind and the juice of 1 lemon
handful of chopped parsley or fresh coriander to taste	handful of chopped parsley or fresh coriander to taste

Cook the mushrooms and garlic together in the oil. Do not over-cook. Add the lemon rind and juice and Tabasco, stir and strain. Reduce the liquid to approximately 2-3 fl. oz (100 ml/ generous US ¼ cup). Return the liquid to the mushrooms and stir in the chopped parsley.

FUNGHI ALLA MARSALA (Italy)

MUSHROOMS IN MARSALA

Ideally the mushrooms should be half *porcini* (*boletus edulis*, *cèpes*) and half cultivated. Nevertheless, this is a good and unusual way to do cultivated mushrooms. Serve with warm French-type bread.

Imperial/Metric	*American*
3 lb (1.5 kilos) mushrooms, finely chopped	3 lb mushrooms, finely chopped
1 onion, finely chopped	1 onion, finely chopped
1 tablespoon tomato concentrate	1 tablespoon tomato concentrate
4 fl. oz (120 ml) olive oil	½ cup olive oil
6 fl. oz (180 ml) medium sweet Marsala	¾ cup medium sweet Marsala
salt and pepper	salt and pepper
1 teaspoon marjoram	1 teaspoon marjoram
1 tablespoon parsley, chopped	1 tablespoon parsley, chopped

Using a wide pan so that the liquids will reduce quickly, fry the onion in the olive oil. Stir in the tomato concentrate. Add the mushrooms and sprinkle with the marjoram and a little salt. Cook fast and when almost cooked pour on the Marsala. Turn up the heat, stirring all the time, and finish the cooking – a matter of less than 2 minutes. Transfer to a serving dish and sprinkle with parsley.

CHAMPIGNONS A LA SUISSE (Switzerland)

MUSHROOMS IN SOUR CREAM

Imperial/Metric	*American*
6-8 slices white bread, cubed	6-8 slices white bread, cubed
2½ lb (approx. 1.25 kilos) mushrooms, whole*	2½ lb mushrooms, whole*
1 medium onion, finely chopped	1 medium onion, finely chopped
1 tablespoon paprika	1 tablespoon paprika
1 tablespoon parsley, chopped	1 tablespoon parsley, chopped
3-4 tablespoons butter	3-4 tablespoons butter
½ pint (300 ml) sour cream	1½ cup commercial sour cream

* Use small button mushrooms. The larger sort will need cutting and will let out juice and ruin this dish.

Make croûtons of the bread cubes and keep warm while you cook the mushrooms. They can be made in advance and re-heated without harm in the oven. The rest of the dish can be made in advance up to the point where you add the cream.

Cook the onion in the butter and when almost done add the button mushrooms and cook for 4-5 minutes. Add the paprika, parsley and sour cream. Bring up to heat but do not let boil. Put the croûtons in the bottom of a serving dish, pour over the mushrooms and cream and serve immediately.

MUSHROOMS A LA GRECQUE (Greece and all over the Mediterranean)

Imperial/Metric
3 lb (1.5 kilos) small cultivated mushrooms, preferably whole*
1 or 2 stalks of celery, chopped
1 large onion, finely sliced
juice of 1 large lemon
6 fl. oz (180 ml) olive oil
6 fl. oz (180 ml) wine vinegar
12 fl. oz (360 ml) water
pinch each of dried thyme and oregano (*rigani*)
teaspoon each of ground coriander and fennel seeds
2 teaspoons double-concentrate tomato paste
parsley, chopped
salt and pepper

American
3 lb small cultivated mushrooms, preferably whole*
1 or 2 stalks of celery, chopped
1 large onion, finely sliced
juice of 1 large lemon
¾ cup olive oil
¾ cup wine vinegar
1½ cups water
pinch each of dried thyme and oregano (*rigani*)
teaspoon each of ground coriander and fennel seeds
2 teaspoons double-concentrate tomato paste
parsley, chopped
salt and pepper

* Bear in mind that sliced mushrooms always give off more juice than those that are whole.

Cook the onion slices gently in the olive oil but do not let brown. Add all the other ingredients except the mushrooms and bring to a rolling boil. Turn down heat and add mushrooms. Cook them 5-10 minutes – they should still hold their shape. Drain into a dish and reduce the liquid to around a quarter pint (just under 150 ml). Once cool, refrigerate overnight. Before serving add some parsley. These will keep for 3-4 days well refrigerated.

CONGUMELOS VILA VICOSA (Portugal)

MUSHROOMS COOKED WITH WINE, WALNUTS AND BACON

Vila Vicosa, one of the prettiest old-fashioned towns in Portugal, is the home of this dish, which is served only in autumn when the pine woods are full of wild mushrooms. The Portuguese use their raw ham for it, but this is ruinously expensive elsewhere and green bacon is a good substitute.

In Portugal this is served on slices of crisp fried bread, which makes it almost too rich. You can serve it in individual dishes accompanied by fresh French bread or toast.

Imperial/Metric	American
2½ lb (1 kilo) mushrooms	2½ lb mushrooms
butter or oil for frying	butter or oil for frying
2 large onions, chopped	2 large onions, chopped
12 fl. oz (360 ml) red wine	1½ cups red wine
2 tablespoons tomato concentrate	2 tablespoons tomato concentrate
8 rashers of unsmoked bacon, grilled and diced	8 rashers of unsmoked bacon, grilled and diced
6 oz (190 g) walnuts, chopped	¾ cup chopped walnut meats
Tabasco to taste	Tabasco to taste
good pinch thyme	good pinch thyme
salt and pepper	salt and pepper

Fry the onions in the butter until transparent. Clean and trim mushrooms and add them whole to the pan, with herbs and seasoning to taste. Put in the Tabasco (this dish should be fairly highly seasoned) and then add the wine and tomato purée. Once the mushrooms are all but cooked, drain off the liquid and reduce this by at least half. Return liquid to mushrooms. Add the bacon and finally the walnuts.

STUFFED OLIVES (USSR: Armenia)

As olives vary so much in size and weight it is impossible to give an exact amount of the large green olives (such as Spanish Reinas), stoned, that would accept the following amount of stuffing. Use the very largest you can find – otherwise it will be too much work. Of olives the size of 'Reinas', allow approximately 6 per head as part of a mixed hors d'œuvre.

Russians and Armenians make this with a pestle and mortar but it can be done in a liquidizer. Personally I prefer this recipe with the addition of the juice of a lemon or some wine vinegar but it is not in the original.

Imperial/Metric	American
yolks of 3 hard-boiled eggs	yolks of 3 hardcooked eggs
8 oz (250 g) butter	1 cup butter
8 oz (250 g) *kilkis** or anchovies	8 oz *kilkis** or anchovies
4 oz (125 g) onion, chopped	4 oz onion, chopped
3 tablespoon tarragon, chopped	3 tablespoon tarragon, chopped
3 tablespoon chervil or parsley, chopped	3 tablespoon chervil or parsley, chopped
cayenne pepper	cayenne pepper
eggs, hard-boiled (to garnish)	eggs, hardcooked (to garnish)

* *Kilkis* are specially preserved tiny fish from Norwegian waters; they were much loved in Tsarist Russia, whence they presumably got to Armenia. Anchovies will do just as well, though you should check on their saltiness and choose the *least* salt. Otherwise soak them for an hour or so in milk and water to rid them of their salt.

Mash down the fish, butter, egg yolks, herbs, onions and cayenne pepper and stuff the olives. Arrange on a dish and garnish with quartered hard-boiled eggs if liked.

BAKED ONIONS IN CREAM (Sweden)

You will need a large baking dish for this recipe.
Serve with French bread. Very good cold-weather food.

Imperial/Metric	American
3 lb (1.25 kilos) white onions, finely sliced	3 lb white onions, finely sliced
approx. 4 oz (125 g) anchovies*	approx. 4 oz anchovies*
2 oz (60 g) butter (or oil/butter or clarified butter)	¼ cup butter (or oil/butter or clarified butter)
1 pint (600 ml) double cream	2½ cups heavy cream
cayenne pepper to taste	cayenne pepper to taste

* Be very careful about the type of anchovies you buy: those in tins with oil are often very salt indeed; those in jars are best – in any event, you must soak them before use for at least an hour.

Cook the onions in a large pan with the butter or oil and butter, or clarified butter which burns less easily. The onions should not brown but should become straw-coloured. Once they are almost cooked, put them in a large baking dish, add the chopped anchovies and pour over the cream to which you have added the cayenne pepper. (For British and American taste this seems a prodigious amount of cream, so I would suggest using rather less and, if necessary, adding more half way through the cooking.) Put in a moderately hot oven (375°F/190°C/Gas 5 for 10 minutes. (After 5 minutes see how much more cream you need, if any.) If the top of the *gratin* is not browning sufficiently, do not be tempted to leave the dish in much longer than 10 minutes but run it under a hot grill for a couple of minutes instead.

FLAN D'OIGNONS (France and Belgium)

ONION FLAN

Although called a flan this has no pastry base – it is more of a flan in the Spanish meaning of the term, being an oniony egg custard. I have found a microwave oven ideal for cooking onions in butter for this sort of dish since they do not burn. About 4 minutes on top heat should do the trick but every make of microwave is different so follow the maker's instruction book.

Imperial/Metric	*American*
1 lb (500 g) large onions, finely sliced	1 lb large onions, finely sliced
1 pint (600 ml) milk	2½ cups milk
8 eggs	8 eggs
3 dessertspoons sunflower oil	3 dessertspoons sunflower oil
6 oz (185 g) butter	6 oz butter
nutmeg, pepper and salt	nutmeg, pepper and salt

Put the onions to cook in the oil and butter mixture on a very low heat – they should not colour but should just more or less melt into a purée. An asbestos or heat mat can help, and a sharp eye and stirring from time to time will prevent catching. Cool thoroughly. Beat the eggs and milk together and the salt, pepper and about ½ teaspoon of freshly grated nutmeg. Add the cooled onions to this mixture and divide between 8 well-buttered ramekins. Place these in a low oven, approximately 250°F/130°C/ Gas ½ for 1 hour.

Some people run the finished flans under the grill to brown the tops but just decorating with a sprig of parsley is all that is required.

OIGNONS A LA MONEGASGUE (Monaco)

MARINATED ONIONS

In Italy they produce small, slightly larger than pickling size onions for this dish, and what is more they sell them ready peeled! Alas, in Monaco and elsewhere they do not, and one must do it oneself.

Imperial/Metric	American
2 lb (1 kilo) small onions	2 lb small onions
5 fl. oz (150 ml) olive oil	scant ¾ cup olive oil
2 fl. oz (60 ml) vinegar	¼ cup vinegar
3 medium tomatoes, chopped	3 medium tomatoes, chopped
2 oz (60 g) currants	2 oz currants
1 tablespoon sugar	1 tablespoon sugar
1 bayleaf	1 bayleaf
thyme (*serpolet* type if possible)	thyme (*serpolet* type if possible)
salt and pepper	salt and pepper
parsley, chopped	parsley, chopped
1 recipe classic vinaigrette (p.401)	1 recipe classic vinaigrette (p.401)

Cook onions in boiling water until three-quarters done. Drain off and sprinkle on sugar. Caramelize the onions very slightly. Add the tomatoes and stir until nearly done. Then pour on the vinaigrette dressing, put in currants, bayleaf, thyme, salt and pepper and cook a little longer – they should not be soft. Cool and finally stir in the parsley. Should be made at least 4 hours before serving.

ONIONS IMAM BAYELDI (Turkey)

Imperial/Metric	American
8 large onions, whole parboiled	8 large onions, whole parboiled

STUFFING

Imperial/Metric	American
remainder of the onions, chopped	remainder of the onions, chopped
3 tablespoons olive oil	3 tablespoons olive oil
2 cloves of garlic, chopped fine	2 cloves of garlic, chopped fine
handful of parsley, chopped fine	handful of parsley, chopped fine
1 teaspoon dried dillweed	1 teaspoon dried dillweed
1 lb (500 g) tomatoes, skinned and chopped	1 lb tomatoes, skinned and chopped
2 oz pine nuts (optional)	2 oz *pignoli* (optional)
2 oz currants	2 oz currants
2 tablespoons vinegar or lemon juice	2 tablespoons vinegar or lemon juice
salt and pepper	salt and pepper
1 dessertspoon white sugar	1 dessertspoon white sugar

Mix all the ingredients and stuff the onions. Pack in a dish and pour in up to 1 pint (600 ml/1¼ US pints) of water to which you have added the dessertspoon of sugar and a little salt. Cook for 45 minutes in a medium oven (350°F/180°C/Gas 4), basting with the water from time to time. You may need additional water.

Serve cold. Better the next day.

BAKED PEARS AND ROQUEFORT CHEESE (USA)

Imperial/Metric	*American*
4 peeled pears, diced	4 peeled pears, diced
4 oz (125 g) Roquefort cheese	½ cup Roquefort cheese
4 oz (125 ml) single cream	½ cup light cream
5 slices white bread	5 slices white bread

Make croûtons first: remove the crusts from the sliced bread, cut into half-inch (1 cm) cubes and fry them in hot oil. Drain well on kitchen paper. Divide them between 8 ramekins. Then divide the pear cubes among the 8 dishes. Put some Roquefort on each and dribble about 1 tablespoon cream on each ramekin. Run under a fierce grill until golden brown and bubbling or alternatively give them 10 minutes in an oven at 400°F/200°C/Gas 6. That should do the trick but look after 7 or 8 minutes to make sure.

CHEESE STUFFED PEPPERS (Yugoslavia: Serbia)

For all I know, these are common all over Yugoslavia. We were taken out to lunch in Belgrade where this (and a cup of coffee afterwards) was the only thing on the menu. My own hostess kept complaining, *sotto voce*, that our hostess was the laziest thing on earth and could not be bothered to do more than one dish – which was an insult in Serbia etc. However, the peppers were so delicious, and there were so many of them, that it did not seem to matter.

Serve with salt and pepper and plenty of warm French bread.

Imperial/Metric	American
16 large peppers	16 large peppers
approx. 1 lb (500 g) thinly sliced sharp, melting cheese*	approx. 1 lb thinly sliced sharp, melting cheese*
pepper	pepper
1 large clove garlic	1 large clove garlic
olive oil	olive oil

* In Yugoslavia they use a cheese called Kačkavalj – which is something like a cross between Bel Paese and Cheddar, only better. Americans are better off for once, since Monterey Jack comes quite close to its Yugoslav counterpart. The sort of cheese used in France for *raclette* would also do.

Cut off the tops off the peppers, remove the seeds and pith. Rub each pepper with a cut clove of garlic and put a slice or 2 of cheese the width and length of the pepper. Brush a couple of large, shallow, fireproof dishes with olive oil or lard. Lay the stuffed peppers inside and brush their tops with olive oil or pour it over. Cook at 400°F/200°C/Gas 6 for 30 minutes. If they are not done by this time, give them a little longer. It depends on the thickness of the pepper.

LECSÓ (Hungary)

RAGOUT OF PEPPERS AND TOMATOES

One of the national dishes of Hungary and one which they also put up in preserving jars for winter when they eat it with a sort of pasta called *tarhonya*. (I've served it on pasta to Italians and they loved it.)

The most common way to find *lecsó* is with rice or *tarhonya* added but these additions make it too substantial for a first course. If bottling or preserving *lecsó*, never use anything with flour or rice with it. It can also be successfully frozen, though some of the taste is lost.

The main problem with *lecsó* is that it is difficult to get the plain thing: people insist on adding frankfurters, bacon, rice, smoked sausage and so on to it. So here's the real McCoy. (Serve with French bread.)

Imperial/Metric	American
3 lb (1.5 kilos) peppers	3 lb peppers
1½ lb (750 g) tomatoes, peeled	1½ lb tomatoes, peeled
2 large onions, finely sliced	2 large onions, finely sliced
4 oz (125 g) bacon (optional)	4 oz bacon (optional)
lard or sunflower oil	lard or sunflower oil
2 tablespoons paprika	2 tablespoons paprika
salt	salt

Cook the onion in the fat. If you want to use bacon, this is the moment to put it in. Remove the seeds and pith from the peppers and slice them. Add them to the pan and cook over a high flame for about 10 minutes, stirring much of the time since they catch easily. Then add the tomatoes and cook at a simmer for another 10 minutes. Add salt and paprika and your dish is ready.

JANSSONS FRESTELSE (Sweden and USA)

JANSSON'S TEMPTATION (POTATO GRATIN)

This recipe is named after an American (of Swedish origin) who was the pastor of a community which believed in eating nothing but the bare essentials to keep body (and soul) together. Tradition has it that he was caught on one occasion stuffing himself with this dish. It is quite heavy and very rich, so it should be followed by something light and, of course, without potatoes.

Imperial/Metric	American
a small tin of anchovy fillets	a small tin of anchovy fillets
2 lb (1 kilo) potatoes, peeled and thinly sliced	2 lb potatoes, peeled and thinly sliced
2 large onions, finely sliced	2 large onions, finely sliced
15 fl. oz (450 ml) double cream	2 cups heavy cream
butter	butter
8 fl. oz (240 ml) milk	1 cup milk

Soak the anchovies in milk, or milk and water, if you think they are too salt. Butter a baking dish thickly and put in a layer of potatoes, then a layer of onion. Put some of the anchovy fillets on top. Continue this way, finishing with a layer of potatoes. Pour over the mixture of milk and cream and dot with butter. Bake at 325-350°F/170-180°C/Gas for 3-4 50-60 minutes.

ANDALUSIAN BAKED TOMATOES (Spain)

Imperial/Metric	American
8 large tomatoes (Marmande type)	8 large tomatoes (Marmande type)
8 oz (250 g) chopped pimento stuffed olives	1 cup chopped pimento stuffed olives
8 slices white bread	8 slices white bread
3 cloves garlic	3 cloves garlic
8 tablespoons olive oil	8 tablespoons olive oil
thyme and parsley	thyme and parsley
salt and pepper	salt and pepper

Slice the top off each tomato and scoop out the seeds. In a food processor or liquidizer turn the bread into breadcrumbs (you can leave the crusts on if you wish) and put them into a bowl. Add the tomato seeds and liquid, chopped olives and pimentos, garlic, thyme, parsley, salt and pepper. Stuff the tomatoes with this mixture. Put them on a baking tray and pour about 1 tablespoon olive oil over each. Bake at 450°F/230°C/Gas 8 for 5 minutes or so.

If the tomatoes are really enormous, you can cut them in half and bake them like that but they will take rather more stuffing and oil.

CHEESE STUFFED TOMATOES (UK)

Serve on lettuce leaves.

Imperial/Metric	*American*
8 large tomatoes (Marmande type)	8 large tomatoes (Marmande type)
12 *petits suisses* cheeses	12 *petits suisses* cheeses
1 teaspoon Dijon mustard	1 teaspoon Dijon mustard
half to whole cucumber (depending on size)	half to whole cucumber (depending on size)
4 fl. oz (120 ml) double cream	½ cup heavy cream
1 tablespoon wine vinegar	1 tablespoon wine vinegar
3 tablespoons olive oil	3 tablespoons olive oil
3 shallots, finely chopped	3 shallots, finely chopped
chives or parsley chopped (for decoration)	chives or parsley chopped (for decoration)

Cut each tomato in half and remove the centre flesh and seeds. Sprinkle slightly with salt and turn upside down to drain. Meanwhile peel and de-seed the cucumber and dice. Put in colander, sprinkle with salt and leave to drain.

Just before serving, mix the *petits suisses* with the shallots and mustard and stir in the cucumber. Fill the 16 halves. Mix the cream with the oil and vinegar and pour over the tomatoes. Sprinkle with chives or parsley.

STUFFED TOMATOES (Portugal)

Imperial/Metric	*American*
8 large tomatoes (Marmande type)	8 large tomatoes (Marmande type)
4 oz (125 g) cream cheese	½ cup Philadelphia-type cheese
12 oz (375 g) peeled prawns	12 oz peeled shrimps
2 tablespoons chives, chopped	2 tablespoons chives, chopped
2 fl. oz (60 ml) double cream	¼ cup heavy cream
vinaigrette (p.401)	vinaigrette (p.401)
salt and pepper to taste	salt and pepper to taste
1 clove garlic (optional)	1 clove garlic (optional)
parsley, chives or watercress (to garnish)	parsley, chives or watercress (to garnish)

In Portugal they skin their tomatoes for this dish but it is not essential. Cut off tops of tomatoes and reserve. Scoop out flesh and seeds, sprinkle with salt and drain. Mix all the other ingredients, except the vinaigrette, and fill the tomatoes. Put on the tomato tops. Arrange in a large dish or on individual plates and spoon over vinaigrette. Garnish with parsley, chives or watercress, whichever is the most plentiful.

TOMATES FARCIES A LA PROVENÇALE (France)

PROVENÇAL STUFFED TOMATOES

Imperial/Metric	*American*
8 large tomatoes (Marmande type)	8 large tomatoes (Marmande type)
8 oz (250 g) sausage meat	8 oz sausage meat
3 oz (90 g) breadcrumbs	½ cup breadcrumbs
1 onion, chopped	1 onion, chopped
2 cloves garlic, chopped	2 cloves garlic, chopped
3 tablespoons *bouillon*	3 tablespoons *bouillon*
thyme	thyme
2 tablespoons chopped parsley	2 tablespoons chopped parsley

Slice off top of tomatoes and reserve. Sauté the onion and garlic in a little oil, add the pulp and seeds of the 8 tomatoes, the herbs and finally the sausage meat, then moisten with the *bouillon*. Stuff the tomatoes with this mixture. Oil the outside of the skins if possible since it makes the finished dish look better. Replace the (oiled) caps and bake in a dish for 30-35 minutes at 300°F/150°C/Gas 2. They are best eaten hot.

TOMATES FARCIES A LA VAUDOISE (Switzerland)

STUFFED TOMATOES

Imperial/Metric	*American*
8 large tomatoes	8 large tomatoes
3 eggs, separated	3 eggs, separated
1 medium onion, finely chopped	1 medium onion, finely chopped
2 oz (60 g) ham, minced	¼ cup ham, minced
2 oz (60 g) Gruyère cheese, grated	¼ cup Gruyère cheese, grated
a little cayenne – no salt	a little cayenne – no salt
third of recipe *sauce béchamel* (p.391)	third of recipe *sauce béchamel* (p.391)
a little parsley or chives (optional)	a little parsley or chives (optional)

Remove slice from top of each tomato and discard. Remove pulp and seeds and drain thoroughly. Add the ham and Gruyère cheese to the cold *sauce béchamel* and then one by one work in the egg yolks. Add chives or parsley (optional). Whip egg whites and fold them into the mixture. Divide between the 8 tomatoes and bake in a hot oven for 15 minutes at 375°F/185-190°C/Gas 5.

Must be eaten straight from the oven and can't be kept waiting.

ATJAR KETIMUN (Malaya and Indonesia)

This spicy mixed vegetable dish goes well with chicken liver satay (p.66) and with prawns (p.127).

Imperial/Metric	*American*
4 cucumbers	4 cucumbers
1 medium onion, finely chopped	1 medium onion, finely chopped
2 teaspoons ground turmeric	2 teaspoons ground turmeric
1 tablespoon fresh ginger	1 tablespoon fresh ginger
2 cloves garlic	2 cloves garlic
2 tablespoons brown sugar	2 tablespoons brown sugar
8 fl. oz (240 ml) white vinegar	1 cup white vinegar
4 fl. oz (120 ml) water	½ cup water
3 or 4 tablespoons salt	3 or 4 tablespoons salt
1 hot chilli (optional)	1 hot chilli (optional)
2 oz (60 g) ground almonds	¼ cup almonds, skinned and ground
cooking oil	cooking oil

Peel cucumbers. Depending on their thickness, cut cucumbers lengthwise into halves or quarters. Remove seeds and cut into thickish slices (about ½-⅔ inches/1.5 cm). Put in a large, shallow dish and sprinkle on salt. Leave for 45-60 minutes, then rinse, drain and dry. Meanwhile heat a little oil and fry the garlic and onion in it. Grate or finely chop the fresh ginger (ground ginger won't really do as well) and add, with the brown sugar. Add all other ingredients and simmer for a few minutes. Pour over the drained cucumber and let them soak in this mixture for at least 3-4 hours before serving.

RATATOUILLE A LA NICOISE (France)

There must be more recipes for *ratatouille* than practically anything else. I was once standing in a queue for vegetables in Nice when a Belgian in front of me was asking the owner what vegetables she needed for this local dish. The man laughed and said, '*Madame, avec cet accent vous n'arriverez jamais!*' (i.e. a foreigner, certainly one from as far away as Belgium, would never be able to make it). Not so – there's no mystery about it, except that the vegetables should have had the benefit of open air and Mediterranean sun rather than that of a greenhouse, deep freeze or tin. The Middle East, Turkey and Algeria have dishes very similar to *ratatouille.*

The finished dish should be slightly sloppy but not wet. If you have too much liquid, pour it off and reduce it down without the vegetables, which on further cooking will probably give out even more liquid.

The onions used are the large white summer type with a very mild flavour, and the garlic is the large sort as well, with an equally mild flavour. If you use the small garlic, 2 or 3 cloves will do very adequately. The thyme used is *serpolet* or *thymus serpyllum*, and the parsley is the flat-leaved sort. If you use curly parsley, you will need at least double the quantity.

Imperial/Metric
equal amounts of the following
   vegetables: about 1½ lb
   (750 g) is a good average:
   aubergine
   courgettes
   tomatoes
   green and/or red peppers
   onions
6 or 8 cloves garlic
4 or 5 sprigs fresh thyme
2 bayleaves (optional)
handful of parsley, roughly
   chopped
salt and pepper
3 fl. oz (90 ml) olive oil

American
equal amounts of the following
   vegetables: about 1½ lb is a
   good average:
   eggplant
   zucchini
   tomatoes
   green and/or red sweet
     peppers
   onions
6 or 8 cloves garlic
4 or 5 sprigs fresh thyme
2 bayleaves (optional)
handful of parsley, roughly
   chopped
salt and pepper
3 fl. oz olive oil

Cut everything into 1 inch (5 cm) cubes, keeping the garlic and onions separate. Fry the 2 latter in olive oil without letting them brown, then add all the other ingredients and cook for approximately 10 minutes, stirring all the while, by which time most of the liquid should have come out of the vegetables. Drain the vegetables and turn into an ovenproof dish. Reduce any liquid to a few tablespoons and pour back over the *ratatouille*. At this stage many Niçois stir in a tablespoon or two of tomato concentrate but it is not in any of the classic recipes. However, if your tomatoes are northern European or American, it may be a good idea.

Cook, covered, in a medium oven, middle shelf, for 45 minutes at 400°F/200°C/Gas 6. Serve hot or cold. Better the next day re-heated but pour off any juice which may have leaked out in the meantime.

11   Soups

Cream Soups

Although the classic way to make a cream soup is to add cream and/or eggs at the end, it is possible to make something similar by using either an ordinary or an enriched *sauce béchamel* (p.392).

For those who do not want added flour, *fromage frais* , now available from 0-60 per cent fat can be used – never use more than 40 per cent fat *fromage frais* in soup, i.e. nothing as rich as 50 or 60 per cent. Used at 0 per cent, you will not get such a rich-tasting soup but it will be acceptable and more interesting than a chicken-stock flavoured vegetable purée.

For those who want no dairy products in their soup, Japanese *tofu* (bean curd) is the answer. Chinese will do equally well but tends to be sold only in block form, whereas the Japanese *tofu* (often made outside Japan) comes in the silken variety which is ideal for addition to soups. However, it should be remembered that beans can cause flatulence in children and the elderly, and that *tofu* is made from *fermented* beans, which can cause even worse flatulence, so you should be careful as to whom you serve this particular food. With the help of a liquidizer or food processor, Chinese bean curd can be incorporated into soup – it comes in several varieties: you will need the freshest and unpickled sort. Between 5 and 19 fl. oz (150-300 ml) – 1 or 2 packets of silken *tofu* – is the right amount for 8 servings.

Consommé

Of course there are cubes and there are tins of consommé but nothing replaces the real thing. Too often the cubes are unpleasantly salt (some have as much as 50 per cent salt) and in most countries are available only in chicken flavour. A list of the ingredients on one of the better makes of chicken bouillon cubes makes interesting reading: 'Salt 43 per cent, flavouring agent, monosodium glutamate [frowned on by many medical authorities], fat and meat of boiling fowl, onion, yeast extract, vegetable extract, starch, parsley, spices.' The real thing can be made after having a roast chicken fairly cheaply.

Beef consommé is, of course, more expensive. In tins, probably Campbell's is the most useful, being reasonably priced, utterly reliable and widely available. In countries where consommé is a tradition, it is, strangely, more difficult to find tins of ready-made consommé: France, Belgium, Germany, Austria, Switzerland and Italy are all organized for the home-made stuff. Campbell's is excellent where you want clarified jellied or set consommé. Its only drawback is that it is instantly recognizable as Campbell's and not your own or anyone else's.

Recipes are given for 3 basic consommés: beef (p.299), chicken, (p.300) and fish (p.308). The last should not be confused with a *court-bouillon* which is used for poaching fish only. The fish consommé can be the base of all fish soups unless otherwise stated.

Vegetable

CREME D'ARTICHAUTS (France)

CREAM OF ARTICHOKE SOUP

This soup is best made shortly before consumption and does not improve with keeping.

Imperial/Metric	American
1½ lb (750 g) artichoke hearts or bottoms	1½ lb artichoke hearts or bottoms
1 medium onion, finely chopped	1 medium onion, finely chopped
2½ pints (1.5 litres) chicken stock	6½ cups chicken stock
2 oz (60 g) butter	¼ cup butter
8 fl. oz (240 ml) double cream	1 cup heavy cream
1 tablespoon parsley, chopped	1 tablespoon parsley, chopped

Cook the onion gently in the butter. Meanwhile boil the artichoke hearts or bottoms until done and purée with some of the chicken stock. When all is nicely amalgamated, add the cream. Add half the parsley and use the rest for decorating the soup.

CREME D'ASPERGES (France)

CREAM OF ASPARAGUS SOUP

You can use either white or green asparagus for this soup. Serve with asparagus tips on each plate and with melba toast.

Imperial/Metric	*American*
1½ lb (750 g) asparagus	1½ lbs asparagus
2 pints (1.2 litres) chicken stock	5 cups chicken stock
8 fl. oz (240 ml) double cream	1 cup heavy cream
2 egg yolks	2 egg yolks
salt and pepper	salt and pepper

Clean, trim and then blanch the asparagus for 3-4 minutes in boiling water, drain, then cook in the chicken stock. Reserve some of the tips for decorating the soup.

Put everything through a mouli, liquidizer or food processor and then sieve the result, as you are bound to have some stringy bits. Heat the soup up. Beat the egg and cream together with a little of the warm soup and then gradually add to the rest.

ICED AVOCADO SOUP (Kenya)

Before embarking on the various avocado soups, it should be said that most versions of guacamole (which in itself is really a sauce) can be thinned down into a soup or thickened up with gelatine into a mousse. That said, it is up to you what additions you make.

Imperial/Metric	American
3 ripe avocados	3 ripe avocados
2 pints chicken stock (cubes will do)	5 cups chicken stock (cubes will do)
8 fl. oz (240 ml) double cream	1 cup heavy cream
2 medium tomatoes, chopped	2 medium sized tomatoes, chopped
1 medium onion, chopped	1 medium onion, chopped
salt and pepper	salt and pepper
cayenne or red pepper, in strips (optional)	cayenne or red pepper, in strips (optional)
parsley (to garnish)	parsley (to garnish)
2 tablespoons wine vinegar (optional)	2 tablespoons wine vinegar (optional)
oil for cooking	oil for cooking

Fry the onion and tomatoes together in a little oil. Peel avocados and put in a liquidizer or food processor with the tomato and onion, and make into a purée. Add half the chicken stock and the cream. Out of the machine add the rest of the stock. Adjust seasoning and add the wine vinegar, salt and pepper etc to taste. Ice and serve with either cayenne sprinkled on top or with tiny thin slices of red pepper (which can easily be mistaken for tomato with disastrous consequences). Garnish with chopped parsley.

ICED AVOCADO SOUP (Mexico)

Serve with toasted *tortillas* for preference in cans in speciality grocers in most countries.

Imperial/Metric	American
3 avocados	3 avocados
3 tins Campbell's Beef Consommé	3 cans Campbell's Beef Consommé
2 Campbell's tins filled with water	2 Campbell's cans filled with water
1 tablespoon vinegar	1 tablespoon vinegar
2 tablespoons olive oil	2 tablespoons olive oil
1 medium tomato, chopped	1 medium tomato, chopped
1 medium onion, chopped	1 medium onion, chopped
2 sliced chillies or chilli powder to taste or Tabasco to taste	2 sliced chillies or chilli powder to taste or Tabasco to taste
fresh coriander or parsley, chopped	fresh coriander or parsley, chopped
salt	salt

Peel the 3 avocados, remove stones (reserve 1), chop roughly and put in the liquidizer or food processor with the consommé and water. Reduce to a purée. Add the olive oil and vinegar and remove contents to another bowl. Add onion and tomatoes and a little fresh coriander or parsley. Put one of the avocado stones back in the mixture and cover well. Chill thoroughly but not for more than 3 hours or it will discolour. Check seasoning and add chillies, chilli-powder or Tabasco to taste. If the soup is not thin enough (it should not be too thick), add a little more water.

SOPA DE AGUACATE Y CAMARONES (Venezuela)

AVOCADO SOUP WITH PRAWNS

Imperial/Metric	American
3 avocados, peeled	3 avocados
2½ pints (1.2 litres) fish stock	6¼ cups fish stock
1 lb (500 g) medium prawns*	1 lb medium shrimps*
1 fl. oz (240 ml) double cream	1 cup heavy cream
1 tablespoon white wine vinegar	1 tablespoon white wine vinegar
1 teaspoon Tabasco (optional)	1 teaspoon Tabasco (optional)
parsley or paprika (to decorate)	parsley or paprika (to decorate)

* If possible do not use shelled prawns (shrimps).

Cook the prawns (shrimps) in the fish stock. Strain, keep the stock and shell the prawns (shrimps). Chop into slightly smaller pieces.

Put a little of the stock in the liquidizer or food processor and liquidize the avocados. Add to the rest of the stock, stir in the cream, vinegar, salt and pepper and a little Tabasco if liked. Adjust seasoning – it should be creamy with a slightly tart aftertaste. Add the prawns (shrimps). Serve chilled, sprinkled with parsley and/or a little paprika.

AVOCADO VICHYSSOISE (USA)

Make a vichyssoise according to the recipe on p.287 but withhold 5 fl. oz/150 ml/generous ½ US cup of the chicken broth and a similar amount of the milk. Add the mashed pulp of 1 ripe avocado pear and purée it along with the rest of the soup. Adjust seasoning and add a tiny pinch of cumin. Check that soup is not too thick and act accordingly. Serve absolutely glacial without chives but with a little cayenne or paprika sprinkled on top.

BARSCZYK (Poland)

BEETROOT SOUP

For this version of Polish beetroot soup you must think in advance since you need to ferment some beetroot prior to making the soup. Also, in early autumn the Poles add fresh mushroom broth to the soup and make tiny mushroom *piroshki* (p.194) from the vegetable itself. Both these things can be done with dried mushrooms but, of course, it is not the same.

FOR FERMENTING

Imperial/Metric	American
1 lb (500 g) raw beetroot	1 lb raw beets
a slice of pumpernickel bread or 1 teaspoon live brewers' yeast	a slice of pumpernickel bread or 1 teaspoon live brewers' yeast
approx. 2 pints (1.2 litres) boiled water	5 cups boiled water

Peel the beetroot and slice it finely into julienne strips, cover with boiled water and float the slice of bread on top. (Alternatively, stir in a teaspoon of live brewers' yeast but the taste is not the same as with black bread.) Cover with a muslin cloth and keep in a warm part of the kitchen where the temperature is constant (obviously not too near a stove). Froth should appear. After 5 days, clear the liquid of the froth, strain through a muslin and put into a clean bottle. It will keep in the refrigerator for several weeks.

FOR THE SOUP

Imperial/Metric	American
3 medium carrots	3 medium carrots
3 medium onions	3 medium onions
4 medium beetroot – about 1 lb (500 g)	4 medium beets – about 1 lb
2 pints (1.2 litres) water	5 cups water
1 pint (600 ml) consommé	2½ cups consommé
8 oz (250 g) fresh or 1 oz (30 g) dried mushrooms	8 oz fresh or 1 oz dried mushrooms
1 tablespoon sugar	1 tablespoon sugar
6-8 parsley stalks	6-8 parsley stalks
1 clove garlic, crushed	1 clove garlic, crushed
2 beef bouillon cubes (optional)	2 beef bouillon cubes (optional)
1 glass heavy red wine or port	½ cup heavy red wine
lemon juice (if necessary)	lemon juice (if necessary)
1 pint (600 ml) fermented beetroot juice	2½ cups fermented beetroot juice

Cut all the vegetables into julienne strips where possible and cook them all, except mushrooms, in the water (or bouillon) and simmer for approximately 1 hour. Strain and discard the vegetables (do not push vegetables through the sieve). Cook the mushrooms in the consommé and then discard them (keep them for another dish). If dried mushrooms are used; wash, soak and follow packet directions – allow approximately 1 oz (30 g).

Add this mushroom liquor, fermented beetroot juice and red wine or port to the mixture. By now you should have approximately 4 pints/2.5 litres/10 US cups of liquid left. If you think you have too much, reduce the amount by boiling down rapidly. It should be a rich, clear, beautifully coloured broth. If it is not tart enough, add a little lemon juice but *never* vinegar ('That's Russian,' say the Poles).

SIMPLIFIED BEETROOT SOUP (Poland)

Serve with piroshki (p.194) or warm French bread.

Imperial/Metric	*American*
2 lb (1 kilo) beetroot*	2 lb beets*
2 large onions, sliced or chopped	2 large onion, sliced or chopped
3 tablespoons sunflower oil	3 tablespoons sunflower oil
4 pints water	5 pints water
3 beef bouillon cubes	3 beef bouillon cubes
bouquet garni	*bouquet garni*
twist of lemon peel	twist of lemon peel
glass of red wine	½ cup red wine
caraway seeds (optional)	caraway seeds (optional)

* The beetroot should be sliced thinly, cubed or cut into julienne strips to extract the maximum flavour.

Fry the onions gently in the oil. Add the water and all the other ingredients except the red wine and put on to boil gently for at least 45 minutes. You should lose a bit of liquid during the cooking. Taste and adjust seasoning. (Some people add a teaspoon of caraway seed at this stage but it is not Polish.) Add the red wine, bring up to heat and strain.

QUICK COLD BORSCHT (USA)

COLD BEETROOT SOUP

Strictly speaking, when borscht is served cold it becomes *kholodnik* but Americans call all beetroot soup borscht.

There are rather a lot of people who absolutely loathe beetroot, so make sure of your guests' tastes first. For beetroot lovers, this is ambrosial.

For 8 people, you will have to whizz up this soup in two halves.

Imperial/Metric	*American*
3 tins Campbell's Beef Consommé	3 cans Campbell's Beef Consommé
1 Campbell's tin full of water	1 Campbell's can full of water
10-12 oz (315-375 g) pickled or unpickled beetroot*	10-12 oz pickled or unpickled beets*
10 fl. oz (300 ml) sour cream	1¼ cups sour cream
salt and pepper	salt and pepper
parsley or dill to decorate	parsley or dill to decorate

* If using unpickled beetroot, add 1 tablespoon wine vinegar.

Rinse beetroot well under running tap to get rid of vinegary taste. Put in blender and liquidize. Add consommé and then water. Finally add sour cream and adjust seasoning.

Serve in soup cups with a blob of sour cream and parsley or dill on top.

POTAGE CRECY (France)

CREAM OF CARROT SOUP

Imperial/Metric	*American*
2 lb (1 kilo) carrots, sliced	2 lb carrots, sliced
2 medium onions, chopped	2 medium onions, chopped
a pinch of salt and bicarbonate of soda	a pinch of salt and bicarbonate of soda
2 pints (1.2 litres) chicken stock	5 cups chicken stock
8 fl. oz (240 ml) single or double cream	1 cup light or heavy cream
a little butter	a little butter
croûtons (optional)	croûtons (optional)
parsley, chopped	parsley, chopped

Fry the onions in a little butter and add to the chicken stock and carrots. When cooked, purée or liquidize and add the cream. Serve with or without croûtons and with plenty of parsley.

POTAGE DUBARRY (France)

CREAM OF CAULIFLOWER SOUP

This should not be made by the sauce method.

Imperial/Metric
1½ lb (750 g) cauliflower, in
  sprigs
2 pints (1.2 litres) chicken stock
pinch of nutmeg
8 fl. oz (240 ml) double or single
  cream
salt and pepper
2 egg yolks
croûtons (optional)
parsley, chopped, or paprika

American
1½ lbs cauliflower, in sprigs
5 cups chicken stock
pinch of nutmeg
1 cup heavy or light cream
salt and pepper
2 egg yolks
croûtons (optional)
parsley, chopped, or paprika

Blanch the cauliflower sprigs in boiling water for 5 minutes. Drain and then cook in the chicken stock with the salt and pepper and a pinch of nutmeg until done. Pass through liquidizer, food processor, *mouli-légumes* or sieve. It should be very smooth. Add the cream and bring up to heat but do *not* let boil. In a little of the warm soup beat up 2 egg yolks well and add to the rest. Serve immediately with croûtons and a sprinkling of parsley and/or paprika.

POTAGE LIEGEOISE (Belgium)

CREAM OF CELERIAC AND POTATO SOUP

This soup cannot be made with *sauce béchamel*.

Imperial/Metric
2 medium onions, chopped
1 large or 2 medium celeriac
8 oz (250 g) diced raw potato
scant 3 pints (1.5 litres) chicken
  stock (cubes will do)
8 fl. oz (240 ml) single or double
  cream
2 egg yolks
pinch of nutmeg
salt and pepper
2 fl. oz (60 ml) gin
parsley, chopped (to garnish)

American
2 medium onions, chopped
1 large or 2 medium celeriac
1 cup diced raw potato
3¾ pints chicken stock (cubes
  will do)
1 cup light or heavy cream
2 egg yolks
pinch nutmeg
salt and pepper
¼ cup gin
parsley, chopped (to garnish)

Peel the celeriac with a knife and put into acidulated water or immediately put it on to boil. It will go brown very easily. Cut up small and cook until well done. Cook potatoes separately. Put both vegetables through the mill, liquidizer or food processor with enough stock to make a purée. In a large saucepan mix the purée with the remaining stock to make approximately 4 pints (2.5 litres/5 US pints). Add the seasoning, being careful if you have used stock cubes for they can be very salt. Keep a little of the cream aside and mix down the egg yolks with it. Add rest of cream, bit by bit, to the soup and bring up to heat but do not boil. Adjust seasoning, add gin and serve with a little parsley.

CREAM OF CELERY SOUP (UK)

Imperial/Metric
approx. 1½ lb (750 g) celery
2 pints (1.2 litres) chicken stock
8 fl. oz (240 ml) single or double
   cream
pinch of nutmeg
parsley, chopped
salt and pepper

American
approx. 1½ lb celery
5 cups chicken stock
1 cup light or heavy cream
pinch of nutmeg
parsley, chopped
salt and pepper

Cook the celery in the chicken stock and reduce to a purée. Sieve it – there are bound to be stringy bits. Add the cream and seasonings and bring up to heat. Do not let boil. Serve with a sprinkling of parsley.

Variation
This soup can be made by using an enriched *sauce béchamel* (p.391), in which case you add the puréed and sieved celery to the sauce.

CELERY AND TOMATO SOUP (USA)

Although the original recipe says you can use canned tomato juice, the taste is not nearly so good as when using fresh tomatoes.

Imperial/Metric	American
8 large tomatoes skinned, roughly chopped	8 large tomatoes skinned, roughly chopped
2 pints (1.2 litres) water	5 cups water
2 tablespoons parsley	2 tablespoons parsley
2 tablespoons fresh basil	2 tablespoons fresh basil
2 tablespoons best olive oil	2 tablespoons best olive oil
1 tablespoon wine vinegar	1 tablespoon wine vinegar
1 large head crisp celery	1 large head crisp celery
salt and pepper	salt and pepper
clove of garlic (optional)	clove of garlic (optional)

Liquidize all the ingredients except the water, celery, salt and pepper. If using garlic, make sure it has been thoroughly mixed in. Heat the water to almost boiling and mix in with the tomato mixture. Let cool and then chill. Just before serving, chop the celery finely and add to the chilled mixture. Correct seasoning – you may wish to add a little more vinegar or pepper. The texture should resemble a *gazpacho* (p.290).

CREAM OF CHERVIL SOUP (Belgium and Northern France)

This soup should not be made on a *sauce béchamel* base.

Imperial/Metric	American
approx. 6-8 oz (200-250 g) chervil, finely chopped	approx. 6-8 oz chervil, finely chopped
3 pints (1.5 litres) rich chicken stock	7½ cups rich chicken stock
8 fl. oz (240 ml) single or double cream	1 cup light or heavy cream
2 tablespoons parsley	2 tablespoons parsley
salt and pepper	salt and pepper
2 egg yolks (optional)	2 egg yolks (optional)

Chop the chervil very fine, preferably with a *mezzaluna* or a knife rather than in a food processor. Heat the soup and cream together, adjust seasoning, bring up to heat and stir in the chervil. Remove from heat immediately and serve at once. (Chervil is like basil in that it reacts badly to heat and loses some of its flavour.) 2 egg yolks can be added if wished but it is not necessary.

COLD YOGHURT AND CUCUMBER SOUP (Iran)

Imperial/Metric	American
2 pints (1.2 litres) thick unflavoured yoghurt	2½ pints thick unflavoured yoghurt
4 fl. oz (120 ml) double cream	½ cup heavy cream
2 eggs, hard-boiled	2 eggs, hardcooked
4 oz (125 g) raisins	4 oz raisins
2 cucumbers	2 cucumbers
1 medium onion, finely chopped	1 medium onion, finely chopped
2 tablespoons parsley	2 tablespoons parsley
2 tablespoons fresh or 1 tablespoon freeze-dried dillweed	2 tablespoons fresh or 1 tablespoon freeze-dried dillweed
water and 10-12 ice cubes	water and 10-12 ice cubes
salt and pepper	salt and pepper

Put raisins to soak in hot water for 10 minutes so they plump up. Chop cucumbers finely or julienne them in a food processor. Put in large bowl and add yoghurt, onion, hard-boiled eggs, herbs, drained raisins etc. Add ice cubes and enough water to bring up to the quantity required for 8. Leave in refrigerator for approximately 2½ hours before serving.

CACIK (Turkey)

CUCUMBER AND YOGHURT SOUP

Imperial/Metric	American
3 medium cucumbers, peeled and seeded	3 medium cucumbers, peeled and seeded
2 pints (1.2 litres) thick unflavoured yoghurt	5 cups thick unflavoured yoghurt
2 tablespoons white wine vinegar (optional)	2 tablespoons white wine vinegar (optional)
1 teaspoon dried mint or freeze-dried dillweed*	1 teaspoon dried mint or freeze-dried dillweed*
salt and pepper	salt and pepper

* The Turks use dill and the Lebanese use dried mint.

Tip yoghurt into large mixing bowl and stir to thin down. Peel and de-seed cucumbers and grate them into the yoghurt. If using dill, add now; if using mint, add when serving. Do not add salt and pepper at this stage. Refrigerate for approximately an hour.

Take out before serving, add seasoning and iced water to bring the soup up to the liquid required for 8. Sprinkle each serving with dried mint if you have not used the dill.

CREME D'ENDIVES (Belgium)

CREAM OF CHICORY SOUP

Proceed as for Cream of Asparagus (p.270) but substitute 1½ lb (750 g) Belgian *witloof* (chicory) and add 1 dessertspoon sugar and a pinch of nutmeg. Serve with croûtons.

VELOUTE DE TOPINAMBOURS (France)

JERUSALEM ARTICHOKE SOUP

Serve with or without croutôns. This soup is fairly rich and will take a bit of thinning down if you suddenly have an extra guest.

Imperial/Metric	American
2 lb (1 kilo) Jerusalem artichokes	2 lb Jerusalem artichokes
1 onion, chopped	1 onion, chopped
1 tablespoon butter	1 tablespoon butter
3½ pints (2 litres) chicken bouillon*	8 cups chicken bouillon*
6 level tablespoons double cream	6 level tablespoons heavy cream
bunch of parsley or mixture of parsley and chervil, both chopped fine	bunch of parsley or mixture of parsley and chervil, both chopped fine

* Cubes will do but watch the saltiness.

Partially cook the artichokes in plain water, rinse in cold water and remove peel. Continue cooking in chicken bouillon. Let the onion cook in the butter without taking too much colour. Once the artichokes are thoroughly cooked, run the whole thing either through the mixer or food processor (in at least 2 separate lots) or through a *mouli-légumes*. Add the onions. The soup can be prepared to this stage the day before and kept covered in the refrigerator.

Heat to serving temperature and add the cream and finally the chopped herbs, remembering that chervil, like basil, does not take kindly to being heated. Adjust seasoning.

KARALÁBELEVES (Hungary)

CREAM OF KOHLRABI SOUP

This is a subtle and delicious soup and worth the trouble of growing kohlrabi in your garden. Kohlrabi can also be stuffed with other vegetables or meat as a first course.

Imperial/Metric	*American*
1½ lb (750 g) peeled kohlrabi	1½ lb peeled kohlrabi
2 pints (1.2 litres) chicken stock	5 cups chicken stock
2 shallots (chopped) or 2 teaspoons instant shallot	2 shallots (chopped) or 2 teaspoon instant shallot
pinch of marjoram	pinch of marjoram
8 fl. oz (240 ml) single or double cream	1 cup light or heavy cream
2 egg yolks	2 egg yolks
paprika or parsley, chopped (to decorate)	paprika or parsley, chopped (to decorate)

Cook the kohlrabi in the chicken stock and reduce to a fine purée. Add the instant shallot or alternatively fry 2 shallots in a little butter until almost done. Add the marjoram and cream. Adjust seasoning. Beat the egg yolks with a little of the warm soup and stir in. Bring up to serving heat but do not let boil. Serve sprinkled with paprika or parsley.

CREAM OF LEEK (UK)

Proceed as for Cream of Asparagus (p.270) but substitute 1½ lb (750 g) leeks for the asparagus.

POTAGE BONNE FEMME (France)

LEEK AND POTATO SOUP

This is a family recipe and so probably differs slightly from the classic version.

Imperial/Metric	American
1½ lb (750 g) leeks	1½ lb leeks
8 oz (250 g) carrots, diced	8 oz carrots, diced
1 lb (500 g) potatoes, diced	1 lb potatoes, diced
3 oz (90 g) butter	3 oz butter
bouillon cube (optional)	bouillon cube (optional)
2½ pints (1.5 litres) water	6¼ cups water
8 fl. oz (240 ml) single cream	1 cup light cream
parsley, chopped	parsley, chopped
a little savory	a little savory
salt and pepper	salt and pepper

Remove most of the green part of the leeks, slice into thin rounds and put to soak in salted water. Rinse several times, then drain. Cook them in the butter but do not let brown. Pour on the water and bring to the boil. (You can add a bouillon cube if you wish, if you prefer a slightly stronger soup.) Bring to the boil and then put in the carrots and cook for 10 minutes at a gentle boil. Then add the potato. Once everything is cooked, put through the liquidizer, food processor, sieve or *mouli-légumes*. Add savory. Taking into account the cream you will be adding, you must judge if you have enough soup and if it has the right consistency. This amount of vegetables can take more water without the soup losing flavour. Get it really hot and then, off the heat, add the cream. Stir in the parsley and serve at once.

MARROW AND WALNUT SOUP (Hungary)

Hungary is a country which shares with Britain a liking for vegetable marrow – though the Hungarians cook it much better. This soup is an original way to use up marrows. It can be served iced as well as hot. Courgettes can be used instead.

Imperial/Metric	American
approx. 1 lb (500 g) vegetable marrow	approx. 1 lb vegetable marrow
1 large onion, finely sliced	1 large onion, finely sliced
3 tablespoons butter or oil	3 tablespoons butter or oil
1 teaspoon marjoram	1 teaspoon marjoram
2 oz (60 g) walnut pieces	2 oz walnut pieces
paprika, parsley, chopped (optional)	paprika, parsley, chopped (optional)
2½ pints (1.5 litre) chicken stock or water	6¼ cups chicken stock or water
1 dessertspoon wine vinegar	1 dessertspoon wine vinegar
½ pint (300 ml) single cream	1¼ cups light cream

Peel the marrow and remove the seeds and pith. Grate into a bowl so you lose none of the juice. Drain slightly and fry gently with the onion in the butter or oil. Sprinkle on the paprika, marjoram and a little salt. Once half done, pour on the stock and cook at a simmer until the marrow more or less melts into the liquid. Chop the walnuts finely. (Do not use machinery or the result will be too fine.) Stir the walnuts into the soup. Add the vinegar and then the cream. Do not let boil. Serve sprinkled with a little more paprika or some parsley.

CREAM OF MUSHROOM SOUP (USA)

Although this can be made with an enriched *sauce béchamel* (p.391) it is much better made as shown below.

Imperial/Metric	American
1½ lb (750 g) mushrooms, sliced*	1½ lb mushrooms, sliced*
2 pints (1.2 litres) chicken stock	5 cups chicken stock
8 fl. oz (240 ml) single or double cream	1 cup light or heavy cream
pinch of thyme, preferably ground	pinch of thyme, preferably ground
butter	butter
salt and pepper	salt and parsley
parsley (to decorate)	parsley (to decorate)

* Use partly wild mushrooms if you can.

Save approximately one-eighth of the mushrooms for decoration. Cook the mushrooms in the stock and reduce to a purée. Add the cream and bring up to heat but do not let boil. Stir in the seasonings. Cook the other sliced mushrooms in a small amount of butter and add to the soup. Sprinkle with parsley before serving.

SOUPE A L'OIGNON GRATINEE (France)

ONION SOUP

Imperial/Metric	American
¾ lb (375 g) onions, sliced or chopped	¾ lb onions, sliced or chopped
oil or butter	oil or butter
1 small glass cognac (optional)	1 small glass cognac (optional)
3½ pints (2.1 litres) stock*	8¾ cups stock*
1 tablespoon meat glaze (*glace de viande*, p.299)	1 tablespoon meat glaze (*glace de viande*, p.299)
bouquet garni	*bouquet garni*
8 rounds of French bread	8 rounds of French bread
4 oz (125 g) Gruyère cheese, grated**	4 oz Gruyère cheese, grated**

* Home-made stock is best but canned or cube stock will do.
** Do not be tempted to use Cheddar or other cheese instead of the Gruyère – the taste is radically different.

Cook the onions in a *little* oil or butter until approximately half done. If you are using the cognac, this is the moment to pour it on and ignite. Let flames die down and then add the warmed stock, meat glaze and *bouquet garni*. Cook at a simmer until the onions are just done. You can prepare the soup in advance to this stage – reheating it only improves it.

At serving time, toast the French bread slices on either one side or both and heap with grated Gruyère. Run them under the grill until the cheese is bubbling and slightly brown. Depending entirely on your personal taste, you can either put these cheese toasts *in* the bottom of the soup bowl and pour the soup over or float them on top of the soup. I think the latter looks nicer and lives more up to the name *gratinée*, but both are correct.

PARSNIP SOUP (UK)

This is a delicious and inexpensive soup and even those who (like me) loathe parsnips are hard put to guess its origins. Had I first known what it was, I would never have put the spoon to my mouth.

Imperial/Metric
approx. 1 lb (500 g) parsnips, peeled and cubed
2 onions, chopped
2 oz (60 g) butter
2½ pints (1.5 litres) chicken stock
1 teaspoon curry powder (hot or mild, to taste)
8 fl. oz (240 ml) double or single cream
parsley, chopped (to decorate)
salt

American
approx. 1 lb parsnips, peeled and cubed
2 onions, chopped
2 oz butter
6¼ cups chicken stock
1 teaspoon curry powder (hot or mild, to taste)
1 cup heavy or light cream
parsley, chopped (to decorate)
salt

Fry the onions in the butter. Put the parsnips on to cook in the stock. Once cooked, purée in the food processor or liquidizer, then add the onions and return to the saucepan. Stir in the curry powder and heat through. Taste and salt if necessary. Stir in the cream and serve sprinkled with chopped parsley.

GREEN PEA SOUP (UK)

This is so much nicer with freshly picked garden peas (i.e. your own). Good-quality frozen ones will do; tinned peas will not.

Imperial/Metric
2-2½ lb (1 kilo plus) peas
2½ pints (1.5 litres) chicken stock (cubes will do)
10 fl. oz (300 ml) single (or double) cream
sprig of mint (optional)
salt and pepper
3 thin slices good ham, diced very small

American
2-2½ lb peas
6¼ cups chicken stock (cubes will do)
1 cup light (or heavy) cream
sprig of mint (optional)
salt and pepper
3 thin slices good ham, diced very small

Cook the peas in the stock with salt and mint if wished and then purée seven-eighths of them with the stock. Add the ham to the soup. Stir in the other peas and add the cream. (For a richer effect you can use double/heavy cream but it is not necessary.) If the result is too thick (depending on the age of the peas), thin down with a little more stock.

ALFOLDI LEVES (Hungary) The Great Plain

POTATO SOUP FROM THE HUNGARIAN GREAT PLAIN

Imperial/Metric	American
2 pints (1.2 litres) water	2½ pints water
1 lb (500 g) potatoes, peeled and diced	1 lb potatoes, peeled and diced
2 medium onions, chopped	2 medium onions, chopped
2 rashers streaky bacon	2 rashers streaky bacon
½ green pepper, chopped	½ green pepper, chopped
1 tablespoon parsley, chopped	1 tablespoon parsley, chopped
8 fl. oz (240 ml) sour cream	1 cup commercial sour cream
1-2 tablespoons flour	1-2 tablespoons flour
salt, paprika	salt, paprika
oil for frying	oil for frying

Cook the potatoes in part of the water. Fry the onion, bacon and pepper in the oil. Sprinkle with salt and about 1 teaspoon paprika and pour on remaining water. Add this mixture to the potatoes once they are cooked. Just before serving mix in the sour cream, off the heat, and the parsley. Once the soup is in the tureen or bowls, sprinkle with a little more paprika.

CALDO VERDE (Portugal)

POTATO AND KALE SOUP

Too often this soup is made of just potatoes, kale and water and is not very attractive. Properly made, it can be delicious. The Portuguese buy their *verde* ready sliced in the market but, providing you have a steady hand and a sharp knife, you can do almost as well as a machine.

Imperial/Metric	American
approx. 1 lb (500 g) cooked mashed potato*	approx. 1 lb cooked mashed potato*
½ pint (300 ml) full cream milk	1¼ cups full cream milk
1 small onion, chopped	1 small onion, chopped
2 oz (60 g) kale or spinach leaves**	2 oz kale or spinach leaves**
2 pints (1.2 litres) chicken stock	5 cups chicken stock
salt and pepper	salt and pepper

* Ideally cook the potatoes in the chicken stock – they taste richer

that way. Mash down *by hand* since machinery turns them into wallpaper paste too easily.

** Slice your washed and dried kale or spinach as fine as possible (almost like hair).

Heat the milk and steep the onion as you would for bread sauce. Once the full flavour of the onion has been extracted, discard it and mix the milk into the mashed potato. Check that the soup is not too thick – if it is, add more chicken stock. (This soup is very elastic and can be stretched to accommodate extra guests.) Heat up. Stir the kale or spinach into the boiling soup and then serve immediately.

VICHYSSOISE (USA but with French origins)

ICED POTATO AND LEEK SOUP

Vichyssoise is really a cold version of the classic French soup *Potage Bonne Femme*. I prefer to use only leeks and leave out the onion and not to use butter.

Imperial/Metric	American
1 lb (500 g) leeks, white only*	1 lb leeks, white only*
1 lb (500 g) potatoes, peeled and diced	1 lb potatoes, peeled and diced
1½ pints (750 ml) rich chicken stock	3¾ cups rich chicken stock
15 fl. oz. (450 ml) full cream milk	2 cups full cream milk
10 fl. oz (300 ml) double cream	1¼ cups heavy cream
3 tablespoons chives, chopped	3 tablespoons chives, chopped
2 fl. oz (60 ml) sunflower or corn oil	¼ cup sunflower or corn oil

* You will need at least double the weight to get 1 lb (500 g) of white leeks. Wash leeks well and let soak for at least an hour in cold water. Shake dry and slice into small rings, using the white part only.

Sauté the leeks very gently and do not let them colour too much or the final soup will be ruined. Add the diced potatoes and then the chicken stock and cook for approximately 30 minutes. Purée with a liquidizer, food processor or vegetable mill. Return the mixture to the saucepan and add the milk; heat through and add half the cream, making sure the soup does not boil. If you want a really smooth end-product, you should pass everything through a sieve once more. Chill thoroughly. Just before serving, add the remaining cream, beating in with a whisk. Stir half the chives into the soup and sprinkle the other half over the 8 individual portions.

VICHYSSOISE A LA RITZ (USA)

VICHYSSOISE WITH TOMATO

To the recipe for Vichyssoise (p.287) after adding the cream, add the following:

Imperial/Metric	American
½ pint (300 ml) tomato juice	1¼ cups tomato juice
1 tablespoon tomato concentrate	1 tablespoon tomato concentrate

CREME D'EPINARDS AU JAMBON (France)

CREAM OF SPINACH SOUP WITH HAM

Imperial/Metric	American
1 lb (500 g) *cooked* spinach	1 lb *cooked* spinach
8 oz (250 g) best-quality ham	1 cup cooked ham
2 pints (1.2 litres) chicken stock	5 cups chicken stock
8 fl. oz (240 ml) double cream	1 cup heavy cream
pinch of nutmeg	pinch of nutmeg
pepper	pepper

Mix the cooked spinach and chicken stock together and purée. Cut the ham into quarter-inch (0.5 cm) dice. Stir into the mixture and add the cream. Add the nutmeg and adjust seasoning. Bring up to heat – do not let boil – and serve.

CREMA DI POMODORI CON BASILICO (Italy)

CREAM OF TOMATO SOUP WITH FRESH BASIL

Imperial/Metric
2½-3 lb (1-1.5 kilos) tomatoes, (plum tomatoes can be used), skinned
2 medium onions, chopped
2 pints or more (1.2 litres plus) chicken stock
15 fl. oz (450 ml) single cream
butter
salt, pepper, sugar, lemon juice (optional)
3 tablespoons basil, freshly chopped

American
2½-3 lb tomatoes, (plum tomatoes can be used), skinned
2 medium onions, chopped
5 or more cups chicken stock
2 cups light cream
butter
salt, pepper, sugar, lemon juice (optional)
3 tablespoons basil, freshly chopped

Cook the onions in a mixture of oil and butter but do not let colour. Add the tomatoes and cook until they turn into a mush. Purée or liquidize and sieve afterwards, so you have no pips. Add the chicken stock, heat up and add cream. Do not let boil. Check how much liquid you have; if it is not enough for 8, add some more chicken stock. Adjust seasoning. You may want salt and pepper plus a little sugar or lemon juice depending on how sweet or tart the tomatoes are. At the last moment stir in the basil and serve sprinkled with a little more basil.

This is equally good cold.

ICED CREAM OF WATERCRESS (UK)

Imperial/Metric
4 bunches watercress
2½ pints (1.5 litres) chicken
   stock
8 fl. oz (240 ml) double cream
salt and pepper
lemon juice (optional)

American
4 bunches watercress
6¼ cups chicken stock
1 cup heavy cream
salt and pepper
lemon juice (optional)

Wash bunches of watercress thoroughly and remove most of the stem. Cook in the chicken stock and reduce to a purée. Add the cream and adjust seasoning, using lemon juice to sharpen the soup if wished. Ice at least 12 hours before use (covered).

CREAM OF WATERCRESS SOUP WITH PRAWNS (UK)

Imperial/Metric
4 bunches watercress
8 oz (250 g) prepared prawns
2 pints (1.2 litres) chicken stock
8 fl. oz (240 ml) single or double
   cream

American
4 bunches watercress
1 cup prepared shrimps
5 cups chicken stock
1 cup light or heavy cream

Wash bunches of watercress thoroughly and remove most of the stem. Cook in the chicken stock and reduce to a purée. Add the cream and adjust seasoning. Heat the chopped prawns in a little butter and divide between 8 soup dishes. Pour on the soup.

Variation
This soup can be made without the prawns, in which case use croûtons instead.

GAZPACHO

Gazpacho – iced soup – can be one of the most delectable dishes on earth but it can at times be quite disgusting. For instance, every time I go through Llerida, as a matter of honour (never having come across a remotely good one) I try to find a decent *gazpacho* but usually end up with something almost uneatable. Apparently they like their soups acid and sour, which is strange since the Catalans are rather better cooks than most Spaniards. The ingredients are very variable; not all *gazpachos* have tomatoes in; not all have breadcrumbs; not all have nuts, but *all* are served with little bowls of various vegetables as a garnish. Here are 4 different *gazpachos* – there must be at least 40.

GAZPACHO ANDALÚZ (Spáin: Andalusia)

SPANISH ICED SOUP

Imperial/Metric	*American*
3 peeled tomatoes	3 peeled tomatoes
2 cloves garlic	2 cloves garlic
1 large green pepper	1 large bell pepper
3 tablespoons stale breadcrumbs	3 tablespoons stale breadcrumbs
1 cucumber, peeled, seeded and chopped	1 cucumber, peeled, seeded and chopped
4 fl. oz (120 ml) olive oil	½ cup olive oil
2 fl. oz (60 ml) wine vinegar	¼ cup wine vinegar
3 eggs	3 eggs
1¾ pints (1 litre) chicken stock*	3½ cups chicken stock (cube will do)*
salt and pepper to taste	salt and pepper to taste

* If you do not wish to use chicken stock (even made with cubes), use a vegetable stock, vegetable juice or even tomato juice. In the latter case omit the tomatoes from the recipe.

Put all ingredients into liquidizer or food processor and reduce to a liquid. Check seasoning – it should be quite tart and slightly peppery. Add the breadcrumbs. Ice well. Garnish with cucumber, green pepper and a large tomato, peeled and diced, with enough croûtons to fill 2 × 5 oz (155 g) ramekins served in little bowls – 2 of each. The guests help themselves to what they fancy most.

BARCELONA GAZPACHO (Spain)

ICED VEGETABLE SOUP

Imperial/Metric	*American*
4 tablespoons fresh breadcrumbs	4 tablespoons fresh breadcrumbs
2 pints (1.2 litres) chicken or vegetable stock	5 cups chicken or vegetable stock
2 large cucumbers, peeled and seeded	2 large cucumbers, peeled and seeded
2 large peppers, chopped	2 large bell peppers, chopped
1 large onion, chopped	1 large onion, chopped
2 tablespoons pine nuts	1 tablespoon *pignoli*
1 tablespoon parsley	1 tablespoon parsley
4 fl. oz (120 ml) olive oil	½ cup olive oil
2 fl. oz (60 ml) wine vinegar	¼ cup wine vinegar
2 egg yolks	2 eggs yolks
chopped black and green olives (to garnish)	chopped black and green olives (to garnish)

Put all ingredients except the breadcrumbs and pine nuts (*pignoli*) in the liquidizer or food processor and blend thoroughly. Stir in breadcrumbs and pine nuts (*pignoli*) and adjust seasoning to your liking. Chill overnight and serve next day with the same garnishes, excluding the tomatoes.

GAZPACHO CORDOBÉS (Spain)

ICED VEGETABLE SOUP FROM CORDOBA

This is an unusual recipe because in the south of Spain they have never been great dairy-food eaters yet this soup contains cream. It is the most beautiful pale green colour.

Imperial/Metric	American
2 large cucumbers, peeled and seeded	2 large cucumbers, peeled and seeded
1 green pepper, peeled and seeded	1 green bell pepper, peeled and seeded
1 clove garlic	1 clove garlic
3 tablespoons fresh breadcrumbs	3 tablespoons fresh breadcrumbs
3 tablespoons ground almonds	3 tablespoons almonds, skinned and ground fine
2 tablespoons olive oil	2 tablespoons olive oil
2 tablespoons white wine vinegar	2 tablespoons white wine vinegar
1 pint (600 ml) iced water	1½ cups iced water
1 pint (600 ml) chicken stock	1½ cups chicken stock (cube)
15 fl. oz (450 ml) single cream	2 cups single cream
parsley (optional)	parsley (optional)
cucumber, croûtons and tomatoes (to garnish)	cucumber, croûtons and tomatoes (to garnish)

In a liquidizer or food processor purée the cucumber, garlic, pepper, olive oil and vinegar. Remove purée to a large bowl and add the iced water and stock, ground almonds, breadcrumbs and finally the cream. You may have to thin the cream down with some of the mixture in the liquidizer in order to get a smooth result. You can add parsley if you wish, though it is not in the recipe.

ESTRAMADURA GAZPACHO (Spain)

ICED SOUP FROM S.W. SPAIN

It is strange that one of the hottest parts of Spain has the most perishable type of *gazpacho*. We had this soup at the parador at Jarandilla, where King Carlos V stayed for a year or two whilst building a monastery at nearby Yuste where he intended ending his days in contemplation and presumably pain, since he suffered from gout, pour soul. His favourite food was anchovies washed down with Spanish *fino*, both of which, we now all know, are absolute death for the gouty.

Imperial/Metric
½ pint (300 ml) mayonnaise (home-made preferably, p.404)
1 large cucumber, peeled and seeded
1 large green pepper, peeled and seeded
2 cloves garlic
3 fl. oz (90 ml) wine vinegar
1 lb (500 g) ripe tomatoes
8 oz (250 g) chicken, cooked and chopped*
3-4 oz (90-125 g) ground almonds
1½-2 pints (900 ml-1.2 litres) chicken stock

American
1¼ cups mayonnaise (home-made preferably), p.404
1 large cucumber, peeled and seeded
1 bell pepper, peeled and seeded
2 cloves garlic
3 fl. oz wine vinegar
1 lb ripe tomatoes
8 oz chicken, cooked and chopped*
½ cup almonds, skinned and ground fine
3½-5 cups chicken stock

* These should be freshly made, not sad left-overs.

Chop pepper, cucumber and tomatoes roughly and purée in liquidizer or food processor. Add ground almonds, garlic (chopped a bit), wine vinegar and mayonnaise. Remove to a large bowl and add chicken stock to bring the amount of liquid up to approximately 4 pints in all (2.4 litres/5 US pints) and add the chicken bits. Personally I reduce the vinegar, since it is a bit too sharp with 3 oz (90 g) but this is a matter of taste. Chill well for several hours and serve with the usual garnishes.

LIGURIAN WINTER SOUP (Italy)

This is somewhat like a minestrone but lighter and has a pesto sauce added at the end. Parmesan cheese can be served with this soup, though the Ligurians tend to use pecorino instead.

Imperial/Metric
2 oz (60 g) white beans
1 large onion, chopped
4 oz (125 g) *pancetta* (streaky bacon), chopped

American
2 oz white beans
1 large onion, chopped
4 oz *pancetta* (streaky bacon), chopped

2 tablespoons olive oil
2 sticks celery, chopped
12 oz (375 g) pumpkin, grated*
1 medium aubergine, peeled
(optional) and diced
2½ pints (1.5 litres) chicken or
beef stock**
approx. 1 lb (500 g) tinned
tomatoes
2 tablespoons pesto sauce
1 dessertspoon sugar
salt to taste

2 tablespoons olive oil
2 sticks celery, chopped
12 oz pumpkin, grated*
1 medium aubergine, peeled
(optional) and diced
6¼ cups stock**
2 cups canned tomatoes
2 tablespoons pesto sauce
1 dessertspoon sugar
salt to taste

* Carrot is sometimes used instead of pumpkin.
** The stock can be made of cubes, in which case you will probably not need salt at the end.

Soak and three-quarters cook the white beans before putting into the soup. Fry the bacon and onion in the olive oil. Add the celery, pumpkin, aubergine and parsley (optional), then the tomatoes and their juice, smashing them into the other ingredients, and the stock. Cook until the beans are done. At the last moment, off the heat, stir in the pesto and serve immediately.

VEGETABLE SOUP (Portugal)

Around the Lisbon area among much of the English colony this is known as 'maids' soup', since it seems to be standard irrespective of the person who cooks it. Excellent though it is, it can be a bit boring night after night.

Imperial/Metric
1 medium onion
1 medium potato
2 medium carrots
2 tomatoes
1 medium turnip
a handful of peas or a handful
of greenstuff*
olive oil
salt and pepper
chicken stock or water for 8
fresh coriander or parsley,
chopped (to serve)

American
1 medium onion
1 medium potato
2 medium carrots
2 tomatoes
1 medium turnip
a handful of peas or a handful
of greenstuff*
olive oil
salt and pepper
chicken stock or water for 8
fresh coriander or parsley,
chopped (to serve)

*The greenstuff is usually turnip tops (much loved by the Portuguese) but sometimes thinly sliced spinach is also used.

Cut all vegetables into small dice or julienne them. Fry them gently in olive oil and sprinkle with salt and pepper. Then pour over the stock or water and cook at a simmer until done. Serve sprinkled with parsley or coriander.

OKROSHKA (Russia)

ICED VEGETABLE SOUP

Imperial/Metric	*American*
2 pints (900 ml) fermented beet liquor (p.273)*	5 cups fermented beet liquor (p.273)*
2 carrots, diced small	2 carrots, diced small
2 onions, diced small	2 onions, diced small
2 medium cucumbers, diced small	2 medium cucumbers, diced small
bunch of spring onions	bunch of scallions
2 teaspoons sharp mustard	2 teaspoons sharp mustard
2 teaspoons sugar	2 teaspoons sugar
4 tablespoons sour cream	4 tablespoons commerical sour cream
3 eggs, hard-boiled	3 eggs, hardcooked
dill to garnish	dill to garnish
salt	salt

* It should be remembered that this liquor is very slightly alcoholic.

Cook the onions and carrots in boiling water. Chill. Peel, seed, salt and drain the cucumbers and dice these also. Chop up the spring onions as best you can, leaving on a little of the green. Mix all the vegetables together with the fermented beet liquor. Separate the hard-boiled egg yolks from the whites. Mix them with the mustard, sugar and salt and stir into the vegetable soup. Chill well.

Ladle out the soup, with a blob of sour cream and a sprinkling of chopped egg whites and dill.

Fruit

SOPA DE ALMENDRAS (Spain)

CHILLED ALMOND SOUP

This is slightly different from the classic Andalusian recipe and, I think, rather more subtle. Shallots are used instead of garlic, and chicken stock instead of water.

Imperial/Metric	American
2 pints (1.2 litres) chicken stock (cubes will do)*	2½ pints chicken stock (cubes will do)*
3 shallots, chopped	3 shallots, chopped
4 tablespoons good olive oil	4 tablespoons good olive oil
4 tablespoons white wine vinegar	4 tablespoons white wine vinegar
8 oz (250 g) blanched almonds	1 cup blanched almonds
8 oz (250 g) white seedless grapes**	8 oz white seedless grapes**
salt	salt
cinnamon	cinnamon

* Make sure your chicken stock is not so robust that it will mask the almond flavour.
** The best grapes to use are Chasselas as they are seedless but others will do, though if they have thick skins they should be peeled.

In 2 tablespoons of the olive oil sweat the 3 shallots. Add half the wine vinegar and reduce to about 1 tablespoon, then add a little of the chicken stock. Put everything into a liquidizer or food processor except the grapes. Chill well and adjust seasoning before serving. You may need a little more oil or vinegar. Add the grapes and serve with a very light sprinkling of cinnamon.

HIDEG MEGGYLEVES (Hungary)

COLD MORELLO CHERRY SOUP

Imperial/Metric	American
1½ lb (750 g) morello cherries*	1½ lb morello cherries*
12 oz (375 g) caster sugar	1½ cups sugar
¾ pint (450 ml) red wine	2 cups red wine
1 pint (600 ml) water	2½ cups water
twist of lemon peel	twist of lemon peel
small piece of cinnamon stick*	small piece of cinnamon stick*
2 egg yolks	2 egg yolks
2 level tablespoons potato starch or arrowroot	2 level tablespoons potato starch or arrowroot
8 fl. oz (240 ml) double cream	1 cup heavy cream

* Tinned cherries will not do, nor will ground cinnamon. Bing

cherries or *amarena* type can be used instead of morello but the flavour will be different.

Cook the cherries in the water with the sugar, lemon peel and cinnamon. Remove the cinnamon and lemon peel plus approximately a quarter of the cherries. Liquidize these in a liquidizer or food processor. To this mixture add the egg yolks, cream and potato starch or arrowroot. If you think there are any lumps, sieve the mixture before returning it to the main soup. Bring everything almost to the boil and remove from heat. Because of the egg yolks, it is essential that the mixture does not boil. Add the red wine. Adjust seasoning if necessary, and add either a little more sugar or a squeeze or lemon juice. Chill very thoroughly before serving.

HIDEG SZAMOCALEVES (Hungary)

COLD STRAWBERRY SOUP

Imperial/Metric	*American*
2 lb (1 kilo) strawberries	2 lb strawberries
15 fl. oz (450 ml) sweet white wine	2 cups sweet white wine
	2½ cups full cream milk
1 pint (600 ml) full cream milk	1 cup heavy cream
8 fl. oz (240 ml) double cream	sugar and a little parsley
sugar and a little salt	2 egg yolks
2 egg yolks	2 tablespoons arrowroot or
2 tablespoons arrowroot or	potato starch
potato starch	salt and lemon juice (optional)
salt and lemon juice (optional)	

Cut the strawberries in to halves or quarters depending on their size and cook in the white wine. When cooked, put through liquidizer, food processor or sieve. Return to heat and add three-quarters of the milk and all the cream. Bring up to almost boiling. Mix down the arrowroot or potato starch with the eggs and reserved milk and pour the hot mixture over it, bit by bit, stirring well to avoid lumps. Serve well chilled.

Some people put a little salt in the mixture and some use a squeeze of lemon juice. You will find it best to do these things once the soup is thoroughly chilled.

Meat, Poultry and Game

BEEF CONSOMME

Because of the bones, you will need a large pot for this soup, although in the end it is reduced down to approximately 4-5 pints

(2-2.5 litres/5-6 US pints). In the end you may have to reduce it a bit more to concentrate the flavour sufficiently.

Right from the beginning you must decide whether you want dark or light consommé. If you want dark, you must fry the ingredients first – or use gravy browning, which is cheating! The taste is, of course, much richer if you fry the ingredients first.

Imperial/Metric	*American*
1 veal knuckle	1 veal knuckle
2-3 lb (1-1.5 kilos) beef bones – ribs are excellent	2-3 lb beef bones – ribs are excellent
1 marrow bone	1 marrow bone
1 lb (500 g) minced beef*	1 lb minced beef*
2 lb (1 kilo) shin of beef on the bone	2 lb shin of beef on the bone
8 oz (250 g) ox liver (optional)	8 oz ox liver (optional)
meat glaze (optional)**	meat glaze (optional)**
3 leeks	3 leeks
2 sticks celery	2 sticks celery
bouquet-garni	*bouquet-garni*
8 pints (4.8 litres) water	5 quarts water
6-8 peppercorns	6-8 peppercorns
1 dessertspoon tomato paste	1 dessertspoon tomato paste

* Better that *you* should mince or chop the beef so you know what you are getting.
** Meat glaze can be purchased in speciality grocers and in some supermarkets. However, there are all sorts of meat glazes on the market, some of which are little better than liquid bouillon cubes. The price is an indicator for meat glaze (or *glace de viande*, for it is usually French or Belgian) is ruinously expensive, and a dessert-spoon to a tablespoon in this quantity of consommé will do the trick.

Remove the meat from the shin bone and keep for a stew or similar. Cover the other ingredients (fried or not) with the cold water and bring to boil. Do *not* skim. Turn down heat and simmer for 4 hours. Strain stock through sieve and then through a double thickness of muslin. Put back into a clean pan and reduce until the flavour is concentrated. Add salt only at the end. Clarify if necessary but let cool once and bring up to heat again. The addition of meat glaze can help increase the flavour. Do not over-sherry or over-Madeira your beautiful home-made con-sommé. The amount is about 3 dessertspoonfuls in a consommé for 8 people. If you are making an aspic, sherry (which can be quite pleasing in a hot soup, though Madeira is far better) ends up tasting sharp and unattractive.

CHICKEN CONSOMME (UK)

Imperial/Metric	American
3-3½ pints (2 litres approximately) water	3¾-4 pints water
the carcasses of 3 roast chickens	the carcasses of 3 roast chickens
or	or
3 lb (1.5 kilos) chicken backs and wings	3 lb chicken backs and wings
2 medium onions, washed but not peeled	2 medium onions, washed but not peeled
8-10 peppercorns	8-10 peppercorns
6 or 8 parsley stalks	6 or 8 parsley stalks
a stick of celery or slice of celeriac	a stick of celery or slice of celeriac
1 small turnip	1 small turnip
salt to taste at end of cooking	salt to taste at end of cooking

If using fresh or frozen chicken parts blanch first in boiling water for 3 or 4 minutes and rinse under the tap. This prevents a lot of scum. Put all ingredients into a large saucepan, bring to the boil and simmer for approximately 1 hour over a gentle heat. Do not cook for more than 1½ hours or you will get the taste of 'bones' rather than chicken to your stock. Strain through a sieve and then through wetted muslin. Clarify or not depending on the ultimate use for the stock.

TO CLARIFY CONSOMME

Imperial/Metric	American
6 egg whites and their shells	6 egg whites and their shells
muslin and coffee filter paper*	muslin and coffee filter paper*
1 or two large bowls to take clarified consommé	1 or two large bowls to take clarified consommé
1 large clean saucepan	1 large clean saucepan

* Melitta make very large filters to go with a large plastic holder which will fit over a basin.

Bring consommé to the boil. Whisk the egg whites as stiff as possible and add crushed eggshells, or alternatively whisk them all up together. Lower heat and let soup just simmer. Stir egg whites carefully into the soup. Let simmer for approximately half an hour, stirring during the first 5-10 minutes to make sure the egg whites do not stick to the bottom of the pan. You should find that egg white and shells have taken all the floating bits of the soup down to the bottom of the pan.

Strain carefully through 2 thicknesses of wetted muslin. Then strain, very slowly and carefully through a coffee filter paper. As the basin fills, pour off into another bowl. You should have a bright and clear broth. If not, start again with the *cleared* soup and a couple more eggshells and whites.

KRAFTBRUEHE MIT LEBERNOCKERLN (Austria)

RICH BEEF CONSOMME WITH SMALL LIVER DUMPLINGS

Your consommé must be really good; the tinned sort will not do; nor will the sort made of scraps of this and that.

Imperial/Metric	*American*
consommé for 8 (p.298)	consommé for 8 (p.298)
4 small bread rolls	4 small bread rolls
5 fl. oz (150 ml) milk	5 fl. oz milk
1 medium onion, finely chopped	1 medium onion, finely chopped
2 egg yolks	2 egg yolks
6 oz (190 g) calves' liver, finely chopped*	6 oz calves' liver, finely chopped*
salt and pepper	salt and pepper
4 tablespoons flour or more	4 tablespoons flour or more
oil (for cooking)	oil (for cooking)
1 tablespoon parsley	1 tablespoon parsley

* On a board: a food processor or mincer will reduce it to a purée.

Remove most of the crust from the rolls and reduce to breadcrumbs in the liquidizer or food processor. Stir in the milk and after a minute or so drain in a sieve. Fry the onion in a little *oil* not butter with the calves' liver. Do not overcook. Mix the onion and liver into the drained breadcrumbs and add the egg yolks together with salt and pepper. You will have to judge how much flour you will need to make small dumplings which will stick together. They should be about the size of a cherry. Poach them in the just simmering soup for 10-15 minutes. Too violent cooking will cloud the soup and break the dumplings.

CONSOMME MADRILENE (France)

BEEF CONSOMME FLAVOURED WITH TOMATO

Serve with hot cheese straws.

Imperial/Metric	American
2½ pints (1.5 litres) beef consommé (p.298)	6¼ cups beef consommé (p.298)
1 lb (500 g) tomatoes (plum sort are good)	1 lb tomatoes (plum sort are good)
1 carrot, grated (optional)	1 carrot, grated (optional)

Nowadays most *Consommé Madrilène* is made with concentrated tomato paste but the real way is to cook chopped tomatoes with the smallest amount of oil possible, pass them through a liquidizer or food processor, then force them through a sieve. Let stand for a few hours and then strain the consommé.

Variation
Some cooks use a grated carrot when cooking the tomatoes for extra sweetness. With a little added gelatine, this makes an excellent jellied consommé. Campbell's consommé works for this but home-made is better and far more subtle.

OKROCHKA MIASNIAYA (USSR: Ukraine)

UKRAINIAN COLD SOUP WITH MEAT

This comes from a famous Russian cookbook by Boris Andrianov, *The Great Russian Plain*, and was one of a dozen or so recipes translated by my daughter's Russian class at school. So far as I know, it has never been published in English.

For the making of *kvass* see under Polish Borscht (p.273) but ferment the bread for around half the time given in that recipe. If you leave it longer, it really does not matter, although the liquid becomes rather more alcoholic! The soup can be 'stretched' with more *kvass* or even good cold bouillon (at a pinch tinned consommé). Many Ukrainians use mint as well as dill – this is a matter of personal taste.

Serve with black rye bread.

Imperial/Metric	American
2 pints (1.2 litres) *kvass*	5 cups *kvass*
12 oz (375 g) boiled beef or pork, finely chopped	12 oz boiled beef or pork, finely chopped
2 large cucumbers, peeled and grated	2 large cucumbers, peeled and grated
1 bunch spring onions, finely chopped	1 bunch scallions
1 medium potato, cooked	1 medium potato, cooked
3 eggs, hard-boiled	3 hardcooked eggs
8 fl. oz (240 ml) double cream	1 cup heavy cream
2 small teaspoons sugar	2 small teaspoons sugar
2 teaspoons Dijon mustard or similar	2 teaspoons Dijon mustard or similar
fresh or freeze dried dill (or mint) to taste	fresh or freeze dried dill (or mint) to taste

Mix the meat with the spring onions (leave on plenty of the green part) and the potato. Separate the cooked yolks of the eggs from the whites, chop the whites finely and stir them into the other ingredients.

In a separate bowl mix the mustard, egg yolk and sugar together and then add the cream and as much dill (or mint) as you like. Finally stir in the *kvass* and add to the chopped ingredients. Cover with clingfilm and leave in the refrigerator for 2-3 hours before serving.

AVGOLEMONO (Greece)

CHICKEN AND LEMON SOUP

The soup of Greece – at times one wonders if there is any other, delicious as it may be. There is: it is *Melokhia*, made from a form of mallow leaves – but it is much less ubiquitous.

Imperial/Metric	American
4 pints (2.5 litres) chicken stock*	10 cups chicken stock*
4 oz (125 g) long-grain rice	½ cup Carolina rice
5 egg yolks	5 egg yolks
3 whites	3 whites
juice of 2 large lemons	juice of 2 large lemons

* Stock from cubes really is not ideal but will do at a pinch. The soup rises and falls on the quality of the stock.

Cook the rice for approximately 15 minutes in the stock at a gentle boil (the liquid will go down). Test the rice for 'done-ness' after this time and continue cooking if necessary. At this stage, if you have too much liquid or want a stronger-flavoured broth, you should drain off the rice, so it will not overcook, and reduce the liquid by rapid boiling.

In a large basin beat the egg yolks and whites really well with a little salt (not if you have used cubes) and pour in the lemon juice. Have the chicken stock hot and from a Pyrex jug pour it onto the eggs little by little, beating all the time. Then pour this mixture into the rest of the soup and heat through. It should thicken *slightly*, but watch that it does not boil or it will curdle.

COLD CHICKEN SOUP (Sri Lanka)

The original recipe has only thick coconut milk in it – no cream. As thick coconut milk is unobtainable in Europe and most of the USA, I have adjusted this recipe to what is available. Those living on the West Coast of the USA can get coconut milk from Hawaii very easily, and it is worth using it in this recipe. It seems rather more complicated than it is, but it can be made 24 hours in advance with no loss of flavour. You can add more or less curry powder according to taste, bearing in mind that chilling slightly lessens the 'heat' of curry. Serve with warm poppadums, which can be bought at all Indian stores, or with prawn crackers.

Imperial/Metric	*American*
2 pints (1.2 litres) chicken stock	5 cups chicken stock
8 oz (250 g) chicken breast	8 oz chicken breast
1 sweet apple, peeled and diced	1 sweet apple, peeled and diced
1 onion, chopped	1 onion, chopped
1 tablespoon or more curry powder	1 tablespoon or more curry powder
1 tablespoon flour	1 tablespoon flour
8 fl. oz (240 ml) coconut milk*	1 cup coconut milk*
8 fl. oz (240 ml) double cream	1 cup heavy cream
a little oil for frying	a little oil for frying

* Make the coconut milk by steeping 4 oz (125 g) unsweetened desiccated coconut in half a pint (300 ml) of hot water. Half way through this steeping, whizz the whole thing in the liquidizer or food processor to accentuate the flavour. Finally, strain and press out the milk. Discard the coconut.

In a little oil fry the onion, when it is half cooked, add the chicken breast and apple. Cook until almost done. Then add the curry powder and flour and cook for 5 minutes, stirring all the time. Bit by bit add half the chicken stock. Let simmer 5-10 minutes. Put this mixture through the liquidizer or food processor and add the cream and coconut milk. Add enough chicken stock to make 8 servings. Chill well.

CREAM OF CHICKEN SOUP (USA)

Imperial/Metric	*American*
1½ pints (900 ml) *sauce béchamel* (p.391)	3¾ cups *sauce béchamel* (p.391)
1½ pints (900 ml) rich chicken stock	3¾ cups rich chicken stock
1 onion, chopped	1 onion, chopped
12 oz (375 g) chicken breast, diced	12 oz chicken breast, diced
3-4 tablespoons double cream	3-4 tablespoons heavy cream
a little butter	a little butter
salt, pepper and nutmeg	salt, pepper and nutmeg
juice of half a lemon	juice of half a lemon
parsley, chopped or sprig (to garnish)	parsley, chopped or sprig (to garnish)

Fry the onion in a little butter but do not let it colour too much. Add the chicken breast and cook in the same way – slowly. Mix the stock and sauce together and heat through. Add the seasonings, onion and chicken bits. Finally add the lemon juice just before serving, garnished with parsley.

CREAM OF CHICKEN AND SWEETCORN SOUP (USA)

To a recipe of Cream of Chicken Soup (above) add 8 oz/250 g/1 US cup whole-kernel sweetcorn. Allow for this in calculating how much stock to use.

JELLIED CHICKEN AND CUCUMBER SOUP (Egypt)

This is a family recipe and I have never seen it in a Middle Eastern cookbook. Nevertheless it was not uncommon dinner-party fare before and just after the Second World War. It is served with hot

Arab bread (now virtually unobtainable in Egypt). I suspect it originated in the French or Turkish community there, rather than with the Egyptians themselves. This can be made in individual servings if wished – glass bowls look very pretty and cool.

imperial/Metric	*American*
2½ pints (1.5 litres) chicken stock	6¼ cups chicken stock
enough gelatine to set this quantity of stock*	enough gelatin to set this quantity of stock*
12 oz (375 g) cooked breast of chicken	12 oz cooked breast of chicken
medium sprig of tarragon or 3 stalks parsley	medium sprig of tarragon or 3 stalks parsley
1 large cucumber	1 large cucumber
parsley, chopped (optional)	parsley, chopped (optional)
wedges of lemon (optional)	wedges of lemon (optional)

* Using Davis gelatine, you will need 2½ sachets (more in hot weather) but other makes may differ. Follow the packet instructions.

Peel, seed and dice finely the cucumber. Sprinkle with salt and let drain in a colander for at least an hour or the leaking vegetable will ruin the gelatine.

Heat the stock and steep the tarragon sprig or parsley stalks in it for about an hour. Heat approximately ½ pint (300 ml) of the stock to boiling and stir in the melted gelatine. Remove tarragon sprig and stir in the rest of the stock. Pour a thin layer into the mould and let set. Mix the cucumber and chicken together and stir into the just-about-to-set jellied stock. If you put the cucumber and chicken into liquid, it will float. Cover with clingfilm and let set thoroughly. Serve with a little parsley on top and a wedge of lemon.

GAME CONSOMME (UK: Scotland)

No one is going to suggest you buy game just to make this consommé. For those with freezers, it is worth saving the legs of pheasant or partridge (never very tender or delicious) over a period so that you have about half a dozen in order to make this soup. Carcasses or roast game birds will do also but you will need several to get a good strong flavour. Go easy on pigeon and grouse, which both give a rather overpowering flavour to a consommé.

This recipe includes a fair amount of bacon, but this can be lessened or left out altogether if wished. You will need to increase the quantity of shin of beef in that case.

Imperial/Metric	*American*
carcasses of three pheasants or legs of 3 pheasants or 3 or 4 partridges or the trimmings of a hare and some game birds	carcasses of three pheasants or legs of 3 pheasants or 3 or 4 partridges or the trimmings of a hare and some game birds
8 oz (250 g) shin of beef	8 oz shin of beef
2 or 3 onions, roughly chopped	2 or 3 onions, roughly chopped
8 oz (250 g) leanish bacon	8 oz leanish bacon
2 or 3 carrots, grated	2 or 3 carrots, grated
2 or 3 sticks celery	2 or 3 sticks celery
2 or 3 cloves	2 or 3 cloves
bunch of parsley	bunch of parsley
pinch of mace	pinch of mace
1 dessertspoon tomato concentrate	1 dessertspoon tomato concentrate
6¼ pints (3 litres) water	6¼ pints water

Cut the meat up into dice. Break down the carcasses. Fry with the onion until slightly brown. Add the carrots and celery. Grill the bacon separately and chop up. Put everything into a large pot and pour on the water. Simmer for 3-4 hours over a low heat. Strain and clear if necessary. Add salt only at the end and *after* any reduction.

GAME SOUP WITH MADEIRA (UK)

Although the consommé for this can be made from scraps and left-over roast birds, this soup also requires uncooked game.

Imperial/Metric	*American*
12 oz (375 g) uncooked tender game	12 oz uncooked tender game
2½ pints (1.5 litres) game consommé	6¼ cups game consommé
1 large onion, sliced	1 large onion, sliced
1 carrot, grated	1 carrot, grated
butter for frying	butter for frying
4 tablespoons Madeira	4 tablespoons Madeira
parsley, chopped	parsley, chopped

Fry the onion rings in a little butter but do not let colour. Chop or mince the game as small as possible and fry in the same pan. Heat the consommé and add the onions and game plus the grated carrot. Let simmer gently for ten minutes with the lid on. Once the carrot is cooked, the soup is ready to serve. Add the Madeira off the heat and serve sprinkled with parsley.

Fish and Seafood

BASIC FISH STOCK

Imperial/Metric	*American*
heads and bones of 3 or 4 white fish (about 1 lb (500 g) in all)	heads and bones of 3 or 4 white fish (about 1 lb in all)
1 whiting, gutted	1 whiting, gutted
1 glass dry white wine	½ cup dry white wine
3 shallots	3 shallots
3-4 oz (90-125 g) mushrooms	½ cup mushrooms
1 grated carrot	1 grated carrot
oil or butter (for sweating)	oil or butter (for sweating)
salt	salt
3 pints (1.5 litres) water	3¾ pints water

Sweat the vegetables in a little oil or butter (depending on the soup you are going to make afterwards). Add the fish heads and bones and the whiting and let cook together. Add the white wine. Transfer all to a saucepan, add the water and simmer for just under half an hour. Take it off the heat and let it sit for half an hour before straining. Later add salt to taste.

COURT-BOUILLON (France)

A BROTH FOR POACHING FISH

It is essential for the final appearance of a fish dish that you strain this liquid before poaching the fish in it – this goes equally for packaged *court-bouillon* – otherwise your fish will be covered with little bits of herbs etc.

Imperial/Metric	*American*
2½ pints (1.5 litres) cold water	5¼ cups water
2 onions, sliced	2 onions, sliced
1 stick celery	1 stick celery
2 or 3 stalks parsley or dill	2 or 3 stalks parsley or dill
8 fl. oz (240 ml) white wine vinegar	1 cup white wine vinegar
6-8 peppercorns or ½ teaspoon Tabasco	6-8 peppercorns or ½ teaspoon Tabasco
Bayleaf (optional)	Bayleaf (optional)

Boil all ingredients together, but gently, for approximately 30 minutes. Strain carefully and use within 3 or 4 days.

Variation
You may add the trimmings of any whitefish to the above recipe to make a richer *court-bouillon* if wished.

VELOUTE DE POISSON (France)

CREAM OF FISH SOUP

Imperial/Metric	American
1½ lb (750 g) firm white fish*	1½ lb firm white fish*
1 pint (600 ml) *saùce béchamel* (p.391)	2½ cups *sauce béchamel* (p.391)
1 carrot, finely chopped	1 carrot, finely chopped
2 egg yolks	2 egg yolks
1½ pints (900 ml) fish stock (p.308)	3¾ cups fish stock (p.308)
8 fl. oz (240 ml) single cream	1 cup light cream
pinch of fresh or dried tarragon (optional)	pinch of fresh or dried tarragon (optional)
1 teaspoon instant shallot	1 teaspoon instant shallot

* Fish such as sole, halibut, whiting, bream, turbot can be used.

Cook the fish in the stock with the shallot, carrot and tarragon if liked. Once cooked, run it through the liquidizer or food processor and incorporate the *sauce béchamel*. Taste and adjust seasoning. Beat the eggs into the cream and pour gently into the hot soup. Do not let boil. Serve at once. The result should be very smooth – if it is not, sieve it before you put in the eggs and cream, but this should not be necessary.

BOTVINIA (USSR)

ICED FISH AND CUCUMBER SOUP

The sturgeon called for in the original recipe is not often available anywhere outside the USSR, I imagine, and not very often there probably. I have substituted salmon (farmed will do excellently) which marries with the cucumber and greenstuff used. Otherwise in all respects the recipe is authentic.

Imperial/Metric	American
¾ lb (375 g) salmon	¾ lb salmon
1½ pints (900 ml) fermented beetroot liquor (p.273)	3¾ cups fermented beetroot liquor (p.273)
bunch of spring onions	bunch of scallions
1½ pints (900 ml) fish stock	3¾ cups fish stock
4 oz (125 g) spinach leaves	4 oz spinach leaves
1 tablespoon fresh horseradish	1 tablespoon fresh horseradish
2 medium cucumbers	2 medium cucumbers
dill to taste	dill to taste
salt, pepper and sugar (optional)	salt, pepper and sugar (optional)

Cook the salmon in the stock, drain, cool and dice fairly small. Keep the stock. Cook the spinach in boiling water with half the spring onions. Once done, drain and run through the liquidizer, food processor or sieve. Add the fermented liquor, the fish stock and the rest of the onions, chopped up fairly small. Peel, seed and either dice or grate (the first is better) and stir into the liquid. Chill everything.

At serving time put some of the fish on each dish and sprinkle with a little horseradish (the quantity given is a bit much for non-Russian tastes possibly), then ladle on the chilled soup and cucumber. It sounds much more complicated than it is and tastes absolutely delicious. Alternatively, serve horseradish separately for people to help themselves.

FISH AND FRESH GINGER SOUP (China)

I have never seen this soup in Hong Kong or Singapore (presumably because of the lack of mussels) but virtually every Chinese restaurant in Japan, where tiny white mussels are plentiful, seems to serve it.

Imperial/Metric	*American*
12 oz (375 g) firm white fish, raw	12 oz firm white fish, raw
3 pints (1.8 litres) fish stock (p.308)	7½ cups fish stock (p.308)
2 lb (1 kilo) mussels	2 lb mussels
2 onions, sliced	2 onions, sliced
12 oz (375 g) sliced mushrooms	12 oz sliced mushrooms
2 tablespoons soy sauce	2 tablespoons soy sauce
approx. 1 oz (30 g) fresh ginger	approx. 1 oz fresh ginger
8 oz (250 g) fresh bean curd	8 oz fresh bean curd
oil (for cooking)	oil (for cooking)
coriander (optional)	coriander (optional)

Clean and beard the mussels and steam them open in a steamer or colander over boiling water. The moment the shells open, stop the cooking. Cook the onions in a little oil and then add the diced fish. Pour the stock over the fish, add the sliced mushrooms and cook gently for slightly less than 5 minutes. Peel the ginger and slice it finely with the potato peeler, then chop it. Add to the soup with the soy sauce. Cut the bean curd into small cubes and divide between the 8 plates. Put the mussels in their shells in the hot soup to warm through and then serve. Fresh coriander can be used if wished.

OURSINADO (France: Provence)

FISH SOUP WITH SEA URCHINS

Sea urchins are common on the Mediterranean coasts and readily available in the local markets. Here is a way to deal with them other than eating them raw (when they taste rather like superior iodine). Like so many things Provençal, this soup is not cheap – but it is delicious and different.

Either serve with toasted French bread or fry or toast slices of French bread and put them in the soup plate before the soup. This makes it a bit crowded, to my mind.

Imperial/Metric	*American*
1 lb (500 g) monkfish	1 lb monkfish
1 lb (500 g) sea bream or John Dory	1 lb sea bream or John Dory
contents of 20-30 sea urchins	contents of 20-30 sea urchins
2½ pints or more (1.5 litres plus) fish stock	6¼ cups fish stock
1 onion, finely chopped	1 onion, finely chopped
1 grated carrot	1 grated carrot
olive oil	olive oil
8 egg yolks	8 egg yolks
parsley, chopped (to decorate)	parsley, chopped (to decorate)

Cook the onion and carrot in the olive oil and add the fish, which you have cut into small chunks. Do not let them colour too much. Once cooked, pour over the fish stock – to feed 8 you may need a little more. Just before serving, remove the fish with a slotted spoon and keep warm. Heat the soup up but do not let boil. Beat the egg yolks and add to the soup. Stir over a gentle heat until slightly thickened. It can curdle and separate very easily. Finally add the sea urchins, which you have liquidized to a purée. Adjust seasoning – it probably won't need salt. Divide the fish between 8 plates and pour the soup over. Sprinkle with a little chopped parsley.

HALÁSZLÉ (Hungary)

HUNGARIAN FRESHWATER FISH SOUP

Carp from fast-flowing rivers (and, therefore, unmuddy in taste) and pike are the most commonly used fish for this soup or *gulyas*. Sturgeon is considered a real treat. Cod, skate, monkfish are excellent for this soup too. There are two schools of thought about *halászlé*. One says it should contain potatoes and the other says it should have only chunks of good quality fish in a fiery soup. If the following course is to be substantial omit the potatoes.

Imperial/Metric	American
2-2½ lb (approx. 1 kilo) mixed fish	2-2½ lb mixed fish
2 large onions, sliced	2 large onions, sliced
2 rashers of streaky bacon, diced	2 rashers of streaky bacon, diced
2 tablespoons sunflower oil	2 tablespoons sunflower oil
4 medium potatoes (optional)	4 medium potatoes (optional)
1 green pepper, sliced	1 bell pepper, sliced
1 medium tomato	1 medium tomato
2 tablespoons paprika	2 tablespoons paprika
cayenne pepper (optional)	cayenne pepper (optional)
3 pints (1.8 litres) stock	7½ cups stock

Put the fish heads and bones into the stock and cook for approximately 20 minutes – chicken stock cubes can be used if no home-made stock is to hand. Strain well. Fry the rashers of bacon with the sliced onions then add the green pepper and tomato and cook a few minutes. Add the fish, cut into chunks, and cook gently until firm. Then add a little of the stock together with the seasonings and paprika. If you like a piquant soup which is the traditional way then you will need to add some cayenne unless you can find really hot paprika (fairly rare out of Hungary). Transfer everything to a larger pot and add the rest of the stock and the potatoes (cut in half). Cook very gently for 20 minutes until the potatoes are done. If you leave out the potatoes you will need to allow 10 minutes cooking only.

Serve with French bread.

SOUPE DE POISSONS A LA PROVENÇALE (France)

PROVENÇAL FISH SOUP

This is the peppery, dark soup you get on holiday in the South of France. It must be one of the few things that is actually cheaper to buy prepared than to make yourself – and much less trouble. For those who have the time – and money, here is the recipe. I repeat, the commercial jars of Provençal fish soup are excellent. Serve with *rouille* (p.408) and slices of French bread toasted in the oven.

Imperial/Metric	American
4-5 lb (2-2.5 kilos) *poissons de roche**	4-5 lb *poissons de roche**
3 large onions, chopped	3 large onions, chopped
1 lb (500 g) fresh plum tomatoes, cut up**	1 lb fresh plum tomatoes, cut up**
1 fennel bulb	1 fennel bulb
3 or 4 cloves garlic	3 or 4 cloves garlic
approx. 4 pints (2.4 litres) water	approx. 10 cups water
8 oz (250 g) vermicelli	8 oz vermicelli
3 or 4 bits of saffron	3 or 4 bits of saffron

* *Poissons de roche* are tiny multi-coloured fish (often with no names) plus small conger eel, crab, *rascasse* (for which there is no translation except scorpion fish, which sounds terrifying) and anything else that is too small to be sold on its own.

** Ordinary Marmande-type tomatoes will do just as well but not the Canary Island or Channel Island sort available in the UK. When Marmande are not available, it is best to use tinned Italian plum tomatoes.

Fry the onion in some olive oil and add the tomatoes. Put this mixture into a pot, add the fish and then the water and put on to boil. Let boil fairly furiously with the lid half on for approximately 20 minutes. Strain everything through a sieve and press on the fish hard to extract everything. You should end up with a thickish soup and a very dry lump of useless fish (throw it away). Put the saffron into this strained liquid and add the vermicelli (I leave out the vermicelli, feeling that bread is fattening enough) and let *simmer* until the pasta is cooked. (Don't use home-made pasta or it will disintegrate under this treatment.)

Now you see why I recommend the bought variety.

SOPA DE PESCADO (Mexico)

WHITING SOUP

Imperial/Metric	American
1 lb (500 g) whitefish (including the whiting)	2 cups whitefish (including the whiting)
1 recipe fish stock (p.308)	1 recipe fish stock (p.308)
2 egg yolks	2 egg yolks
1 dessertspoon flour	1 dessertspoon flour
2 cloves garlic, crushed	2 cloves garlic, crushed
2 medium onions, chopped	2 medium onions, chopped
1 green pepper, chopped	1 bell pepper, chopped
4 large tomatoes, chopped small	4 large tomatoes, chopped small
2 tablespoons parsley	2 tablespoons parsley
4 sprigs fresh coriander (*cilentro*)	4 sprigs fresh coriander (*cilentro*)
1 teaspoon oregano	1 teaspoon oregano
olive oil	olive oil
1 tablespoon lime or lemon juice	1 tablespoon lime or lemon juice
4 or 5 slices of bread	4 or 5 slices of bread

Simmer the fish in the broth and when done remove to a basin. Mix the fish and half the parsley with the egg yolks and some salt and pepper. Use the flour to bind if necessary. Shape into tiny balls. In a large saucepan fry the garlic and onions and add the pepper. Add the tomatoes, and finally the broth and lime or lemon juice. Allow to simmer very gently for 15 minutes.

Just before serving cut 4 or 5 slices of bread into croûtons and fry them in olive oil. Add the fishballs and serve the soup with the croûtons or hand them separately.

WHITE FISH AND GREEN PEA SOUP (USA: West Coast)

Imperial/Metric	American
1 recipe *sauce béchamel* (p.391)	1 recipe *sauce béchamel* (p.391)
1 recipe fish stock (p.308)	1 recipe fish stock (p.308)
1 lb (500 g) sole, plaice or halibut	1 lb sole, plaice or red snapper, flounder etc
4 oz (125 g) green peas	4 oz green peas (frozen will do)
4 fl. oz (120 ml) dry white wine	½ cup dry white wine
3 tablespoons cream (optional)	3 tablespoons cream (optional)

Remove head and fillet fish. Use bones in the stock. Poach fish in the wine and a little of the stock. When cooked, purée in liquidizer or food processor. Add sauce and rest of fish stock. Cook peas separately in water or a little stock. Adjust seasoning. Add the peas to the soup and serve, stirring in a little cream at the end. The soup should be like a thin cream. If it is too thick, add a little more fish stock.

CULLAN SKINK (UK: Scotland)

SMOKED HADDOCK SOUP

Imperial/Metric	*American*
approx. 2 lb (1 kilo) smoked haddock	approx. 2 lb Finnan haddie
1 medium onion, finely sliced	1 medium onion, finely sliced
2 tablespoons butter	2 tablespoons butter
8 oz (250 g) mashed potato	1 cup mashed potato
1½ pints (900 ml) full cream milk	3¾ cups full cream milk
8 fl. oz (240 ml) double cream	1 cup heavy cream
1 pint (600 m l) water	2½ cups water
chopped chives	chopped chives

Cook the fish in the milk – you should not need to soak it if it is real and on the bone. Cured fillets may need soaking. Skin, fillet and flake fish when cooked. Cook the onion in the butter and when almost done pour on the milk and water and add the fish. Stir in the mashed potatoes and then put everything through the liquidizer or food processor. Return to the saucepan and heat through, adding the cream at the end. Serve sprinkled with chives.

CREAM OF CLAM SOUP (USA)

Minced clams from America are currently available in tins more or less throughout Europe, though you may have to go to a large supermarket or speciality grocer to get them. A very quick, easy and inexpensive soup.

Imperial/Metric	American
2 8 oz (250 g) tins minced clams	2 cans minced clams
2 pints (1.2 litres) fish stock	5 cups fish stock
2 or 3 shallots, finely chopped	2 or 3 shallots, finely chopped
8 fl. oz (240 ml) double cream	1 cup heavy cream
salt and white pepper	salt and white pepper
parsley (to decorate)	parsley (to decorate)

Strain the minced clams and their juice and reserve. Cook slightly in the fish stock with the shallots. Add the cream and heat through. Adjust seasoning and serve sprinkled with parsley.

CRAB AND SWEETCORN SOUP (USA)

A very quick and easy soup.

Imperial/Metric	American
8 oz (250 g) Alaska crab meat (white)	1 cup Alaska crab meat (white)
7-8 oz (250 g) tinned sweetcorn, whole	1 cup canned sweetcorn
1 pint (500 ml) *sauce béchamel* (p.391)	2½ cups *sauce béchamel* (p.391)
1 pint (500 ml) chicken stock (cubes will do)	2½ cups chicken stock (cubes will do)
juice of 1 lemon	juice of 1 lemon
8 fl. oz (240 ml) single or double cream	1 cup light or heavy cream
parsley and red pepper (to garnish)	parsley, and red pepper (to garnish)

Make the *sauce béchamel*. Drain the crab and chop slightly, not too small. Drain the sweetcorn and fold into hot *sauce béchamel*. Add the chicken stock, bit by bit. Add the lemon. Stir. Add the crab and *warm* through – do not let boil. Add extra cream if wished. Garnish with a sprig of parsley and a sprinkle of red pepper.

BISQUE DE HOMARD (France)

CREAM OF LOBSTER SOUP

Lobster bisque in cans is expensive and not even the real thing. For more or less the same price you can make the real thing and know exactly what it contains.

The French demand that the lobsters should be cut up *live*. As this practice makes very little difference to the taste of the finished bisque and I think it is unnecessarily cruel to the poor animal (it is bad enough, after all, that we eat them, without dabbling in torture), I use cooked lobster.

Imperial/Metric	*American*
2 lobsters, each weighing around 1½ lb (750 g)	2 lobsters, each weighing around 1½ lb
4 or 5 shallots, chopped	4 or 5 shallots, chopped
1 carrot, grated	1 carrot, grated
2 tablespoons cognac	2 tablespoons cognac
4 fl. oz (120 ml) dry white wine	½ cup dry white wine
1½ pints (900 ml) full cream milk	3¾ cups full cream milk
8 fl. oz (240 ml) fish stock	8 fl. oz fish stock
4 or 5 sprigs of parsley, tied together	4 or 5 sprigs of parsley, tied together
2 sprigs fennel	2 sprigs fennel
butter for frying	butter for frying
8 fl. oz (240 ml) double cream	1 cup heavy cream
2 egg yolks	2 egg yolks
2 tablespoons Madeira or port	2 tablespoons Madeira or portwine
parsley, chopped (to garnish)	parsley, chopped (to garnish)
a little flour (optional)	a little flour (optional)

Remove the lobsters' shells and dice the meat into small pieces. (The shell will be used later.) Fry the shallots and carrot in a little butter, add the lobster and once hot pour over the cognac and ignite. Pour over the white wine and let cool.

Break the centre part of the lobster shell into small pieces and then run it through the liquidizer or food processor – you will find the claws do no good to machinery. Put this crushed lobster shell and the claws (crushed or not) into the milk and fish stock, add the parsley and fennel and *simmer* gently for 40 minutes, stirring from time to time. Some recipes use a little flour in this milk and stock mixture. If you wish to do so, mix the flour down with a little cold stock and stir until it is well incorporated. At the end of this time strain through a very fine sieve or coffee filter paper. Add the lobster mixture to this and heat through. Make sure you have enough for 8 servings – if not, add a little fish stock. Add the cream and egg yolks and adjust seasoning. Finally put in the Madeira or port and serve sprinkled with a little parsley.

BILLIBI (France)

CREAM OF MUSSEL SOUP

When you make this soup, bear in mind that you will have almost half the mussels over for use in another dish, such as a risotto or salad. Although delicious hot, it is even better cold and seems less rich – which of course it isn't.

Imperial/Metric	*American*
4 lb (2 kilos) mussels	4 lb mussels
6 or 8 shallots, chopped	6 or 8 shallots, chopped
15 fl. oz (450 ml) white wine	2 cups white wine
6 or 8 parsley stalks	6 or 8 parsley stalks
15 fl. oz (450 ml) water	2 cups water
15 fl. oz (450 ml) single cream	2 cups light cream
salt	salt
1 teaspoon Tabasco	1 teaspoon Tabasco
thyme or fennel (optional)	thyme or fennel (optional)
3 egg yolks	3 egg yolks
parsley, chopped (to garnish)	parsley, chopped (to garnish)

In a large pan put the wine, water, shallots, parsley and scrubbed mussels. Bring to the boil, covered, and after 7-8 minutes check that the mussels have opened. Give 2-3 minutes more and then discard any that have not opened. Carefully strain the liquid left to remove the sand. Take mussels from their shells and purée *half* of them with their cooking liquid. Return this purée to the pan and bring to the boil. Add the cream and heat through. Add the Tabasco and then adjust seasonings. (Some people like a little thyme or fennel.) Beat the egg yolks and add to the hot soup. Do not let boil. Serve hot with parsley sprinkled over it and one or two mussels per serving.

Alternatively ice and serve a few hours later with the same garnishing.

CREAM OF SHRIMP OR PRAWN (USA)

Imperial/Metric	*American*
3 lb (1.5 kilos) whole prawns	3 lb medium shrimps
3 pints (1.8 litres) fish stock	7½ cups fish stock
10 fl. oz (300 ml) double cream	1¼ cups heavy cream
nutmeg or dill or parsley, chopped (optional)	nutmeg or dill or parsley, chopped (optional)
salt and pepper	salt and pepper

Cook the prawns (shrimps) in the stock – drain and reserve the stock. Peel and clean the prawns (shrimps). Purée three-quarters of them in the liquidizer or food processor with the stock. Save the others to stir into the soup at the end. Heat through, stirring all the time. This soup can be made in advance up to this point. Once hot add the cream, seasonings and whole prawns. Serve sprinkled with dill or parsley if wished.

This soup can also be served iced but remember to season it rather more highly.

12 Salads

I am married to someone who says he loathes salads when he means he loathes lettuce. A large percentage of men do not like too much rabbit food so when serving salads one must make them sufficiently interesting (i.e. containing non-green ingredients such as prawns, eggs, tunny, crab, olives, anchovies, cucumber, avocado, sweet peppers, etc.). Strangely most non-salad eaters will eat tomatoes not counting them as salad (very subjective reasoning) and dressed cooked vegetables. Whether it is something to do with the colour or the bitterness I cannot say but I have found also that most non-salad eaters will eat the Italian *radicchio* and also Belgian endive.

For the best salads one must also look to the Americas, as well as to Europe, without going overboard by indulging in mixtures of cream cheese, nuts and raspberry jelly. California and Mexico are particularly good at mixed salads and the Scandinavian countries make wonderful fish salads though there one does get a bit tired of the eternal cucumber and potato salads which appear at least twice a day everywhere.

Nothing tired should ever go into a salad – not even into a wilted one or a *salad tiède*. On the contrary the latter seem to require almost rigid greenstuff in order to keep some crispness when the warm ingredients are added.

Dressings should go on at the very last moment or be served separately.

Vegetable and Fruit

WALDORF SALAD (USA)

Imperial/Metric	American
5 or 6 Jonathan apples*	5 or 6 Jonathan apples*
2 pints (1.2 litres) iced water	5 cups iced water
juice of 2 lemons	juice of 2 lemons
1 bunch white celery	1 bunch white celery
6 oz (375 g) walnut pieces	6 oz walnut pieces
8 fl. oz (240 ml) mayonnaise (p.404)	1 cup mayonnaise (p.404)
4 fl. oz (120 ml) double cream	½ cup heavy cream
salt	salt
paprika (to garnish)	paprika (to garnish)

* Jonathan apples are not obtainable everywhere – Worcester Pearmains or similar red apples will do just as well.

Peel the apples; dice them – not too small – and put into the iced water into which the 2 lemons have been squeezed. Chop the celery into similar-sized pieces. Mix the mayonnaise and cream together and stir in the nuts. Drain the apples well and pat dry if necessary. Add them with the celery to the cream and walnuts. Add salt to taste. Chill for at least 4 hours and then bring up to room temperature before serving.

ENSALADA DE BERENJENAS CON VAINITAS (Venezuela)

AUBERGINE AND GREEN BEAN SALAD

Imperial/Metric	American
2 lb (1 kilo) aubergines	2 lb aubergines
1 lb (500 g) green beans	1 lb French beans
1 large onion, finely chopped	1 large onion, finely chopped
2 fl. oz (60 ml) olive oil	¼ cup olive oil
1 red sweet pepper (fresh or tinned, sliced or chopped	1 red bell pepper (fresh or tinned, sliced or chopped
1 recipe vinaigrette (p.401)	1 recipe vinaigrette (p.401)

Do not peel the aubergines but cut into half-inch (1 cm) slices and then into fingers. Sprinkle with salt and let drain in a colander for about an hour. Rinse and dry on paper towels. Fry the onion in the olive oil and add the aubergine. You may need a little more oil, though try to avoid putting in too much otherwise a greasy dish results. Add the red pepper. Cut the beans into 1-2 inch pieces (2-5 cm) and cook in boiling water until they are just done (they should not be soft). Drain and add to the aubergines.

At this stage there are two schools of thought. Some cooks put the vinaigrette on hot, others put it on the cooled vegetables. I prefer the latter but it is a matter of personal taste.

Variations
Some people also add a little chopped raw onion at the end, others sometimes add chopped, stoned olives. I have a friend who adds toasted almonds to this dish. It seems anything is allowed.

GUACAMOLE (Mexico)

AVOCADO DIP OR SALAD

Imperial/Metric	*American*
3 large avocados, peeled	3 large avocados, peeled
1 tomato (optional)	1 tomato (optional)
1 medium onion, chopped	1 medium onion, chopped
green and/or red chillies or Tabasco*	green and/or red chillies or Tabasco*
1 tablespoon vinegar	1 tablespoon vinegar
2 tablespoons olive oil	2 tablespoons olive oil
salt	salt

* I use Tabasco since it is easier to control the amount of hotness which results, but chilli-fans will know how much to use of the real thing.

In a liquidizer or food processor combine the avocados with the tomato, onion, oil and vinegar. Add salt to taste at the last.

Variations
Many things can be added to *guacamole*, such as crispy fried bacon cut into tiny cubes, *chicharrones* (*grattons* from rendering pig fat into lard), tortilla chips etc. It's up to you.

AVOCADO AND MELON SALAD WITH ORANGE DRESSING (Kenya)

I have also had this salad in America, so who copied whom I have no idea. The taste should be a combination of creamy avocado, sweet melon and very slightly astringent dressing.

Imperial/Metric	American
4 large avocados, halved	4 large avocados, halved
1 large Cassaba or Persian melon or 2 Charentais or Ogen melons	1 large Cassaba or Persian melon or 2 Charentais or Ogen melons
juice of 2-3 oranges	juice of 2-3 oranges
2 tablespoons very mild olive or sunflower oil	2 tablespoons very mild olive or sunflower oil
salt	salt
fresh mint, leaf or chopped	fresh mint, leaf or chopped

With a small melon-baller, remove the flesh of the melon(s) and put in a bowl. Then do the same with the avocados, taking care not to damage the shells, which you will be using to serve. Turn the avocado and melon in the orange juice and then add the oil and salt at the last moment (the salt will draw out the melon liquid, so do not do this too much in advance). Serve in the half avocado shells sprinkled with a little fresh mint.

AVOCADO, ORANGE AND GRAPEFRUIT SALAD (USA: Florida)

A fiddly salad but worth the trouble.

Imperial/Metric	*American*
4 avocados	4 avocados
4 grapefruits (fresh or well-drained tinned)	4 grapefruits (fresh or well-drained tinned)
8 oranges	8 oranges
vinaigrette (p.401)	vinaigrette (p.401)
Iceberg-type lettuce	Iceberg-type lettuce
parsley, chopped (optional)	parsley, chopped (optional)

Peel and remove the pith and inner skin from the segments of the orange and (fresh) grapefruit. Slice the avocados last of all. Arrange prettily on a large platter or on individual serving dishes and pour over the vinaigrette. Sprinkle with parsley if liked.

ENSALADA DE AGUACATE Y PIÑA (Mexico)

AVOCADO AND PINEAPPLE SALAD

This is a common salad in Mexico, and frequently in the country tinned pineapple is used but fresh pineapple is nicer.

Imperial/Metric	*American*
4 avocados, slightly firm	4 avocados, slightly firm
1 small pineapple, skinned and cubed	1 small pineapple, skinned and cubed
1 orange, peeled and cubed	1 orange, peeled and cubed
1 lemon, peeled and cubed	1 lemon, peeled and cubed
1 large lettuce	1 large lettuce
vinaigrette (p.401)	vinaigrette (p.401)
fresh mint (to garnish)	fresh mint (to garnish)

Remove the avocados' pulp and cut into small cubes. Mix the pineapple, orange and lemon together with the vinaigrette. Taste and sweeten if the result is too sharp. Serve on large lettuce leaves.

Should be made about an hour before serving.

INSALATA TRICOLORE (Italy)

AVOCADO, TOMATO AND MOZZARELLA SALAD

Imperial/Metric	American
3 avocados, sliced	3 avocados, sliced
6-8 large tomatoes, sliced	6-8 large tomatoes, sliced
approx. 1 lb (500 g) mozzarella cheese, sliced*	approx. 1 lb mozzarella cheese, sliced*
vinaigrette	vinaigrette
parsley, chopped	parsley, chopped

* Try to get mozzarella made from buffalo milk, since the taste is so much richer.

On a large platter or on individual plates arrange the cheese, tomatoes and sliced avocados in lines so they look like the Italian flag, i.e. green, white, red. Serve a vinaigrette separately into which you have stirred a little parsley.

BEAN SALAD (Mexico)

A simple salad excellent in winter and a boon to those in a hurry, since it almost all comes out of tins! It should be followed by something light, without beans, potatoes or rice.

Imperial/Metric	American
1 medium tin red kidney beans	1 medium can red kidney beans
1 medium tin chickpeas (garbanzos)	1 medium can chickpeas (garbanzos)
1 medium tin sweetcorn	1 medium can sweetcorn
1 medium onion, cut in rings	1 medium onion, cut in rings
1 large sweet red pepper, sliced	1 large red bell pepper, sliced
vinaigrette	vinaigrette
2 tablespoons parsley, chopped	2 tablespoons parsley, chopped

Drain and rinse the contents of the tins and mix in a large bowl. Mix in the vinaigrette, sweet pepper and 1 tablespoon of the parsley. Strew the onion rings on top, plus the rest of the parsley, and serve.

BEAN SALAD (Turkey)

Each guest mixes his vegetables into the beans.

Imperial/Metric	American
8 oz (250 g) raw haricot beans	8 oz raw haricot beans
2 cloves garlic	2 cloves garlic
1 tablespoon sugar	1 tablespoon sugar
1 teaspoon allspice	1 teaspoon allspice
4 large or 8 small eggs, hard-boiled	4 large or 8 small eggs, hard-cooked
1 recipe lemon vinaigrette (p.403)	1 recipe lemon vinaigrette (p.403)
2 tomatoes	2 tomatoes
1 large onion, cut in thin rings	1 large onion, cut in thin rings
a handful of black olives	a handful of black olives
parsley, chopped	parsley, chopped

Cook the haricot beans with the sugar and garlic until done. Dress while still hot and leave overnight.

Next day pile the beans onto the middle of a dish and surround with quarters of egg and tomato and onion rings. Decorate with black olives and sprinkle with parsley and serve.

FATTOUCHE or FATTOUSH (Syria and the Lebanon)

BREAD SALAD

A very uninspiring name for something so delicious and refreshing. It must be made with Arab or pitta bread – any other sort becomes soggy and unpleasant. In its home countries the predominant herb is purslane, which grows wild in Europe but is not much cultivated (*pourpier* in French, it is relatively common in that country). Parsley is not a bad substitute. Even without purslane the salad is delicious.

No two recipes for *Fattouche* are the same, and this is a *Fattouche* of my childhood – there are plenty equally as genuine.

Imperial/Metric	American
3 or 4 slices Arab or pitta bread	3 or 4 slices Arab or pitta bread
1 lb (500 g) tomatoes	1 lb tomatoes
2 or 3 cucumbers	2 or 3 cucumbers
1 large green pepper	1 large green pepper
juice of 2 lemons	juice of 2 lemons
4 tablespoons parsley, chopped	4 tablespoons parsley, chopped
2-4 tablespoons purslane, chopped (optional)	2-4 tablespoons purslane, chopped (optional)
1 large mild onion, sliced	1 large mild onion, sliced
up to 4 fl. oz (125 ml) olive oil	up to ½ cup olive oil
salt	salt
1 large-leaved lettuce	1 large-leaved lettuce
dried mint (optional)	dried mint (optional)

Soak the onion in salted water for 15 minutes. Peel, seed and slice the cucumber, sprinkle with salt and let drain 30 minutes. Cut the tomatoes into quarters (or eighths). Make a dressing with the lemon juice, oil olive and salt. Drain, rinse and dry the cucumbers and onions. Toss all the vegetables, except the lettuce, in the lemon dressing and add the parsley and purslane, if used. Grill the bread until quite crisp and either tear or cut into bite-sized pieces. Line a bowl or individual plates with lettuce leaves. Mix the grilled bread into the salad and serve at once. Can be sprinkled with dried mint if wished.

CELERI REMOULADE (France)

This is the classic celeriac salad cut into julienne strips and served with a rather mustardy mayonnaise. The ready-prepared stuff is none too delicious due to the usually poor quality of the mayonnaise used. However, both the Swiss and the Germans, who use a great deal of this vegetable, sell ready-prepared celeriac, and all you have to do is rinse it, dry it and put on your own mayonnaise.

Imperial/Metric	*American*
3 large celeriac	3 large celeriac
8 fl. oz (240 ml) home-made mayonnaise (p.404)	1 cup home-made mayonnaise (p.404)
8 fl. oz (240 ml) sour cream	1 cup sour cream
2 tablespoons or more strong Dijon mustard	2 tablespoons or more strong Dijon mustard
juice of 1 lemon	juice of 1 lemon
parsley, chopped (to garnish)	parsley, chopped (to garnish)

Unless you are very skilled, it is difficult to produce thin enough julienne strips without machinery. Peel the celeriac with a knife and cut into manageable pieces. Put through the julienne disc of your food processor and immediately blanch for 2 minutes in boiling water acidulated with the juice of 1 lemon. Rinse quickly under the cold tap until absolutely cold, then dry on a cloth or on paper towels. Mix the sour cream, mayonnaise and as much Dijon mustard as your taste demands and add the dried-off celeriac. Leave 2-3 hours before serving and sprinkle with parsley just before bringing to table.

SALADA DO PALMITO (Brazil)

HEARTS OF PALM SALAD

In Brazil hearts of palm are sold daily in the markets and are freshly boiled for salads and soups and for adding to other vegetable dishes. They have a subtle, nutty flavour which you either love or hate. They are not expensive, provided you can find them, but always look at the date on the tin. They should never be purchased more than a year old. A large tin will feed 4 people. They are very popular – and very inexpensive – in France.

Imperial/Metric	*American*
2 tins hearts of palm	2 cans hearts of palm
4 tomatoes, sliced	4 tomatoes, sliced
1 onion, sliced	1 onion, sliced
1 recipe vinaigrette (p.401)	1 recipe vinaigrette (p.401)
parsley, chopped (to garnish)	parsley, chopped (to garnish)

Slice the hearts of palm either lengthwise or in rings according to taste. Arrange the tomatoes and onions on plates with the hearts of palm on top. Cover with vinaigrette and sprinkle with parsley.

Variation

Imperial/Metric	*American*
2 tins hearts of palm	2 cans hearts of palm
1 sweet red pepper	1 red bell pepper
5 tablespoons olive oil	5 tablespoons olive oil
2 tablespoons lime juice	2 tablespoons lime juice
salt and cayenne	salt and cayenne
1 teaspoon mustard (optional)	1 teaspoon mustard (optional)
lettuce leaves	lettuce leaves

Cut the hearts of palm and the red pepper into thinnish slices and cover with dressing made of lime juice, olive oil etc. Chill well before serving. Serve on lettuce leaves.

INSALATA DI GIRASOLI (Italy)

JERUSALEM ARTICHOKE SALAD

Very easy and very economical, especially if you have a garden full of these things and can't think what to do.

Imperial/Metric	American
approx. 2 lb (1 kilo) Jerusalem artichokes	approx. 2 lb Jerusalem artichokes
1 recipe mayonnaise (p.404)	1 recipe mayonnaise (p.404)
1 clove garlic, crushed	1 clove garlic, crushed
approx. 1 dessertspoon mustard	approx. 1 dessertspoon mustard

Unless you have an automatic peeler, it is probably easiest to cook the artichokes first and then peel them and cut into slices. Mix with the mayonnaise to which you have added the crushed garlic and mustard.

FRESH MUSHROOM SALAD (Italy)

Always use cultivated mushrooms for salads since most wild mushrooms need preliminary washing and sometimes soaking before being cooked, which ruins the texture of any salad.

Imperial/Metric	American
2 lb plus (1 kilo plus) mushrooms	2 lb plus mushrooms
1 recipe vinaigrette (p.401)	1 recipe vinaigrette (p.401)
1 tablespoon parsley, chopped	1 tablespoon parsley, chopped
1 teaspoon fresh marjoram, chopped (optional)	1 teaspoon fresh marjoram, chopped (optional)

Slice the mushrooms thinly, preferably not more than an hour before you are going to serve them. At the last moment dress them and sprinkle the herbs on the top.

THREE PEPPER SALAD (Yugoslavia and Hungary)

This is an interesting salad, excellent with pickled or smoked fish, hams, terrines and pâtés. In Hungary the generic salad is in fact yellow peppers with a similar dressing but the peppers are totally raw in summer and pickled in winter. This salad is much eaten in southern Hungary, the home of pepper-growing for paprika purposes, and obviously owes a lot to Serbian influences.

Imperial/Metric	American
3 lb (1.5 kilos) peppers*	3 lb peppers*
1 onion	1 onion
juice of 1 lemon	juice of 1 lemon
6 tablespoons or more olive oil	6 tablespoons or more olive oil
sugar	sugar
salt and pepper	salt and pepper
2 cloves garlic, finely chopped	2 cloves garlic, finely chopped
parsley, chopped	parsley, chopped

* The peppers should be of 3 colours, red, green and yellow, in equal quantities.

Bake or grill the peppers until soft and then put a cloth or cling-film over them for 10 minutes, so skinning them will be easier. Remove top and seed and slice in thin rounds. Slice the onion the same way. Dress with the lemon and oil dressing to which you have added the garlic and parsley.

SALAD OLIVIER (Russia)

RUSSIAN SALAD

Monsieur Olivier was chef to the last Tsar of Russia. He invented this salad which is found all over the world, almost always in a debased form. As will be seen, it bears little resemblance to the awful tinned stuff or what many restaurants serve up.

Imperial/Metric	American
12 oz (375 g) chicken breast	12 oz chicken breast
8 oz (250 g) home-cooked ham, diced	8 oz home-cooked ham, diced
8 oz (250 g) baby carrots, cubed	8 oz baby carrots, cubed
12 oz (375 g) new potatoes, cubed	12 oz new potatoes, cubed
8 oz (250 g) baby beetroot, cubed	8 oz baby beets, cubed
1 cucumber, cubed	1 cucumber, cubed
3 or 4 spring onions, chopped	3 or 4 scallions, chopped
8 fl. oz (240 ml) home-made mayonnaise (p.404)	1 cup home-made mayonnaise (p.404)
8 fl. oz (240 ml) sour cream	1 cup sour cream
1 teaspoon freeze-dried dillweed	1 teaspoon freeze-dried dillweed
1 tablespoon parsley, chopped	1 tablespoon parsley, chopped
4 eggs, hard-boiled	4 eggs, hardcooked

Sprinkle the cubed cucumber with salt and let drain for 30 minutes. Steam the chicken breast and when cool enough to handle cut into small cubes and set aside. Cook all the vegetables separately. Once they are cool enough, combine all of them except the beetroot with the diced ham, chicken and cucumber. Stir in the mayonnaise, sour cream and herbs. Put this mixture into a shallow dish and surround with cubes of cooked beetroot which you have previously patted dry on paper towels so the colour will not run. Decorate with quartered hard-boiled eggs and serve.

ENSALADA RUSA (Spain)

SPANISH RUSSIAN SALAD

This has nothing to do with the Russian Salad we got at school and sometimes still get in British restaurants. It probably has nothing to do with Russia either.

Imperial/Metric	American
1 lb (500 g) waxy potatoes	1 lb waxy potatoes
2 tinned red peppers known as *pimientos morrones**	2 canned red peppers known as *pimientos morrones**
2 fresh green peppers	2 fresh bell peppers
1 onion	1 onion
4 tablespoons cooked peas or broad beans	4 tablespoons cooked peas or fava beans
about 20 green olives, stoned	about 20 green olives, pitted
pickled gherkin, chopped to taste	pickled gherkin, chopped to taste
scant 1 pint (500 ml) mayonnaise (p.404)	good pint mayonnaise (p.404)
lettuce leaves	lettuce leaves
parsley, chopped (to decorate)	parsley, chopped (to decorate)

* I can only think that using *pimientos morrones* keeps the canning companies in business; there is no reason why you should not use fresh red peppers when they are in season.

Boil your potatoes as for salad; let cool and dice. Dice the onion and peppers and add all the other ingredients. Bind together with mayonnaise and refrigerate for approximately an hour, covered with clingfilm. Serve on lettuce leaves sprinkled with parsley.

WILTED SPINACH SALAD (USA)

This recipe comes from the Blue Fox Restaurant in San Francisco. They give it to anyone who asks for it, and I now hand it on.

Imperial/Metric
2 lb (1 kilo) fresh, small spinach
8 oz (225 g) streaky bacon
4 fl. oz (120 ml) olive oil
3 tablespoons wine vinegar
salt and pepper

American
2 lb fresh, small spinach
8 oz streaky bacon
½ cup olive oil
3 tablespoons wine vinegar
salt and pepper

Make sure there are no coarse stalks etc left on the spinach. Tear or cut it into bite-sized pieces, wash and dry well. Dice the bacon and fry in half the olive oil. When it is crisp and done and the oil is hot, pour the whole over the spinach, tossing until the spinach starts wilting. Add a little more oil if necessary (it depends how much fat the bacon has given out), then some vinegar and salt and pepper. Serve immediately. This can be prepared in advance up to the last-minute frying of the bacon.

SPINACH, BACON AND SOUR CREAM SALAD (USA)

This is made in precisely the same way as the Blue Fox Wilted Spinach Salad except that sour cream is substitute for olive oil and the bacon should be slightly more fat. Once the bacon is cooked, pour on 5 fl. oz (150 ml/just over ½ US cup) of thick sour cream. Heat through but do not let boil, and stir everything into the torn spinach leaves. Although the recipe does not call for it, I like to cook a small chopped onion in a little oil before starting the bacon.

COOKED SPINACH SALAD (Lebanon and Turkey)

Imperial/Metric
2 lb (1 kilo) cooked weight,
   spinach
2 oz (60 g) pine nuts
2 oz (60 g) currants (optional)
8 fl. oz (240 g) thick,
   unflavoured yoghurt
1 onion, chopped (fried or raw)
olive oil
1 lemon

American
2 lb cooked weight, spinach
2 oz *pignoli*
2 oz currants (optional)
8 fl. oz thick, unflavoured
   yoghurt
1 onion, chopped (fried or raw)
olive oil
1 lemon

Wash the spinach well and tear into small pieces – make sure there are no thick stems. Have a large pan of boiling water ready and (in approximately 4 lots) put the spinach in to blanch for 1 minute – *do not cook* (irrespective of the title of this recipe!). Refresh in cold water as you go along. Finally pat all the spinach dry and stir in the yoghurt, a little lemon juice, the pine nuts (*pignoli*) and chopped fried or raw onion. Serve with a little more oil poured over if wished.

Variation
The Turks put currants in this dish plus a little sugar sometimes to counteract the sourness of the lemon.

TOMATO AND ANCHOVY SALAD (Italy)

Simple but delicious peasant food.

Imperial/Metric	*American*
3 lb (1.5 kilos) Marmande-type tomatoes	3 lb Marmande-type tomatoes
1 tin anchovy fillets	1 can anchovy fillets
vinaigrette (p.401)	vinaigrette (p.401)
1 medium onion	1 medium onion
handful of black olives	handful of black olives

Slice the tomatoes (peeled or not) and lay them in a dish. Cover with thinly sliced onion rings and then make a trellis of anchovy fillets over the whole dish. Pour over the vinaigrette and then put a black olive in each diamond formed by the anchovies.

POIVRONS A L'ANCHOIADE (French and Spanish Basque country)

PEPPER AND ANCHOVY SALAD

Imperial/Metric	*American*
12 red sweet peppers	12 red bell peppers
4 oz (125 ml) olive oil	½ cup olive oil
1 flat tin anchovy fillets	1 flat can anchovy fillets
4 oz (125 ml) double cream	½ cup heavy cream
2 tablespoons lemon juice or vinegar	2 tablespoons lemon juice or vinegar
black pepper, freshly ground	black pepper, freshly ground
parsley, freshly chopped	parsley, freshly chopped

Cut each pepper in half lengthwise and remove the stalk, seeds and pith. Paint a large, ovenproof shallow dish with olive oil and lay the pepper halves on it, flat side down. Paint liberally with olive oil and bake in a hot oven until limp but still with a little resistance. Cool.

In a liquidizer or food processor combine the anchovy fillets, olive oil, lemon juice and cream. You may well need more cream (or milk) to lengthen it – it depends entirely on the anchovies. The object is to get a liquid, strong-tasting sauce. Pour this sauce over the cooled peppers, cover with clingfilm and leave for at least 3 hours. Serve sprinkled with freshly chopped parsley and with a peppermill to hand.

SALADE DE TOMATES (France)

Imperial/Metric	*American*
2½-3 lb (1-1.5 kilos) tomatoes	2½-3 lb tomatoes
1 medium onion, cut in rings	1 medium onion, cut in rings
1 recipe vinaigrette (p.401)	1 recipe vinaigrette (p.401)
1 tablespoon parsley, chopped	1 tablespoon parsley, chopped

You may peel the tomatoes if you wish but the recipe does not call for it. Slice or quarter the tomatoes and toss in the vinaigrette. Strew with onion rings and parsley.

ITALIAN TOMATO SALAD

Imperial/Metric	*American*
2½-3 lb (1.2-1.5 kilos) large tomatoes	2½-3 lb large tomatoes
1 bunch fresh basil	1 bunch fresh basil
1 medium onion, thinly sliced in rings	1 medium onion, thinly sliced in rings
vinaigrette (p.401)	vinaigrette (p.401)

Peel the tomatoes by cutting a cross in the bottom and dipping them in boiling water or holding them over a gas flame. Slice carefully and lay in a dish. Whizz up the vinaigrette in a liquidizer or food processor and add the washed basil. Pour over the tomatoes and decorate with onion rings. Can be made an hour or two ahead of serving.

TABBOULEH (Lebanon)

CRACKED WHEAT SALAD OR PARSLEY SALAD

In fact, *tabbouleh* is found all over the Near East in various forms. It is made of cracked wheat called *burghul* by the Lebanese and Syrians and *bulgur* by the Turks. In countries where *couscous* is the national dish, the special *couscous* semolina (which is virtually instant) can be used instead of *burghul* from health food shops. This is generally available in shops and supermarkets throughout much of France, and the coarse or medium variety is the sort to buy. Pour on boiling water (or stock), stir and leave to cool. Then dress it in the usual way for *tabbouleh*. *Tabbouleh* must be one of the few salads improved by standing a short while.

You can accompany this dish with hard-boiled eggs and/or olives but for many this then becomes too substantial for a first course. It is probably worth noting that people seem to eat a great deal of *tabbouleh* if second helpings are offered, so the main course which follows should be light.

Imperial/Metric	American
8 oz (250 g) cracked wheat or coarse *couscous* semolina*	8 oz cracked wheat or coarse *couscous* semolina*
8 oz (250 g) tomatoes, quartered	8 oz tomatoes, quartered
1 large cucumber, peeled and diced	1 large cucumber, peeled and diced
1 large onion, chopped	1 large onion, chopped
1 green pepper, finely sliced	1 green pepper, finely sliced
approx. 8 oz (250 g) parsley, chopped	1 cup parsley, chopped
1 teaspoon dried mint	1 teaspoon dried mint
1 recipe lemon vinaigrette (p.403)	1 recipe lemon vinaigrette (p.403)
large lettuce leaves for serving	large lettuce leaves for serving
hard-boiled eggs (optional)	hardcooked eggs (optional)
black olives (optional)	black olives (optional)

* If using *burghul*, soak it in cold water for approximately 30 minutes. If using *couscous* semolina, follow packet instructions using boiling water. Do not use stock cubes: they will unbalance the vegetable flavour of the finished dish.

Sprinkle the cucumber with salt and let drain for 30 minutes. Drain the *burghul* and squeeze out any residual moisture. The *couscous* is ready when it has absorbed *all* the liquid. Spread out and let cool, then mix in the vinaigrette and the vegetables and herbs, reserving the mint for final decoration. Mix really well.

Serve either in a salad boiler lined with lettuce or individually on lettuce-lined plates.

Cheese

GREEK SALAD

Delicious and very healthy.

Imperial/Metric	*American*
1 large cos lettuce	1 large romaine lettuce
1 large cucumber	1 large cucumber
8 oz (250 g) feta or Salakis* cheese	8 oz feta or Salakis* cheese
12 oz (375 g) tomatoes	12 oz tomatoes
handful of black olives	handful of black olives
fresh basil or parsley, chopped, to taste	fresh basil or parsley, chopped, to taste
1 recipe lemon vinaigrette (p.403)	1 recipe lemon vinaigrette (p.403)

* French version of the Greek feta and very good.

Wash the lettuce, drain and tear or cut into 1 inch (2 cm) pieces. Peel the cucumber, halve it and remove seeds, then cut into dice. Slice the onion and put into cold salted water to crisp up. Cut the tomatoes into quarters or eighths (unpeeled), and cut the feta or Salakis into small chunks. Add basil or parsley. Mix all ingredients together and toss in the vinaigrette.

INSALATA DI MOZZARELLA FRITTA (Italy)

WARM SALAD OF MOZZARELLA CHEESE, TOMATO AND ANCHOVY

Imperial/Metric
10-14 oz (315-440 g) Mozzarella
   di Bufala (buffalo is better
   than cows' milk mozzarella)
1½ lb (750 g) firm but ripe
   tomatoes, such as Marmande
1 tin or jar anchovies
a little milk
1 onion, finely sliced
1 recipe vinaigrette (p.401)
a little oregano
4 oz (125 g) flour
2 large eggs
6 oz (190 g) white breadcrumbs
parsley, chopped (to decorate)

American
10-14 oz Mozzarella di Bufala
   (buffalo is better than cows'
   milk mozzarella)
1½ lb firm but ripe tomatoes,
   such as Marmande
1 can or jar anchovies
a little milk
1 onion, finely sliced
1 recipe vinaigrette (p.401)
a little oregano
½ cup flour
2 large eggs
1½ cups white breadcrumbs
parsley, chopped (to decorate)

Cut the tomatoes into quarters or eighths, depending on size. (Do not slice.) Put in salad bowl with onion. Soak anchovies in milk to rid them of excess salt and cut into short lengths. Make vinaigrette and pour over tomatoes and onions. Stir in the anchovies and put in a little oregano.

Fry the cubes of mozzarella as in the recipe for *Salade Tiède au Fromage Frit* (below). Once all have been fried, toss them with the salad and serve at once, sprinkled with parsley.

SALADE TIEDE AU FROMAGE FRIT (France)

SALAD WITH FRIED CHEESE

Imperial/Metric
salad greens for 8, such as
   Escarole or crisp lettuce
   and/or Lambs lettuce (corn
   salad) and/or watercress
approx. 1 lb (500 g) Camembert,
   Brie or Neuchatel (the log-
   shaped sort*
1 recipe vinaigrette (p.401)
4 oz (125 g) flour
2 large eggs
1 teaspoon salt
6-7 oz (190-220g) dried
   breadcrumbs (home-made)

American
salad greens for 8, such as
   Escarole or crisp lettuce
   and/or Lambs lettuce (corn
   salad) and/or watercress
approx. 1 lb Camembert, Brie
   or Neuchatel (the log-shaped
   sort*
1 recipe vinaigrette (p.401)
½ cup flour
2 large eggs
1 teaspoon salt
1½ cups dried breadcrumbs
   (home-made)

* You may find, as others have before you, that the amount of cheese shown is too generous – there's no reason why you should not reduce the amount (or increase it) to suit your personal taste.

Wash and spin-dry salad greens and prepare vinaigrette. Cut the cheese into 1-1½ inch (2-3 cm) squares. Beat eggs well. Put the flour on a large plate or board, and the breadcrumbs on another. Roll each cube of cheese in the flour, then in the egg, making absolutely sure that the egg covers every bit of the cube, then roll them in the breadcrumbs. Refrigerate for 30 minutes. Then repeat the flour, egg and breadcrumbing process all over again. This should ensure that the cheese cannot escape. Either refrigerate until you need them or start to fry them in hot oil for a few minutes. Do only a few at a time so as not to lower the temperature of the oil. Keep the cooked pieces warm in a medium oven. Once all are done, dress the salad and add the cheese as quickly as possible. Serve immediately.

Fish and Seafood

CAESAR SALAD (USA)

Imperial/Metric	American
2 large cos lettuces	2 romaine lettuce
4 slices white bread	4 slices white bread
2 oz (60 g) butter	¼ cup butter
3 or 4 anchovy fillets or 3-4 oz (90-125 g) paste	3 or 4 anchovy fillets or 3-4 oz paste
1 recipe lemon vinaigrette (p.403)	1 recipe lemon vinaigrette (p.403)
2 eggs	2 eggs
2 tablespoons Worcester sauce	2 tablespoons Worcester sauce
2 tablespoons Parmesan cheese, grated	2 tablespoons Parmesan cheese, grated

Smash down the anchovy fillets with the butter or use anchovy paste if you are in a hurry. Spread the bread with this, cut into small dice and bake in a slow oven, 250°F/130°C/Gas ½, until dry. (This can be done the night before with advantage.) Beat the Worcester sauce into the lemon vinaigrette and add the Parmesan cheese. Cut or tear the lettuce into 1 inch (2 cm) pieces and put into a salad bowl. Put the eggs (which should be at room temperature) into boiling water for 1 minute. Crack eggs over salad bowl and scrape off any bits adhering to the shell. Put in the anchovy croûtons and then add the dressing and toss well. Serve immediately.

BALTIC HERRING SALAD (Germany, Denmark, Sweden etc)

Imperial/Metric	*American*
1 lb (500 g) salted or pickled herring, cubed	1 lb salted or pickled herring, cubed
8 oz (250 g) beetroot, chopped	8 oz beets, chopped
8 oz (250 g) potato, cooked and chopped	8 oz potato, cooked and chopped
4 fl. oz (120 ml) double cream	½ cup heavy cream
4 tablespoons white wine vinegar	4 tablespoons white wine vinegar
mustard to taste	mustard to taste
a little dill	a little dill
a few sliced gherkins	a few sliced gherkins

Mix together the herring, beetroot and potatoes. Make a dressing of the cream, mustard, vinegar and dill and incorporate into the salad. Sprinkle a little dill on top and a few sliced gherkins (2 or 3).

COURLAND SALAD (Lithuania and Estonia)

This salad is virtually identical to the Baltic Herring Salad except that it has 8 oz (250 g) cubed veal in it (the amount of a good veal cutlet either baked in aluminium foil in the oven or poached in a little chicken broth). The dressing is the same but instead of gherkins dill pickle is used – but only a small amount. You may need a little more dressing since the salad should be very moist. Serve with pumpernickel bread. I have substituted chicken for veal with good results. It's the herring that imposes its taste.

LITHUANIAN HERRING SALAD (Lithuania and Poland)

Beer goes better with this than wine.

Imperial/Metric
8 oz (250 g) pickled herring
8 oz (250 g) potato, cooked and cubed
8 oz (250 g) raw apple, cubed
1 large dill pickle, cubed
1 medium onion, finely sliced
4 eggs, hard-boiled
8 fl. oz (240 ml) sour cream
2 tablespoons Dijon-type mustard
2 teaspoons sugar
2-3 tablespoons vinegar

American
8 oz pickled herring
8 oz potato, cooked and cubed
8 oz raw apple, cubed
1 large dill pickle, cubed
1 medium onion, finely sliced
4 eggs, hardcooked
1 cup commercial sour cream
2 tablespoons Dijon-type mustard
2 teaspoons sugar
2-3 tablespoons vinegar

Mix all the salad ingredients, except hard-boiled egg, and then make a dressing from the sour cream, mustard, vinegar and sugar. You will not need salt. Serve either on one dish surrounded by halved eggs or on individual plates topped with half an egg.

SALAD TIEDE DE LOTTE (France)

SALAD WITH MONKFISH PIECES

Imperial/Metric
salad greens for 8
1½ lb (750 g) monkfish
2 shallots, chopped fine
4 fl. oz (120 ml) fresh orange juice
1 tablespoon honey
a little grated orange peel (optional)
butter
1 recipe vinaigrette (p.401)

American
salad greens for 8
1½ lb monkfish
2 shallots, chopped fine
½ cup fresh orange juice
1 tablespoon honey
a little grated orange peel (optional)
butter
1 recipe vinaigrette (p.401)

Cut the monkfish into bite-sized cubes and dry them well. Fry the shallot in the butter and add the monkfish. Cook until done, then add the honey and orange juice. Dress the salad with the vinaigrette and add a little grated orange peel if liked (you may not want it so orangey). Put in the hot monkfish pieces and the juice, toss and serve.

SALADE NIÇOISE (France)

There is a great deal of misunderstanding about *salade niçoise* even among the French – perhaps above all among the French. I live part of the time in Nice and find real Niçois get quite cross at times for what passes as their particular salad. Certain rules apply. For instance, *either* anchovies *or* tunny fish are included but never the two at the same time. And no Niçois ever puts cooked potatoes in his salad (which is a good thing since that would make it a rather heavy first course). Cooked green beans are now allowed and sometimes beetroot, though neither is traditional. Best with hot, crusty French bread and something light to follow.

Imperial/Metric
8 oz (250 g) anchovy fillets or 8 oz (250 g) tunny fish (fresh or tinned)
2 red peppers
3 medium tomatoes
4 eggs, hard-boiled
small onion, sliced
1 head of lettuce
handful of black olives
8 oz (250 g) cooked green beans or 1 raw celery heart
1 recipe vinaigrette (p.401)

American
8 oz anchovy fillets or 8 oz tuna fish (fresh or tinned)
2 red bell peppers
3 medium tomatoes
4 eggs, hardcooked
small onion, sliced
1 head of lettuce
handful of black olives
8 oz cooked green beans or 1 raw celery heart
1 recipe vinaigrette (p.401)

Arrange the salad prettily with the hard-boiled eggs, anchovies and black olives on top. Pour over the dressing and toss at the last moment.

VASTKUSTSALLAT (Sweden)

SWEDISH WEST COAST SALAD

This is a luxury summer salad which depends on the absolute freshness of all its ingredients.

Imperial/Metric	American
8 oz (250 g) lobster tail	8 oz lobster tail
12 oz (375 g) prepared medium prawns	12 oz prepared medium Gulf shrimps
large head of Iceberg or Boston lettuce	large head of Iceberg or Boston lettuce
8 oz (250 g) cooked weight green peas	8 oz cooked weight green peas
12 oz (375 g) asparagus tips	12 oz asparagus tips
8 oz (250 g) raw mushrooms, sliced	8 oz raw mushrooms, sliced
4-8 eggs, hard-boiled	4-8 eggs, hardcooked
1 recipe vinaigrette (p.401)	1 recipe vinaigrette (p.401)
lemon wedges (optional)	lemon wedges (optional)
fresh or freeze dried dill (optional)	fresh or freeze dried dill (optional)

Line a salad bowl with the lettuce leaves and then arrange the other ingredients like the spokes of a wheel. Sprinkle with dillweed if wished and then pour over the vinaigrette. Alternatively serve the vinaigrette separately.

HEARTS OF PALM SALAD WITH LOBSTER OR PRAWNS (Brazil)

To a plain Hearts of Palm Salad (p.329) with or without watercress, add 8 oz (250 g) sliced lobster meat or deveined prawns (shrimps).

AGUACATES RELLENOS CON ENSALDA RUSA (Cuba)

RUSSIAN SALAD WITH PRAWNS

Just as real Russian Salad has chicken breast in it, so Cuban Russian Salad has prawns as an integral part.

Imperial/Metric	American
4 avocados, halved	4 avocados, halved
1 recipe Russian Salad (p.332)	1 recipe Russian Salad (p.332)
8 oz (250 g) prawns	1 cup shrimps

Combine shelled, deveined prawns (shrimps) with Russian salad and stuff the unpeeled avocado halves. Serve at once.

SALADE TIEDE DE CREVETTES ET D'ASPERGES (France)

WARM SALAD OF PRAWNS AND ASPARAGUS IN RASPBERRY VINEGAR

Imperial/Metric	American
salad greens for 8	salad greens for 8
1-1½ lb (500-750 g) prepared, deveined prawns	1-1½ lb prepared, shrimps
1 lb (500 g) cooked asparagus tips (fresh, tinned or frozen)	1 lb cooked asparagus tips (fresh, canned or frozen)
2 shallots, finely chopped	2 shallots, finely chopped
vinaigrette made with raspberry vinegar (p.401)	vinaigrette made with raspberry vinegar (p.401)
2 tablespoons raspberry vinegar	2 tablespoons raspberry vinegar
butter	butter

Cook the shallots in the butter and then add the asparagus tips and warm through. Finally add the prawns. Once hot, deglaze with 1-2 tablespoons raspberry vinegar. Dress the salad and add the prawns and asparagus and their juice. Toss and serve.

PRAWN AND CAULIFLOWER SALAD (USA)

Too often this salad has coarse-tasting cauliflower. The secret is to use 2 small cauliflowers rather than one large one, to blanch them before cooking them in fresh boiling water. Finally the dressing should be home-made and not from a bottle.

Imperial/Metric	American
2 small cauliflowers	2 small cauliflowers
12 oz (375 g) medium, prepared prawns, deveined	1½ cups medium, prepared shrimps, deveined
8 fl. oz (240 ml) home-made mayonnaise (p.404)	8 fl. oz home-made mayonnaise (p.404)
8 fl. oz (240 ml) double or sour cream	8 fl. oz heavy or commercial sour cream
2 eggs, hard-boiled	2 eggs, hardcooked
1 tablespoon parsley, finely chopped	1 tablespoon parsley, finely chopped
1 tablespoon sharp mustard	1 tablespoon sharp mustard

Divide the cauliflower into sprigs, discarding any green or hard white bits, throw into boiling water and blanch for 2-3 minutes. Drain and refresh. Put into new boiling, salted water and cook until just done – the sprigs should have a bit of bite to them. Drain and rinse in cold water and lay on a cloth or paper towels to dry. Mix the mayonnaise, cream and mustard together and, once the cauliflower is cool, stir it into the mayonnaise mixture. Add them to the cauliflower mayonnaise. Pile into an attractive dish. Force the yolks of the 2 hard-boiled eggs through a sieve and sprinkle the cauliflower mayonnaise with them. Then strew on some finely chopped parsley and serve at once.

Cold cauliflower does not retain its pristine taste for long, so it should be served within 2-3 hours of becoming cold.

SHRIMP AND ASPARAGUS SALAD (CUBA)

This comes from pre-Castro Cuba. It seems too luxurious for present-day life in that country.

Imperial/Metric	*American*
1 lb (500 g) prawns, cooked	1 lb shrimps, cooked
2 lb (1 kilo) asparagus spears, cooked*	2 lb asparagus spears, cooked*
1 cucumber	1 cucumber
12 fl. oz (360 ml) home-made mayonnaise (p.404)	1½ cups home-made mayonnaise (p.404)
4 fl. oz (120 ml) sour cream	½ cup commercial sour cream
1 tablespoon fresh coriander or parsley, chopped	1 tablespoon fresh coriander or parsley, chopped
Tabasco	Tabasco
1 large Iceberg-type lettuce	1 large Iceberg-type lettuce

* Ideally the asparagus should be mostly tips, green and tender all the way through. For once tinned asparagus is quite good in this dish.

Peel, seed and slice the cucumber, sprinkle with salt and let drain at least half an hour. Cut the asparagus into lengths to match those of the prawns. Make sure you have removed the vein on the back of each prawn. Rinse and dry the cucumber and reduce to a purée in the liquidizer or food processor. Let drain a little. Mix this purée with the sour cream and mayonnaise, parsley or fresh coriander and add Tabasco to taste. Stir in the shrimps and asparagus and serve on lettuce-leaf cups sprinkled with a little more parsley.

SHRIMP, WATERCRESS AND EGG SALAD (USA)

Serve with wholemeal bread and butter.

Imperial/Metric	*American*
2 large bunches watercress	2 large bunches watercress
8 egg, hard-boiled	8 egg, hardcooked
1 lb (500 g) prawns	1 lb medium Gulf shrimp
1 recipe vinaigrette (p.401)	1 recipe vinaigrette (p.401)

Cook the prawns (shrimps) at home if possible so that you end up with approximately 1 lb (500 g) prepared weight. Devein. Let cool. Hardboil the eggs and once cooked run cold water on them for at least 5 minutes so no murky grey ring appears between the yolk and the white. Remove stems from watercress, wash well and dry. Place in salad bowl. Add the shrimps and toss well. Then add quartered eggs, being careful not to break them in the mixing. Serve at once.

TONNO E FAGIOLI (Italy)

TUNA AND BEAN SALAD

Seen in every *trattoria* round the world because it is so easy to make: all the ingredients except the onion and the parsley can come out of a tin without it being obvious.

Imperial/Metric	*American*
1½ lb (750 g) borlotti or white haricot beans, cooked	1½ lb borlotti or white haricot beans, cooked
approx. 14 oz (240 g) tuna	approx. 14 oz tuna
1 large mild onion, cut in rings	1 large mild onion, cut in rings
a handful of parsley, finely chopped	a handful of parsley, finely chopped
6 tablespoons Tuscan olive oil	6 tablespoons Tuscan olive oil
2 tablespoons lemon juice or wine vinegar	2 tablespoons lemon juice or wine vinegar

Rinse the beans well before stirring in the salad dressing. On top place small chunks of tuna at intervals. On top of this rings of onion and finally a scattering of parsley over everything.

Variation
Some people add hard-boiled eggs cut in half or strips of red pepper, but this is not the real thing.

INSALATA DI FRUTTA DI MARE (Italy: Liguria)

SEAFOOD SALAD

Within reason this seafood salad can have any firm fish or shellfish in it but usually some form of squid or octopus is included – it depends entirely on the state of your pocket and the season. Here is a very typical example which includes prawns, mussels on the shell (Italians prefer to have at least one of the ingredients on the shell) clams (*arselle* in Ligurian, or *vongole*), pink baby squid (*fragoline*) and a base of larger, sliced squid.

Imperial/Metric	*American*
48 mussels	48 mussels
8 oz (250 g) tiny pink squid	8 oz tiny pink squid
1 lb (500 g) white squid	1 lb white squid
8 oz (250 g) frozen clams	8 oz frozen clams
1 lb (500 g) medium prawns, prepared weight	1 lb medium shrimps, prepared weight
1 very ripe lemon	1 very ripe lemon
4 fl. oz (120 ml) olive oil	4 fl. oz olive oil
2 tablespoons parsley, chopped	2 tablespoons parsley, chopped
1 or 2 cloves garlic, chopped or crushed	1 or 2 cloves garlic, chopped or crushed
1 glass white wine	1 glass white wine
onion rings (optional)	onion rings (optional)

Fry the garlic in a little of the olive oil. Add the white wine and stew a little until the liquid is reduced to half.

Clean the squid by washing under running water, removing the tentacles and pulling out the transparent backbone. Discard the head as it has a hard beak which is unpleasant to find in your mouth. Cut the squid and its cleaned tentacles into tiny pieces. Cook in the white wine/garlic mixture and add a little more of the olive oil and half the parsley.

Rinse the frozen clams and add 5 minutes before the squid have finished cooking. These latter can take anything up to 45 minutes depending on age, and you may well have to keep adding water so they do not catch. Finally put the cleaned and bearded mussels on top and cook with a lid on for 3-4 minutes until they have opened. Do not overcook: remove immediately they are open and set aside. Devein the prawns and add to the other shellfish. Dress with the rest of the oil, the lemon juice and the rest of the parsley. Let cool naturally and then refrigerate, covered, for 2-3 hours before serving. Sprinkle with more parsley and, if you wish, onion rings before serving.

Variations

Some Italians add a little tomato to the dressing – some take the mussels off their shells – some serve crab in these salads, some mushrooms; others use a form of whitebait as a base for *insalata frutta di mara*. The latter, called *gianchetti*, have become prohibitively expensive and, like lobster, are almost a thing of the past.

Meat and Poultry

CHICKEN, CELERY, WALNUT AND SOUR CREAM SALAD (USA)

All the ingredients have a great affinity for each other, and the salad is very moreish. Cook the chicken specially rather than use left-overs.

Imperial/Metric	*American*
1 lb (500 g) cooked chicken breast	1 lb cooked chicken breast
1 head of crisp celery	1 head of crisp celery
4 oz (125 g) walnut pieces*	4 oz walnut pieces*
½ pint (300 ml) sour cream**	½ pint sour cream**
salt and pepper	salt and pepper
parsley, chopped (to garnish)	parsley, chopped (to garnish)

* If the walnuts are not the newest, put them to soak in boiling water and skin them. Alternatively wait to do this recipe until the new season's walnuts are in.
** If preferred, you can substitute mayonnaise (p.404) for half the sour cream.

Cube the chicken and celery into equal-sized bits. Mix with the walnut pieces and stir in the sour cream, salt and pepper. Sprinkle with a little parsley before serving.

This can be made at lunchtime, covered with clingfilm, for serving in the evening.

SALADE BOURGUIGONNE (France: Burgundy)

CHICKEN LIVER SALAD

This makes a very good salad to accompany the *Jambon Persille* (p.185) but can also be served on its own.

Imperial/Metric	American
2 lettuces with good hearts, not Iceberg or Webbs	2 lettuces with good hearts, not Iceberg or Webbs
4 chicken livers	4 chicken livers
3 oz (90 g) butter	3 oz butter
1 recipe *vinaigrette* (p.401)	1 recipe *vinaigrette* (p.401)
2 egg yolks	2 egg yolks
2 teaspoons strong Dijon mustard	2 teaspoons strong Dijon mustard
parsley, chopped (to garnish)	parsley, chopped (to garnish)

Rinse the chicken livers and pat dry. Cut into small dice and cook in the butter. Wash and dry the lettuce leaves, keeping them whole if possible unless they are very big. In a medium-sized bowl mix the egg yolks with the mustard and then bit by bit add the *vinaigrette*. Add the still-warm chicken livers. Pour this sauce *over* the salad, sprinkle with parsley and serve.

SALADE DE MAGRET DE CANARD FUME (France)

SMOKED DUCK BREAST SALAD

Smoked duck breast can be purchased in packets in most large supermarkets in France and in many speciality grocers elsewhere. Some breasts have rather more fat on them than others, and it is wise to choose a lean variety, to save yourself money as well as the work of cutting off surplus fat. The best smoked duck breast comes from the Landes and the Périgord. Two packets (i.e. 8-10 oz/250-310 g) will do for 8 people. You cut each sliver into small pieces, toss into a salad of lettuce, *radicchio*, corn salad etc and dress with a fairly sharp French dressing (p.401). Serve with crusty French bread.

INSALATA DI PROSCIUTTO, CRESCIONE E NOCI (Italy)

HAM, WATERCRESS AND WALNUT SALAD

Imperial/Metric	American
6 oz (375 g) fresh ham, diced*	6 oz fresh ham, diced*
2 bunches watercress	2 bunches watercress
6 oz (375 g) walnuts, chopped	¾ cup chopped walnut meats
1 recipe vinaigrette (p.401)	1 recipe vinaigrette (p.401)
1 mild onion, sliced (optional)	1 mild onion, sliced (optional)

* Some Italians use raw ham but it is very difficult to cut and separate the dice. In any event, use ham from the bone rather than from a packet.

Trim the stalks from the watercress, wash well, dry and taste. According to its piquancy, restrict or increase the pepper or mustard in your vinaigrette. Mix all ingredients together and decorate, if wished, with sliced onion which you have previously soaked for 30 minutes in salted cold water.

Salad Dips

BAGNA CAUDA (Italy)

A DIP AND RAW VEGETABLES

I don't think any Piedmontese would think of this as a first course but more of a snack for any time of the day from about 10 a.m. till well after midnight. It is presumably rather healthy, as the amount of the very rich dip you eat is small, and the raw vegetables must do you good, but it is not for delicate digestions. You will need a fondue casserole and its accompanying spirit lamp to keep the dip warm.

Serve with the Torinese *grissini* (Italian breadsticks) which are imported by most countries.

The most commonly used vegetable for this dish is the *cardo* (edible thistle – cardoon), but since *cardi* are not usually available out of Italy (nor indeed are Alba truffles – there are plenty of genuine Piedmontese versions of this dish that leave them out), you must make your choice from broccoli, cauliflower, celery, baby artichokes (raw), fennel, cabbage, cucumber, sweet peppers, spring onions, radishes, carrots etc.

Imperial/Metric	American
4 fl. oz (120 ml) olive oil	½ cup olive oil
4 fl. oz (120 ml) single cream	½ cup whipping cream
4 oz (125 g) butter	½ cup butter
3 or 4 cloves garlic, finely chopped	3 or 4 cloves garlic, finely chopped
10-12 anchovy fillets	10-12 anchovy fillets
1 Alba truffle 1 inch (2 cm) diameter, finely sliced	1 Alba truffle 1 inch (2 cm) diameter, finely sliced

Soften the garlic in the olive oil and butter. Rinse the anchovy fillets well and chop them finely, then add them to the saucepan.

Pour in the cream and heat up but do not let boil. If you are using a truffle, now is the time to put it in.

Transfer the mixture to your fondue pot and put it over spirit lamp or candle flame. It should not separate if you don't let it get too near to boiling; on the other hand, the dip must be kept very hot.

Arrange the vegetables on large plates around the pot – everyone takes his pick and dips.

MUJADDARAH (Lebanon & Syria)

ESAU'S LENTILS

This is said to be the 'mess of pottage' for which Esau sold his birthright. It is eaten with cucumber and other raw vegetables either as a starter or as an entire, very healthy lunch. It should be served lukewarm or cold accompanied by a variety of *crudités* and plenty of warm Arab bread and of course nothing heavy to follow.

Imperial/Metric	American
1 lb (500 g) green or brown lentils (not yellow)	approx. 2 cups green or brown lentils (not yellow)
2 oz (90 g) long-grain rice	¼ cup rice
2 large onions, chopped	2 large onions, chopped
6-8 fl. oz (180-240 ml) olive oil	¾-1 cup olive oil
juice of 1 lemon	juice of 1 lemon
salt	salt
parsley, chopped	parsley, chopped

Cook the lentils and rice separately, as they cook at different speeds. When cooked, mix them together. Fry the onion in some of the olive oil (though I use raw onion) and when cooked stir into the rice and lentil mixture. Add the rest of the oil, the parsley, salt and lemon juice. The end result should be slightly sloppy. Taste and adjust seasoning to your personal taste: I prefer less oil and more lemon juice.

13 Pancakes, Pasta and Rice

Pancakes

Pancakes, crêpes, *frittele, crespelle, palacsintak, Palatschinken* – call them what you will – are simply fried batter, usually with something inside or on top or both. France, Belgium and Central Europe are the pancake countries, (not forgetting the *blinis* of Russia). Although unusual fillings are suggested, you could make your own up quite easily. The secret is to end up with a crisp pancake and creamy filling or to have both creamy by baking with cream or a cream sauce on top.

BATTER FOR 16 PANCAKES

Imperial/Metric
8 oz (250 g) plain flour
2 eggs
½ pint (300 ml) milk
½ pint (300 ml) water*
1 tablespoon sunflower oil (to fry)**

American
1 cup plain flour
2 eggs
½ pint milk
½ pint water*
1 tablespoon sunflower oil (to fry)**

* My grandmother used soda water and never let her batter stand.

** She used lard to fry savoury pancakes and a mixture of butter and oil for the sweet sort. Now, with non-stick crêpe pan, the fat you use is unimportant as so little of it is used.

Beat ingredients together either by hand or machine. Put in the thinnest layer possible of the mixture, spread over the pan by tipping right and left; when bubbles appear on the top, turn the pancake over. Pile up for use later.

KÁPOSZTÁS PALACSINTAK (Hungary)

CABBAGE PANCAKES

Not a very exciting name. There are 2 ways to make them. The easier (and less interesting) is to mix finely cooked cabbage into a slightly thickened pancake batter and fry in the normal way, serving with a little sour cream. This means last-minute work for the hostess. My grandmother's version is rather more luxurious. Serve with plenty of sour cream on the table.

Imperial/Metric	*American*
1 recipe pancakes (p.352)	1 recipe pancakes (p.352)
1 lb (500 g) cabbage, cooked and chopped	1 lb cabbage, cooked and chopped
caraway seed (optional)	caraway seed (optional)
paprika	paprika
butter	butter
4 fl. oz (120 ml) sour cream	4 fl. oz sour cream
sour cream (for serving)	sour cream (for serving)

Your cabbage should have a little caraway seed in it, if liked, salt and plenty of paprika and butter. Cook your pancakes, fill them equally with the cabbage and put in a shallow dish. Put a good blob of sour cream on each and heat through in the oven – about 10 minutes at 400°F/200°C/Gas 6.

CRESPOLINI CON PORCINI (Italy)

PANCAKES WITH WILD MUSHROOMS

The word *crespolino* does not appear in the Italian dictionary but that was how I saw this dish described on an Italian menu.

Imperial/Metric
1 recipe pancakes (p.352)
8 oz (250 g) wild mushrooms
   (*boletus edulis*)
8 oz (250 g) cultivated
   mushrooms
1 tablespoon plain flour
8 fl. oz (240 ml) double cream
parsley, chopped, salt and
   pepper
butter (for cooking)

American
1 recipe pancakes (p.352)
8 oz wild mushrooms (*boletus
   edulis*)
8 oz cultivated mushrooms
1 tablespoon plain flour
1 cup heavy cream
parsley, chopped, salt and
   pepper
butter (for cooking)

Cook the mushrooms together in a little butter. When cooked, drain and set aside, keeping the liquid. To a little butter add the flour and make a roux. Add the mushroom liquid and the cream and continue to cook. Add the parsley, salt and pepper and put back the mushrooms. Make the pancakes meanwhile and keep hot in the oven by putting them in a dish and covering them with foil. Quickly fill them and lay them in a shallow fireproof dish. Dot the top generously with butter and run them under the grill until crisp and brown.

Variation
You can if you wish add a little Madeira or Marsala to the mixture but do not overpower the taste of the mushrooms.

KAPROS JUHTÜRÖS PALACSINTAK (Hungary)

LIPTAUER CHEESE PANCAKES

Liptauer cheese should really be made from sheeps' cheese but this is a counsel of perfection and any good cream cheese will do. Also, strictly speaking, these pancakes are made at the stove and served immediately. I have slightly adapted them, therefore, for the host or hostess who does not want to spend all their time frying at the last moment.

Imperial/Metric
1 recipe pancakes (p.352)
1 recipe Liptauer cheese (p.157)
4 fl. oz (120 ml) thick *sauce
   béchamel* (p.391)
1 teaspoon freeze-dried dill or 1
   tablespoon fresh dill
2 egg yolks
sour cream

American
1 recipe pancakes (p.352)
1 recipe Liptauer cheese (p.157)
½ cup thick *sauce béchamel*
   (p.391)
1 teaspoon freeze-dried dill or 1
   tablespoon fresh dill
2 egg yolks
sour cream

Make the pancakes. Make the *sauce béchamel* and mix with the cheese, herbs and egg yolks. Stuff the pancakes. Lay in a shallow dish and put on a lid or cover with aluminium foil. Cook them in a hot oven for 10 minutes at 425°F/220°C/Gas 7. Meanwhile heat the grill. Remove pancakes from oven, spread on a little sour cream or dots of butter and run them under the grill until the tops are brown.

CHICKEN LIVER IN CRISPY PANCAKES (UK)

Imperial/Metric	*American*
1 recipe pancakes (p.352)	1 recipe pancakes (p.352)
2 medium onions, finely chopped	2 medium onions, finely chopped
1 lb (500 g) chicken livers	1 lb chicken livers
approx. 6 oz (190 g) fresh breadcrumbs	approx. 6 oz fresh breadcrumbs
4 oz (125 g) melted butter	4 oz melted butter
2 tablespoons brandy	2 tablespoons brandy
2 egg yolks, beaten	2 egg yolks, beaten

Cook the onions in a little butter, add the chopped chicken liver and cook until just stiffened. It is essential not to cook the chicken liver too much at the beginning or it will end up dry and tasteless. Flame with the brandy. Let cool. The dish can be made in advance to this stage, and all that is needed is to assemble everything.

Cook the pancakes, then divide the cooled chicken liver and onion mixture between them and roll them up cigar fashion. Dip in beaten egg and then roll in breadcrumbs. Make sure that you cover every bit of pancake with egg yolk so that nothing can escape. Lay them in a large shallow, well-buttered dish. Sprinkle a few more breadcrumbs over the whole and dot with butter. Bake in a hot oven at 400°F/200°C/Gas 6 for 10 minutes or until the pancakes are nicely brown and crisp.

DELICES DE BRUXELLES (Belgium: Brussels)

HAM AND MUSHROOM FILLED PANCAKES

Imperial/Metric	American
1 recipe pancakes (p.352)	1 recipe pancakes (p.352)
1 lb (500 g) mushrooms	1 lb mushrooms
16 very thin slices of ham	16 very thin slices of ham
2 shallots, chopped	2 shallots, chopped
8 fl. oz (240 ml) double cream	1 cup heavy cream
8 fl. oz (240 ml) single cream	1 cup light cream
1 tablespoon Gruyère cheese, grated	1 tablespoon Gruyère cheese, grated
1 tablespoon parsley, chopped	1 tablespoon parsley, chopped
salt and pepper	salt and pepper

Cook the mushrooms with the shallots until they have got rid of all their juice. Drain and reduce the liquid to a quarter. Put aside. Make the pancakes. Lay a slice of ham on each pancake and put the mushrooms on top. Roll up and put in a shallow dish, seam side down. Mix the mushroom juice and salt and pepper with the 2 creams and pour over the pancakes. Sprinkle on the Gruyère cheese and bake for 25-30 minutes at 400°F/200°C/Gas 6. Watch carefully that it does not burn; if necessary, turn down the heat towards the end.

CREPES AU JAMBON ET AU ROQUEFORT (France)

HAM AND ROQUEFORT CHEESE CREPES

This recipe is identical with *Delices de Bruxelles* (above) except that there are no mushrooms or parsley rolled up in the pancakes, just ham and a dessertspoonful of Roquefort cheese. Roll them up and put in a shallow dish, pour over the cream mixture and bake at 400°F/200°C/Gas 6.

CREPES AUX CREVETTES (France)

PRAWN PANCAKES

Imperial/Metric	*American*
1 recipe pancakes (p.352)	1 recipe pancakes (p.352)
1 recipe *sauce béchamel* (p.391)	1 recipe *sauce béchamel* (p.391)
1 lb (500 g) medium prawns, shelled	1 lb medium shrimps, shelled
8 fl. oz (240 ml) single cream	1 cup light cream
8 fl. oz (240 ml) double cream	1 cup heavy cream
2 shallots, chopped	2 shallots, chopped
1 tablespoon parsley	1 tablespoon parsley
1 teaspoon Tabasco	1 teaspoon Tabasco

Make a (thickish) *sauce béchamel* and mix in the shelled, deveined prawns (shrimps); add the shallots, parsley and Tabasco. Stuff pancakes with this and lay them in a shallow dish, seam side down. Pour over the mixture of the 2 creams and bake at 400°F/200°C/Gas 6 for 25 minutes, until the top is nicely browned.

GALETTES VALAISANNES (Switzerland)

BAKED GALETTES

Imperial/Metric	*American*
10 oz (315 g) flour	1¼ cups flour
7 oz (200 g) butter	¾ cup butter
4 egg yolks	4 egg yolks
5 oz (155 g) Gruyère cheese, grated*	¾ cup Gruyère cheese, grated*
4 tablespoons double cream	4 tablespoons heavy cream
7 oz (220 g) cooked ham	1 cup cooked ham
parsley	parsley
salt and pepper	salt and pepper
butter for cooking	butter for cooking
nutmeg	nutmeg

* There are Swiss who swear by *chopping* the Gruyère rather than grating it.

Warm your mixing bowl in very hot water and dry well. Cut the butter into smallish dice and beat to a cream with a wooden spoon. Add the flour bit by bit, then the egg yolks, grated cheese and cream. Work into a firm paste. Chop the ham finely and add to the paste. Let rest while you heat the oven to approximately 250°F/120°C/Gas ½. Butter 2 or even 3 Swiss roll (jelly roll) tins or baking sheets and divide the paste into little heaps of about a good dessertspoon each. Flatten a little with the back of your spoon or a knife. Cook for 15-20 minutes until nicely browned.

BLINIS (USSR)

Strictly speaking, you should have a couple of small crêpe pans measuring approximately 4 inches (10 cm) across, but this is a counsel of perfection. If you make your pancakes with buckwheat flour, a single ordinary-sized crêpe will be sufficient – otherwise allow ¾ inch (3-4 cm) crêpes. Buckwheat flour is available in healthfood stores and some supermarkets. Ordinary strong wheat flour can be substituted. Serve with caviar (any sort) and *cold* sour cream, smoked fish and sour cream, smoked salmon and sour cream or sometimes just melted butter. I have a Russian friend whose speciality is *blinis* with raw onions and sour cream (a recipe, she says, born of extreme poverty when first in the United States), and very delicious they are. Russians, like many other people, soak their onions for several hours in salted water before eating them raw. It is supposed to render them more digestible.

Imperial/Metric	*American*
12 oz (375 g) buckwheat flour	1½ cups buckwheat flour
3 eggs, separated	3 eggs, separated
1 pint (600 ml) full cream milk	2½ cups full cream milk
1 teaspoon salt	1 teaspoon salt
1 oz (30 g) baker's yeast*	1 oz baker's yeast*
1 teaspoon sugar	1 teaspoon sugar

* Dried yeast can be used but you will get a slightly different result.

Heat the milk to just above tepid (about 100°F/40°C. Mix the yeast with the sugar in a cup and gradually add some of the milk. Let it 'prove' for a few moments – bubbles should appear on the surface. Put the flour in a bowl and make a batter with the rest of the milk and 3 egg yolks. Add the yeast/milk mixture and put in a warm, draught-free place to rise. Cover with clingfilm. The rising should take around half an hour but in a cold atmosphere could take considerably longer.

'Knock down' the batter and add the egg whites which you have beaten into stiff, but not too dry, peaks. The batter should have the consistency of thick cream, certainly thicker than normal pancake batter. For the 4 inch (10 cm) pans you will need a scant 2 tablespoons of batter for each *blini*. Cook for approximately 90 seconds and then turn over. Keep warm in a low oven.

Pasta

Basically there are three sorts of pasta; the fresh home-made sort known in Italy as *pasta fatta in casa* or *pasta casalinga*, dried pasta with eggs added and finally pasta made from durum wheat and water. The hard durum wheat provides the gluten to prevent the pasta falling apart in boiling water; the other sorts, made of softer wheat, rely on the egg to act as the holding-together agent.

Home-made pasta is easily made by anyone who has an aptitude for pastry making. It can also be made in a special pasta-making machine. These vary: in some you put in your mixed dough, in others you throw in the ingredients and pasta comes out according to what you have dialled – everything from *lasagne* or *pappardelle* to *vermicelli*. Finally you can make pasta with the aid of a mixer which has a dough-kneading hook or in a food processor. Both give a good elastic dough, which is what you need. When rolling out hand-made or mixer/food processor-made dough, you must have plenty of flour on the surface.

To Cut Pasta

When cutting pasta other than for *ravioli, lasagne* or *cannelloni* you should roll out the dough as thinly as possible and trim to a neat rectangle. You can use the other pieces in the next rolling out. Roll up this sheet of dough Swiss roll fashion (jelly roll fashion) but not too tightly. Slice off pieces of the thickness you require – you will not get much thinner than *tagliatelle* without a great deal of experience though the Italians can produce fresh pasta as thin as vermicelli by hand. Your knife should be very sharp indeed. Sprinkle with flour and heap these 'nests' two or three on top of each other to dry. Alternatively lay them out individually to dry for at least 45 minutes to 1 hour. If you cook the pasta at a too soft stage it takes in too much water and becomes 'wodgy'. One of those things which is simpler to do and demonstrate than to describe.

Shop-bought dried pasta, *pasta asciutta*, is a heavier product, ideal for filling hungry tummies (of teenage children, for instance), but has little place at a dinner party, simply because it is so filling. The recipes given in this section are for home-made pasta or shop-bought egg pasta.

Pasta requires a great deal of water to cook so that it does not stick together. Too little water gives you a gluey, unattractive mass. Count around 2 pints per 4 oz (1 litre per 125 g). Fresh pasta cooks very quickly indeed, so vigilant watching is required. Many people put a tablespoon of oil or butter in the water, which they feel helps keep the pasta separate.

CANNELLONI

The squares of dough (p.361) for *cannelloni* should measure about 4 inches (10 cm) square.

Purchased *cannelloni* come in tube shapes and need to be almost cooked before being used. They are really quite floppy and difficult to use, and the home-made sort not only taste better but are far easier to handle.

Cook them in boiling water until they are just *al dente* – then rinse them in cold water and lay on a damp cloth. Then put a line of filling down the centre, fold them over and put them in a well-buttered dish, seam side down. Pour over a sauce or cream.

Cannelloni can be filled with virtually anything that goes with pasta as long as it is not too sloppy: chicken liver, game, fish (as for the *ravioli* recipes), minced meat, ham, vegetables – the list is endless. Tomato sauce is not obligatory, as you will see from the following recipes.

RAVIOLI

Ravioli and *raviolini* can be bought ready-made. Some are really quite nice, particularly those made with spinach and cheese or with ham. However, there is much ravioli on the market not worth making a sauce for.

Ravioli are remarkably easy (if a little time consuming) to make at home. The dough remains the same but, strictly speaking, you need a *raviolatore* (ravioli dish) to get them all the same size. This is a metal dish with equally spaced depressions in it. Put a layer of dough over it, then drop a teaspoonful of your filling into each depression, paint a little egg white on the spaces in between, put on another layer of dough and roll your pin over the whole. Hey presto! you have 16 or 20 ravioli. Alternatively, if you have a good eye and do not mind a slightly raggedy result, you can make ravioli using a pastry cutter or the rim of a small glass. Unless you have a square cutter, the normal rectangular ravioli are not possible.

Making your own pasta allows you to have unusual fillings such as vegetables or fish which, because of their tendency quickly to become stale – if not actually bad, are not to be found in the shops. Some Italian housewives paint the whole of their dough on the inside with egg white (or yolk) but I think this tends to make a slightly heavy end-product.

1½ lb (750 g) of the pasta dough (below) should produce enough ravioli for 8 as a first course (except for Italian appetites). Roll the dough as thin as possible and keep your filling fairly dry also. The cooking and the sauce with the ravioli will take care of any dryness at the beginning.

BASIC PASTA DOUGH

Imperial/Metric	*American*
1½ lb (750 g) plain flour	6 cups flour
4 or 5 eggs	4 or 5 eggs
1 dessertspoon salt	1 dessertspoon salt

Mix the flour and salt with 4 of the eggs. If a fifth is needed, add it. The dough should be firm, rather like pastry. You may have to add a little more flour after the fifth egg to get the right consistency. The whole thing depends on the quality of flour (which varies from country to country) and what constitutes a medium egg. You may even need a small amount of water.

Knead on a board so that everything is very smooth. Cover with a damp cloth or tea-towel and leave for an hour.

You will probably need to cut the dough into thirds or even quarters. Roll out a piece at a time on a floured board or work surface as thinly as possible. (If you have a pasta-making machine, use it according to instructions with these amounts. You will almost certainly need to pass the dough between the rollers 2 or 3 times.) You cannot roll it too thin: Italians say you should be able to see the headlines of a newspaper through it. Flour the top very slightly and then roll it up loosely, like a Swiss roll (jelly roll). Slice off rounds at the thickness you want and pile these 'nests' up gently on top of each other. They should dry for about an hour at least before using them – 3-4 hours is even better, which is ideal for the person giving a dinner party who can make the pasta in the early afternoon. Continue in this fashion until all the dough is used up. *Lasagne* and *cannelloni* should be laid out to dry on a floured worksurface for a few hours before use.

The cooking time of this pasta depends on the thickness but 3-4 minutes for the thin sort and 5-6 minutes for the thick sort, *pappardelle*, is a good average. Test as you go along, remembering that pasta will continue to cook (and go soggy) if left in hot water. Shop-bought pasta takes a little longer, and instructions are usually given on the packet. For the Italian taste this will be *al dente*, which is sometimes too raw for non-Italians. Again you must be the arbiter.

These instructions may seem fussy and complicated but pasta-making is a fairly simple process. Home-made raw pasta freezes excellently.

CANNELLONI ALL 'ALPINA (Italy)

CANNELLONI STUFFED WITH CHEESE AND HAM

Imperial/Metric	American
1 recipe basic pasta (p.361) cut into *cannelloni*	1 recipe basic pasta (p.361) cut into *cannelloni*
6 oz (190 g) Fontina* cheese, chopped	6 oz Fontina* cheese, chopped
6 oz (190 g) Gruyère cheese, grated	6 oz Gruyère cheese, grated
12 oz (375 g) good-quality ham, chopped	12 oz good-quality ham, chopped
1 pinch of nutmeg	1 pinch of nutmeg
1 tablespoon parsley	1 tablespoon parsley
8 fl. oz (240 ml) double cream	1 cup heavy cream
8 fl. oz (240 ml) single cream	1 cup light cream
salt and pepper	salt and pepper

* Fontina is a Piedmontese cheese used for fondue because of its perfect melting qualities. Use any similar *mild* creamy cheese –

Philadelphia or mild Gouda for instance. Cook the *cannelloni* in the normal way. Mix the cheeses, parsley and ham together and fill the *cannelloni* – allow only 2 per person, since the dish is rather rich. Sprinkle a pinch of nutmeg over before rolling up. Arrange in a shallow dish. Mix the 2 creams together and add salt and pepper. Pour over the *cannelloni* and bake in a hot oven (400°F/200°C/Gas 6) for 20 minutes.

CANNELLONI MARIA-PIA (Italy)

CANNELLONI FILLED WITH HAM, PISTACHIO NUTS AND HERBS

Imperial/Metric	*American*
1 recipe basic pasta (p.361), cut for *cannelloni*	1 recipe basic pasta (p.361), cut for *cannelloni*
8 oz (250 g) ham, chopped	8 oz ham, chopped
4 oz (125 g) pistachio nuts, shelled weight, chopped	4 oz pistachio nuts, shelled weight, chopped
6 fl. oz (180 ml) *sauce béchamel*	¾ cup *sauce béchamel*
1 tablespoon parsley, chopped	1 tablespoon parsley, chopped
pinch of thyme	pinch of thyme
pinch of nutmeg	pinch of nutmeg
8 fl. oz (240 ml) single cream	1 cup light cream
8 fl. oz (240 ml) double cream	1 cup heavy cream
Parmesan cheese, grated	Parmesan cheese, grated

Make the *sauce béchamel*, let it get cold, then mix the ham, pistachio nuts, parsley, nutmeg and thyme. Fill the *cannelloni* and put in a well-buttered shallow dish. Pour over the mixture of the 2 creams, sprinkle with Parmesan and bake at 400°F/200°C/Gas 6 for approximately 20 minutes until nicely browned.

CANNELLONI CON VERDURA (Italy)

CANNELLONI WITH SPINACH

Imperial/Metric	*American*
1 recipe basic pasta (p.361) cut as *cannelloni*	1 recipe basic pasta (p.361) cut as *cannelloni*
4 oz (125 g) spinach, cooked and chopped	4 oz spinach, cooked and chopped
4 oz (125 g) onion, chopped	4 oz onion, chopped
2 oz (60 g) pine nuts	2 oz *pignoli*
2 oz (60 g) sultanas	2 oz seedless raisins
8 fl. oz (240 ml) *sauce béchamel* (p.391)	1 cup *sauce béchamel* (p.391)
1 recipe fresh tomato sauce* (p.389)	1 recipe fresh tomato sauce* (p.389)
Parmesan cheese, grated	Parmesan cheese, grated

* Personally I prefer cream to tomato sauce. Tomato sauce goes better, I find, with the meat- or fish-filled *cannelloni*, but this is a matter of personal taste.

Make the *sauce béchamel* and while it is cooling make the *cannelloni*. Then mix the spinach, onion, pine nuts and sultanas into the *cold* sauce and fill the *cannelloni*. Put them seam side down in a well-buttered shallow dish and pour over the tomato sauce. Bake for 20 minutes at 400°F/200°C/Gas 6.

LASAGNE BOLOGNESE (Italy)

BAKED PASTA WITH MEAT SAUCE

Imperial/Metric	*American*
1 recipe basic pasta (p.361), cut into *lasagne*	1 recipe basic pasta (p.361), cut into *lasagne*
1 pint (500 ml) *ragù bolognese* (p.408)	1 pint *ragù bolognese* (p.408)
1 pint (500 ml) *sauce béchamel* (p.391)	2½ cups *sauce béchamel* (p.391)
4 oz (125 g) Parmesan cheese, grated	4 oz Parmesan cheese, grated
butter	butter

Cook the *lasagne* in plenty of salted water and drain. Lay each piece separately on a cloth (otherwise they will stick together). Butter an ovenproof dish and put in a layer of *lasagne*. Cover with a layer of *ragù*, then a layer of *lasagne*, then a layer of *béchamel*, then a layer of *lasagne, ragù, lasagne, béchamel,* until everything is used up. End with *béchamel* on top. Sprinkle the Parmesan thickly and dot with butter. Cook for 15 minutes in a hot oven (475°/250°C/Gas 9). This dish can be prepared ahead of time but you will need a slightly lower oven temperature and a slightly longer time. It should come out brown and bubbling.

RAVIOLI ALLA FONDUTA (Italy)

RAVIOLI IN A CHEESE FONDUE SAUCE

Very delicious and very rich. In the season some Piemontese scrape Alba truffle over this dish.

Imperial/Metric	*American*
2 lb (1 kilo) spinach-filled ravioli (p.360)	2 lb spinach-filled ravioli (p.360)
1 lb (500 g) Fontina cheese	1 lb (500 g) Fontina cheese
8 fl. oz (240 ml) milk	1 cup milk
4 oz (60 g) butter	½ cup butter
1 egg yolk	1 egg yolk
cayenne pepper and salt	cayenne pepper and salt

An hour before cooking the *ravioli* (which should be freshly made and of the finest quality) cut the crust off the Fontina cheese and cut into dice. Put these dice to steep in the milk. Cook the *ravioli* to the *al dente* stage and meanwhile melt the Fontina and milk together in a non-stick saucepan, stirring all the time. Add the butter and egg yolk and remove from heat, beating all the time. Put the drained *ravioli* into a dish and stir in the *fonduta* (cheese mixture). Serve as hot as possible with freshly ground black pepper as a garnish.

RAVIOLI ALLA GIUSEPPINA (Italy)

RAVIOLI FILLED WITH BACON AND MOZZARELLA WITH A FRESH TOMATO SAUCE

Who Giuseppina was I have no idea, but her recipe is excellent.

Imperial/Metric	American
1 recipe basic pasta (p.361), cut into *ravioli*	1 recipe basic pasta (p.361), cut into *ravioli*
8 oz (250 g) unsmoked streaky bacon, diced	8 oz unsmoked streaky bacon, diced
4 oz (125 g) unsmoked lean bacon, diced	4 oz unsmoked lean bacon, diced
8 oz (250 g) mozzarella cheese, chopped	8 oz mozzarella cheese, chopped
a little chopped sage (optional)	a little chopped sage (optional)
1 recipe fresh tomato sauce (p.389)	1 recipe fresh tomato sauce (p.389)
parsley, chopped (to garnish)	parsley, chopped (to garnish)
Parmesan cheese, grated	Parmesan cheese, grated

Fry the bacon a little. Let cool. Mix with the mozzarella and add the sage. Make, stuff and cook the *ravioli* in the usual way. Heat the sauce and pour over the *ravioli*. Sprinkle with parsley and serve with a little Parmesan cheese.

FISH RAVIOLI WITH PRAWN SAUCE (Italy)

Imperial/Metric	American
1½ lb (750 g) pasta dough, cut into *ravioli* (p.360)	1½ lb pasta dough, cut into *ravioli* (p.360)
1 egg, separated	1 egg, separated
1 small onion, chopped	1 small onion, chopped
12 oz (375 g) white fish (cod, for example)	12 oz white fish (cod, for example)
1 tablespoon parsley	1 tablespoon parsley
1 tablespoon lemon juice	1 tablespoon lemon juice
1 teaspoon lemon rind, grated	1 teaspoon lemon rind, gr ·ted
salt	salt

Make the *ravioli*. Chop onion and fish together, add parsley and lemon juice and rind, the egg yolk and a little salt. Put tiny spoonfuls of this mixture in each *ravioli* depression, paint the outside of the squares with beaten egg white and put on the top. Alternatively do the same thing with little rounds you have made with the rim of a glass; brush egg white round the edge and fold over into a half-moon shape. Once the *ravioli* are made, let dry for half an hour at least before cooking.

Cook *ravioli* in plenty of boiling salted water. Once the water comes up to the boil again, do not let it boil violently but turn down the heat *slightly*. The cooked *ravioli* float upwards and should be scooped off as they are done. Always taste before counting them as cooked, and give them a few moments more if necessary – nothing is more disgusting than uncooked flour.

SAUCE

Imperial/Metric
8 oz (250 g) medium prawns, shelled and deveined
½ recipe *sauce aurore* (p.391)
8 fl. oz (240 ml) double cream

American
8 oz medium shrimps, shelled and deveined
½ recipe *sauce aurore* (p.391)
1 cup heavy cream

To the hot *sauce aurore* add the prawns cut into smallish pieces, and then at the end the cream. Bring up to heat and serve over *ravioli*.

SALMON RAVIOLI WITH DILL SAUCE (Italy)

We originally had this recipe as *penne* with salmon, cream and dill. The owner of the restaurant on the Riviera dei Fiori had spent 12 years in Scandinavia. When I asked whether such a combination would make a good *ravioli*, I was told it would be stupendous but impossible for a restaurant unless it was part of a set menu. On a set menu you could not offer non-travelled Italians dill, apparently. And without a set menu you would have 'keeping' problems.

It is odd how Italians adapt all new food to pasta. When I saw avocados in a supermarket in Italy for the first time, many years ago, there was a leaflet, by the Israeli firm Carmel with a dozen recipes using avocados, and half were for pasta. Ostensibly the Italians are very stick-in-the-mud about food, and the one way to get them to eat something new is to present it with or on pasta. Thereafter their prejudices play second fiddle to their taste buds.

Imperial/Metric
1½ lb (750 g) pasta dough, cut into *ravioli* (p.360)
12 oz (375 g) cooked salmon*
4 tablespoons double cream
2 tablespoons fresh breadcrumbs
1 dessertspoon tomato concentrate (optional)**

American
1½ lb pasta dough, cut into *ravioli* (p.360)
12 oz cooked salmon*
4 tablespoons heavy cream
2 tablespoons fresh breadcrumbs
1 dessertspoon tomato concentrate (optional)**

* Any other dense fish could be used instead.
** I leave out the tomato from the mixture but add an egg yolk instead. I also add a little nutmeg.

Mash up the salmon, cream, breadcrumbs and tomato concentrate. The mixture should be slightly sloppy but not wet. Make the ravioli as in the basic recipe and put spoonfuls of the mixture in the depressions. Brush with beaten white of egg and put on the top layer of dough. Continue until all the dough and filling are used up. Do not use too much filling or your *ravioli* will burst. Cook until done – drain and stir in a little butter to keep the *ravioli* separate.

SAUCE

Imperial/Metric	*American*
8 fl. oz (225 ml) single cream	1 cup light cream
8 fl. oz (225 ml) double cream	1 cup heavy cream
salt and pepper	salt and pepper
dill, chopped	dill, chopped

Mix the creams and add salt, pepper and chopped dill to your taste. Pour over the *ravioli* and serve.

RAVIOLINI TRICOLORE (Italy)

RAVIOLINI IN A CREAM, BASIL AND TOMATO SAUCE

Raviolini are always purchased. They are usually filled with spinach and ricotta cheese. In Italy you can get them in a plain cream colour or what is known as *paglio*, which is a mixture of green, white, and red – like the Italian flag. The sauce is made of the same colours too. It looks rather nasty as you put it onto the hot *raviolini*, but once melted it turns a delicious shrimp pink with dark green flecks of basil.

For approximately 1½ lb (750 g) *raviolini* you will need a sauce as follows:

Imperial/Metric	*American*
8 fl. oz (240 ml) double cream*	1 cup heavy cream
8 fl. oz (240 ml) single cream*	1 cup light cream
1 bunch/handful large-leafed basil	1 bunch/handful large-leafed basil
1 tablespoon (or more) tomato concentrate	1 tablespoon (or more) tomato concentrate
salt	salt

* If you use all double cream, you will find there is a chance of its 'turning' and separating.

Wash basil well and remove leaves. In a liquidizer or food processor mix the ingredients together until a smooth emulsion is obtained. Pour over just-cooked *raviolini* and serve immediately. The heat of the *raviolini* will heat the sauce.

RAVIOLINI WITH HERB AND CREAM SAUCE

Proceed as for the previous recipe but choose your own herb, chopped. The only proviso is that the herb must be absolutely spanking fresh, not freeze-dried or packeted. Parsley and marjoram are a good combination, and summer savory is good.

Mix equal amounts of single and double (light and heavy) cream and the chopped herb.

TAGLIATELLE WITH CHICKEN, BRANDY AND CREAM (Italy)

Imperial/Metric	*American*
1 recipe pasta dough, cut into *tagliatelle* (p.360)	1 recipe pasta dough, cut into *tagliatelle* (p.360)
1 small onion, chopped	1 small onion, chopped
1 whole breast of chicken	1 whole breast of chicken
4 fl. oz (120 ml) brandy	½ cup brandy
10 fl. oz (300 ml) double cream	1¼ cups heavy cream
a little dried thyme	a little dried thyme
salt and pepper	salt and pepper
Parmesan cheese, grated (optional)	Parmesan cheese, grated (optional)

Cook the onion in a little butter. Cut the chicken breast into small dice (alternatively this can be done cooked). Sauté with the onions in butter, together with a little thyme, salt and pepper until cooked. Flame with the brandy. Pour in the cream and bring up to heat.

Once the pasta has been cooked, drain well and stir in this sauce. Serve with or without grated Parmesan cheese – I think it is better without.

PASTA WITH ANCHOVIES AND CREAM (Italy)

Imperial/Metric	*American*
1 recipe basic pasta (p.360)	1 recipe basic pasta (p.360)
1 tin anchovy fillets	1 can anchovy fillets
15 fl. oz (450 ml) double cream	2 cups heavy cream
plenty of freshly ground	plenty of freshly ground
pepper	pepper
milk	milk

Soak the anchovies in milk to lessen their saltiness. Chop up small. Pour warmed (not hot) cream over the hot cooked pasta and add the anchovies. Serve with freshly ground pepper but no cheese.

PASTA WITH ANCHOVIES, EGG AND MASCARPONE (Italy)

You can add Parmesan cheese if you want, but it is not in the usual recipe.

Imperial/Metric	*American*
1 recipe basic pasta (p.360)	1 recipe basic pasta (p.360)
1 4 oz (125 g) tin anchovy fillets*	1 4 oz can anchovy fillets
3 egg yolks	3 egg yolks
8 oz (250 g) mascarpone (or cream cheese)	8 oz mascarpone (or cream cheese)

* Anchovies in brine are best for this dish but they are not always obtainable. Soak if necessary to get rid of the saltiness.

Beat the egg yolks well and add to the mascarpone (or cream cheese). Add the anchovies. You should get something that looks like Liptauer cheese.

Have the pasta very hot. Stir in this mixture and serve at once.

PASTA WITH WALNUTS AND CREAM (Italy)

This is a version of the Genovese walnut sauce but less aggressive. Italian amounts are given – the Italians tend to like less abundant sauce with their pasta than do other nationalities. There is no reason why you should not increase the quantities if you wish. Parmesan or Pecorino cheese can be served with this.

Imperial/Metric	American
1 recipe basic pasta (p.360)	1 recipe basic pasta (p.360)
6 oz (190 g) walnuts, shelled	1½ cups 'English' walnuts
8 fl. oz (240 ml) double cream	1 cup heavy cream
1 tablespoon wine vinegar	1 tablespoon wine vinegar
salt and pepper	salt and pepper

If the walnuts are old, peel them by pouring boiling water over them first. New season's walnuts do not need this treatment. Pulverize in a liquidizer, food processor or mortar and gradually add the cream, salt, vinegar and pepper. Stir into hot pasta.

PASTA ALL'AMATRICIANA (Italy)

PASTA WITH TOMATOES AND BACON

This dish, being a southern one, from Amatrice in the Abruzzi, is normally made with factory-made spaghetti but since it has one of the most delicious sauces it is a pity to confine it to *pasta asciutta*. Pecorino cheese is served with this dish but Parmesan tastes good also, although it is not authentic.

Imperial/Metric	American
1 recipe basic pasta (p.360)	1 recipe basic pasta (p.360)
8 oz (250 g) lean green bacon, diced small	8 oz unsmoked lean bacon, diced small
1 medium onion, finely chopped	1 medium onion, finely chopped
12 oz (375 g) firm tomatoes, peeled and chopped	12 oz firm tomatoes, peeled and chopped
1 small red pepper (optional)	1 small red pepper (optional)
olive oil	olive oil

Fry the bacon in a little olive oil. Do not make it too crisp. Put aside. In the same oil fry the onion but do not let it really brown. Add tomatoes and cook until a slightly mushy sauce is obtained – about 10 minutes. Just before serving add the bacon (and the washed, seeded and sliced hot pepper if wished).

Normally you dress half the pasta first and then put the rest of the sauce on top of the other half.

PASTA WITH CHICKEN LIVER AND RED WINE SAUCE (Italy)

Imperial/Metric
1 recipe basic pasta (p.360)
8 oz (250 g) chicken livers
8 fl. oz (240 ml) red wine
1 onion, chopped
1 tablespoon tomato
   concentrate
4 oz (125 g) mushrooms,
   chopped
2 fl. oz (60 ml) brandy
salt, pepper, thyme, sage
butter

American
1 recipe basic pasta (p.360)
8 oz chicken livers
1 cup red wine
1 onion, chopped
1 tablespoon tomato
   concentrate
4 oz mushrooms, chopped
¼ cup brandy
salt, pepper, thyme, sage
butter

Clean and chop the chicken livers. Fry the onion in a little butter and then add the chicken livers. Do not overcook. Flame them with the brandy and let it go out. Then add the mushrooms and herbs. Let cook a little and finally add the red wine and simmer for 5-6 minutes. Stir into the cooked pasta and serve with or without cheese.

PASTA WITH CRAB SAUCE (Italy)

No Parmesan cheese with this dish!

Imperial/Metric
1 recipe basic pasta (p.360)
1 lb (500 g) fresh or frozen crab
   claws*
2 fl. oz (60 ml) olive oil
2 medium onions, chopped
2 or 3 sticks celery, chopped
garlic, chopped
8 oz (250 g) tomatoes, chopped
2 tablespoons tomato
   concentrate
4 fl. oz (120 ml) dry sherry
juice of a lemon
parsley

American
1 recipe basic pasta (p.360)
1 lb fresh or frozen crab claws*
¼ cup olive oil
2 medium onions, chopped
2 or 3 sticks celery, chopped
garlic, chopped
8 oz tomatoes, chopped
2 tablespoons tomato
   concentrate
½ cup dry sherry wine
juice of a lemon
parsley

* It does not matter if your crab gives more than 1 lb (500 g) of meat but there must not be less.

Fry the onions, celery and garlic if liked until golden. Add the tomatoes and tomato concentrate together with the sherry (wine). Let simmer approximately 15 minutes. Add the crab and simmer for a few minutes. Pour in the lemon juice, add parsley and serve.

PASTA CON RAGÙ DI SELVAGGINA (Italy)

PASTA WITH GAME SAUCE

Imperial/Metric	*American*
1½ lb (750 g) pasta (p.360)	1½ lb pasta (p.360)
1 recipe *sauce espagnole* (p.394)	1 recipe *sauce espagnole* (p.394)
approx. 8 oz (250 g) or more of cooked game, cubed small*	approx. 8 oz or more of cooked game, cubed small*
butter	butter
garlic (optional)	garlic (optional)
small glass of port	small glass of port
Parmesan cheese, grated	Parmesan cheese, grated

* Use partridge, pheasant, grouse (unknown in Italy!) or pigeon.

Heat the game in a little butter (you may add a little garlic if you wish). Make the *sauce espagnole* and pour on. Let simmer for 15 minutes and add the port. Simmer another 5 minutes and pour over the cooked pasta. Sprinkle with Parmesan cheese.

PASTA WITH HAM, PEAS AND CREAM (Italy)

Serve with Parmesan cheese if wished.

Imperial/Metric	*American*
1 recipe pasta (p.360)	1 recipe pasta (p.360)
8 oz (250 g) cooked weight peas*	8 oz cooked weight peas*
6 oz (190 g) cooked ham, diced	6 oz cooked ham, diced
8 fl. oz (240 ml) double cream	1 cup heavy cream

* The really good makes of *petits pois extra-fins* are excellent for this dish but so are home-grown fresh peas (cooked without mint).

Cook the peas and add the ham. Heat the cream slightly and stir into the hot cooked pasta.

PASTA WITH RAGU BOLOGNESE (Italy)

PASTA WITH MEAT SAUCE

Imperial/Metric	American
1 recipe pasta (p.360)	1 recipe pasta (p.360)
1 recipe *ragù bolognese* (p.408)	1 recipe *ragù bolognese* (p.408)
Parmesan cheese, grated	Parmesan cheese, grated

Mix the *ragù* with the cooked pasta and serve with Parmesan cheese.

PASTA WITH MUSSEL SAUCE (Italy)

We had this once at Alassio with the mussels still in their shells. Although absolutely delicious, it was very messy to eat – as indeed are *spaghetti alle vongole*, for that matter. It is, in fact, *Moules Marinières* with a small amount of tomato paste added to the juice. The owner had been a waiter and then chef at a restaurant near Dieppe and had brought the recipe home.

Imperial/Metric	American
1 recipe pasta (p.360)	1 recipe pasta (p.360)
1 recipe *Moules Marinères* (p.108)	1 recipe *Moules Marinières* (p.108)
1 tablespoon tomato concentrate (optional)	1 tablespoon tomato concentrate (optional)
8 fl. oz (240 ml) double cream.	1 cup heavy cream

Cook the mussels. The moment they have opened, remove from the heat and take them out. Strain the juice carefully to avoid any sand and heat up.

Have the pasta hot at this stage. Stir the tomato concentrate (optional) into the hot liquid and make sure it has thoroughly amalgamated before adding the cream. Do not let boil. Add the mussels and pour over the hot pasta and serve. (No cheese.)

PASTA WITH SEAFOOD SAUCE (Italy)

In Italy clams (*vongole*) and mussels (*cozze*) are sold in small quantities specifically for making sauces such as this. However, it is quite possible to do as the Italians did before the coming of the deep freeze and extract the mussels and clams yourself from their shells, though one gets a bit resentful of the work involved.

Imperial/Metric	American
1 recipe pasta (p.360)	1 recipe pasta (p.360)
1 onion, chopped	1 onion, chopped
1 lb (500 g) fresh tomatoes, chopped	1 lb fresh tomatoes, chopped
1 teaspoon fresh marjoram (not oregano)	1 teaspoon fresh marjoram (not oregano)
8 fl. oz (240 ml) white wine	1 cup white wine
4 oz (125 g) frozen mussels or 1 pint in shells	2½ cups mussels
4 oz (125 g) clams	4 oz clams
4 oz (125 g) medium prawns	4 oz medium shrimps
2 tablespoons parsley, chopped	2 tablespoons parsley, chopped
4 oz (125 g) mushrooms, chopped	4 oz mushrooms, chopped
2 fl. oz (60 ml) olive oil	¼ cup olive oil

Fry the onion until soft, add the tomatoes and reduce to a syrupy sauce. Add the white wine and then the seafood. Finally add the mushrooms and parsley and once cooked stir in or pour on top of the cooked pasta. (No cheese.)

PASTA WITH TUNNYFISH AND TOMATO SAUCE (Italy)

Very economical and delicious.

Imperial/Metric	American
1 recipe pasta (p.360)	1 recipe pasta (p.360)
7 oz (220 g) tunnyfish (tuna)	7 oz tuna
1 recipe tomato sauce (p.389)	1 recipe tomato sauce (p.389)
a little oil	a little oil
1 tablespoon capers	1 tablespoon capers

Drain the tunnyfish and fry in a little olive oil. Add the tomato sauce gradually. Get it very hot and add the capers just before serving.

Gnocchi

GNOCCHI ALLA ROMANA (Italy)

BAKED SEMOLINA GNOCCHI

The Italian housewife can buy ready-made semolina *gnocchi* at the supermarket and all she has to do is slice it and bake it according to the recipe. The recipe below shows how to make it (and bake it) at home and it must be said that the quality is rather superior to the purchased sort.

Imperial/Metric	*American*
8 oz (250 g) semolina (not too fine	8 oz semolina (not too fine)
1¾ pint (1 litre) full cream milk	4½ cups full cream milk
6 oz (190 g) butter	¾ cup butter
4 oz (125 g) Parmesan cheese, grated	½ cup Parmesan cheese, grated
2 oz (60 g) Gruyère or similar cheese	¼ cup Gruyère or similar cheese
3 egg yolks	3 egg yolks
salt	salt
pinch of nutmeg	pinch of nutmeg
a few breadcrumbs	a few breadcrumbs

Bring the milk to the boil and pour in the semolina in a stream, stirring all the time. Add the nutmeg and about a third of the butter. Turn down the heat and cook until done – about 20 minutes. Stir all the time and make sure the bottom of the saucepan does not 'catch'. Once cooked, remove from the heat and beat in the Gruyère cheese. When a little cooler, beat in the egg yolks, one by one.

Take two Swiss roll (jelly roll) tins and wet them under the tap. Alternatively line with Bakewell paper. Pour half the mixture into each tin. Smooth out and let get quite cold. This will take about 2 hours. The thickness should be approximately half an inch (1 cm) – not more. Cut into squares, lozenges or rounds with a cutter.

To serve 8 you will probably need 2 ovenware dishes, unless you have a very large one. Melt the rest of the butter. Put the squares or lozenges in rows, slightly overlapping into a very well buttered dish. In between the *gnocchi* put a little melted butter and a sprinkling of cheese. When all the *gnocchi* are used up, pour melted butter over the top, sprinkle with the rest of the Parmesan and the breadcrumbs and bake in a hot oven (400°F/200°C/Gas 6) until golden brown. Serve at once.

GNOCCHI WITH GORGONZOLA AND PARSLEY

Make your gnocchi as in *Gnocchi alla Romana* (p.376). Put them in a well buttered dish and pour over the following sauce:

Imperial/Metric	American
8 oz (250 g) *dolcelatte* Gorgonzola cheese	8 oz *dolcelatte* Gorgonzola cheese
12 fl. oz (360 ml) single cream	1½ cups light cream
2 tablespoons parsley, chopped	2 tablespoons parsley, chopped

Mix the cheese and cream, preferably in a liquidizer or food processor. Stir in the parsley and pour over the *gnocchi*. It should not cover them. Bake 15-20 minutes at 400°F/200°C/Gas 6, when it should be golden on top. Serve at once.

Can be prepared in advance but do not put the sauce on until you are ready to bake.

GNOCCHI DI POLENTA (Italy)

Usually *gnocchi* are made of semolina or potatoes. This recipe is unusual because it uses *polenta* flour (what the Italians call *farina gialla*) but it is dished up to look like *Gnocchi alla Romana*.

Imperial/Metric	American
1 lb (500 g) fine to medium *polenta*	1 lb fine to medium *polenta*
3 pints (1.5 litres) water	3¾ pints water
8 oz (250 g) veal, minced	8 oz veal, ground
8 oz (250 g) cooked ham, chopped	8 oz cooked ham, chopped
4 oz (125 g) Parmesan cheese, grated	½ cup Parmesan cheese, grated
salt and pepper	salt and pepper
butter	butter

Boil the water. Once it is boiling, pour in the *polenta* in a fine stream, stirring all the time. Turn down heat slightly and continue to stir all the time – otherwise you will get lumps. Once you have a smooth mass, leave it to cook for ¾ hour, stirring from time to time. An asbestos or heat mat is useful to prevent catching.

Once cooked add the meats (it is not necessary to cook them beforehand). Add half the Parmesan cheese. Spread the mixture on a *wetted* board about ¾ inch (2 cm) thick. Either cut out with a glass (2 inch/5 cm diameter) or in lozenges. You will need a basin of water to dip your glass or cutter into from time to time.

Place the rounds or lozenges in an ovenproof dish in rows so they are slightly overlapping each other. Sprinkle liberally with Parmesan cheese and then dot equally liberally with butter. Bake for 20 minutes in a hot oven at 400°F/200°C/Gas 6.

Dumplings

KNEDLE OD POVRACA (Yugoslavia: Croatia)

VEGETABLE DUMPLINGS

Not an easy dish to succeed with first time round but with practice it becomes quite easy.

Imperial/Metric	*American*
4 oz (125 g) carrots	4 oz carrots
4 oz (125 g) onions	4 oz onions
4 oz (125 g) cabbage	4 oz cabbage
4 oz (125 g) mushrooms	4 oz mushrooms
8 oz (250 g) butter	1 cup butter
2 fl. oz (60 ml) milk	¼ cup milk
3-4 slices white bread	3-4 slices white bread
2 eggs	2 eggs
12-14 oz (375-440 g) flour	1½-1¾ cups flour
stock for cooking dumplings (cubes will do)	stock for cooking dumplings (cubes will do)
2 oz (60 g) fresh breadcrumbs	½ cup fresh breadcrumbs

Dice the vegetables small and cook each separately. Cook the mushrooms in a little butter, then add the other vegetables. Let cool. Cut the bread into cubes and fry in butter to make crisp croûtons. Beat the 2 eggs with the milk in a mixing bowl and add enough flour to get a stiff mixture. Add the vegetables and croûtons and form into balls, flouring your hand to prevent their sticking. Have the stock boiling and drop the balls in a few at a time. Turn down heat slightly. Once cooked, drain and keep warm until all are done. Fry the breadcrumbs in the remaining butter, sprinkle over the cooked vegetable dumplings and serve.

VIRTINIAI (Lithuania)

LITHUANIAN DUMPLINGS OR RAVIOLI

I had a Polish stepmother who had a Lithuanian nanny. A great many of her recipes came from this source and were handed on to me. *Virtiniai* are rather like large *ravioli*, cooked in broth and served with large quantities of soured cream. My stepmother associated this recipe with coming home from school in the autumn term when the woods were full of mushrooms. Cultivated mushrooms will do, but a mixture of cultivated and wild or cultivated and dried wild are best.

Serve with a large bowl of sour cream and plenty of freshly ground pepper.

DOUGH

Imperial/Metric	American
1 lb (500 g) plain flour	2 cups plain flour
2 eggs, beaten	2 eggs, beaten
2 oz (60 g) butter	¼ cup butter
4 pints (2.4 litres) bouillon (cubes will do)	5 pints bouillon (cubes will do)

Melt the butter and put into the beaten eggs. Add a couple of tablespoons of water. Make a well in the flour and mix. You may need a little more water to get a dough-like pastry (or pasta dough).

Roll out as thinly as possible. Either cut into squares or stamp out rounds with the rim of a glass – about 2½-3 inches (6.5 cm) is a good size. Put a spoonful of the mushroom filling on each and fold over in a triangle shape or into a half moon. I find the edges stick together better with a little egg brushed on them. Press the edges with the tines of a fork.

Cook in boiling bouillon about 12 at a time until they are done. Floating to the top is not a sure sign, so taste.

FILLING

Imperial/Metric	*American*
12 oz (375 g) fresh mushrooms, chopped	12 oz fresh mushrooms, chopped
1 package (1 oz) (25 g) dried Italian mushrooms	1 package (1 oz) dried Italian mushrooms
2 oz (60 g) butter	¼ cup butter
2 shallots or spring onions	2 shallots or scallions
1 egg, beaten	1 egg, beaten
1 tablespoon potato flour*	1 tablespoon potato flour*

* If you have no potato flour, use cornflour (cornstarch) instead or even instant mashed potato – the object is to mop up any juice which will ruin the *virtiniai*. Cool and use for the filling.

Soak dried mushrooms for an hour or so, drain and chop up. They look awful but will taste delicious. Cook the shallots or onions in the butter and then add the fresh mushrooms. Once done, add the dried mushrooms and some salt and pepper. Pour off the juice. Mix down the cooled juice and the potato flour and return to the pan and let it thicken. Cool and use for the filling.

VARSKIECIAI (Lithuania)

COTTAGE CHEESE DUMPLINGS AND SOUR CREAM

Another Lithuanian recipe from the same source as *Virtiniai*. They are served in shallow soup plates with sour cream and/or melted butter but sour cream is best. I like the addition of a little parsley to the dough or the sour cream but that is not genuine.

The dough can be made in advance, covered with a damp cloth and kept in a cool place until ready for use. Alternatively you can even cut them out and keep them covered before using. I once tried making this dough in the food processor. The result was heavy and lacked the freshness of the original. If there are any over, they can be brushed with butter and baked for a moment in a hot oven or can even be fried next day. Lithuanians have (or used to have) them for breakfast.

Imperial/Metric	*American*
1½ lb (750 g) cottage cheese	1½ lb cottage cheese
12 oz (375 g) plain flour	1½ cups plain flour
2 eggs	2 eggs
salt	salt
4 pints (2.4 litres) salted water (for cooking – have it ready)	5 pints salted water (for cooking – have it ready)

Break down the cottage cheese into smaller lumps – do not beat smooth. Add the eggs and stir in. Then add flour – a little at a time. In the end you should have a dry dough with occasional blobs of cottage cheese in it. Roll out quickly on a well-floured board. Cut into rounds or squares as for the *virtiniai* but about ¼ inch (0.5 cm) thick. Drop into boiling water: when they float up, they are done. Put on a shallow plate in a warm place with a little melted butter to stop them drying out. Continue cooking in this way.

Risotti

The whole point of a *risotto* is that it should not be dry and fluffy but slightly creamy with a very rich flavour. The texture of Italian *Arborio* rice may not be to everyone's taste, particularly those who have lived in the Middle East, but there is no doubt that it has an ability to absorb and keep flavours as no other rice has. For *risotto* you must use Italian *Arborio* rice, or otherwise you will be making a sloppy sort of pilaff.

The ingredients of an Italian *risotto* are always part and parcel of the dish, and *risotto*, with the exception of *risotto alla milanese* which is served with *Osso buco* is never served as a rice accompaniment. For the latter you order *riso in bianco* (which you will surely regret as it is not one of Italy's better dishes).

All the following *risotto* are based on the following recipe to which you add other ingredients, sometimes at the beginning but mostly at the end.

BASIC RISOTTO

Imperial/Metric	*American*
1 lb (500 g) *Arborio* rice	2 cups *Arborio* rice
1 large or 2 medium onions, finely chopped	1 large or 2 medium onions, finely chopped
8 fl. oz (240 ml) white wine	1 cup white wine
6 oz (190 g) unsalted butter	¾ cup sweet butter
approx. 3 pints (1.8 litres) chicken or beef stock*	4 pints chicken or beef stock (cubes can be used)*
salt and pepper	salt and pepper

* You can use cubes but it is worth making stock from a chicken carcass especially for this dish.

Melt the butter in a thick-bottomed pan (Dutch oven) and cook the onions until golden but not brown. Add the rice and stir until glistening. Then add the wine and turn off the heat for a moment.

Stir well. Add *half* the stock. (If you are using cubes, watch for the salt and do not add any to the dish until the end.) Cook for 10 minutes over a low heat. The mixture should be slightly sloppy.

At this stage you must decide whether to continue cooking on the top of the stove or in the oven. Personally I plump for the stove every time because you can check on the state of the rice more easily. On a medium heat the rice will need approximately 30 minutes to cook by Italian standards (they like it *al dente*) but a little more for non-Italian tastes.

Not more than 10 minutes before the end of the cooking time do you add the other ingredients, otherwise you will lose the fresh taste, particularly of herbs.

Italians frequently add Parmesan cheese to the risotto before serving but I think it is better to put freshly grated Parmesan on the table for non-Italians to help themselves.

RISOTTO ALLA CONTANDINA

RISOTTO PEASANT STYLE

Imperial/Metric	American
1 recipe *risotto* (p.381)	1 recipe *risotto* (p.381)
4 oz (125 g) French beans, cooked	½ cup French beans, cooked
4 oz (125 g) asparagus tips, cooked	½ cup asparagus tips, cooked
4 oz (125 g) green peas, cooked	½ cup green peas, cooked
4 oz (125 g) Parmesan cheese, grated	½ cup Parmesan cheese, grated
2 tablespoons parsley, chopped	2 tablespoons parsley, chopped

Cook in a basic *risotto* for 20 minutes and add the other ingredients.

RISOTTO ALLA GENOVESE (Italy)

RISOTTO WITH ARTICHOKES, PEAS AND SAUSAGE

This is a useful dish because you can cook the whole thing in advance until it has to go into the oven. Where you start cold, increase the oven temperature slightly and give it a little longer.

Imperial/Metric	American
1 recipe *risotto* (p.381)	1 recipe *risotto* (p.381)
8 oz (250 g) sausage meat or a mixture of minced pork and veal	1 cup sausage meat or a mixture of minced pork and veal
8 oz (250 g) fresh green peas, cooked	1 cup fresh green peas, cooked
3 oz (90 g) mushrooms, sliced	3 oz mushrooms, sliced
approx. ½ pint (300 ml) *ragú Bolognese*	approx. ½ pint *ragú Bolognese*
2 tablespoons Parmesan cheese, grated	2 tablespoons Parmesan cheese, grated

To a basic risotto when it is approximately two-thirds cooked add the other ingredients *which you have already cooked separately*. Mix everything together and put in a fireproof dish. Bake in a moderate oven approximately 325°F/170°C/Gas 3, uncovered, for about 15 minutes. A *slight* crust should form. Test that the rice is cooked and serve with grated Parmesan.

RISOTTO D'AOSTA (Italy)

RISOTTO WITH HAM, FONTINA CHEESE AND ALBA TRUFFLES

This dish is made only in the autumn. Serve with a dry white wine – or even champagne!

Imperial/Metric	American
1 recipe *risotto* (p.381)	1 recipe *risotto* (p.000)
4 oz lean, chopped ham	½ cup lean, chopped ham
6 oz (190 g) farmhouse Fontina cheese*	¾ cup farmhouse Fontina cheese*
1 Alba truffle the size of a golf ball**	1 Alba truffle the size of a golf ball**

* Farmhouse Fontina is not easy to find. The next best thing is Swiss Vacherin, which is probably even more difficult to find.
** Alba truffles are not easy to find either and cost the earth. They are white and are seldom preserved for eating out of season.

Assuming you can get good Fontina, I'm sure this dish with good-quality mushrooms *under* the Fontina would be very good also.

Make the *risotto*, add the ham and divide into 8 portions on 8 fireproof dishes. Cover the rice with thin slices of Fontina and run it under the grill until it melts but does not turn brown. Over each, 'peel' some slivers of truffle – the Piedmontese and

Valdostani have special shaving instruments for dealing with truffles 'economically' – a potato peeler is probably the nearest non-Italians can get.

RISOTTO CON PROSCIUTTO E GREMOLATA (Italy)

RISOTTO WITH HAM, LEMON AND PARSLEY

When I was very new to cooking and making *Osso buco* for the first time, I added the *gremolata* (a mixture of lemon rind and parsley which the Milanese sprinkle on a lot of their veal dishes) to the *risotto alla Milanese* instead of to the *osso buco*. The result was rather nice and certainly different. Later I added the ham and have since served the dish to Italians who have been very complimentary. (Italians are notoriously tolerant and polite guests!)

To a basic *risotto* (p.381), with or without the saffron demanded for a *risotto alla Milanese*, add just before serving:

Imperial/Metric	American
grated rind of 1 lemon	grated rind of 1 lemon
2 tablespoons parsley, chopped	2 tablespoons parsley, chopped
4 oz (125 g) cooked ham, diced	½ cup cooked diced ham
Parmesan cheese, grated (optional)	Parmesan cheese, grated (optional)

RISOTTO CON PROSCIUTTO E FUNGHI (Italy)

RISOTTO WITH HAM AND MUSHROOMS

Strictly speaking, this *risotto* should be made in the autumn, when *porcini* (*boletus edulis* or *cèpes*) are plentiful, but this is a counsel of perfection and most of us have to manage with ordinary cultivated mushrooms.

To a basic *risotto* (p.381), in which have included the Parmesan and which is almost cooked, add, hot, the following:

Imperial/Metric	American
8 oz (250 g) mushrooms, cooked and sliced	1 cup mushrooms, cooked and sliced
8 oz (250 g) lean ham, chopped or diced	1 cup ham, chopped or diced

Any liquid from the mushrooms can go into the *risotto* and will soon be absorbed. Serve with more Parmesan.

RISOTTO CON POMODORI E PROSCIUTTO (Italy)

RISOTTO WITH HAM AND TOMATOES

To a basic *risotto* (p.381), in which you have included the Parmesan, add:

Imperial/Metric	American
8 oz (250 g) ham, chopped or diced	1 cup ham, chopped or diced
1½ lb (750 g) firm tomato	3 cups firm tomato
basil to taste, chopped (optional)	basil to taste, chopped (optional)
a little oil	a little oil

Remove the seeds and cut tomatoes up roughly. You can skin them if you want, but they tend to let out more liquid than ever. Over a high heat cook the tomato pieces, add the ham and after a couple of minutes add to the *risotto* and stir. Just before serving, add the chopped basil, if used.

RISOTTO VERDE (Italy)

RISOTTO WITH HERBS

To an all-but-cooked basic *risotto* (p.381) add the following:

Imperial/Metric	American
6-7 oz (190-220 g) spinach, cooked*	¾ cup cooked spinach*
2 sticks celery, chopped	2 stick celery, chopped
1 carrot, grated	1 carrot, grated
2 tablespoons parsley	2 tablespoons parsley
2 cloves garlic, finely chopped	2 cloves garlic, finely chopped
butter or oil (to cook)	butter or oil (to cook)

* I prefer the chopped spinach to be cooked with the other ingredients rather than boiled separately but that is a personal foible – it makes the final stirring in easier.

In a small amount of butter or oil, cook the garlic and celery; add the carrot. The celery should remain slightly crunchy. Combine all ingredients with the *risotto* and cook. Serve with Parmesan cheese separately.

Variation
Some Italian recipes for this dish call for just under 4 fl. oz (100

ml/½ US cup) of *ragù* to be incorporated into this dish but I think it kills the taste of the herbs.

RISOTTO CON SEPPIE (Italy)

RISOTTO WITH INK FISH OR SQUID

This can be made with fish stock made from the bones of any white fish and the heads and tentacles of the squid. Choose small squid as these are the most tender. If you want to use the ink, do so when making the basic *risotto*. It looks a bit murky and sepulchral but tastes delicious. However, know your guests before you do it! Serve with lemon, but no cheese.

Imperial/Metric	*American*
1 recipe risotto (p.381)	1 recipe risotto (p.381)
1 small carrot, grated	1 small carrot, grated
2 or 3 cloves garlic, chopped	2 or 3 cloves garlic, chopped
8 oz (250 g) mushrooms, sliced	1 cup mushrooms, sliced
approx 1½ lb (750 g) squid*	approx. 1½ lb squid*
a little oil	a little oil
4 fl. oz (120 ml) dry white wine	½ cup dry white wine

* See p.347 on how to deal with squid.
   Make the *risotto*. Fry the garlic and carrot in the oil. Turn up heat and add the fairly finely sliced squid. Cook for a minute or 2, then pour in the white wine, stir, add the mushrooms and cook over a rather more gentle heat for 10 minutes. Try a piece of squid: if it is done, add them and their sauce to the *risotto*; if not, add a little more liquid (wine or water) and continue to cook until they are just done.

RISOTTO CON SCAMPI (Italy)

RISOTTO WITH LARGE PRAWNS

Imperial/Metric	*American*
1 recipe *risotto* (p.381)	1 recipe *risotto* (p.381)
1 lb (500 g) uncooked scampi tails	1 lb uncooked Gulf shrimps tails or Dublin Bay prawns
4 fl. oz (120 ml) cognac or stock brandy	½ cup cognac or stock brandy
a little butter	a little butter
1 tablespoon parsley (optional)	1 tablespoon parsley (optional)
2 lemons	2 lemons

Make the *risotto*. Remove heads and shells of scampi (shrimps) and make a fish stock (p.306) with them. Slice the scampi (shrimps) into about 3 pieces each. In a little butter fry the scampi (shrimps); once they have become opaque, pour in the brandy and set alight. Add them to the finished *risotto* and stir in the parsley if wished. Serve with wedges of lemon.

RISOTTO CON FRUTTI DI MARE (Italy)

RISOTTO WITH SHELLFISH

To a basic *risotto*, preferably made with a fish stock (from the head, tails, bones, shells etc of the fish and crustaceans – see p.308) and all but cooked, add the following:

Imperial/Metric	American
approx. 1 dozen mussels (with/ without shells)*	approx. 1 dozen mussels (with/ without shells)*
1 dozen large scampi*	1 dozen large shrimps*
approx. 3-4 oz (90-125 g) cooked squid or calmar or inkfish*	½ cup cooked squid or calmar or inkfish*
½ lobster or crawfish	½ lobster or crawfish
1 stick celery (optional)	1 stick celery (optional)
2 lemons	2 lemons

* You should end up with a minimum of 1 lb (500 g) of seafood. The mixture is up to you, depending on your pocket.

Chop the celery very small and add to the *risotto*. Add the cooked fish and heat through. Once the *risotto* is cooked, serve with wedges of lemon (no Parmesan).

14 Sauces, Dressings and Mayonnaises

Sauces and Dressings

Imagine Green Goddess salad without the dressing – just a boring arrangement of fish, no matter how fresh or well cooked it is, it will not tempt or come alive without the dressing. Imagine a plain boiled lobster with *nothing* – not even melted butter, the simplest form of sauce. The Anglo-Saxons are inclined to be dismissive of sauces, believing them to have been invented by the French to mask poor meat or fish, (and this from a people who think nothing of pouring Worcester sauce or ketchup over everything!). Nothing could be further from the truth. How much more delicious a *sole Dieppoise* is than one plainly poached and unadorned, as is a smoked trout with walnut, cream and horseradish sauce than the same thing with a mere squeeze of lemon juice.

Sauces and dressings should form an integral part of the dish and should be served in a properly generous quantity. Those that follow are either basic or required by the recipes in this book. They are not Holy Writ and can be adapted to suit other recipes and the personal taste of the reader.

Sauces

COULIS DE TOMATES FRAICHES (France)

Imperial/Metric	*American*
1 lb (500 g) ripe tomatoes	1 lb ripe tomatoes
2 teaspoon tomato concentrate	2 teaspoon tomato concentrate
2 fl. oz (60 ml) olive oil	¼ cup olive oil
2 or 3 shallots	2 or 3 shallots
6-8 stalks parsley	6-8 stalks parsley
2 stalks basil (optional)	2 stalks basil (optional)
8 fl. oz (240 ml) chicken stock*	1 cup chicken stock*
salt and pepper	salt and pepper

* Cubes will do but watch the salt.

Skin the tomatoes (this is essential to the finished sauce). Cook the shallots in the olive oil very gently, add the skinned tomatoes, and the parsley and basil tied together, and cook gently for 5 minutes or so. Add the chicken stock and the tomato concentrate and stew gently for a quarter of an hour. Sieve the result if you wish and reduce further if you want a thicker sauce but do not do so over a fast heat or the fresh taste will be ruined. Remove the parsley and basil stalks before serving.

Variation
At the end of cooking a basic *coulis de tomates fraîches* add 2 tablespoons chopped basil and 2 tablespoons chopped parsley. There is no need to cook the sauce in the first place with the herbs on stalks.

SALSA CRUDA (Bolivia)

This is a very common sauce throughout the whole of South America and originates, I think, from Mexico. It is very elastic as to ingredients and thickness or sloppiness – tomatoes, chillis and green herbs being the constants.

Imperial/Metric	American
3 or 4 large ripe tomatoes, peeled and chopped	3 or 4 large ripe tomatoes, peeled and chopped
1 large onion, chopped	1 large onion, chopped
large bunch of fresh coriander or parsley, chopped	large bunch of fresh coriander or parsley, chopped
2 or more chilli peppers, chopped, or Tabasco to taste	2 or more chilli peppers, chopped, or Tabasco to taste
1 tablespoon wine vinegar	1 tablespoon wine vinegar
1 tablespoon water (optional)	1 tablespoon water (optional)
1 tablespoon fine white sugar	1 tablespoon fine white sugar
salt to taste	salt to taste

Lemon or fresh lime juice can be substituted for the vinegar. The water is used only if you wish to have a slightly wetter sauce than usual. Mix all the ingredients together stirring in the chopped herbs last of all with the salt. (You can use a mixture of both herbs though fresh coriander is more common.) This sauce should be served fairly soon after it is made or the fresh quality is lost.

SAUCE AMERICAINE (France)

Imperial/Metric	American
2 lb (1 kilo) French or Italian tomatoes	2 lb French or Italian tomatoes
4 fl. oz (125 ml) olive oil	½ cup olive oil
1 medium onion	1 medium onion
1 medium carrot	1 medium carrot
2 cloves garlic	2 cloves garlic
4 fl. oz (150 ml) cognac	½ cup cognac
12 fl. oz (450 ml) white wine	1¼ cups white wine
4 fl. oz (150 ml) chicken stock	½ cup chicken stock
4 tablespoons parsley, chopped	4 tablespoons parsley, chopped
empty prawn or lobster shells	empty prawn or lobster shells
salt and pepper to taste	salt and pepper to taste
a little butter (optional)	a little butter (optional)

Chop finely or grate the carrot and onion and fry gently in half the oil. Add the garlic and roughly chopped tomatoes and all the other ingredients except the parsley and cognac. Cook for approximately 30 minutes by which time the liquid should have thickened. Discard the lobster or prawn shells and put everything through the liquidizer or food processor. If not thick enough reduce further over heat. Add the cognac, salt and pepper to taste and parsley. Heat through. If liked a little butter can be added at the end to make the sauce shine.

The use of tomato purée or concentrate gives this sauce a very commercial taste.

SAUCE AURORE (France)

To an enriched *sauce béchamel* (p.392) add 2 tablespoons tomato concentrate and blend well.

SAUCE AURORE (Hungary)

Imperial/Metric	American
1 recipe enriched *sauce béchamel* (p.392)	1 recipe enriched *sauce béchamel* (p.392)
1 oz butter	1 oz butter
2 cloves garlic, crushed	2 cloves garlic, crushed
8 oz (250 g) tomatoes, peeled and chopped	8 oz tomatoes, peeled and chopped
1 tablespoon tomato concentrate	1 tablespoon tomato concentrate
1 dessertspoon paprika	1 dessertspoon paprika

Make the *sauce béchamel*. Cook the garlic in the butter and add the tomato concentrate and tomatoes. Cook to a mush, drying out as much as possible. Stir in the paprika and then the enriched *sauce béchamel*. Cook for a further 10 minutes or so until thickened.

SAUCE BECHAMEL (France)

WHITE SAUCE

A real *sauce béchamel* should have veal or chicken stock in it – not to such an extent that it becomes a *sauce velouté* but certainly at least half the liquid *should* be stock. Nowadays, even in France, a *béchamel* is made with butter, flour, milk and sometimes a chicken stock or veal stock cube – the latter being available only at expensive grocers in France.

As we all know, there are many travesties of this all-purpose sauce, so perhaps the recipe for a good one would not come amiss. Use the same tablespoon for measuring butter and flour, and for accuracy melt the butter before measuring. This recipe makes about 1¼ pints/750 ml/3 US cups) of sauce and counts as '1 recipe *sauce béchamel*' when used in recipes elsewhere.

Imperial/Metric	American
6 level tablespoons melted butter	6 level tablespoons melted butter
6 level tablespoons plain flour	6 level tablespoons plain flour
1 chicken stock cube (optional)	1 chicken stock cube (optional)
scant 1¼ pints milk	scant 1¼ pints milk
nutmeg	nutmeg
salt and white ground pepper	salt and white ground pepper

Heat the milk gently and stir in the nutmeg. (Melt the chicken cube in it, if using.) Set aside. Stir the flour into the melted butter, make a *roux* and cook for a few moments. Add the hot milk bit by bit and stir all the time. Cook on a very low heat for at least 10 minutes or there can be a taste of raw flour. Add pepper to taste (and salt if you have not used a chicken stock cube).

Can be stored, covered for 2-3 days in a refrigerator for use later on.

ENRICHED SAUCE BECHAMEL – SAUCE SUPREME

Make a basic *sauce béchamel*, with or without the stock cube, and use only 1 pint/600 ml/2½ US cups of milk. Add 4 fl. oz/120 ml/½ US cup of double (heavy) cream. To this can be added *poivre vert*, shrimps, *baies rouges* etc.

SAUCE BEARNAISE (France)

EGG, BUTTER AND TARRAGON SAUCE

Imperial/Metric	American
12 oz (750 g) unsalted butter, softened*	1½ cups sweet butter*
2 shallots, finely chopped	2 shallots, finely chopped
3 tablespoons tarragon flavoured wine vinegar	3 tablespoons tarragon flavoured wine vinegar
6 tablespoons dry white wine	6 tablespoons dry white wine
1 tablespoon tarragon, finely chopped*	1 tablespoon tarragon, finely chopped*
6 egg yolks	6 egg yolks
salt and white pepper	salt and white pepper

* If using salted butter, omit the salt from this recipe, and if using dried tarragon, use approximately 1 level teaspoon.

In a little of the butter sweat the chopped shallots, then add the vinegar, white wine and tarragon. Cook at a moderate heat and reduce to 3-4 tablespoons – the butter will help it not to stick or burn. Put this mixture into a double saucepan with very hot but not boiling water underneath and add the beaten egg yolks, stirring all the time. Once warm, add the butter bit by bit until all is incorporated, and cook until thickened, stirring constantly. Alternatively, you can add all the butter first and heat up and then add the egg yolks bit by bit – whichever you find easier. The sauce should thicken but should never get hot or it will curdle. Add salt and pepper to taste.

This can be made 60-90 minutes in advance and kept warm – longer than that and the taste suffers.

BEURRE BLANC (France)

This is a wonderfully simple sauce comes from the Loire Valley and is ideal for all poached, steamed, microwaved or baked fish. It is normally used for freshwater fish but is just as good with sea fish. Onions will not do instead of shallots, but Muscadet is not a vital ingredient – any good white, slightly acid wine will do.

Imperial/Metric	*American*
4 or 5 medium shallots, chopped	4 or 5 medium shallots, chopped
1 lb (500 g) butter, unsalted preferably	2 cups sweet butter
4 tablespoons white wine vinegar	4 tablespoons white wine vinegar
4 tablespoon white wine	4 tablespoons white wine

Cut the butter into small cubes – I make 32 out of a 1 lb piece by cutting each pat into 4 and then 4 again and put into a cool place. Cook the shallots in the liquids until they are reduced to a soft mash and the liquid has three-quarters disappeared. Let the shallots in the liquid cool to tepid and then beat in the butter, bit by bit, beating all the time, until you have a thick white mass. If the shallots or butter are too warm you will end up with an oily mess. This can sometimes be saved by holding the bowl's or saucepan's base in iced water for a moment. Everything depends on having the ingredients at a temperature which allows their perfect amalgamation without them actually melting together. I have tried using a food processor for this and to a degree it works but you must beat for at least 5 minutes *by hand* at the end or you will end up with a grainy result. Also your ingredients should be even colder than for beating by hand. Experiment with small quantities for 2 people – say ¼ of this recipe before embarking on *beurre blanc* for 8. *Poivre vert* added is excellent.

SAUCE ESPAGNOLE (France)

BROWN SAUCE

This sauce is the basis for many others including Bigarade, Madeira, Perigueux, *sauce aux cépes* (wild mushroom sauce), etc.

Imperial/Metric	American
4 oz (125 g) unsmoked bacon	4 oz unsmoked bacon
2 tablespoons butter	2 tablespoons butter
1 tablespoon sunflower oil	1 tablespoon sunflower oil
3 tablespoons flour	3 tablespoons flour
1 medium carrot, grated	1 medium carrot, grated
1 large onion, chopped	1 large onion, chopped
1 pint (600 ml) beef or veal stock	2½ cups beef or veal stock
1 pint (600 ml) strong red wine	2½ cups strong red wine
2 tablespoons cognac (optional)	2 tablespoons cognac (optional)
1 stick celery	1 stick celery
2 tablespoons tomato concentrate	2 tablespoons tomato concentrate
6 or 7 parsley stalks, tied together	6 or 7 parsley stalks, tied together
1 bayleaf	1 bayleaf
pinch of thyme	pinch of thyme
salt and pepper at end of cooking	salt and pepper at end of cooking

Home-made stock is best but Campbell's consommé is an acceptable substitute and this should be diluted with an equal amount of water. Put the stock on to simmer with the herbs and celery. Cut the bacon into small dice and put to cook in the butter and oil. Once a little of the fat has run out add the onion. When they are slightly coloured, sprinkle on the flour and brown *gently* – the process should take at least a quarter of an hour. If you are using the cognac take the pan off the heat, pour over the cognac and ignite. When the flames have died down, pour over the red wine, stir well and let it bubble for a couple of minutes. Strain the stock, add it and heat again. Stir in the grated carrot and the tomato concentrate.

Cook over a very low heat for two-and-a-half hours – the sauce should just simmer and at the end should have been reduced by one third. Strain *twice* before serving.

Some people stir in a tablespoon of butter at the end to make a more glistening sauce.

GUACAMOLE SAUCE (Mexico)

Imperial/Metric
1 recipe Guacamole (p.323)
3 medium tomatoes, skinned
1 tablespoon wine vinegar
2 tablespoons water
2 tablespoons fresh coriander
   or parsley, chopped

American
1 recipe Guacamole (p.323)
3 medium tomatoes, skinned
1 tablespoon wine vinegar
2 tablespoons water
2 tablespoons fresh coriander
   or parsley, chopped

Mix all ingredients in a liquidizer or food processor and use the sauce as soon as possible. In Venezuela they often add two chopped hard-boiled eggs folded in at the last minute.

SAUCE HOLLANDAISE (France)

EGG, BUTTER AND LEMON SAUCE

To be absolutely sure, make this sauce in a double boiler or with a *bain-marie*. People are very greedy with *hollandaise* – this recipe will serve 8 very generously.

Imperial/Metric
12 oz (375 g) unsalted butter
6 egg yolks
juice of 1 lemon*
salt and pepper

American
1½ cups sweet butter
6 egg yolks
juice of 1 lemon*
salt and pepper

* You will not necessarily use all the lemon juice.

Melt approx. 2 oz (60 g) of the butter in the double saucepan. Cut the rest of the butter into small cubes and let soften (but not melt – think ahead and do this sometime before you start the sauce) and put them on a warm plate. Put the egg yolks into the pan and stir well. Let them heat, stirring all the time. Once they start thickening, add the butter, cube by soft cube, stirring without cease. You should end up with a sauce thick enough to coat the back of a spoon. From time to time you can add a teaspoon of cold water, which will prevent the whole thing getting too hot but if you are careful it is not necessary. Once thick enough, remove the pan from the source of heat and stir in a little lemon juice, salt and pepper – taste and add a little more as necessary. Serve as soon as possible – it can be kept warm in a *bain-marie* but this does nothing for the taste.

AMERICAN SAUCE HOLLANDAISE

The same ingredients as for a classic *sauce hollandaise* – only the method is different, since a blender or liquidizer is used.

Heat the *softened* butter. If the butter is hard, cut it into small cubes or you will have to get it too hot to melt it all. Get the butter hot but do not let it even begin to brown. Drop the egg yolks onto the blades of the machine and pour the hot butter in a fairly slow, steady stream. Stop the machine, add the lemon juice and salt, blend and taste. Add more lemon juice as necessary. As can be seen, the temperature of the butter is everything – and do not overblend. If the sauce thickens up too much (you will be very lucky if it does), pop it back into the machine with a tablespoon of hot water and blend it down – adding another tablespoon if the first was not enough.

SAUCE MALTAISE (France)

SAUCE HOLLANDAISE WITH ORANGE

Make a *sauce hollandaise* by either method but instead of using lemon incorporate the juice of one blood orange and the grated rind of half an orange. If you cannot find blood oranges, use an ordinary one but the look and taste are different.

SAUCE MEURETTE (France)

BURGUNDIAN SAUCE

This is a sauce that can be made in advance and heated up later. It is excellent with fish as well as eggs, particularly if you want to serve red wine with fish – and freshwater fish is even better than sea fish.

Imperial/Metric	American
2 oz (60 g) mushrooms, finely chopped	2 oz mushrooms, finely chopped
1 medium onion	1 medium onion
1 clove garlic, crushed	1 clove garlic, crushed
½ medium carrot, grated	½ medium carrot, grated
10 fl. oz (300 ml) red wine*	1¼ cups red wine*
2 tablespoons *marc de Bourgogne* or cognac	2 tablespoons *marc de Bourgogne* or cognac
1 tablespoon flour	1 tablespoon flour
butter for frying	butter for frying
pinch thyme and bayleaf	pinch thyme and bayleaf

*The red wine should preferably be a Burgundy but it does not have to be an expensive one.

Fry the onion, garlic and carrot with the butter but do not let them brown too much. When the vegetables are almost cooked, add the mushrooms and cook a little longer. Pour on the *marc de Bourgogne* or brandy and ignite. When the flames have died down, stir in the flour and then moisten with the red wine. Add the herbs and cook gently until all the raw taste of flour has disappeared – you may need a little more wine.

SAUCE MORNAY (France)

To a normal *sauce béchamel* (p.391) add 3 oz (90 g) grated Gruyère cheese and 2 oz (60 g) grated Parmesan cheese and cook until the cheese has thoroughly melted.

SAUCE MOUSSELINE (France)

SAUCE HOLLANDAISE WITH WHIPPED CREAM

A very tricky sauce to do well but worth the effort.

Imperial/Metric	American
1 recipe *sauce hollandaise* (p.395)	1 recipe *sauce hollandaise* (p.395)
1 tablespoon lemon juice	1 tablespoon lemon juice
12 fl. oz (360 ml) whipped cream	1½ cups whipped cream

Have the *hollandaise* as warm as you dare, having added a little more salt and 1 tablespoon more of lemon juice. Then incorporate the whipped cream. Do this off the heat, whipping all the time. Do not try for a too warm sauce.

MUSHROOM SAUCE 1

Imperial/Metric
1 medium onion, chopped
6 oz (190 g) white mushrooms, sliced
6 tablespoons butter
6 tablespoons flour
1 chicken stock cube (optional)
1 pint (600 ml) or more milk
salt and pepper

American
1 medium onion, chopped
6 oz white mushrooms, sliced
6 tablespoons butter
6 tablespoons flour
1 chicken stock cube (optional)
2½ cups or more milk
salt and pepper

Cook the onion in the butter without browning and add the mushrooms. Once almost cooked, add the flour and make a *roux*. Continue as for a *sauce béchamel* (p.391). You will probably not need so much milk as for an ordinary *béchamel* as the mushrooms will supply some liquid.

MUSHROOM SAUCE 2

Imperial/Metric
1 medium onion, finely chopped
6 oz (190 g) mushrooms
6 tablespoons butter
6 tablespoons flour
1 pint (600 ml) chicken or beef stock (pp.298-300) or tinned consommé
1 tablespoon tomato concentrate
pinch thyme and bayleaf
4 fl. oz (120 ml) Madeira
salt and pepper

American
1 medium onion, finely chopped
6 oz mushrooms
6 tablespoons butter
6 tablespoons flour
2½ cups chicken or beef stock (pp.298-300) or tinned consommé
1 tablespoon tomato concentrate
pinch thyme and bayleaf
½ cup Madeira
salt and pepper

Cook the onions in half the butter without browning them and then add the mushrooms.

Make a *roux* with the rest of the flour and let it brown slightly. Add the onions and mushrooms and then the heated stock. Add the herbs and tomato concentrate and cook for 15 minutes over a gentle heat, stirring frequently. Once cooked, add the Madeira, salt and pepper to taste and cook for a minute or 2 more before serving.

SAUCE NANTUA (France)

A SAUCE FOR FRESHWATER FISH

A wonderful and classic sauce and well worth making.

Imperial/Metric	*Imperial/Metric*
1 recipe *sauce béchamel* (p.391)	1 recipe *sauce béchamel* (p.391)
4 oz (125 g) crayfish butter*	4 oz crayfish butter*
approx. 4 oz (125 g) crayfish tails*	approx. 4 oz crayfish tails*
1 tablespoon brandy**	1 tablespoon brandy**
1 teaspoon tomato concentrate	1 teaspoon tomato concentrate

* Crayfish butter is available at speciality grocers and, whilst it costs a lot, it costs less than if you were to make it yourself. Crayfish tails can also be found frozen but lobster tail is almost as good.
** Do not be any more generous with the brandy thinking it will improve the flavour if you use more – it will kill the crayfish taste.

Cook the *sauce béchamel* over a gentle heat and let it reduce by half. Then add all but 2 tablespoons of the cream and brandy and stir in the crayfish butter bit by bit. Put in the crayfish tails and stop cooking. Fold in the last bit of cream and serve at once.

ORANGE AND PORT WINE SAUCE (UK)

Not unlike Cumberland sauce except that it has no redcurrant jelly in it.

Imperial/Metric	*American*
2 or 3 shallots, chopped	2 or 3 shallots, chopped
2 oz (60 g) butter	¼ cup butter
1 tablespoon flour	1 tablespoon flour
1 tablespoon Dijon mustard	1 tablespoon Dijon mustard
juice of 2 oranges	juice of 2 oranges
grated rind of 1 orange	grated rind of 1 orange
8 fl. oz (240 ml) port	1 cup port
salt	salt

Cook the shallots in the butter until almost melted away, then add the flour and make a brown *roux*. Add the orange juice and rind, the mustard and finally the port wine. You should end up with a pouring sauce – not at all thick. Cook until all taste of flour has disappeared and then serve.

SAUCE PROVENÇALE (France)

Imperial/Metric	American
1 medium onion, chopped	1 medium onion, chopped
2 cloves garlic	2 cloves garlic
12 oz (375 g) tomatoes	12 oz tomatoes
1 sweet red pepper	1 red bell pepper
1 sweet green pepper	1 green bell pepper
pinch thyme and summer savory	pinch thyme and summer savory
olive oil or olive oil and butter	olive oil or olive oil and butter
1 teaspoon sugar	1 teaspoon sugar
salt and pepper to taste	salt and pepper to taste
2 tablespoons parsley, chopped	2 tablespoons parsley, chopped

Peel the tomatoes and remove the seeds. Chop roughly. Cook the onions with the garlic and olive oil/butter and then add the other vegetables and cook until done. Add the seasonings, except the parsley. Serve as is or run it through the liquidizer or food processor to make a smoother sauce. Stir in the parsley just before serving.

SAUCE SOUBISE (France)

FRENCH ONION SAUCE

Imperial/Metric	American
2 lb (scant 1 kilo) onions, chopped	2 lb onions, chopped
3 tablespoons melted butter	3 tablespoons melted butter
3 tablespoons plain flour	3 tablespoons plain flour
1 chicken stock cube (optional)	1 chicken stock cube (optional)
12 fl. oz (360 ml) milk	1½ cups milk
3-4 tablespoons double cream	3-4 tablespoons heavy cream
salt and pepper	salt and pepper

Cook the onions in the butter very gently, stirring all the time. Once almost done, add the flour and blend well. Then add the hot milk (with or without the chicken cube) and season to taste. Run the whole thing through the liquidizer or food processor, or sieve it. Return to the heat and cook for approximately 10 minutes until all taste of raw flour had disappeared. Just before serving, stir in the cream.

Variation

Cook 1 lb (500 g) onions as in the previous recipe and then run them through the liquidizer or food processor. Stir in ½ pint/300 ml/1¼ US cups thick cream, salt and pepper to taste and heat very slightly before serving. This sauce is inclined to separate on keeping, so make it at the last moment.

SHRIMP OR PRAWN SAUCE

To an enriched *sauce béchamel* (p.392) add 4-6 oz (125-190 g) chopped-up prawns or whole small shrimps, heat through and serve. A dessertspoonful of tomato purée can be added if the sauce is preferred pink.

Dressings

CLASSIC VINAIGRETTE (France)

OIL AND VINEGAR DRESSING FOR SALAD

Imperial/Metric	*American*
1 teaspoon dry or Dijon mustard	1 teaspoon dry or Dijon mustard
pinch of salt	pinch of salt
1 part vinegar	1 part vinegar
3-4 parts olive oil*	3-4 parts olive oil*

* Olive oil can be replaced by half olive oil and half sunflower or peanut oil if wished.

Mix the salt and mustard, add the vinegar and stir and finally add the oil, beating all the time to get a good emulsion. Alternatively use a liquidizer or food processor.

AMERICAN DRESSING

Imperial/Metric	*American*
3 tablespoons or more wine vinegar	3 tablespoons or more wine vinegar
half a clove garlic	half a clove of garlic
salt and pepper	salt and pepper
1 teaspoon icing sugar	1 teaspoon confectioners' sugar
1 teaspoon Dijon mustard	1 teaspoon Dijon mustard
2 teaspoons tomato ketchup	2 teaspoons tomato ketchup
6 tablespoons olive oil	6 tablespoons olive oil

Crush the garlic and mix with the salt, sugar, mustard, ketchup and vinegar. Add the olive oil and let steep for half an hour or so. Remove the garlic and dress the salad.

GREEN GODDESS SALAD DRESSING (USA)

Frequently used for fish or chicken combined with salad greens, this dressing can also be used for a plain green salad with which you have lobster or prawns or monkfish or breast of chicken – a lovely light first course.

Imperial/Metric	American
8 fl. oz (240 ml) mayonnaise (p.404)	1 cup mayonnaise (p.404)
8 fl. oz (240 ml) sour cream	1 cup sour cream
3 spring onions	3 scallions
10-12 anchovy fillets	10-12 anchovy fillets
2 tablespoons parsley	2 tablespoons parsley
2 sprigs tarragon	2 sprigs tarragon
1 clove garlic, roughly chopped	1 clove garlic, roughly chopped

Combine all the ingredients in a liquidizer or food processor until they are very smooth and a beautiful pale green colour.

LEBANESE DRESSING

Equal parts of olive oil and lemon juice are used as a basic dressing to which are added salt and pepper, occasionally some sugar (to counteract the sourness of the lemon), crushed garlic and/or chopped onion. Almost always the salad is sprinkled with dried or fresh mint (usually the former). Much parsley is used as well.

SWISS DRESSING

Imperial/Metric	American
2 tablespoons olive or other oil	2 tablespoons olive or other oil
4 fl. oz (120 ml) cream	½ cup cream
juice of a medium lemon	juice of a medium lemon
sugar to taste	sugar to taste
salt and pepper	salt and pepper
parsley, chopped	parsley, chopped

Mix all ingredients together, except the parsley, and let steep for an hour. Stir in the parsley and serve on green salads.

TOFU SALAD DRESSING (USA)

Imperial/Metric	*American*
5 oz (155 ml) silken tofu	5 oz silken tofu
2 tablespoons wine vinegar	2 tablespoons wine vinegar
4 fl. oz (120 ml) olive or light oil	4 fl. oz olive or light oil
1 good teaspoon Dijon mustard	1 good teaspoon Dijon mustard
1 tablespoon fresh parsley,	1 tablespoon fresh parsley,
chopped	chopped

If you are not using a machine, at least use a balloon whisk to mix all the ingredients.

For a tomato salad chopped basil can be exchanged for the parsley.

Mayonnaises

If you are not going to use at least half olive oil in your mayonnaise, you might as well buy one of the good makes available in jars. Mayonnaises made wholly of heavy olive oil are no longer to most people's taste and there is a tendency to use half olive oil and half sunflower seed, corn or peanut oil. I find that sunflower seed oil does not quarrel with the olive oil and makes for a light but olive-oil-tasting mayonnaise.

Also, with an eye on cholesterol, there is a tendency to use fewer eggs. One egg will easily absorb 8 fl. oz/240 ml/1 US cup of oil. The oil, being non-animal, is less dangerous than the egg. Going further, olive oil is better for you than any of the others – though of course more expensive.

For any mayonnaise the ingredients should all be at room temperature.

CLASSIC MAYONNAISE

For approximately 1½ pints/900 ml/3¾ US cups. Quantities can be halved but mayonnaise will keep for 2-3 weeks in a covered jar in a refrigerator.

Never use heavy, fruity oil or the mayonnaise will taste unattractive and greasy. Heavy oil is meant for dressing salads such as beans, pasta etc which need a fruity oil – a green salad doesn't. Nowadays a lot of the better oils come with drippers incorporated. If you do not have a bottle like this, it is worth putting the oil into a specially purchased container which has a spout such as you get on soy sauce, certain vinegars etc. Kitchen equipment shops often sell *aceiteras* from Spain. Alternatively you need a very steady hand.

This is a basic mayonnaise which can have many things added to it, such as herbs, whipped cream etc. It can also be made entirely with vinegar or entirely with lemon juice if wished rather than half quantities of each.

Imperial/Metric	*American*
15 fl. oz (450 ml) light olive oil	2 cups light olive oil
15 fl. oz (450 ml) sunflower seed oil	2 cups sunflower seed oil
4 egg yolks	4 egg yolks
1 tablespoon dry mustard or Dijon mustard	1 tablespoon dry mustard or Dijon mustard
1 teaspoon sea salt	1 teaspoon sea salt
juice of a lemon	juice of a lemon
2 tablespoons white wine vinegar	2 tablespoons white wine vinegar
pepper	pepper

Warm the bowl in which you are going to make the mayonnaise and dry it well. Stir the eggs together with the mustard and salt and start *dripping* the oil in drop by drop and mixing it well into them. After about 4 fl. oz/120 ml/½ US cup has been dripped in, the eggs should start thickening up. Stir constantly. Once the eggs have really thickened, you can pour the oil in, in a very thin, steady stream. When all the oil has been used up, add the lemon juice and vinegar, again *drop by drop* – taste and correct seasoning.

If the mayonnaise is too thick, you can thin it with a little warm, *not hot*, water – about 1-2 tablespoons maximum. In any event it is a good idea to put a little water in a mayonnaise as it helps stabilize the emulsion and prevents it separating.

If your mayonnaise fails, it can be due to many things but mostly it is caused through faulty and too fast mixing or having the bowl, eggs and oil too cold (or too hot) – around 75-80°F/22-27°C is ideal – what the Italians used to call 'silk-worm temperature'. Sometimes a mayonnaise can be saved by starting with another egg and dripping in the (un)made mayonnaise drop by drop – or by doing this with the bowl over hot water until the mayonnaise 'takes' again, but it is best not to be impatient and take time at the beginning. Mayonnaise can be rushed only with a liquidizer or food processor.

MACHINE-MADE MAYONNAISE

Imperial/Metric
8 fl. oz (240 ml) olive oil
8 fl. oz (240 ml) sunflower seed
   oil
2 medium egg yolks
juice of ½ lemon
2 teaspoons or more dry or
   made mustard*
salt
2 tablespoons white wine
   vinegar

American
1 cup olive oil
1 cup sunflower seed oil
2 medium egg yolks
juice of ½ lemon
2 teaspoons or more dry or
   made mustard*
salt
2 tablespoons white wine
   vinegar

* If you prefer pepper to mustard, you can substitute cayenne or some Tabasco.

Warm the bowl of the machine by standing it in hot water for a moment or 2 – dry well and then drop the 2 yolks onto the blades. Pour in the lemon juice, mustard and salt (to taste) and then add the oil in a thin stream whilst running the machine, then increase the stream as the mixture thickens. Finally add the vinegar just before the last of the oil. You may need to add 1-2 tablespoons hot water if it ends up too thick, remembering that this mayonnaise tends to thicken on standing in the refrigerator.

CHILLI MAYONNAISE (Mexico)

Imperial/Metric
15 fl. oz (50 ml) mayonnaise
   (p.404)
2 teaspoon Tabasco
3 tablespoons tomato ketchup
2 hot green peppers

American
2 cups mayonnaise (p.404)
2 teaspoons Tabasco
3 tablespoons tomato ketchup
2 hot green peppers

Mix the first three ingredients in the machine or by hand and then add de-seeded green peppers cut-up very small indeed. Let stand for an hour or so before serving.

CUCUMBER MAYONNAISE (USA)

Imperial/Metric	American
1 large cucumber, grated	1 large cucumber, grated
8 fl. oz (225 ml) mayonnaise	1 cup mayonnaise
8 fl. oz (225 ml) double cream	1 cup heavy cream
salt, white pepper	salt, white pepper
dill or parsley, optional	dill or parsley, optional

Some Americans use soured cream instead of the richer sort. Drain the grated cucumber for approximately 1 hour. Press and pat as dry as possible with paper towels. Mix the double cream, mayonnaise, salt, pepper and dill or parsley, if used, then stir in the cucumber. Serve at once with cooked lobster, prawns, shrimps, cold white fish, salmon, trout etc.

HERB MAYONNAISE

This is only one of many herb mayonnaises: you can make your own out of your favourite herbs. If you add capers, it will do duty for *sauce tartare*.

Imperial/Metric	American
15 fl. oz (450ml) basic (p.404) or machine-made (p.406) mayonnaise	2 cups basic (p.404) or machine-made (p.406) mayonnaise
2 tablespoons parsley, roughly chopped	2 tablespoons parsley, roughly chopped
1 tablespoon chervil, roughly chopped	1 tablespoon chervil, roughly chopped
1 teaspoon tarragon, roughly chopped	1 teaspoon tarragon, roughly chopped
6 or 8 stalks watercress	6 or 8 stalks watercress
bunch of chives	bunch of chives

Pour boiling water on the unchopped herbs, leave for a couple of minutes, then pour off and chop roughly. Add the chives and put the whole lot through the liquidizer or food processor. In the absence of machinery, you will need to chop everything very small and stir it into the mayonnaise, leaving the chopped chives until last.

RAGÙ BOLOGNESE

ITALIAN MEAT SAUCE.

Non-Italian *ragù bolognese* is usually made from beef ground too coarsely and in too great a quantity. Italians never swamp their pasta in sauce. It is a good idea to run either the meat or the finished sauce through the food-processor (never the liquidizer!) for *a few seconds* to get a smooth, Italian result.

Imperial/Metric	*American*
1 lb (500 g) minced beef	1 lb ground chuck or top round
4 oz (125 g) chicken liver, chopped	4 oz chicken liver, chopped
1 medium onion, finely chopped	1 medium onion, finely chopped
1 small carrot, finely chopped	1 small carrot, finely chopped
1 stick celery, finely chopped	1 stick celery, finely chopped
2 tablespoons tomato concentrate	2 tablespoons tomato concentrate
4 fl. oz (120 ml) wine, white or red	½ cup wine, white or red
4 fl. oz (120 ml) double cream	½ cup heavy cream
oregano and thyme to taste	oregano and thyme to taste
a little parsley and nutmeg (optional)	a little parsley and nutmeg (optional)
salt and pepper	salt and pepper
stock (optional)	stock (optional)
butter and oil for frying	butter and oil for frying

Fry the chopped vegetables in the butter/oil mixture and let brown evenly. Add the beef and brown slightly, stirring all the time. Add the chicken liver and the herbs with some parsley or nutmeg if you wish. Then add the wine and stir in the tomato concentrate. Let simmer over a low heat (preferably with a mat) for at least 30 minutes. You will need to stir the mixture from time to time and add a little more wine or stock. Before serving stir in the cream.

ROUILLE (France)

ROUILLE COMES FROM THE FRENCH WORD FOR RUST

Serve with fish soups or slices of grilled or baked fish.

Imperial/Metric	American
4-5 large cloves mild garlic	4-5 large cloves mild garlic
2 medium hot red peppers (the Spanish or southern Italian type)	2 medium hot red peppers (the Spanish or southern Italian type)
4 tablespoons olive oil	4 tablespoons olive oil
1-2 slices of bread from sandwich loaf or from French loaf	1-2 slices of bread from sandwich loaf or from French loaf
½ pint (300 ml) chicken or fish stock	1¼ cups chicken or fish stock

Warm the stock. Put everything, except the stock, into the liquidizer or food processor and reduce to a mush. Alternatively, crush the ingredients in a mortar. Add the stock bit by bit until you get the desired consistency – it should be on the thick side.

Quite commonly seen in France and also commercially made are *rouilles* made on a mayonnaise base instead of stock. Delicious as they may be they are not true *rouilles*.

SAUCE NIÇOISE (France)

Much used in Nice and its surroundings instead of the ordinary mayonnaise.

Imperial/Metric	American
15 fl. oz (450 ml) mayonnaise (p.404)	2 cups mayonnaise (p.404)
1 lb (500 g) tomatoes	1 lb tomatoes
2 cloves garlic	2 cloves garlic
1 sweet red pepper, cut up	1 red bell pepper, cut up
salt and a little Tabasco	salt and a little Tabasco

Peel the tomatoes, chop roughly and cook with the garlic. Add the red pepper and cook everything until reduced to a purée. Continue cooking to dry off the vegetables, watching that it does not catch. Once reduced to about a quarter or its original size, let cool and then incorporate into the mayonnaise. Add Tabasco and salt if necessary.

Glossary

BAIES ROUGES DE L'ILE DE BOURBON: Usually available only in France these small pink peppers have a slightly sweet and not at all hot taste. They add an indefinable flavour to fish and poultry pâtés – they would be wasted in a strong, country terrine – and are excellent added to cream sauces. Often combined with *poivre-vert* (*q.v.* below) either in equal quantities or two thirds *baies rouges* to one third *poivre-vert*. The Ile de Bourbon hasn't existed since the French Revolution at which time its name was changed to Réunion.

BAIN-MARIE: Real *bains-marie* are used in catering establishments whereas the domestic cook must make do with a double saucepan or double boiler which is not quite the same thing. Boiling water should *never* touch the utensil in which the fragile food is being cooked but should create heat in the space between the utensil and the water. As many cooks know to their cost, it is quite easy to curdle a delicate sauce in a double saucepan. *Bains-marie* are very often responsible for stomach upsets since sauces etc, kept at blood heat for a long period can develop all sorts of nasty bacteria.

Reheating sauces made with egg liaisons should always be done with a *bain-marie* or double saucepan. Never be impatient with such a sauce or disaster will surely follow. Never try the microwave unless you really like exotic forms of scrambled egg. Many of the sauces such as *hollandaise, béarnaise, paloise* etc, should *not* be hot but lukewarm – it is the food they accompany which should be piping hot – and the plates too.

BEURRE MANIE: An equal mixture of flour and melted butter mixed together and used in small quantities to thicken sauces etc, at the last moment. It can be made in advance and kept covered with clingfilm for three or four days. Best broken into small pieces of about half a teaspoonful when using. I am not over-fond of this method, as I think it leaves a slightly raw flour taste to the dish, but sometimes it is the only method available for last minute thickening.

BEURRE-NOISETTE: The first stage in browning butter and one which should not be continued for too long or you will end up with burnt butter which is most unpleasant. The butter should be the colour of a hazelnut and should then be removed from the heat source.

CEVICHE: A method of 'cooking' fresh (not frozen) fish by soaking it in either lime, lemon or bitter orange juice – vinegar would do the same thing but leave an unpleasantly strong taste. The juice is poured off before re-dressing the fish for serving.

CLARIFIED BUTTER: Although I have not specified the use of clarified butter throughout this book (it is not vital if you cook with a mixture of butter and oil), it is better than using ordinary butter which can all too easily burn and ruin a dish. The concentrated butter which is on sale in many countries is a form of clarified butter in as much as the water has been extracted from it and it can be used as such.

There are two ways of clarifying butter and the first is the simplest. Cut 8 oz (250 g) or 1 cup of butter (preferably unsalted) into small cubes and heat to the bubbling stage. Remove the saucepan from the heat and let cool until the sediment has gone to the bottom. Strain the butter fat through a muslin-lined sieve and refrigerate.

The other method is a little more trouble, but rather more certain in its result. To 1 lb (500 g) or 2 cups of butter (preferably unsalted) allow 1 pint (600 ml) or 2½ cups of water. Cut the butter into cubes and heat with the water until boiling point is reached. Allow to cool, pour into a pudding basin and refrigerate. A few hours later a 'lid' of butter will have formed. Take off and remove any sediment clinging to the underside of the lid (it is unlikely there will be any) and pat dry. Heat gently and once melted put a folded tea-towel over the top of the saucepan. Any remaining water will be absorbed by the cloth.

Clarified butter will keep for months in a covered container in the refrigerator.

COURT-BOUILLON: A liquid for poaching (usually) fish. See recipe (p.309).

CREME FRAICHE: I love to sit in an Air France aeroplane on the way back to London and wait for someone to wail 'This cream's off!' It always happens. I find thick, Channel Island or Loseley-type cream far too rich nowadays and in fact, prefer *crème fraîche*. This is the cream the French prefer. Each manufacturer uses a special, slightly different culture and I find Isigny has the best flavour though others swear by Gervais, Chambourcy etc. It is slightly less fat than British double cream and comes in both thick and liquid versions in France though I believe only the thick version is exported. Ordinary cream is available in France – Yoplait is the nearest to British cream.

CRUDITES: Cleaned and prepared raw vegetables usually served with a sauce such as vinaigrette, *Bagna Cauda, Fondue* etc.

DEGLAZE: The dilution with wine, water, cream or other liquid of the fish or meat juices left in the pan after frying or baking. Scrape the pieces into the sauce and reduce or add liquid. Depending on the requirements of the finished dish the final sauce can be strained or left as is.

DEVEINING SHRIMPS AND PRAWNS: If you take a prawn (or medium or large shrimp) in your hand you will see that it is divided more or less into 2 parts – the head section and the abdominal. The abdominal section in turn is made up of 6 segments – this is the edible part. Across the top part of this abdominal section, under the carapace (shell), runs the alimentary canal of the animal and since prawns are scavengers the contents of this canal should always be removed before eating.

This is called deveining. Provided you leave the carapace on you can leave in this thin black line of waste and remove once the prawn is cool enough to handle. However, if you are going to cook the raw prawn or shrimp from scratch without its carapace you should remove it so it does not contaminate the food. Something like 80 per cent of all prawn and shrimp allergies can be put down to eating the contents of the prawns' intestines. The other 20 per cent simply shouldn't eat shellfish or crustaceans – lobster, mussels and oysters being the worst offenders. Usually if you can eat oysters, mussels etc, but have a problem with prawns it is due to poor cleaning. It is worth pointing out that most restaurants and most Chinese recipes do *not* use deveined prawns. There is nothing to stop you from deveining the prawns yourself though it is difficult without a running tap!

FAT-BACK: The hard layer of fat between the skin and the flesh of the pig on its back. It has the advantage of holding its shaping through cooking and is often used in pâtés and in larding dry joints of meat. In France it is also used, cut in very thin sheets, to wrap round roasts of beef, pork, veal etc. In much of central

Europe and northern Italy it is slightly pickled and smoked with a little of the flesh attached and known as *speck*.

FLARE OR FLAIR FAT: The best sort comes from bacon pigs and is the fat usually used for lard. It comes from the loin and from around the kidneys and is very white.

FROMAGE FRAIS: A purely commercial product of French origin. This is a form of fresh cheese made with a special culture so the taste varies from make to make. The fat content can be from 0 to 80 per cent though 40 and 50 per cent are the most commonly sold. Useful for soups and other recipes where it can be used instead of cream.

FUMET: Reduced stock – usually used in this book in connection with fish.

GELATINE: Usually of animal origin. Vegetarians should use agar-agar. As gelatine (gelatin) varies for country to country in both its presentation (leaves, powder or crystals) and its setting potential it is best to follow the instructions on the packet. When making aspic, allowance should be made for its own setting potential and probably half quantities of gelatine are enough. It is best to experiment before using expensive ingredients. It is worth pointing out that Cox's Gelatin (USA) and Davis Gelatine (UK) are not interchangeable as to quantities. Always add the gelatine to the liquid, which should be hot, and not the other way round though this is less important with leaf gelatine which should be slightly broken up before being put to melt.

GRATIN: A dish (often of vegetables in sauce) finished off under a grill to brown it. Not necessarily made with cheese though this is not uncommon.

JULIENNE: Cut into thin strips. Mostly applied to vegetables and best done on a food processor's julienne disc.

MEDAILLONS: Small steaks of meat or fish about the size of a large medal – particularly applied to veal.

MEZZALUNA: (Italian for half-moon). A most useful two-handled chopping knife shaped like a half-moon which makes chopping quick and easy and doesn't reduce the food to the mush sometimes produced by a food processor. Small sized *mezzalune* sometimes come with a bowl to fit and this can be useful for chopping herbs or garlic.

MI-CUIT: Half cooked – usually applied to duck liver and certain vegetables.

MOULI-LEGUMES: A type of metal sieve with a handle which pushes the food through. Very useful for those who have no machinery but also very useful for doing small quantities. Comes in various sizes.

EN PAPILLOTE: In the old days food was sealed into a paper case and baked – nowadays this is replaced by aluminium foil. Keeps in all the juices.

PETIT-SALE: The belly and ribs of pork which are salted and spiced for a couple of months – the salt draws out the juices and forms a brine. You can produce this yourself very easily by following instructions from Jane Grigson's wonderful book *Charcuterie and French Pork Cookery*. There is *no* British equivalent although our pork will produce excellent *petit-salé*. Green streaky bacon can be used as a substitute.

POIVRE-VERT: The French introduced and commercialized this Madagascan spice and for a long time kept the market to themselves. Malaysia now produces *poivre-vert* which are the unripe seeds of the pepper tree. The best are freeze-dried and the cheapest are packed in brine. The best quality still come from Madagascar. Much used in sauces, pâtés and terrines.

SALADE TIEDE: A salad, usually of green stuff, to which hot or warm items are added at the last moment.

Index